D1328411

JUL 2002

THE CHALLENGE OF CHANGE

Perspectives on Family, Work, and Education

WOMEN IN CONTEXT: Development and Stresses

THE CHALLENGE OF CHANGE

Perspectives on Family, Work, and Education

EDITED BY

MATINA HORNER

Radcliffe College
Cambridge, Massachusetts

CAROL C. NADELSON

AND

MALKAH T. NOTMAN

New England Medical Center
Tufts University School of Medicine
Boston, Massachusetts

PLENUM PRESS • NEW YORK AND LONDON

Library of Congress Cataloging in Publication Data

Main entry under title:

The Challenge of change.

(Women in context)
    Includes bibliographical references and index.
    1. Women—United States—Congresses. 2. Family—United States—Congresses. 3.
Women—Employment—United States—Congresses. 4. Education of women—United
States—Congresses. 5. United States—Social conditions—Congresses. I. Horner,
Matina. II. Nadelson, Carol C. III. Notman, Malkah T. IV. Series.
HQ1426.C454 1983   305.4'2'0973   83-8994
ISBN 0-306-41237-3

©1983 Plenum Press, New York
A Division of Plenum Publishing Corporation
233 Spring Street, New York, N.Y. 10013

Printed in the United States of America

We dedicate this volume to

Jean Humphrey Block, Ph.D.,

whose untimely death in December 1981 deprived us of
an esteemed colleague and a dear friend.

Contributors

Mary Jo Bane, Ph.D. • John F. Kennedy School of Government, Harvard University, Cambridge, Massachusetts

Jessie Bernard, Ph.D. • The Pennsylvania State University, University Park, Pennsylvania

†Jeanne H. Block, Ph.D. • Institute for Human Development, University of California at Berkeley, Berkeley, California

William H. Chafe, Ph.D. • Oral History Program, Duke University, Durham, North Carolina

Elizabeth Douvan, Ph.D. • Survey Research Center, Institute for Social Research, University of Michigan, Ann Arbor, Michigan

Jacqueline Fleming, Ph.D. • 392 Central Park West, New York, New York

Carol Gilligan, Ed.D. • Graduate School of Education, Harvard University, Cambridge, Massachusetts

Matina S. Horner, Ph.D. • President, Radcliffe College; Department of Psychology, Harvard University, Cambridge, Massachusetts

Joseph Katz, Ph.D. • Human Development Department, State University of New York, Stony Brook, New York

Nathan Keyfitz, Ph.D. • Department of Sociology, Harvard University, Cambridge, Massachusetts

†Deceased

Jean Lipman-Blumen, Ph.D. • LBS International, Bethesda, Maryland 20814

Valory Mitchell, Ph.D. • Institute of Personality Assessment, University of California at Berkeley, Berkeley, California

Carol C. Nadelson, M.D. • Department of Psychiatry, New England Medical Center, Tufts University, Boston, Massachusetts

Malkah T. Notman, M.D. • Department of Psychiatry, New England Medical Center, Tufts University, Boston, Massachusetts

Robert Rapoport, Ph.D. • Institute of Family and Environmental Research, London, England

Rhona Rapoport, Ph.D. • Institute of Family and Environmental Research, London, England

Patricia Salt, Ph.D. • Department of Psychiatry, New England Medical Center, Tufts University, Boston, Massachusetts

Abigail J. Stewart, Ph.D. • Department of Psychology, Boston University, Boston, Massachusetts

Joseph Veroff, Ph.D. • Survey Research Center, Institute for Social Research, University of Michigan, Ann Arbor, Michigan

Preface

This book is a compilation and update of a group of provocative papers presented at the Radcliffe College invitational conference, "Perspectives on the Patterns of an Era: Family, Work, and Education." A scholarly event saluting Radcliffe's centenary, the conference examined a range of indicators of social change, particularly as they relate to women in America in the last two decades. The program was interdisciplinary, bringing together scholars from economics, history, psychology, sociology, and psychiatry.

Each conference participant was asked to explore, theoretically and empirically, the lessons of our social history and, as much as possible, to separate myth from reality with regard to recent changes in patterns of family life, work, and education. Particular emphasis was given to the examination of the rapid changes—or what have been assumed to be the rapid changes—of the last two decades. In addition, participants analyzed the perceived and actual costs and benefits associated with changing lifestyles, for women and men as individuals and for society as a whole. Finally, they considered the implications of their findings for the future and identified areas for further research.

In recent years, scholars and researchers have developed a broadened theoretical understanding of the social history of our nation. Many earlier assumptions have been challenged—perhaps none more than those assumptions about women's lives and women's participation in society. Certainly one goal of this book is the clarification of erroneous and outdated assumptions about men's and women's capacities and about the roles men and women can play in the family, the workplace, and elsewhere in society. Our more ambitious goal, however, is to stimulate the reader to consider in greater depth questions about the nature and effects of social change, and in this way to stimulate further research efforts. In short, we hope this volume will serve as a catalyst for new ideas and as a facilitator of new learning.

The attention given by the chapters in this book to the topics of family, work, and education recognizes that these aspects of our society, each critical to the development of individual identity and self-esteem, continue to be highly interdependent. As always, any shift that occurs in the options and barriers present in any one of these areas greatly influences the nature and extent of opportunities that will be available in the others.

A number of variables have greatly influenced the roles that men and women have assumed within each of these spheres over the years. One cannot disregard these factors and their interaction and at the same time obtain an understanding of *what* has changed, what the underlying reasons for the changes have been, what consequences these changes have had, and what possibilities exist for the future. In any analysis of change, a range of political, economic, psychological, and social factors must be taken into consideration; and social change must be studied from a number of perspectives to gain a truer picture of its impact.

One theme emerges as dominant throughout the book: Change itself, especially when it is rapid, presents a society with new challenges and brings us face to face with fundamental issues that require serious reconsideration, often of our most cherished values and assumptions. Within a broad framework of shared reactions, individuals and institutions respond and adapt in unique ways to these challenges. When change proceeds slowly, both individuals and institutions have time to plan and to develop alternative ways of behaving, thinking, and feeling, as well as to find new systems of support and reinforcement for their present views of themselves and others. In times of rapid change, however, the need for immediate responses to entirely new situations often precludes the possibility of evolving satisfactory modes of adaptation. This often creates anxiety and generates conflict. Rapid change brings about the sudden loss of much of what is familiar and expected in our relationships and defined roles, often making it impossible for us to "grieve" over the loss of previously dependable sources of support.

At such times of transition, few guidelines and reference points seem consistently applicable. It is as though the generation gap assumes qualitatively different proportions. What was meaningful to previous generations, or even to one's own generation a decade ago, is no longer entirely relevant, not only because of individual development or age differences but because so much has changed. When there is little applicable antecedent history and an absence of a shared societal vision of reality, it is difficult to plan for change or even to assess its impact.

The new options and alternative lifestyles available to women, and especially to educated women today, have had an exhilarating and positive effect on our society. Extending the horizon of women's expression and achievement has great benefits for all.

At the same time, we are well aware of a growing sense of alarm that the new choices open to women today will have a deleterious effect on the family as an institution and on individual family members as well. As evidence for this alarmist view, proponents point to an ever-growing list of "stress indicators": alcoholism, drug abuse, depression, suicide, family violence, marital problems, divorce. (Unfortunately, "stress" has become the catchall term used to describe problems and negative consequences associated with change. This ignores work showing the positive effects of stress for stimulating growth.) In response to the concerns expressed, intensified attention has also been directed at identifying possible new coping strategies and ways of facilitating adaptation: counseling, self-help centers, lifelong learning, day care, and support for altered roles for men within marriage and in the workplace are among the most frequently cited. These currents of thought and suggested remedies are reflected in various ways through the contributions of our authors.

Several chapters of this book deal primarily with demographic and historical facts, figures, and issues. In the past, life expectancy was low, disease was rampant, children often failed to survive to adulthood, and, even though fertility control was not possible, the world population was small and expanded slowly. Even at the beginning of this century, health care was generally poor in this country, and occupational risks were high. Here, as in all industrialized nations, population increase was considered a desirable goal. All this has changed: Life expectancy in the United States is now approaching 80 years. Serious and fatal diseases of the young are unusual; most children survive to adulthood, and fertility control is possible.

Historically, when economic resources are plentiful, social consciousness with regard to equal opportunity tends to be high, but when they are scarce, it tends to recede. Consider, for example, the events of the second quarter of the century, encompassing the Great Depression and the Second World War. This period had a tremendous impact on the professional aspirations and educational opportunities available to women. By 1930, women made up 45% of the professional and semi-professional workers in the United States. With the Depression, however, and then again following the Second World War, women—married women in particular—were discouraged from "taking jobs away from men." Their participation in graduate study similarly dwindled and the proportion of doctoral degrees awarded women fell. Only recently has it regained the level reached in the 1930s. In 1950 with the postwar surge of demand for education, especially scientific training for men, the percentage of all degrees awarded to women, graduate and undergraduate, dropped precipitously.

At the same time the postwar era brought the baby boom, a unique, unanticipated, and wholly unprecedented population explosion that lasted 15 years and was followed immediately by 15 years of the steepest decline in the birthrate in America's history. The baby boom produced an unprecedented bulge in the American age structure which significantly altered American life, affecting the economy and workplace, the nature of competition, politics, family structure, and the expectations of the nation's people. Within a decade, the center of gravity of our population had shifted from the more traditional 35- to 40-year-olds to 17-year-olds. Those under 20 became the dominant group in society, representing about 40% of the population. American society as a whole began to assume the characteristics of a younger, more rebellious generation that stayed in school longer than any other, yet faced the chilling possibility that it might become the first downwardly mobile generation in our history.

The 1960s began as a decade of extraordinary optimism and self-confidence about the nation's capacity for social progress and it ended in tragedy, turbulence, and confusion. The 1970s continued to be a decade of social change so dramatic that it challenged fundamental habits of thought and behavior and greatly affected many of the expectations we had of one another, of our partners at home and at work, and of our cultural, educational, and other social institutions. This was a time when the search for oneself assumed such importance for so many that it also earned for the seventies the title "the Me decade." During this period the issues involved and the need for defining personal and societal limits became apparent. We are now led to ask: Where will the 1980s go? Few doubt it will be a "Decade of Hard Choices."

This extraordinary period of United States history presented a variety of new issues analyzed by the contributors to this volume, whose retrospective understanding helps illuminate our possible future direction.

As editors, we have considered the themes that emerge in the chapters of this book, and have become increasingly convinced that to understand the effects of change on individuals one must be sensitive to the wide variety of possible responses available to the challenges created. For some the challenges mobilize energy and increase motivation. For others they evoke primarily conflict and distress. For all individuals, on varying occasions, both responses are probably experienced.

From the recognition that change can have both these components and that it can be frustrating as well as fulfilling, we arrived at a number of questions: On what basis can individuals, at a time of major social change, define and evaluate a sense of identity and self-esteem? How do individuals conceptualize and experience feelings of loss, isolation, and loneliness, which become particularly salient in the context of changing—often shrinking—networks of family relationships? How do men and women deal with the implicit tension between autonomy and commitment? How is this effort affected by the rapidly increasing array of options? How do individuals replace rejected or conflicted values and beliefs so as to retain self-esteem, commitment, meaning, and morality in their lives?

These questions about the challenge of change are but a few that we believe are addressed in the chapters that follow. We hope that our readers will have other questions and will be stimulated to seek answers both here and in their own work.

We would like to thank Mary Cox, Janet Gornick, and Hilary Evans for their sustained effort, enormous help and patience in the preparation of this book.

MATINA S. HORNER
CAROL C. NADELSON
MALKAH T. NOTMAN

Contents

PART I

Emerging Issues

The demographic and economic conditions of any era greatly influences both our attitudes and the quality and content of our lives. Today's mood is one of uncertainty and concern about the nation's economic and political future. Instead of perceiving a sense of expanding horizons, unfettered optimism, and an unqualified confidence in technology and economic growth, we note a growing tendency toward lowered expectations, heightened apprehension about the future, greater conservatism in social, political, and intellectual attitudes, diminished confidence or trust in our institutions, and a growing "psychology of limits." One recent survey reports that 72% of the respondents agreed that "the land of plenty is rapidly becoming a land of want." A Gallup poll in August, 1979, reported that 60% of the population felt the nation was "in deep and serious trouble." Just three years before, only 40% of those polled had held that view. In 1979, for the first time in polling history, a majority of those polled (55%) felt that "next year will be worse than last"—a reversal of previous polls in which at least a 60% majority looked forward to a better tomorrow.

The chapters of this book by Nathan Keyfitz and William H. Chafe serve to document many of the economic, political, and social trends—both drastic and subtle—that have influenced and characterized the changing face of America over the last several decades. Keyfitz, in "American Demographic Directions," discusses the changing patterns in births, abortions, divorce, survivorship, education, and employment. His summary of recent American demographic directions lays a sound factual foundation for understanding many particular aspects of change. Chafe, in his chapter, "The Challenge of Sex Equality," outlines the movement toward equality between the sexes as it has evolved—or failed to evolve—through America's social history.

With a growing set of options for both men and women, accompanied by a growing need for decision making and risk taking, there has come a shift away from rigidly stereotyped sex roles and toward greater freedom of choice for both sexes. The revitalization of the women's movement in the latter part of the 1960s was an important challenge to age-old assumptions about sex roles, for it established new expectations and possibilities for the personal and professional fulfillment of both men and women. We have only begun to examine the effects that these shifts will have on individual developmental patterns and on interpersonal relations. It is premature to speculate whether and when these new expectations will become realities, especially as they interact with the forces of a difficult and uncertain economic future.

In coping with changes in their personal and professional roles, men and women continue to confront difficult decisions as they attempt to choose between important values, and, when necessary, between their rights and the responsibilities they have to themselves and to others. How much attention should be given to fulfilling social obligations? How much freedom of personal expression is one entitled to and what are the costs? How much of what one sees as unacceptable for oneself should be tolerated in others' behavior?

These and other moral dilemmas, which are discussed by Carol Gilligan in her chapter on women's moral judgments, have come to have particular poignancy for individuals today in the context of the recent history of evolving equality between the sexes. Will the pursuit of equality between the sexes mean the deterioration of what we have cherished in family life? Will women bring to the workplace a new emphasis on the values of nurturance, cooperation, and human interdependence, or will they be overtaken by the institutional pressures and competitive values that have ruled the lives of men at work? These questions are asked frequently. While the answers to them will come in part from careful collection and analysis of data, we must also ask the much broader question: What do we mean by equality between the sexes?

One area in which this question has particular relevance is that of work. Many observers today view the increased possibilities of jobs for women as a solution to the problem of inequality; they believe that women with jobs are more fulfilled and happier than women who do not work for pay. Others are convinced that on the road to true equality everything is moving along exceedingly well. Still others, however, think that at this moment women's progress is blocked by a serious regression. This diversity of views suggests the necessity of reassessing the validity of current assumptions about what the "new woman" and "new man" are doing, thinking, and feeling.

Figures from a number of sources give a relatively conservative picture and challenge many widespread assumptions about the extent of social change that has occurred. They suggest that society may not have been as effective in lowering the hurdles to top levels of power and status as many assume. Despite many advances, women continue to earn significantly less than men, and the already small number of women professionals, managers, and entrepreneurs is in some cases declining.

Jean Lipman-Blumen's chapter, "Emerging Patterns of Female Leadership in Formal Organizations," analyzes some of the cultural constraints inhibiting women from attaining leadership roles in the workplace. From Lipman-Blumen's work it becomes clear that purposefully bringing about social change, even in the wake of overt policy change, may be exceedingly difficult. While the availability of nontraditional roles may have increased greatly in recent years, the effort to change the attitudes of individuals surrounding those who assume these roles may constitute a slow and tiresome process.

Chapter 1

American Demographic Directions

NATHAN KEYFITZ

For the demographer these are eventful days. All-time records are being established on the basic population variables. For 10 years the American birth rate has been about 15 per 1,000, lower than it had ever been before; the expectation of life, after some hesitation, is rising again, and that of women could well reach 80 years in the near future; legal abortions are near the 1.5-million mark; one-sixth of all births are to unmarried women. In addition to these facts affecting the biological variables of birth and death are changes in social aspects of population: the divorce rate sets a new record each year; women have entered the labor force in unheard-of proportions, and even mothers of young children now take jobs; unconventional living arrangements are widespread.

Women have every reason to be interested in the statistics on which these statements are based. The divorce rate, the new labor market, the extension of life, indeed every one of the demographic changes mentioned in this chapter represents large changes in women's lives. Many of the changes are clearly a part of women's liberation. It is hard to say what causes what in such matters: in some instances divorce or the threat of divorce causes women to seek work where they would not otherwise do so; in other instances the fact that they work enables them to contemplate a divorce that carries little economic penalty. Do women seek jobs in order to attain independence, or do they need the money, the independence coming of itself once they take a job? The connections are evident, though the causal structure underlying them is not easily uncovered.

The following sketch of major demographic changes in the United States relies on various official sources of information, mostly summa-

NATHAN KEYFITZ, PH.D. • John F. Kennedy School of Government, Harvard University, Cambridge, Massachusetts 02138.

rized in the *Statistical Abstract of the United States* (U.S. Bureau of the Census, 1980). Unless otherwise stated, page references given along with the numbers in what follows are from the 1980 issue of the *Abstract*.

BIRTHS

The United States birthrate troughed at 14.8 per 1,000 population in 1975 and 1976, lower even than 1935 in the dark days of the Depression, when it was 18.7 (p. 61). The absolute number of births was about 3.1 million per year in mid-decade and then showed some rise—to about 3.5 million by 1980.

Births are low despite the many women of childbearing ages. The Total Fertility Rate—number of births that women would average on current age-specific rates—is 1.8 (p. 61), against the 2.1 needed to keep the population from declining in the long run. Official statistics show the decline of the TFR from its high level about 1960 to below replacement in the 1970s. If the age distribution were that corresponding to present birthrates, the American-born population would be declining at about 6% per year.

For the labor force or the educational system it is the absolute number of births, not the rate, that is operative. With the widespread use of contraception, births fluctuate with the fluctuations of the economy and of fashion. Expressed in round numbers, births were about 3 million after World War I, dropped below 2.5 million during the 1930s, then rose in the 1950s to well above 4 million, and now have fallen back almost to 3 million. Though mortality and immigration have some effect, birth numbers are what largely determine subsequent age distribution. Age distribution in turn affects the personal fate of individuals, and the national life as a whole.

JOB VERSUS CAREER

The male cohort born in the 1930s has several advantages over the larger cohorts that precede and that follow it. Thus when on reaching age 20 in the 1950s it sought its first job, it was welcomed into those positions suited to beginners; since employers needed so many beginners, the services of individuals from the male cohort were correspondingly in demand. A few years later these same individuals attained easy promotion because there were a large number of new entrants—the birth cohorts of the 1940s and 1950s. Those fortunate few of the 1930s were pushed upward to posts as supervisors, teachers, and managers as they were required to direct the increasing entrants into the labor force during two decades. Today the cohort of the 1930s is in its 40s and large cohorts of senior managers (born in the 1920s) will retire ahead of them. This will mean many vacancies at the top into which those of the 1930s will be drawn. Thus at three distinct stages in their careers the fortunate small cohort benefits from an updraft created by the larger cohorts following and preceding it. The resultant optimism, even euphoria, encouraged it to have large families, and Richard Easterlin (1980) has related the high births of the 1950s to this cause.

Women born in the 1930s do not seem to have shared the good fortune of the men. The hierarchy within which promotion takes place exists for fewer female occupations; fewer women are on a ladder to be climbed almost automatically with increasing age. A male office worker can hope to become supervisor, then manager. The typist, waitress, or nurse has no equally obvious possibility of promotion. The matter has not been investigated in detail, but apparently the women members of the cohort of the 1930s were not drawn upward like their brothers. My suggested reason is that the mechanism benefiting small cohorts depends on the sequence of tasks and rewards that we call a career. Careers and the promotions they entail imply a hierarchy at any one time. Those in occupations that do not lead upward, i.e., that are not parts of careers, are less affected by the size of their cohort.

Continuity in the timing of work and the sequence of stages in the life cycle is more easily attained by men than by women. A women who takes 10 years out to have children and get them launched into school is then out of step with her male contemporaries. She has to fall back into competition with a younger cohort whose training may be more up-to-date. Her husband, moreover, may well have opportunities to advance his career in distant cities, and it would be only by rare coincidence that her career would be best served by the same move. When she moves with her husband she will most probably fall into a noncareer job— typist or waitress, even though she is overqualified for such work.

ABORTION

A prime indicator of the changes in social attitudes, on a matter close to people's deepest moral sensibilities, was the acceptance of legal abortion in the 1970s. The number of legal abortions, 745,000 in 1973, had risen to 1,410,000 by 1978 (p. 70). Few statistical series have risen so much in so short a span of years. Abortions had been taking place all along—no one knows quite in what numbers—and one cannot even be sure that the total increased with legalization. What is important is the acceptance as legal of an activity hunted down by the police as recently as a decade ago. To what extent legal abortion merely takes the place of illegal we do not know. Two-thirds of abortions are to women under 25 years of age (p. 69), as against only about one-half of births, and this suggests that education in contraception will help lower the abortion rate. For most states 70% or more of abortions were to unmarried women. In relation to population, abortion has been three times as frequent among black as among white women.

The high level of abortion and the availability of contraception cause the number of unwanted children to be lower than it would otherwise be. A retrospective survey of mothers 15–44 years of age in 1976 (p. 68) found an average of 2.51 births in all, of which .30 were unwanted. This ratio, one birth in eight unwanted, applies to the average of the past 25 or so years and is undoubtedly higher than the current fraction of unwanted births. The important point for our purpose is the movement toward free choice for women in an area where the constraints on them through the whole of history have been far greater than those on men.

THE FUTURE OF CHILDBEARING

The number of births that will occur in the United States during the coming years depends on two factors: the number of women of childbearing age and the number of children they average. According to the projections of the U.S. Bureau of the Census, the number of women at the prime childbearing ages of 22–24 at last birthday (i.e., the interval between exact ages 22 and 25) increased from 3,289,000 in 1960 (when they were the small cohort born between 1935 and 1938) to 6,060,000 in 1979, and then goes on to peak at about 6,204,000 in 1985 (p. 30). After that the number will inevitably decline, to fewer than 5 million by the end of the century. The same can be said of women in the older childbearing ages, except that their numbers will peak later.

In short, because the number of potential mothers in the 1980s tracks the births of the 1950s and 1960s, we have before us a 10% increase in the number of mothers before these start to decline. The big unknown is what will happen to the average rate at which they bear children. It would not require a large fall for the total number of births to stay constant at about 3.5 million, at least until the mid-1980s, and then drop below that.

No one can say what *will* happen, and past predictions have often been very wrong, but we gain some confidence here by noting that the decline of the birthrate has been associated with several other trends. The increase in women's participation in the labor force will be discussed later; now it is enough to say that the entry has been dramatic and seems irreversible. The fall in the birthrate is somehow associated with a system in which marriage tends to be no more important to women than to men (rather than much more important to women, as in the past).

Whatever the relative status of the sexes, one would think that under monogamy the same numbers of married men and married women would be counted in the country, but this is not so. In 1979 there were 51,181,000 married women and only 50,329,000 married men (p. 43). The difference for blacks is proportionately greater than for the population as a whole: 4,282,000 married women against 3,893,000 married men. The figures are similar for the population of Hispanic origin, where 2,575,000 married women are shown against 2,337,000 married men.

The census figures are obtained by asking individuals what their marital status is, and the discrepancy must be due to loosely attached couples in which men more often than women declare themselves to be single or divorced. The figures suggest that marriage has been a claim on the part of the woman, a concession on the part of the man. The 1980 Census shows a somewhat larger difference than earlier estimates: 52.8 million married females, against 51.8 million married males.

After years of earlier and earlier marriage the age is now rising, especially for women. The median age of American women at first marriage, for a long time below 20.5 years, reached 20.8 years by 1975, and by 1978 it was 21.4 (p. 83).

Not inconsistent with this is an increasing proportion of births to unmarried women, 16.3% in 1978 against 5.3% in 1960 (p. 66), with 44% to teenagers. Insofar as these result from ignorance of contraception they can be expected to diminish with the spread of information. An increasing number [in 1979, 1,346,000 against 523,000 in 1970 (p. 44)] of unmarried persons living together is part of a trend that is unlikely to lead to high fertility.

DIVORCE

Whichever parent has custody of them, children are a handicap to divorced people for either work or remarriage. The sense that a marriage may break up (and divorce is not usually a complete surprise) inevitably discourages childbearing. The causation works both ways: people avoid having children because of possible divorce; they are also more likely to resolve marital conflict by divorce if they have no children.

Before World War II there were less than one-tenth as many divorces as marriages, and the ratio has steadily risen, until by 1979 there were 1,170,000 divorces and 2,359,000 marriages (p. 83). And since about a third of the marriages were remarriages, one might relate divorce to first marriage and conclude that most couples break up in divorce.

This would be hasty; it is not correct to relate current divorces to current marriages, since the divorces issue from the marriages of some years back. Moreover, the divorces are not evenly distributed among the marrying population; some individuals have a propensity to divorce and some of the population never divorces. The more sophisticated calculation of the Bureau of the Census (1978, p. 9) shows that out of 100 first marriages of women born 1945–1949, 38.3 would eventually end in divorce if the rates of 1975 continued to apply. The rate for those who have been divorced once is the same or higher. Says the Bureau of the Census, "About four-tenths of the persons [around the age of 30] who had entered their second marriage, after their first marriage has ended in divorce, may expect eventually to have their second marriage also end in divorce."

Families with female heads are given as 4,507,000 in 1960 and 8,458,000 in 1979 (p. 45). In the past (though not in 1980, when the change in wording will result in some loss of comparability) the census has taken as the head of the family or household the adult male worker present, if there was one, so we suppose there was none in families classified as having a female head. Some of the increase is of older women who are widows and is simply the result of improved mortality among women. By 1979 there was one female householder for every three male householders. Among the 19,987,000 female householders were 8,821,000 widows, 4,379,000 divorcées, and 4,436,000 never married (p. 46).

CONCERN ABOUT THE BIRTHRATE

Whatever the direction of causation, the factors of low fertility, women working, and high divorce rates, and the availability of contraception and abortion, all fit together. The birthrate is unlikely to turn upward unless the other trends also reverse themselves. The persistence of the whole set of trends is the basis of the prediction that births will remain low.

Could effective measures be taken to raise them? The Soviet Union, more concerned than we are about the same low birthrate, has tried hard. Apartments are more easily obtained by couples with children; schooling is free; there are even special schools that look after children from 7:00A.M. to 7:00P.M. The birthrate of European Russia, nonetheless, continues as low as that of the United States. So does that of Canada, despite family allowances going back to the early 1940s.

The "peril of the declining birthrate," as Michel Debré calls it (*New*

York Times, June 6, 1978), reminds some Frenchmen unpleasantly of the demographic competition in which France lost to Germany during the century preceding World War II. France has tried paid pregnancy leaves, family allowances, and tax advantages for families with children. These could well have had an effect, but its relatively small extent makes one question whether direct financial incentives can do much to raise the birthrate unless they rise to the level of the wages women can earn in industry. Debré asks for extra votes for citizens who have large families. His bill introduced into the legislature would give fathers one extra vote for each son and mothers one extra vote for each daughter, until the children were old enough to vote themselves.

The chief conclusion from international experience is that lowering the birthrate in the first instance is difficult, and raising it once it has fallen is equally difficult. A policy measure attempting to act on one variable (the birthrate) that is tied to a whole complex of other variables (divorce, women working, etc.) encounters great inertia. To turn one basic social tendency around is hard enough; to alter a whole configuration may well be impossible.

Yet one suggestion is provided by the example of the military. Men are induced to go into the armed services in considerable part by generous pension rights for the ex-soldier after only 20 years of service. Could women be attracted to motherhood in the same way? A modified version of the military scheme might include a Mothers' Bill of Rights after childbearing service that would provide college tuition and stipend, as well as support until the veteran mother had established herself in a new career, even a life pension whether or not she took up other work.

WOMEN'S HIGH SURVIVORSHIP

The expectation of life at birth for women in 1978 was 77.2 years as against 69.5 for men (p. 72), a difference of nearly 8 years. No one knows for sure whether this is due to heredity (superior biological constitution of women) or environment (that men lead harder lives, the hard life including more smoking and drinking). The difference was only about 1 year in 1920; it jumped to 4 years in 1930, where it remained for over a decade, then to 6 years by 1950. The increasing differential is shared with other industrial countries, and applies equally to white and non-white women.

Can women's greater longevity be due to their taking better care of themselves, for instance, having more medical attention than men? In 1977 the average days of hospital care per person in the United States was 1.1 for males, 1.4 for females, averaging all ages (p. 118). But boy babies were in hospital more than girl babies, and the same applies to male children up to age 15. It is between ages 15 and 45 that the female excess appears, due to childbearing and gynecological operations. Since women live longer, there are more of them who use hospitals in older age.

It happens that the excess mortality of males is almost exactly the same as that of smokers over nonsmokers, and the fact that at least in the past a larger proportion of men have been smokers accounts for some of the differential. But it is still true that among persons of given smoking status mortality is higher for men than for women (Office of Federal Statistical Policy and Standards, 1977, p. 206). For instance, among those who never smoked, averaging all ages from 35 to 84, the death rate was 14.8 per 1,000 for males and 9.6 per 1,000 for females. Males were 3 times as numerous among homicide and suicide victims (p. 186) and showed 2½ times as many accidental deaths. The sex difference in mortality obtains despite the fact that a higher fraction of women than men are obese (OFSPS, 1977, p. 210).

Interestingly enough, women more often assess their own health as fair or poor than do men (OFSPS, 1977, p. 211). More women said that they felt near a nervous breakdown (p. 212). What we need are more data on mortality according to type of activity. We need to compare women in given occupations with men in the same occupations. Pending more factual detail it has to be admitted that we simply do not know why women live longer than men.

EDUCATION

On the educational front, as in survivorship, real progress appears. The National Center for Education Statistics (OFSPS, 1978, p. 120) shows the substantial change in the sex composition of colleges and universities that took place between October 1966 and October 1976. At the earlier date white males attending were 3,536,000 and white females were 2,172,000; by 1976 the numbers had grown to 4,658,000 and 3,986,000. Both sexes show a large increase, but females much the larger—to the point where equality is in sight for overall attendance at institutions of higher education. Blacks started out closer to sex equality, but with a much lower fraction of each cohort attending; 154,000 males and 128,000 females in 1966, as against 489,000 and 573,000 in 1976. Apparently black females have attained equality in this one sphere, both with whites and with black males.

The National Center for Education Statistics reports some clear gains at the bachelor's degree level for certain professions. Between 1971 and 1976 women increased from 5% to 14% in the field of law, from 9%

to 20% in business and management, from 4% to 14% in architecture and environmental design (OFSPS, 1978, p. 328).

The proportion of women is much lower at the doctoral level. Only 9.1% of doctorates were gained by women in 1950, 10.2% in 1960, and 26.4% in 1978 (p. 174). Though progress is considerable, equality is hardly in sight.

LABOR FORCE

The United States labor force (including those working or looking for work) has been increasing by well over 2 million per year, and by mid-1980 reached 106 million; as recently as 1960 it was only 72 million (p. 394). There are two separate and unrelated causes for the rapid increase—the high births of the 1940s and 1950s and the current entry of women. In round numbers, men in the labor force increased by 13 million between 1960 and 1980, and women by 21 million. Nearly all of the net increase of men occurred in the ages under 35—the number of males beyond age 35 in the work force was constant over the two decades. Women on the other hand have increased at all ages, though most dramatically at ages under 35. The changes since 1960 are embraced in Table 1, expressed in millions of persons (p. 394). The black labor force included among the above has also increased, again more on the female side than on the male. The changes can be briefly summarized by saying that since 1960 the labor force has become younger, more female, and more black.

To what extent can the dramatic rise in employment be merely an offset to shorter hours? Not much: In 1960 average hours worked in all industries (omitting farming) were 38.6 per week; by 1979 they were 35.7 (p. 411), a decline of 8%. This offsets very little of the increase of 67% in the labor force. In fact even the trifling decline of 8% in hours per week over the 19 years is in one sense spurious. Manufacturing taken by itself changed negligibly in the same period: it averaged 39.7 hours worked per week in 1960 and 40.2 in 1979. Finance and insurance fell only from 37.2 to 36.3 hours per week (p. 411). There was a shift of labor force from

Table 1. Changes in the Age Distribution of the United States Labor Force, 1960–1980

	1960		1980		Change 1960–1980	
	−35	35+	−35	35+	−35	35+
Males	19.0	29.9	30.7	30.8	11.7	0.9
Females	8.9	14.5	22.8	20.7	13.9	6.2

manufacturing to finance and other shorter-hour activities, and a good part of overall decline is due merely to this shift. (Unfortunately, average hours worked in government are omitted from the source table.)

Unemployment, bad as it has seemed over the past few years, is trifling over the long term in comparison with the growth of the labor force. Unemployment increased by 4 million from 1960 to its peak in 1975, while employment went up by 19 million (p. 394). Optimists focus on the increase of 19 million working rather than on the added 4 million unemployed. The major problem is less the total unemployment than its distribution. It is heaviest among those groups that have most recently entered the labor force—the young and women, as well as blacks. For 1979 males show some 5.1% unemployed; females, 6.8%; minority races, 11.3%.

One way of presenting employment data is in the form of participation rates: the ratio of labor force to population in age, sex, and racial categories. Here the most dramatic differences are shown between the sexes: from 1960 to 1979 the percentage of men in the labor force went down from 82.6% to 78.0%, due to more years at school and earlier retirement (p. 394). The same schooling and retirement trends also affect women, but nonetheless their overall percentage in the labor force went up from 36.0% to 49.9%.

The entry into jobs in such large proportions is a recent change for American women. In 1960, with only 38% of women in the labor force, the United States was behind such other industrial countries as Britain, Sweden, and Germany, and far under Japan's 53%. Since then the U.S. has climbed steadily to 46% in 1975, while Japan declined to 46% and West Germany to 37%. Italy had always been low, with 31% in 1960; by 1974 it was lower yet at 25% (OFSPS, 1977, p. 390). Middle-class Italians have tended to protect their women, and they apparently use their new prosperity to protect them further. However, a main factor is the shift away from agriculture, where women have always participated heavily. The most that can be said is that women's liberation has clearly taken the form of a movement into jobs in the United States; if the statistics can be trusted, liberation elsewhere may be defined differently and could even take the form of withdrawal from the labor market.

The rise in U.S. female participation rates appears for all ages. For instance, the percentage working of women married with spouse present in 1960 was 31.7% for ages 20–24 and 33.1% for ages 25–44; by 1979 it had gone up to 60.8% and 58.4% for these two groups (p. 401). One would expect a higher proportion of working women among those old enough to have children who have left home, but this seems not to be the case; the fraction of women aged 45–64 who are working is lower than the fraction of younger women. Perhaps by age 45 the husband has reached such a high salary level that the wife's economic assistance is not needed; more likely we have here a cohort difference, because the older women have different attitudes. (Riley, 1980, p. 6, speaks of "cohort norm formation.") In the latter case—if the women 45–64 are working in lower proportions than those younger because they are of a cohort with more domestic orientation—we can expect to see a further rise in the female labor force when the new generation accustomed to holding a job moves into the older age group.

It is still true that the proportion of married women working is lower than that of single women, but the difference is narrowing. For 1960, taking ages 25–44, the participation of married women was 33.1% as against 83.2% of single women; by 1979 the corresponding numbers were 58.4% of married women and 81.8% of single women (p. 401). Extrapolating a quarter century into the future suggests that the difference in labor force participation by marital status will disappear altogether.

This applies to married women with young children, as well as those whose children have left home or have not yet been born. Of women with husbands present and children under 6 years of age, the proportion in the labor force has gone up from 12% in 1950 to 19% in 1960 and 43% in 1979, and the trend is still sharply upward at over 1% per year (p. 403). The portion of women with children under 6 working was 43%; with children 6–17 only, it was 59%; with no children under 18, 47%. It is curious that women with children 6–17 show a higher proportion working than those with no children. An unkind suggestion might be that they want to get away from their children; more realistically, they probably need the money to fill a gap in the family's finances; in fact, those working women with no children at home are older, and the cohort effect mentioned above could well apply.

Bumpass and Sweet (1977) report a study of the way women combine paid work and childbearing through the course of the life cycle. They find that the percentage of women who worked before marriage had gone from 80% in the 1950s to 86% by the late 1960s; the fraction working between marriage and first child went from 66% to 80%, and between first and second child from 37% to 51%. The mean time of exit from the labor force was at 5.8 months of pregnancy, apparently the same in the 1950s and 1960s. Higher rates of unemployment during pregnancy were found for women pregnant with a first child, women married to men with very low incomes or with higher-than-average incomes, and black women.

From being workers and mothers successively, women are more often coming to be workers and mothers simultaneously. Time studies by Philip Stone (1972) and others have shown that the two combined account for very long hours per week. Stone reports a cross-national study that includes Western and socialist countries. Four of his results are:

- A woman's employment cuts into the amount of time she is with her children by over a third. The socialist countries have not managed to let her be with them more than in Western countries.
- Being employed decreases a woman's total "free-time" activities by about half.
- Being employed even cuts into the amount of time a married woman has for sleep, the effect being particularly severe in socialist countries.
- In the Western countries, reluctance to accept women's employment may be the cause of special marital strains. The socialist woman gives precious weekend time to her children or to her spouse and children together, while the Western woman gives it more exclusively to her spouse.

Ways in which women are busy and likely to become busier are suggested by Alice Rossi (1978):

> [T]he critical figure in . . . inter-generational links is a woman. As mental hospitals have shifted from being largely inpatient to outpatient institutions, as veterans return with various kinds of physical and mental disabilities, as children are born with deformities or mental retardation, as older people become chronically disabled, as youth remains unemployed, as the elderly slip below the poverty line, who is picking up the burden and providing the human services? If they are at all able to do so, it is the women in American families.

THE POSTINDUSTRIAL ECONOMY

Technical advance has brought a stage in economic evolution in which farming occupies only 4% of the total labor force (p. 406), and now manufacturing is peaking in absolute numbers and declining as a proportion of the labor force. In 1960 there were 16,796,000 workers in manufacturing and in 1979 there were 20,972,000, but much of the rise took place in the 1960s (the 1970 figure was 19,367,000 [p. 411]).

In the postindustrial society, the strategic resource in the economy is neither land nor capital but knowledge. A large part of production may be imputed to information processing. This knowledge theory of value covers every part of the economy: the weather forecaster with his computer models of atmospheric movements contributes to agriculture, just as the expert in control theory helps the automobile industry. Electronic pattern recognition is initiating a new wave of automation.

The high productivity that results must sooner or later lead to a condition of saturation with material goods. In the nature of things, we require only so much food, so many refrigerators to store it in, so many automobiles to fetch it from the supermarket. Notwithstanding the move up from bread to meat and a variety of changes of fashion, we reach adequate supplies in one commodity after another. The question for the future is going to be whether social emulation will be strong enough to push demand upward, or whether the economic problem will be regarded as solved. Up to now the trend of hours of paid work and the preoccupation with unemployment, along with inflationary pressures, suggest that economic questions are increasingly salient.

If primary (agricultural) and secondary (manufacturing and construction) work is slowing down, what are all those new people (youth and women) doing in the labor force? They mostly fall under three headings: participation in the wholesale and retail trades went up by over 5 million between 1970 and 1979 (from 15,040,000 to 20,137,000), and a 5.5 million increase was shown in the services and 3 million in government. Thus trade, services, and government together account for 13.5 million of the 19 million increase of labor force over 9 years, while manufacturing accounts for only 1.5 million (p. 415).

TERTIARY WORK

What women now have an opportunity to work at is an important factor in their movement into the labor force. Taking the critical group—those who have a choice whether or not to work—of married women with husband present, we find that only 12% are factory operatives as against 36% who are clerical workers, both in 1979. In 1955, 22% were operatives, 25% clerical workers. Women are more and more underrepresented in manufacturing and overrepresented in finance and insurance, retail trade, services, and government (p. 405).

Some 3.5 million married women with husband present were professional and technical workers in 1976. In a high proportion of cases their husbands were also professional and technical workers, so that there are well over 3 million households in the United States with husband and wife both enjoying substantial salaries. Has this movement of women into professional fields brought a revival of domestic services? Even though the income tax authorities make little concession to them, one would have thought that many such couples would have a live-in domestic servant. Yet women live-in servants numbered only 167,000 in the census of 1960, and had dropped by more than half, to 73,000, by the census of 1970. Women private household workers living out were more numerous, 1,585,000 in 1960, but they, too, had fallen substantially by

1970—to 1,093,000 (p. 410). Many of these are foreign-born and have little choice in the labor market.

The conclusion from this is that the American woman wants to escape from her home and, however low her social class, however disadvantaged she may be by color or birthplace, wants less and less to work in someone else's home. The tertiary sector is often referred to as "service," yet domestic servants, barbers, and taxi drivers are all rapidly decreasing in numbers. (The dictionary meaning of "service" has given over to a new and somewhat ironic meaning, as in "Internal Revenue Service.")

Those who want to see women in the upper reaches of the work hierarchy along with men will not get much comfort from a more detailed breakdown of the labor force by occupation. It is true that women professional and technical workers of all marital statuses went from 2.7 million in 1960 to 6.5 million in 1979, which is to say that they more than doubled; but it is also true that the lower category of clerical workers went from 6.6 million to 14.2 million (p. 18). The proportion of women in higher level occupations has increased, but not dramatically.

EARNINGS

Correspondingly, there has been little advance in the earnings of women compared with those of men. Comparability is not easy to attain in the aggregate figures, but consider the contribution to family income made by husband and wife when both are working. For white families the wife contributed 25.7% in 1970 and 24.9% in 1974—the only dates available. There is no sign of a favorable trend; working husbands continue to contribute three times as much income as working wives. This is partly, but only partly, because a larger fraction of wives than husbands were working part time, either voluntarily or not.

Counting full-time workers only, median earnings of all men ages 25 and over were $322 per week in 1979, against $197 for women. This reflects both different kinds of work and different pay for the same work. It shows slight improvement from 1970; men went up by 101%, women by 105% (p. 424).

A recent National Academy of Sciences report gives 1977 median salaries for doctoral scientists and engineers at $26,000 for men and $20,700 for women. In the humanities the difference was less, $22,100 for men and $18,300 for women.

Swafford (1978) shows how widespread is the differential compensation of men and women. Differences of definition introduce some uncertainties into international comparison, but official published figures are remarkably consistent from country to country. For white-collar or technical workers, women's earnings were 62% of men's earnings in 1976 in Great Britain, 69% in Sweden, 65% in Switzerland. For all workers over 25, they are 61% in the United States.

It is hard to obtain data for the USSR, but evidence adduced by Swafford (1978) suggests 66%. The difference between the sexes is explained by a Soviet writer:

> As is well known, there exist many occupations which require primarily men's or women's work. As examples, we need merely point to such occupations as mechanic, miner, steel founder, driver, and others which are almost all in the sphere of men's activity. The work of these and similar occupations is complex, heavy, demanding and at times requires great physical strength; that gives rise to higher pay. On the other hand, the occupations of weaver, typist, and library worker as a rule are filled by women. Although these occupations demand significant concentration and attention, all the same their work is comparatively light, which explains women's relatively low level of pay.

The women's movement in the United States would hardly find this explanation satisfactory.

In the United States at least some of the difference is related to genuine competition in the female labor market and restriction in the male. Of 21.8 million dues-paying labor union members in the United States in 1979 some 16.6 million were men and 5.1 million were women (p. 429). Relating these to the 59.5 million men and 43.4 million women in the labor force, men members of unions make up 28% of workers, 12% for women. Is the proportion of women low because they are so largely in clerical and other white-collar occupations where there is effectively open admission? Are these less unionized because there are more women in them or because they are closer to management? Do women unionize less because they are less committed to the labor market? The overall statistics cannot answer such questions, but they are useful in at least pointing to some important differences.

THE TYPING OF OCCUPATIONS

The arduousness of work in an earlier generation kept out those women who had husbands capable of supporting them, but today work is mechanized. Trucks, if not already so equipped, can be fitted with controls suited to women. The dead hand of the past is on us: up to this generation construction was hard work for which men were physically better adapted than women; the industry came to be rigidly organized, and a universal understanding came into existence that building was men's work. Technology has made (or can make) many of the building trades equally suited to women and men, but that fact by no means brings about an automatic change in social expectations.

Society does not start out each day from a zero base. The activities of the previous phase of history created interests that are a living force to influence this phase. When the United States had no significant weapons industry there was no arms lobby; the national defense budget is what ultimately pays for the lobby and ensures the expansion of the defense budget. If there had been no previous phase of the construction industry in which muscular strength was a requisite there would now be no structure of employers and unions to keep women out when muscles have become unimportant.

New industries are less tied to the past. The airlines defined as women's work many activities that were men's work on the railroads; the railway ticket collector and club-car attendant or waiter gave way to the airline hostess. It seems to have required the elimination of the passenger railroads and their replacement by the airlines for women to have this opportunity.

Why Women Work

Note that the increase in women's work outside the home occurs despite their persistently lower wages and despite a decreasing return due to the income tax. The tax is formally symmetrical between men and women, but the symmetry is lost if the husband is already working when the wife makes her decision. She may well think of her entire income as taxed at the couple's marginal rate. Between lower wages and income tax she receives a small net return for her work and yet goes into the labor market notwithstanding.

The most obvious explanation of why women work is that they need the money. Prices are going up all the time; it seems harder for families to make ends meet. But what appears to the individuals concerned to be the reason for working cannot possibly explain the overall trend, for women work more now when real average income is high than they did years ago when it was low. The question then becomes: Why do people need the extra income in the 1970s if they did not need it in the 1920s or the 1950s when they were much poorer? Why do they need it in the United States and not in Italy, where the income per head is only half as high?

The statement that people work because they need the money can be rescued by saying that the richer one is, the higher one's demands; but such an explanation after the fact is suspect. There is no way of measuring the increase in people's needs outside of their observed entry into the labor force, so rather than the needs' explaining the entry, the two are different ways of stating the same fact. I side with those from

Marx onward who have seen work as important for its own sake (Riley, 1980).

VOTING

Participation of women in political society may be expected to rise with their more independent participation in the economy. American women have not voted in as large proportions as men, but in recent years the gap has narrowed. Thus according to a sample (p. 519), 69.8% of men of voting age stated that they had voted in the presidential election of 1968 compared to 66.0% of women; in 1972 the numbers were 64.1% and 62.0%; in 1976 they were 59.6% and 58.8%. The voting population was increased to include those 18 and over in 1972 and there was a downtrend on the whole, but the narrowing difference between men and women is probably real.

CONCLUSION

Through colorless official statistics we have glimpsed drastic changes taking place in American society. Some of these changes show progress for women as well as for men—in longevity, in education, in labor-force participation. Other changes are less admirable. Women seek to have the sorts of contacts and careers outside the home that men have always taken for granted, but their progress toward these is spotty. They have made gains in employment, but have higher rates of unemployment than men; they have advanced in education, both as students and as teachers, but have made less progress in the construction trades, as business executives, and in the higher reaches of government.

The statistics cited here hint at the essential difficulty of combining motherhood and careers. They cannot alone say what ought to be done to hasten the attainment of equality, but they prompt me to suggest that in some future day being a mother will be regarded as one phase of a career. The soldier or flier works for 20 years in the armed forces and then continues for the remaining 25 or so years of his work life in private industry. He has a pension that subsidizes his subsequent work by continuing a large fraction of the salary that he has been paid in the military, a cost justified by security needs.

If this is taken as a model, a woman would be paid a salary by the state for the time (typically less than 20 years) that it takes to bear children and raise them to the age where they no longer require much maternal attention. During the time the children are in her care she might undertake subsidized part-time study with a view to her later work. With something like the GI Bill of Rights to further more intensive education when she has completed her service as a mother, she could then launch herself on what would be seen as the second half of her career. Corresponding support would be provided to the energetic woman who could carry on motherhood and career simultaneously; some of the support would be financial, some of it subsidies to day-care centers and other ancillary services. These measures are a recognition that the community needs childbearing and childraising and ought to compensate them just as it compensates other useful work. They will come to seem less extravagant as time passes and American births continue to be below replacement level. The future of the country depends at least as much on its mothers as on its soldiers. We await a President who will press Congress for a real increase of 10% per year in national expenditures on children.

REFERENCES

Bumpass, L. L., & Sweet, J. A. *Patterns of employment before and after childbirth* (CDE Working Paper 77–20). Madison, Wisc. Center for Demography and Ecology, 1977.

Easterlin, R. A. *Birth and fortune: The impact of numbers on personal welfare.* New York: Basic Books, 1980.

National Center for Education Statistics. *The condition of education.* Washington, D.C.: U.S. Government Printing Office, 1978.

Office of Federal Statistical Policy and Standards, Bureau of the Census, U.S. Department of Commerce. *Social Indicators, 1976.* Washington, D.C.: U.S. Government Printing Office, 1977.

Office of Federal Statistical Policy and Standards, Bureau of the Census, U.S. Department of Commerce. *Statistical Reporter,* June 1978, No. 78–9.

Riley, M. W. *Implications for the middle and later years.* (Conference Report, Women: A Development Perspective, In press.)

Rossi, A. S. *Problems and prospects: American families in the 1980s.* Keynote Address, Northeast Home Economics Association, Hartford, Conn., 1978.

Stone, P. J. On being up against the wall: Women's time patterns in eleven countries (Unpublished manuscript, 1972.)

Swafford, M. Sex differences in Soviet earnings. *American Sociological Review,* 1978, 43(5), 657–673.

U.S. Bureau of the Census. *Population profile of the United States: 1977* (Current Population Reports P–20, No. 324). Washington, D.C.: U.S. Government Printing Office, 1978.

U.S. Bureau of the Census. *Statistical abstract of the United States.* Washington, D.C.: U.S. Government Printing Office, 1980.

Chapter 2

The Challenge of Sex Equality
Old Values Revisited or a New Culture?

WILLIAM H. CHAFE

As America moves toward a new century, few developments appear
more significant for the future of our society than the changes that have
occurred in the distribution of sex roles over the past 40 years. In many
areas the lives of women have been virtually transformed since World
War II. In 1940 it was a mark of opprobrium for married middle-class
mothers to work. Today more than half of such women are in the labor
force. In 1940 participation of women in law and medicine was almost
unheard of. Today professional schools in both areas are increasingly
populated by women students. In 1940 feminism was a word of suspicion that occasioned laughter, if not scorn. Today politicians and media
commentators make a point—on the surface at least—of paying homage
to the idea of equal rights.

Yet if a shift in sex roles has been a hallmark of the past three
decades, it is by no means clear that change has brought progress toward equality, or for that matter *any* significant alteration in the underlying values governing our society. Together with race and class, gender
roles still shape our lives in fundamental ways. Whether we are born
male or female, black or white, poor or rich, determines the entire pattern of our existence, shaping the power we may exercise, the vocations
we can aspire to, the "life chances" we have—even the emotions we are
taught to cultivate. The values associated with sex roles in particular are
implicit in every aspect of our daily lives. Notions of competitiveness,
individualism, success, achievement, dominance, and victory reflect di-

WILLIAM H. CHAFE, PH.D. • Oral History Program, Duke University, Durham, North
Carolina 27710.

rectly our underlying presuppositions about masculinity and femininity. Clearly not a great deal will have changed in our world if the old values prevail and some women simply join as new participants in traditional ways of doing things. In the midst of changes in sex roles that sometimes appear revolutionary, therefore, it becomes imperative to pose the larger issue of where we are going: Will a shift in the roles men and women occupy affect in any significant way a culture whose social and economic structures to this day still operate according to "masculine" values.

HISTORICAL CHANGE

The pervasiveness of the changes that have occurred in sex roles should no longer be a matter of dispute. The shift began during World War II when 6.5 million women went to work for the first time, nearly three-quarters of them married, and 60% of them over age 35. These were women who had been taught in their childhood that it was a violation of nature to work after marriage—unless one were black or poor. During the Depression, especially, women were urged to stay in the home so that men might have a better chance for a job. Then it suddenly became a matter of patriotic necessity that women leave the home and take jobs in order to win the war. After four years of employment, the vast majority (80%) decided that they liked to work, and enjoyed the recognition of a paycheck. They welcomed the opportunity for companionship, and wished to remain on the job. In service to patriotism, a revolution in behavior had occurred. And once the genie was out of the bottle, there was no putting it back in.

During most of the 20 years after World War II a kind of cultural schizophrenia gripped the country. While popular magazines, politicians, and preachers of consumerisum drove home the ideology of the "feminine mystique," the same middle-class women who allegedly were finding new fulfillment in domesticity were in fact returning to the labor force in increasing numbers. During the 1950s women's employment rate rose four times faster than that of men. More important, those women who entered the labor force were the same group who had first joined in large numbers during World War II—middle-aged, middle-class, married white women. Although the magazines and advertisers continued to sell the romance of homemaking, homemakers themselves were increasingly becoming a part of the labor force. Most were offered jobs far below their abilities, at wages that showed contempt for their work. On the other hand the jobs they held were the indispensable precondition for large numbers of American families to enter the world of middle-class consumerism that advocates of the "feminine mystique" trumpeted so loudly.

During the 1960s the gap between attitudes and behavior finally evoked a broad-scale social movement designed to correct ancient inequalities. The new women's movement was a direct offshoot of the civil rights movement. Women took as their model both the organization and the strategy that had guided the early civil rights movement. Martin Luther King, Jr., preached the immorality of treating any group of people as unequal to others simply because of a physical characteristic. That message obviously applied to sex as well as to race. Perhaps more important, the younger women who had joined the student demonstrations in the South became increasingly radicalized as they saw their sex used as a basis for discrimination against them *within* the movement, even as they worked to eliminate the wider problem of social discrimination based on race. The recruits who made up the women's liberation movement on campuses and in cities during the middle and late 1960s came from the civil rights movement, and drew from it an acute understanding of the shortcomings of traditional American society, as well as of the fallacies of traditional American values.

Although at first dismissed as a joke, the new feminism quickly achieved a significant impact on American society. Consciousness, once raised, could not be destroyed, and even if the vast majority of women did not attend consciousness-raising sessions, they shared in twos and threes the dawning awareness that theirs was a social condition created by unjust and far-reaching discriminatory practices which could be eliminated only by collective action. The "problem that had no name" suddenly became a product of the society in which one was reared rather than an individual idiosyncracy. At first in small groups, and then through national coalitions of concerned women, activists began to agitate for legislative and cultural change on issues involving sex bias.

The impact of the women's movement was perhaps best dramatized in a series of public opinion polls. In 1962 a Gallup survey of American women had shown that by a margin of nearly two to one American women did not feel that they were discriminated against or treated unequally. Eight years later, after the movement had begun to draw significant attention, the proportion of women who perceived widespread discrimination grew to 50%. By 1974 the earlier margin of two to one had been reversed so that two out of three women responding to the new poll affirmed their commitment to measures designed to secure equality. Moreover, even if some felt uncomfortable with the women's liberation movement itself as "radical" or "too kooky," a vast majority endorsed feminist programs such as the Equal Rights Amendment, the repeal of abortion laws, sharing of household responsibilities, and equal access to careers.

By the 1970s for the first time in more than half a century shifts in attitude and behavior began to reinforce each other, creating a mutually supportive cycle. The surge in women's employment that had started with World War II reached new heights. By 1975, 49% of all wives were employed (as opposed to 15% in 1940) and nearly 60% of all mothers of children 6–17 years old were in the work force. The progression of women's employment had followed its own peculiar cultural logic. During the late 1940s and 1950s the greatest increase had occurred among women over 35 whose children were in school, and whose employment did not directly challenge the emotional values associated with early mother–child relationships. During the late 1960s and 1970s, however, the greatest increase occurred among younger women in the prime childbearing and childrearing ages. The sharpest rise of all occurred among women 20–24 years old, whose employment increased from 50% in 1964 to 61% in 1973. At the same time, employment of mothers with children under 3 more than doubled, from 15% in 1959 to 31% in 1974, and that for mothers of children 3–5 moved from 25% to 39%. Clearly the social notion about women's "place" being in the home no longer had a base in reality. Indeed, female labor market participation had begun to approach in shape that of men, taking the form of an inverted "U" rather than an "M."

At the same time commitment to careers among younger women became increasingly pronounced. The proportion of women enrolled in law schools and medical schools grew by 300% between 1969 and 1974, and most law schools projected an enrollment that would be 50% women by 1980. In a growing number of surveys, women indicated that their career would be just as important as a choice of potential marriage mate, and that training for the career might well take precedence over marriage. In fact a trend toward later marriages was already evident. By 1971 more than half of all women 20 years of age were single, as contrasted with only one-third in 1960. In addition more and more women were either living with men out of marriage, living alone, or living with female roommates.

Changes in career aspirations and job patterns coincided with a shift in both attitude and behavior about sexuality. Most observers concluded that a second sexual revolution had occurred in America during the 1960s. One study of women students at a large urban university showed a significant increase after 1965 in the number of women having intercourse in a "dating" or "going steady" relationship; at the same time guilt feelings about sex sharply declined. Another nationwide sample of freshmen college women in 1975 disclosed that one-third endorsed casual sex based on short acquaintance, and over 40% believed that couples should live together before getting married. Most indicative of changing mores, perhaps, was a survey conducted by Joseph Katz in 1976 of eight colleges. Katz found not only that 76% of women had engaged in intercourse by their junior year (the male figure was also 76%) but that women were appreciably more active sexually than men. New attitudes toward abortion, homosexuality, and premarital and extramarital sex all testified to the change. As one other indicator, *Our Bodies, Ourselves,* a handbook published by a woman's health collective on the importance of women controlling their own bodies, sold nearly 1,000,000 copies between 1971 and 1976.

Each of these changes in turn related directly to one of the most important and startling shifts of all—the plummeting birthrate. After World War II a baby boom spread across the country, peaking in 1957 with a birthrate of 27.2 children per 1,000 people. There then ensued a prolonged downturn, which in 1967 resulted in the birthrate of 17.9, the lowest since the Great Depression. At the time demographers disagreed about the reasons for the decline, some citing the development of oral conceptives; others, economic and social instability. But all agreed that there would be a new baby boom in the early 1970s when the children born 20 years earlier began to reproduce. Yet instead of rising, the birthrate continued to decline, reaching an all-time low by the mid-1970s and achieving the reproduction level required—over time—for zero population growth.

There appeared to be a direct relationship between the declining birthrate and changing attitudes toward marriage, sexuality, employment, and childbearing. Throughout the 1960s women married later, delayed the birth of their first child, and bore their last child at an earlier age. Whether as cause or effect, this trend coincided with many women finding careers or interests away from the home. The rewards of an independent life outside the family tended to emphasize the advantages of a small number of children. These advantages in turn were reinforced by the ideology of feminism and the population control movement. Two Gallup polls in 1967 and 1971 highlighted the shift in values. The earlier survey showed that 34% of women in the prime childbearing years anticipated having four or more children. By 1971, in contrast, the figure had dropped to 15%. Two years later 70% of the nation's 18- to 24-year-old women indicated that they expected to have no more than two children, and in a public opinion poll conducted by Daniel Yankelovich (1974) in 1973, only 27% of college women considered that having children was an important value in their lives. By 1975 the fertility rate of women had fallen to exactly half of what it had been 20 years earlier. Thus by the end of the 1970s job patterns, career aspirations, marriage trends, attitudes toward sexuality, and the fertility rates all tended to coincide with, and reflect, a new awareness of sex equality as an issue, and a new commitment toward roles for women vastly different from those that became normative in late-19th-century Victorian America.

Needless to say college women were, and are, in the forefront of these changes. Between 1968 and 1980 the number of women college graduates was expected to increase by two-thirds (twice the rate of increase for men), providing a growing pool of potential career women. By 1975, 86% of all college women 24 years of age were employed. The growing ranks of applicants for professional schools testified to the commitment of the new generation of college women to independent careers, including careers formerly dominated by men. In fact whether one looked at jobs, careers, sexual practices, divorce rates, or attitudes toward women's liberation, higher education appeared always to correlate with the most advanced or "liberated" attitudes and practices.

In the eyes of at least some people the changes that occurred, as well as the attitudes that accompanied them, signified that the major obstacles to sex equality had been overcome. The cry of "reverse discrimination" signified a growing belief by many that women and blacks now had the advantage over white men, and that white Anglo-Saxon Protestant males were suddenly in the position of victims. On college campuses sex equality had become almost a part of the American creed—a belief that almost no one dared to challenge directly. The Katz (1976) survey of college students indicated that 86% of men as well as 92% of women believed that fathers should spend as much time as mothers in bringing up their children. It was almost as though sex discrimination and inequality were relics of a long-forgotten past, and that the new generation of college men and women had inaugurated an era of complete sex equality and liberation.

THE PERSISTENCE OF INEQUALITY

Nothing of course could be further from the truth. In the years of greatest change in women's employment patterns, the actual earnings of women declined relative to men. Although some barriers to equal opportunity had been eliminated through the Department of Health, Education and Welfare's HEW enforcment proceedings, most patterns of discrimination remained intact. In addition, cultural presumptions about women's "place" continued to pervade the society, providing fuel for those who opposed affirmative action. The number of "token" women on corporate boards may have increased, but the aggregate statistics showed no appreciable change in the number of women who were full

THE CHALLENGE OF SEX EQUALITY

professors or business executives. Indeed if, as some have argued, the entire economy of consumerism is based on treating women as sex objects, there seems to have been an acceleration rather than diminution of sex oppression during the "liberated" 1970s. From Noxema's "take it all off" to Catherine Deneuve's "all my men wear English Leather," the selling of sex has become synonymous with rising profits.

In fact the problem of continued sex inequality rests as much *within* the younger generation as in society as a whole. The movement toward sex equality has two edges—one egalitarian, the other elitist. The young must face a decision as to which path to take. Growing out of the counterculture and student movements of the 1960s there has developed some sentiment toward a more egalitarian and cooperative society that would place less emphasis on victory and competition. One poll taken by Daniel Yankelovich (1974) showed that nearly 80% of college young people and 74% of noncollege young people would welcome less emphasis on money within society. Almost half of all young people also said that they would give priority to self-fulfillment over economic security in choosing a job. Many women and men seemed committed in principle to the idea of a society of greater sharing.

Yet the same generation that says it is alienated from traditional free-enterprise values has also given evidence of being very committed to behaviors that perpetuate those values. Observers on most major campuses have noted a new obsession with grades, an end to political and social activism, and the revival of traditional attitudes toward fraternities and sports. It seems as though everyone wants to go to medical school or law school and make $100,000 before reaching 30. The conflict between the two approaches could hardly be more glaring. Yet it speaks directly to the underlying issue involved in the quest for sex equality. Will young women and men assume leadership in promoting and supporting new values that could undercut the gross inequalities that exist in American society based on sex, race, and class? Or will they join the mainstream and embrace the traditional values that created those inequalities in the first place. Stated another way, will the students of Radcliffe, Duke, Yale, and Smith devote their efforts toward ensuring that more women participate in the top 5% of the existing system, or will they join a movement to change the values that produced and have rationalized that 5% in the first place?

HISTORICAL PRECEDENTS

Fortunately or unfortunately, there exists an historical precedent for the kind of choice that today's younger generation must make. At the turn of the century another great movement for sex equality began to crest. It too was characterized by leadership from college women. As women's colleges were founded throughout the country in the last quarter of the 19th century, they attracted students infused with a conscious sense of mission and obligation. The very act of going to college set the first generation of college women apart from others as a select group with a special responsibility. Between 1890 and 1910, a Vassar professor recalled, women students "proudly marched in militant processions and joyfully accepted arrest and imprisonment for the sake of 'votes for women', free speech, and to help a strike" (Rogers, 1940, p. 115). Through such organizations as the College Equal Suffrage League these women provided a cutting edge for the social changes that were to come with the social welfare movement. In addition most ventured into careers that broke new patterns. More than 50% of the graduates of women's colleges prior to 1900 remained single, preferring to employ their energies and talents in a career rather than submerge their individuality in marriage. They invented the profession of social work, attended medical schools, became architects, political leaders, and social welfare organizers. On trial before the world, such women were dedicated to proving that women had as many brains as men and could hold their own in the "rough" world of politics and business. Only those who took part in the early college experience for women, one Wellesley historian wrote, could know "how exciting and romantic it was to be a professor in a woman's college during the last half century"

Understandably, the first generation of college women looked to their successors to carry on the battle. Between 1900 and 1920 enrollment of women in public colleges increased by 1,000% and in private colleges by 482%. Many of these students took part in the suffrage crusade leading to the enactment of the Nineteenth Amendment in 1920. But after the vote had been gained, the activist spark seemed to disappear. Ironically, the absence of enthusiasm coincided with, and probably reflected, the extent to which college education for women had become a norm rather than an aberration. In a new era supposedly devoted to "equality" the atmosphere of special purpose began to evaporate. "Feminism has become a term of opprobrium for the young," one author observed in 1927 (Bromley, 1927, pp. 152–160). Instead of sacrifice and dedication to a cause, young students seemed more concerned with having a good time. "We are not out to benefit society . . . or to make industry safe," one student commented (O'Hagan, 1928). And Virginia Gildersleeve, the head of Barnard College, remarked that the new generation of college students was characterized by "blasé indifference, self-indulgence, and irresponsibility" (Gildersleeve, 1934).

Instead of the social reformer, the flapper characterized the new era. Although she held a job, smoked cigarettes, and used profanity, she did not embrace the social reforms of the generation before. The women's movement had ceased to hold any attraction for the "juniors," one League of Women Voters officer lamented. Instead, the flappers personified a lifestyle totally alien to that of the older generation. "I mean to do what I like . . . undeterred by convention," one short story heroine remarked (Chambers, 1925). "Freedom—that is the modern essential. To live one's life in one's own way" (Gildersleeve, 1934). In popular history the 1920s gained a reputation as the era of the "emancipated woman." But whatever emancipation occurred was both strictly personal and also temporary.

The feminist movement itself, meanwhile, divided into bitter factions. The National Women's Party devoted itself single-mindedly to the passage of the Equal Rights Amendment and rejected coalition with those groups that supported social welfare laws, maternity- and infancy-health legislation, or the birth control movement. "Social feminists" in turn tended to deemphasize issues of women's rights, and more and more devoted themselves to fighting the National Women's Party and defending the idea of "protective" legislation for working women. The end result was the rapid loss of any degree of popular support for either faction of the women's movement. Leaders of the National Women's Party were denounced as elitists who cared only for the narrow rights of a few, while supporters of the Women's Trade Union League, the League of Woman Voters, and other social feminist organizations failed to find an issue that would rekindle the social fervor or support of the mass of American women. The optimism of the suffrage era had passed. Neither the college women who were supposed to carry the torch, nor the older leaders, were able to carry forward effectively the battle to restructure the institutions and values of American society.

THE CHOICE BEFORE US

The experience of the 1920s seems disturbingly pertinent to that of the 1980s. Today as then college women and men have inherited the benefits of a decade of social activism without carrying that activism forward toward the goals it espoused. Today as in the 1920s there is a tendency to equate personal freedom with social progress. "Doing your own thing" has become a cultural watchword identified in the public eye with greater sexual freedom, experimentation with drugs, "hanging loose," or simply "looking out for number one." Today as well as then there exists a tendency to emphasize personal gain, individual happiness, and self-gratification rather than to think critically of social institutions and their impact on large classes of people. The 1920s was the era of "the emancipated woman." The 1970s and '80s are the age of "sexual liberation."

Yet history is not necessarily destined to repeat itself. Even if there are trends discernible today that bear a striking resemblance to those of the 1920s, the final decision has not yet been made. If the public opinion polls of Daniel Yankelovich and others are to be believed, many young people are still confused about which direction they wish to pursue, and are still alienated from some of the traditional values of success and competitiveness associated with the past. The contemporary student generation may compulsively pursue high grades to get into law or medical school, but as one student remarked, "that's not because we believe in it. It's because we don't see any alternative" (Personal communication, Duke University student, 1978).

For there to be an alternative, of course, there must be a social movement with a coherent vision of a different social order. Up until now most reform efforts in America have operated on the premise that the existing system of values is sound, that only slight correctives are required in order to restore health to the body politic, and that legal redress of grievances will be sufficient to incorporate all Americans within the "equal opportunity" network. Thus most of America's greatest moments of reform have centered on such issues as winning the suffrage, abolishing child labor, guaranteeing access to public accommodations, etc. Each of these efforts has been a significant and indispensable step toward change. But all have presumed that beneath it all the system is sound, and that once legal rights are granted everyone will be treated as equal under the law and have the same opportunities.

The underlying question then becomes: What do we mean by equality, or equal rights? In the case of sex, can we have equal relationships between men and women without a collective vision that emphasizes mutual fulfillment and responsibility rather than personal self-aggrandizement? Can we have equality between partners when winning is still emphasized as the most important goal, and rising up the corporate ladder is seen as more important than developing rewarding personal relationships? More generally, can we have equality as long as the botton 40% of the wage earners in America bring home only 14% of the income and control less than 3% of the wealth, and the top 5% controls 20% of the income and 53% of the wealth? Can we have equality as long as welfare laws discourage men from staying with their families and as long as the government grants the right of abortion—de facto—only to those who can afford to pay for it?

All of these questions point to the implicit contradiction, or at least potential incompatability, between liberty and equality. Through much of our past history we have managed to escape the contradiction by relying on the concept of equality of opportunity—the notion that individuals starting from the same place would then distinguish themselves by their personal talent. Yet equal opportunity has never in fact existed in a society where the vast majority of people—blacks, women, native Americans, most minority groups, and most workers—have never started from a place of opportunity parallel to that experienced by a rich, white, and male elite. As long as there was still land to settle or new industries to build we were able to retain a faith that the next spurt of economic growth or the next new invention would make it possible for those who historically had been left out finally to find a way into the American dream. But now even that illusory notion has lost all credibility. We find ourselves with the prospect of continuing economic crisis and a sharp limit to the possibility of further growth. One out of every seven jobs in America is connected to the automobile industry. In the face of a worldwide recession, how can the economy continue to grow at its past rate? In short, we appear to be at a turning point, not only on the issue of how men and women relate to each other, but how that relationship in turn intersects with and mirrors the entire structure of values that guide the conduct of our social and economic institutions.

One of the virtues of the chaotic 1960s was to highlight the interrelationship of specific social grievances and larger cultural values. Although the connection was never fully developed in any movement's literature, it helped to explain why so many devotees of particular causes in the middle and late 1960s eventually abandoned their immediate goals as hopeless within the existing framework of society, and set out instead to create a new culture—a counterculture. Whatever we think of the shortcomings of that effort, especially its own form of self-indulgence, condescension, and upper-middle-class luxury, the instinct to draw ties between specific injustices and overall cultural assumptions was sound. The Vietnam War was not a temporary aberration or a sound policy gone momentarily awry. It grew out of a framework of values about American power, Third World peoples, and the right of the United States to tell the rest of the world how to behave that has its own history going back at least as far as the Indian wars and the 1846 Mexican War. In short, one of the major contributions (albeit a failed one) of the 1960s was a focus on our larger values, and on the assumptions provided an underpinning for institutions that rewarded "body counts," victory at all costs in football contests, and money-making as the great barometer of success.

Within this larger context the women's movement contributed its own crucial insights. If the problem of sex discrimination grew out of patterns in the male world that kept women quiet or ignored them, movement advocates reassured, then women must meet by themselves and gather strength from within. Furthermore the solidarity that brought strength must also be the basis for devising a more satisfactory and meaningful set of ground rules for interaction. If one of the problems of the existing system was a "masculine" culture based on hierarchy, winning, and competition, the women's movement would seek sanction for new modes of behavior based on collective decision-making, cooperation, and mutual respect and tolerance. These were ideals not always achieved in practice. But they carried forward in significant ways the underlying and critical perception that people's behavior flowed from the value assumptions learned in the culture.

Perhaps the most pivotal manifestation of this insight was the movement's repeated emphasis on the interrelationship of the private and public sectors of people's lives. As movement adherents stated over and over again, the personal is political and the political is personal. One cannot live a compartmentalized existence, advancing a philosophy of liberation on the outside, if one is living a condition of oppression on the inside. This premise in turn provided a nexus that all other movements of the 1960s lacked, or at least found more difficult to locate—namely, that there was a place very close to home where one's own thoughts and actions could relate directly to the largest conflicts over macrostructures and cultural values. By zeroing in one one's own family, home, or living situation as the starting place of the revolution, the women's movement forged that connection between the immediate grievance and the larger cultural framework that had eluded other 1960s activists.

In making such a connection the women's movement also dramatized that enormous difficulties were inherent in moving toward sex equality. For the male–female situation, by this definition, gathered unto itself the full complexity and contradictions of the society as a whole when questions of equality arise—contradictions such as individualism versus collective action, competition versus cooperation, external achievement versus internal satisfaction. If there is no way that we can envision equality between the sexes without a major alteration in the way men and women relate to each other in the home as well as in the way institutions operate to facilitate a greater distribution of resources between the sexes, then the dimensions of our challenge can be fully revealed by looking at our own personal situations and the choices we are called upon to make. And it is here that the point of contact is made with today's generation of college students.

For illustrative purposes let us take a model young man and woman, both college graduates, who choose to get married at the age of 24. They plan on having two children, one when they are 27, the other when they are 30. They plan to have both children enrolled in school by the time the parents reach the age of 35.[1] Both spouses believe in sex equality and look forward to maximizing their individual potential for success, he as a doctor and she as a lawyer. In order for one to attend professional school, however, the other must work. Consistent with past practice, the wife takes a job in an advertising firm while the husband attends medical school. The first child arrives as planned, in the middle of the husband's internship and prior to his establishing a "successful" career. It suddenly appears that with a child at home, the only way the wife will achieve her career goals will be for the husband to drop out of medical school for a period of time and take primary responsibility for the child while the woman begins her law school career. Obviously, significant tensions develop in the relationship as those choices are negotiated, but there is enough commitment to their initial collective vision on the part of both partners for them to proceed. After the first two years of law school the couple decides that they will use day care facilities for the children and that both of them will attend school on a part-time basis, sharing household responsibilities. As each concludes his or her schooling, it becomes obvious that a full-time, 16-hour-a-day career for either spouse will destroy any possibility for a meaningful family life or significant personal interaction. At this juncture both succeed in finding career openings that demand only a part-time commitment of 6 hours per day. After some haggling, they work out a flexible work schedule which permits each parent to spend a significant portion of the day with the children and still leaves time for the spouses to interact successfully with each other as well as to find meaning and fulfillment in their careers. They live happily ever after.

Obviously, such a scenario presumes a radical transformation both of the personal values that today's young people bring to their relationship, as well as a readiness on the part of social and economic institutions to encourage, or at least make possible, the development of equality between men and women. On a personal level both the man and the woman would have to place a higher priority on their mutual commitment to each other's fulfillment than on the traditional American value of individual achievement through success over one's competitors. Instead of rising quickly and sharply in one's chosen profession, each would accept the spreading out of his or her education, along with the

[1]As is already clear, this discussion itself discriminates against large groups of people—those who prefer living alone, are divorced, or are gay. To account for each possible living situation would be impossible, and since overall rates of marriage as well as heterosexual behavior seem to have remained stable, I am presuming a nuclear family situation in this description. The problems that arise in this "family," however, would in all likelihood arise in any "family" generically defined—that is, people living together with a bond of common commitments and expectations.

diminished possibilities of prestige that would accompany such a delay, in order to live up to their "shared vision." Yet the delay would be possible in the first place only if the law school or the medical school recognized, and was willing to adjust to, a new pattern of student priorities and values. In all likelihood, moreover, such academic institutions would support innovation only if other social and economic institutions gave evidence of flexibility. Indeed the success of our couple in achieving their collective goals would be dependent on hospitals, medical practices, law firms, and corporations being willing to establish flexible job schedules and to support part-time careers. For that to happen, in turn, the government and political leaders would have to provide tax support as well as implement such social policies as universal day care. In short, an egalitarian marriage that started out with a generalized commitment to equal opportunity for both spouses would, in order to be implemented, entail a radical restructuring of the institutions that dominate our society, as well as the values that shape our images of what it means to be a man or a woman, a success or a failure, happy or unhappy.

The point of this lengthy example is that the issue of sex equality cannot be separated from larger issues of equality in the society. Any movement toward sex equality automatically presumes a sharp redefinition of both our personal and public lives. For the only way we can move toward equality in personal relationships is through establishing a collective goal that takes precedence over—though it does not preclude—the realization of individual goals. The development of such a collective vision, moreover, will automatically impinge upon the daily routine of work and government, as well as the values implicit in those public sectors. These new routines in turn will necessarily alter the emphasis on competitiveness, winning, and individual prowess that now so dominate our economy. That change in turn will inevitably alter the psychosexual image we have of ourselves. Thus when we talk of man as nurturant and expressive and women as assertive and independent, when we speak of flexible work hours and shared careers as well as part-time graduate school and universal day-care centers, when we discuss nonsexist childrearing and coeducational sports, when we raise all these related issues, we are highlighting the extent to which the issue of sex equality automatically bears upon and threatens to alter the entire structure of social values that we have been taught to equate with the American way.

It may be that none of us is really ready to consider such a longrange perspective, or the relation of our personal values to the shape of our society 100 years from now. Yet it seems to me that any serious inquiry into the issue of equality between men and women must eventually drive us to those kinds of questions. We are once again at a turning point in our history. The choices we make will determine the future—not only the choices on affirmative action, or in our personal decision about having children or sharing careers or housework—but also the decisions we make as educational leaders of powerful institutions. Radcliffe, like Duke and Yale and Emory and Northwestern, must come to grips with past history as well as future possibility. Will we who represent those institutions continue to define them as upper-class, elite gathering places for a small segment of the population committed to upholding an older structure of power and the values that have produced that power?

Or will we advance another vision, committed to the values of diversity and equality, and based on the notion that our schools can be possible leaders in the move toward a more democratic culture and more democratic institutions. We have a rare opportunity to choose between building a new culture, or presiding over the calcification of old values. On the basis of the history that has gone before, it would seem that the past is not that great that it deserves to be enshrined.

REFERENCES

Bromley, D. D. Feminist—new style. *Harper's* 106 (Oct. 1927), pp. 152–160.
Brownlee, W. E., & Brownlee, M. M. (Eds.). *Women in the American economy.* New Haven: Yale University Press, 1975.
Chafe, W. *The American woman: Her changing social, political, and economic roles, 1920–1970.* New York: Oxford University Press, 1972.
Chafe, W. *Women and equality.* New York: Oxford University Press, 1977.
Evans, S. *Personal politics.* New York: Knopf, 1979.
Freeman, J. *The politics of women's liberation.* New York: David McKay, 1975.
Friedan, B. *The feminine mystique.* New York: W. W. Norton, 1963.
Gildersleeve, V. The college girl of the crisis. Address delivered on February 4, 1934. In *Gildersleeve papers.* New York: Columbia University.
Katz, J. *Evolving relationships between women and men.* Paper presented at the Rockefeller Foundation Conference on Educating Women for the Future, Bellagio, Italy, March 1976.
Lerner, G. Placing women in history: Definitions and challenges. *Feminist Studies* 1975 3 (1/2).
Moran, B., & Gornick, V. (Eds.). *Woman in sexist society.* New York: Basic Books, 1971.
Nye, F. I., Hoffman, L., & Baker, S. J. *Working mothers.* San Francisco: Jossey-Bass, 1974.
Pleck, J., & Sawyer, J. (Eds.). *Men and masculinity.* Englewood Cliffs, N.J.: Prentice-Hall, 1974.
Rogers, A. *Vassar women.* Poughkeepsie, 1940.
Rossi, A. Equality between the sexes: An immodest proposal. In *The woman in America.* R. J. Lifton (Ed.), Boston: Houghton-Mifflin, 1965.
Rossi, A. A. Biosocial perspective on parenting. *Daedalus,* 1977.
Smith-Rosenberg, C. The female world of love and ritual. *Signs 1* (Autumn, 1975).
Yankelovich, D. *The new morality.* New York: 1974.

Chapter 3

Do Changes in Women's Rights Change Women's Moral Judgments?

CAROL GILLIGAN

The century marked by the Radcliffe centennial is spanned roughly by the publication of two novels, both written by women and posing the same moral dilemma: a heroine in love with her cousin Lucy's man. In their parallel triangles, these novels provide a historical frame in which to consider current research on women's moral judgments and offer a way of addressing the centennial question as to what has changed and what has stayed the same.

In *The Mill on the Floss* (Eliot, 1860/1965), Maggie Tulliver "clings to the right." Caught between her love for Lucy and her "stronger feeling" for Stephen, Lucy's fiancé, she is unswerving in her judgment that "I must not, cannot, seek my own happiness by sacrificing others." When Stephen says that their love, natural and unsought, makes it "right that we should marry each other," Maggie replies that while "love is natural, surely pity and faithfulness and memory are natural too." Even after "it was too late already not to have caused misery," Maggie refuses to "take a good for myself that has been wrung out of [others'] misery," choosing instead to renounce Stephen and return alone to St. Oggs.

While the minister, Mr. Kenn, considers "the principle upon which she acted as a safer guide than any balancing of consequences," the narrator's judgment is less clear. George Eliot, having placed her heroine in a dilemma which admitted no viable resolution, ends the novel by drowning Maggie, but not without first having cautioned her reader that "the shifting relation between passion and duty is clear to no man who

CAROL GILLIGAN, PH.D. • Graduate School of Education, Harvard University, Cambridge, Massachusetts 02138. This essay, originally presented at the Radcliffe Pre-Centennial Conference, is also published in a revised version as Chapter Five of Carol Gilligan's book, *In a Different Voice* (Cambridge: Harvard University Press, 1982).

is capable of apprehending it." Since "the mysterious complexity of our life" cannot be "laced up in formulas," Eliot concludes that moral judgment cannot be bound by "general rules" but must instead be informed "by a life vivid and intense enough to have created a wide fellow-feeling with all that is human."

Given that in this novel the "eyes of intense life" that were Maggie's look out at the end from a "weary, beaten face," it is not surprising that Margaret Drabble, steeped in the tradition of 19th-century fiction but engaged in the issues of 20th-century feminism, should choose to return to Eliot's story and explore the possibility of an alternative resolution. In her novel *The Waterfall* (1969), she recreates Maggie's dilemma in *The Mill on the Floss*, but, as the title implies, with the difference that the societal impediment has been removed. Thus Drabble's heroine, Jane Grey, clings not to the right but to Lucy's husband, renouncing the renunciations and instead "drowning in the first chapter." Immersed in a sea of self-discovery, "not caring who should drown so long as I should reach the land," Jane is caught by the problem of judgment as she seeks to apprehend the miracle of her survival and find a way to tell that story. Her love for James, Lucy's husband, is narrated by two different voices, a first and third person who battle constantly over the issues of judgment and truth, engaging and disengaging the moral questions of responsibility and choice.

While the balance between passion and duty has shifted between 1860 and 1969, the moral problem in both novels remains the same. Across the intervening century the verdict of selfishness impales both heroines. The same accusation that compels Maggie's renunciation orchestrates Jane's elaborate plea of helplessness and excuse ("I was merely trying to defend myself against an accusation of selfishness, judge me leniently, I said, I am not as others are, I am sad, I am mad, so I have to have what I want"). Yet the problem with activity and desire that the accusation of selfishness implies not only leads Jane into strategies of evasion and disguise but also impels her to confront the underlying premise on which it is based. Taking apart the moral judgment of the past that had made it seem, "in a sense, better to renounce myself than them," Jane seeks to reconstitute it in a way that could "admit me and encompass me." Thus she strives to create "a new ladder, a new virtue," one that could include activity, sexuality, and survival without abandoning the old virtues of responsibility and care.

> If I need to understand what I am doing, if I cannot act without my own approbation—and I must act, I have changed, I am no longer capable of inaction—then I will invent a morality that condones me. Though by doing so, I risk condemning all that I have been. (Drabble, 1969, pp. 52–53)

I have embarked on this contrast partly in search of similar texts that could support comparative statements over time but also because of the continuing power for women of the judgment of selfishness and the morality of self-abnegation which it implies. This is the judgment that regularly appears at the fulcrum of novels of female adolescence, the turning point of the *Bildungsroman* that separates the invulnerability of childhood innocence from the responsibility of adult participation and choice. The notion that virtue for women lies in self-sacrifice has complicated the course of women's development by pitting the moral issue of goodness against the adult question of responsibility. In addition, the ethic of self-sacrifice is directly in conflict with the concept of rights which has supported in this past century women's claim to a fair share of societal justice.

The problem I wish to explore arises from the tension between a morality of rights that dissolves "natural bonds" in support of individual claims and a morality of responsibility that knits such claims into a fabric of relationship where the distinction between self and other is blurred by the realization of their interdependence. In this chapter I will show how this conflict appears in the moral judgments of contemporary Radcliffe women and indicate how its resolution affects the course of their development. In doing so I trace the continuation through time of an ethic of responsibility as the center of women's moral concern, anchoring the self in a world of relationship and giving rise to the activity of care, and then show how this ethic is informed by the recognition of the justice of the rights approach.

My interest in this problem is tied to the repeated observation in the field of psychology that women's conceptions of self and morality are different from those of men. The recurrent discovery that women have less sense of justice than men (Freud, 1925; Kohlberg & Kramer, 1969; Piaget, 1932), while previously interpreted as indicative of a deficit in women's development, may point instead to a difference in their perception and construction of moral conflict and choice. The differences observed in women's experience of the relationship between self and other (Chodorow, 1974; Gutmann, 1965) and the continuing importance of attachment and affiliation in women's lives (Miller, 1976) are consonant with the reports of sex differences in cognitive and perceptual style, indicating that women "orient more to both sides of relationships of interdependence" (McClelland, 1975), attend more to the contextual aspects of meaning (Block, 1977), and develop a greater "interpersonal" than "impersonal" cognitive competence (Witkin, 1979).

I first became interested in the subject of differences in women's moral judgments when I noticed at Harvard in 1970, while teaching in a

course on Moral and Political Choice offered for sophomores by Law-
rence Kohlberg, that of the 20 students who dropped the course, 16
were women. Since these women had sought out this experimental,
elective course and completed the written moral judgment interview,
thus evincing an interest in studying morality, I wondered what had
sent them away. Presumably they had expected something different
from what they had found, and since few men had left, perhaps the
women's disappointment stemmed from a disparate conception of morality that was at odds with the view presented in the course.

When these women subsequently were contacted and interviewed,[1] their thinking about morality diverged from Kohlberg's orientation to individual rights, counterposing an ethic of responsibility and
care to his conception of justice as fairness. Morality, in the view of these
women, "had to do with responsibilities and obligations," with "conflicts between personal desires and social things, personal desires of
yourself versus personal desires of others." The paramount moral obligation which the women enunciated was the injunction "not to hurt,"
and the dilemma they repeatedly cited as central in their own lives was
the conflict between hurting others and hurting themselves. Thus they
sought in morality a way of resolving the tension they encountered in
striving to be true to themselves while at the same time adhering to their
"moral principle of not hurting other people." Among these women
there was substantial agreement that the "morally right" solution was
one which enabled "everyone to come out better off" but also considerable doubt as to whether "it was possible both to not lie and not hurt."

The women's overriding concern with not hurting led to a reluctance to make judgments at all, a hesitance "to take stands on controversial issues," and a "willingness to make exceptions all the time." These
Radcliffe women of the early 1970s qualified their moral statements repeatedly, even to the point of saying that "I could never argue that my
belief on a moral question is anything another person should accept. I
don't believe in absolutes. . . . if there is an absolute for moral decisions, it is human life."

While in one sense such seemingly excessive qualification appeared
indicative of a general moral relativism or a personal reluctance to take a
stand, from another perspective it suggested a capacity to envision alternative viewpoints and to imagine the considerations or constraints that
would render them legitimate. Since the judgments of the women who
remained in the course were similar to the judgments of those who left,
these observations lingered in my mind. The moral concerns of all of the

[1] I am grateful to Deborah Lapidus, a graduate student at Harvard at the time, who
collaborated in this project and interviewed the students.

women seemed somewhat at odds with the political and moral atmosphere of the campus in the fall of 1970, but it was not clear what part of the college population had enrolled in this particular course.

Kohlberg had reported with Kramer in 1969 that women's moral judgments typically fell at the third of his six-stage developmental sequence where morality was conceived in interpersonal terms and equated with helping and pleasing others. This apparent arrest in women's moral development was attributed by Kohlberg and Kramer to the fact that most women's lives at that time were spent within the interpersonal bounds of family life. While the call to social activism of the late 1960s and the resurgence of the women's movement at that time might have been expected to propel women toward Kohlberg's higher stages of moral judgment where moral problems were conceived in societal terms or resolved in accordance with universal principles of justice, the surprising finding of the study that followed the development of the students who had taken the course was the persistence in the women's moral thinking of a strong and clear interpersonal orientation—a concern with the effects of actions on others and an insistent awareness of the psychological and social context of moral conflict and choice. When the women were asked to resolve Kohlberg's hypothetical moral dilemmas, they sought to ground these dilemmas in a narrative of social relationship in order to establish the bounds of moral responsibility and to assess the likelihood of various resolutions' eventuating in suffering and hurt.

The senior year follow-up interview with one of the women who had taken the course illustrates some of the dimensions of moral understanding among Radcliffe women in 1973, the year that the Supreme Court decided in favor of legalizing abortion and thus in support of a woman's right to terminate a pregnancy she chooses not to continue. This student indicated that she had taken Kohlberg's course because she was "looking for different ways of thinking about things" and was interested "in arguments that protect individual freedom," arguments that she saw as compatible with "Kohlberg's system."

Claiming to "suffer from a low self-image," she reports in the senior year interview a sense of moral progress and growth which she attributes to having had "to review a lot of what I thought about myself" as a result of having become pregnant and deciding to have an abortion. Attributing the pregnancy to "a lapse of self-control, decision-making, and very much stupidity," she considered abortion to be a desperate and life-saving solution ("I felt very much to save my own life that I had to do it"), but one which she viewed as "at least in the eyes of society, if not my own, a moral sin."

Given her "great personal feeling of being very evil," her discovery that "people would help me out anyway did great things for my feelings toward them and myself." In the month that she spent waiting and thinking about the abortion, she thought "a lot about decision-making, and for the first time, I wanted to take control and responsibility for my own decisions in life." As a result, her image of herself changed,

> because now that you are going to take control of your life, you don't feel like you are a pawn in other people's hands. You have to accept the fact that you have done something wrong, and it also gives you a little more integrity because you are not fighting off these things in yourself all the time. A lot of conflicts are resolved, and you have a sense of a new beginning . . . based on a kind of conviction that you can act in a situation.

Thus she "came out basically supporting myself, not as a good or bad human being, but simply as a human being who had a lot to learn either way." Seeing herself as capable of choice, she becomes responsible for herself in a new way, but while the experience of choice led to a greater sense of personal integrity, her judgment of these choices stays remarkably the same. While she has come to a more inclusive and more tolerant understanding of herself and a new conception of relationships that will, she believes, allow her to be "more obvious with myself and more independent," the moral issue remains for her one of responsibility.

In this sense she considers the pregnancy and abortion to have "come to my aid" in illuminating her previous failure to take responsibility:

> It was so serious that it brought to light things in myself, like feelings about myself, my feelings about the world. . . . What I had done, I felt, was so wrong that it came to light to me that I was not taking responsibility where I could have gone on like I was, not taking responsibility. So the seriousness of the situation brings the questions right up in front of your face. You see them very clearly, and then the answers are there for you.

Seeing her own irresponsibility as having eventuated in a situation where she could see no way of acting that would not cause hurt, she began "getting rid of old ideas" about morality that now seemed an impediment to her goal of living in a way that would not "cause human suffering." In doing so, she calls into question the opposition of selfishness and morality, discerning that "the word 'selfish' is tricky" and beginning to consider "individual freedom and decision . . . [as not] all that incompatible with morality." In her expanded conception morality becomes "the sense of concern that comes from your sense of caring, your sense of concern for another human being and your sense of concern for yourself."

Continuing to articulate an ethic of care that centers on the avoidance of hurt, she extends that ethic to include herself within the compass of her moral concern. Given her awareness of interdependence, rights are subsumed to responsibilities in a morality where the questions remain: How much suffering are you going to cause, and why do you have the right to cause human suffering? Responsibility, however, now is tied to the knowledge of self and others that allows one to discern the causes of suffering and to anticipate what actions are likely to result in hurt.

The focus on responsibility as the center and substance of moral concern was evident as well in a subsequent study of women's thinking about abortion decisions. In 1975 Gilligan and Belenky interviewed 29 women who were at the time considering whether to continue or abort a pregnancy (see Belenky, 1978; Gilligan, 1977; Gilligan & Belenky, 1980). The study was designed to discover whether women constructed this decision in moral terms (as indicated by the use of words such as "should," "ought," "better," "right," "good," "bad," and so forth), and if so, to determine the nature of their moral construction. With a sample of women who were diverse in age, race, and social class, ranging from teenagers who had dropped out of school to graduate students, including married and single women, some with children, others without, there was across this wide variation a consistency in the women's construction of the moral problem posed by the abortion decision as a problem of responsibility and care.

While responsibility and care meant different things to the women in this sample, depending on their conceptions of self and their understanding of relationships, morality remained an issue of care, and the abortion dilemma, a dilemma of responsibility and relationship. The decision itself was considered to pose a problem of inclusion or exclusion that hinged on the issue of relationship since the decision to continue the pregnancy was predicated on the assumption of responsibility for taking care of the child. In the awareness that the life of a child depended on someone assuming responsibility for care, the morality of the decision, whether it entailed continuing or aborting the pregnancy, was assessed not in terms of justice and rights but rather in terms of which resolution best seemed to exercise care and avoid hurt.

While for some women the concern with care and with hurt centered unreflectively on their own needs, usually because of their own sense of vulnerability and powerlessness in the world, for others it was shaped by a concern for others and a wish to maintain relationships with them. Then the distinction between selfishness and responsibility arose to articulate a morality of relationships in which goodness was equated with caring for others and opposed to concern for oneself. In this construction the abortion decision readily created a moral crisis by posing a choice in a situation where there seemed no way of acting that would not cause hurt. Through a reiterative language of selfishness and responsibility, the moral problem was defined as one of responsibility for taking care of others and avoiding hurt to them. The infliction of hurt was considered to be selfish and immoral in its reflection of unconcern, while the expression of care, in contrast, was seen as the fulfillment of moral responsibility. Then the critical question became whether the woman could include herself in the universe of people for whom she considered it moral to care.

The moral judgments of the women in the abortion decision study thus showed a remarkable continuity with the responses of the Radcliffe students to questions concerning their own experiences of moral conflict and choice. Facing a conflict over the continuation of a pregnancy where hurt seemed inescapable, the women in the abortion study saw themselves as having in some sense to decide between self and other. Since hurt was inevitable, from a moral point of view the problem was repeatedly expressed as one of choosing "the lesser of two evils," a choice which then carried with it responsibility for "choosing the victim." In this sense the pregnancy decision created a moral crisis, but one which highlighted both the issue of responsibility and the connection between self and other from which the sense of responsiblity emerged. In doing so it exposed the problem in the opposition of self and other which sustained the distinction between "selfish" and "selfless" choice.

The right to include oneself in the compass of a morality of responsibility and care was a critical question for Radcliffe students in the 1970s. This question arose in differing contexts and posed at once a problem of inclusion which could be resolved through the logic of justice as fairness and a problem of relationship whose solution required a new understanding of responsibility and care. In the continuing study of moral judgment and choice among the students who had taken Kohlberg's course (see Gilligan & Murphy, 1979; Murphy & Gilligan, 1980), one of the women describes at age 27 how her thinking about morality had changed. Referring to her understanding of morality at the time when she entered college, she says:

> I was much more simple-minded then. I went through a period in which I thought there were fairly simple answers of right and wrong in life. I even went through a period that now strikes me as so simplistic; [I thought] that as long as I didn't hurt anybody, everything would be fine. And I soon figured out or eventually figured out that things were not that simple: that you were bound to hurt people, they were bound to hurt you, and life is full of tension and conflict, and people are bound to hurt each other's feelings, intentionally, unintentionally, but just in the very way things work out. So I abandoned that idea.

This abandonment occurred during her first college years when she got involved in a love affair with some guy . . . [who] wanted to settle down and get married, and I could not imagine a worse fate, but I was really quite fond of him. And we broke up, and he was so upset by it that he left school for a year, and I realized that I had hurt him very badly and that I hadn't meant to, and I had violated my first principle of moral behavior but that I had made the right decision.

Explaining that she "could not have possibly married him," she felt that there was, in that sense, an "easy answer" to the dilemma she had faced. Yet in another sense, given her moral injunction against hurting, the situation presented an insoluble problem, allowing no course of action that would not eventuate in hurt. This realization led her to question her former absolute moral injunction and to "figure out that this principle [of not hurting others] was not all there was to it." The limitation she saw directly pertained to the issue of personal integrity as she realized that "what that principle was not even attempting to achieve was, like, 'to thine own self be true.'" Indicating that she had "started thinking more about maintaining your personal integrity," she says that this experience had led her to conclude that "you can't worry about not hurting other people; just do what is right for you."

Yet given her continuing equation of morality with caring for others, her continuing belief that "acts that are self-sacrificing and that are done for other people or for the good of humanity are good acts," her abandonment of the principle of not hurting others was tantamount to an abandonment of moral concern. Recognizing the rightness of her decision but also realizing its consequence of hurt, she can see no way to maintain her own integrity while at the same time continuing to adhere to a morality of caring for others. Seeing the dilemma which Mary McCarthy (1946) describes in *Memories of a Catholic Girlhood* as the "trap of adult life, in which you are held, wriggling, powerless to act because you can see both sides," yet recognizing the necessity for action, she chooses to avoid the solution of compromise which McCarthy depicts in her novel and chooses instead to resolve the dilemma by "just doing what is right for you."

Yet the residual opposition of morality and integrity leaves her in fact with a feeling of compromise. Recounting her experience as a lawyer, she describes the dilemma she faced when she realized that the opposing counsel in a trial had overlooked a document providing critical support for his client's "meritorious claim." Deliberating whether or not to tell her opponent of the document that would help his client's case, she realized that the adversary system of justice was not only impeding "the supposed search for truth" but also inhibiting the expression of her concern for the person on the other side. Choosing in the end to adhere to the system, partially in recognition of the vulnerability of her own position within it, she sees herself as having failed to live up to her ideal of selfless and self-sacrificing behavior. Thus her depiction of herself contrasts with her description of her husband as "a person of absolute integrity [who] would never do anything he didn't feel was right" as well as with her description of the people she admires: her mother, whom she sees as "a very caring person," and Albert Schweitzer, whom she considers to be "selfless" and "a great man . . . [for] going to Africa and living in conditions that I would consider difficult to live in and treating, helping those who needed help with very little reward for it, really."

On her own behalf she says, somewhat apologetically, that she has become, since college, more tolerant and more understanding, less ready to blame people whom formerly she would have condemned and more capable of seeing the integrity of different perspectives. While as a lawyer she has access to the language of rights and sees the value of personal integrity, the concept of rights remains in tension with an ethic of responsibility and care. The continuing opposition of selfishness and responsibility thus leaves her with no way to reconcile the injunction to be true to herself with a morality of care.

The clash between a morality of rights and an ethic of responsiblity erupted in a moral crisis described by another woman who had taken the course. In her senior-year interview she also articulates a moral ideal of selfless and self-sacrificing behavior, exemplified by her mother, who illuminates her conception of the ideal person:

> If I could grow up to be like anyone in the world, it would be my mother, because I've just never met such a selfless person. She would do anything for anybody up to a point that she has hurt herself a lot because she just gives so much to other people and asks nothing in return. . . . So, ideally, that's what you'd like to be, a person who is selfless and giving.

At the same time, however, she considers that "there are faults with the way she is," since her mother "in hurting herself can hurt people very close to her." Recognizing that self-sacrifice can also hurt others, she nevertheless describes herself, in comparison to her mother, as "much more selfish in a lot of ways." The hope of resolving the tension between selfishness and care is expressed, however, in her belief that "the best person you could possibly be is the person who will do the most good for other people . . . [while] fulfilling your own potentialities."

In Kohlberg's course she had set out to examine morality in terms of the questions: How much do you owe yourself and how much do you owe other people? Defining morality as a problem of obligation, she attempts, through the equation of self and others, to challenge the premises underlying the contrast between selfishness and responsibility. However, a crisis that occurred in her family at the time of the course called into question the logic of this endeavor by demonstrating the inadequacy of the entire terminology. The crisis was caused by the suicide of a relative at a time when the resources of the family were already strained by the illness of her grandfather who was in need of continual care. While the morality of suicide had been discussed in the course from the perspective of individual rights, this suicide appeared to her instead an act of consummate irresponsibility. Trying to bring her feelings of rage into connection with her logic of reason, she had written a paper for the course about the moral crisis which this conjunction of thought and feeling provoked. Thus she describes to the interviewer the impasse of her discovery that her old way of thinking "just didn't work anymore":

> You know, that whole semester we had been discussing what's right and what's wrong, what's good, and how much do you owe yourself and how much do you owe other people, and then my [relative] killed himself, right then, you know, and that's a moral crisis, right? And I didn't know how to handle it because I really ended up hating him for having done that, and I knew I really couldn't do this. I mean, that was wrong, but how could he do this to his family? And I really had to seriously reevaluate that whole course because it just didn't work anymore. You know, all these nice little things that we had been discussing are fine when you talk about it. I remember, we had little stories to evaluate like, if you were on a mission and were leading a patrol and somebody had to go and throw a hand grenade or something. Well, that's fine, but you know, when it's something like this that's close to you, it just doesn't work anymore. And I had to seriously evaluate everything I had said in that course and why, if I believed all that, how could I end up with such an intense hatred?

Given the awesome dimensions of this problem, the underlying logic of the equation of how much is owed to self versus other began to unravel and then fell apart:

> All of a sudden, all the definitions and all the terminology just fell apart. It became the type of thing that you couldn't place any value on it to say, yes, it was moral, or no, it was not. It's just one of those things that is just irrational and undefineable.

What she realized was that whatever the judgment, the action itself was irreversible and had consequences that affected the lives of others as well. Since rights and responsibilities, selfishness and self-sacrifice were so inextricably confounded in this situation, she could find no way of thinking about it except to say that while in one sense it seemed a moral crisis, in another it appeared "just irrational and undefinable."

Five years later she says that these events which ravaged her family had also changed her life by bringing into focus for her "the whole thing about responsibility. When the opposition of selfishness and morality prevailed, she had "not wanted to take responsibility for [her] grandfather" and thus had considered herself selfish but she also had been unwilling to take responsibility for herself and thus in the end had been irresponsible to others. Seeing that "it was too easy to go through [life] the way I had always done . . . [letting] someone else take responsibility for the direction of my life," she challenged herself to take responsibility and "changed the direction of my life."

The underlying construction of morality as a problem of responsibility and the struggle for women in taking responsibility for their lives were evident in the responses of other Radcliffe students who took part in a study conducted by Murphy and Gilligan in the spring of 1978 (see Gilligan *et al.*, 1982). By comparing the responses of three of the women who participated in this study, it is possible to see how the opposition of selfishness and responsibility complicates for women the issue of choice, leaving them suspended between an ideal of selflessness and the truth of their own participation in the events of their lives.

The developmental problem which this opposition of morality and truth creates is evident in the attempt of all of these women to find a way of overcoming this opposition, to be more honest with themselves while searching for a way to resolve the tension they feel between the search for integrity in their own lives and their continuing connection to their parents. While all three women have difficulty with choice and tie their difficulty to the wish not to hurt others, their varying resolutions of this dilemma reveal the binding nature of the opposition between selfishness and responsibility, the way in which the concept of rights enters in to challenge the virtue of selflessness, and how the extension of responsibility recasts the dilemma and changes the moral problem.

The first woman, a sophomore, defines morality as a consciousness of power,

> a type of consciousness, a sensitivity to humanity, that you can affect someone else's life, you can affect your own life, and you have the responsibility not to endanger other people's lives or to hurt other people. So morality is complex; I'm being very simplistic. Morality involves realizing that there is an interplay between self and other and that you are going to have to take responsibility for both of them. I keep using that word "responsibility"; it's just sort of consciousness of your influence over what's going on.

Tying morality to an awareness of power but equating responsibility with not hurting others, she considers responsibility to mean "that you care about that other person, that you are sensitive to that other person's needs and you consider them as a part of your needs because you are dependent on other people." The equation of morality with caring for others leads her to consider selfishness as the opposite of responsibility, an opposition manifest in her judgment that the experience of personal gratification compromises the morality of actions which otherwise could be considered responsible ("[tutoring] was almost a selfish thing because it made me feel good to do something [for others] and I enjoyed it").

Thus morality, seen as arising from the interplay between self and other, is reduced to an opposition between self and other, tied in the end to dependence on others and equated with responsibility to care for them. The moral ideal is not the collaboration or cooperation of interdependence but rather the fulfillment of the obligation to repay one's debt to society by giving to others without taking anything for oneself in return. The binding quality of this construction is evident as she begins her description of herself by saying "I am not very honest with myself." The experience of dishonesty emerges from the apparent contradiction in her image of herself as

> a person who has a lot of ideas about the way I would like things to be and who wants to, just through love, make everything better, but also, I am a selfish person and a lot of the time I don't behave in a loving manner and I'm trying to sort of deal with that.

In her effort to deal with the problem of selfishness, she describes a continuing struggle "to justify my actions" and "a hard time making choices." Seeing herself as having the power to hurt but wishing to do none, she has difficulty explaining to her parents "why I really have to take the year off, why it's really important to me," since she feels that her staying in college is important to them. Caught between her wish not to hurt others and her wish to be true to herself, she tries to clarify her own motivation, "to be honest with myself about why I am unhappy here, what is going on, what do I want to do." Seeing Harvard as a "selfish" institution where competition overrides cooperation so that "working for yourself, doing for yourself . . . you don't help other people," and wishing herself to be "caring, sensitive and giving," she can find no way in the complication of this situation to integrate an ideal of personal and moral integrity with an ethic of responsibility and care. The sense of continuing tension is evident in her aspiration to be both honest and caring, "someone who is committed to certain ideas but is able to relate to other people and to respect other people's ideas and yet not compromise and not be just submissive and just accommodate to other people."

The complication of this struggle as it becomes entangled in the conflict between responsibilities and rights pervades the dilemma described by the second woman, who was at the time a Radcliffe senior. Asked whether she had ever "faced a decision about what to do where the moral principle was not clear," she refers to her conflict with her parents over where she should go to medical school. Explaining her parents' position, she sets up a contrast between moral and selfish justifications:

> They had moral justifications of principle and justifications for wanting me here that were both good and not so good. The good ones I can put in the classification of morals, and the bad ones in the classification of selfishness.

Casting the dilemma in the language of rights, she considers that her parents

> have a right to want to see me a certain way, at certain times. I think the bad part was sort of the abuse of that right which kind of brings up the selfish-ness issue and my moral part which was that I didn't view my going away as breaking up the family in any sense.

Thus equating rights with wishes and morality with responsibility for sustaining relationships, she indicates that it was not her "aim or goal or my anything to break up the family," adding that "I thought and I still think in some respects that I would grow more by being in a different place with different people." Contrasting the "positive aspect of separation," her attempt to take responsibility for her own growth, with "the negative on my side," she considers that hers

> was a sort of selfish, in part, motivation or a not-high-enough motivation. Our family was not only given but sort of life-long given, and it was sort of my moral obligation, all things being relative, to equally accept that aspect of not going, to be staying here, and I was letting some of my unselfishness take control of the situation.

Her emerging sense that selfishness and unselfishness might be relative rather than absolute judgments, a matter of interpretation or perspective rather than an issue of truth, extends into two conceptions of morality, one centered on rights, the other on responsibility. The shift between these conceptions marks her response to the interviewer's question as to what was the moral decision and what were the conflicts that it entailed.

> The moral decision was whether I had the right to act as an independent party when I did not see my leaving as doing harm to other parties but just being a zero. They, on their part, saw it as a negative, although I did not perceive it that way. The conflict was not in my interpretation but in the fact that we had a different interpretation of the morality, and it was very close in terms that I thought both interpretations were relatively equally stacked, and I guess I opted for theirs by staying here, and I guess that was the conflict.

Saying that before she had thought "there is always one moral, one higher and that higher can be a quarter of one percent, I do believe that it is possible to closely match things out," she had nevertheless found in this situation that "it gets impossible to make a moral decision." Having subsumed her right to act as an independent party to her belief that in doing so she would not hurt others, she nevertheless acceded to her parents' interpretation of responsibility, explaining that the "critical reason" for her decision to stay lay in the fact that in setting up the dilemma as a balance of selfishness, she had concluded that hers was "the greater selfishness."

> They were really, really hurt by the whole situation, and I didn't feel the loss so greatly, not going. So I guess I began to view my selfishness as more than their selfishness. Both selfishnesses started out being equal but somehow or other they appeared to be suffering more.

Thus the rights construction, itself cast in the language of responsibilities as a balance of selfishnesses, in the end gives way to considerations of responsibility, the question of who would suffer more. The attempt to set up the dilemma as a conflict of rights turned it into a contest of selfishnesses, precluding the possibility of a moral decision since either resolution could be construed as selfish from one or the other perspective. Consequently, the concern with rights, action, and choice was overridden by a concern with responsibility, and she resolved the dilemma by "letting some of my unselfishness take control" since she saw her parents as more vulnerable than herself.

Dismissing the hurt to herself as one of omission ("not having a new experience is not a hurt in the absolute sense"), she contrasts it with the act of commission, the responsibility she would feel for causing her parents what seemed to them "a fairly great loss." Considering responsibility to be "attached to morality," she sees responsibilities as setting up "a chain of expectations, and if you interrupt that, you interrupt a whole process for not only yourself but for all those around you." As a result considerations of rights, based on an assumption of independence, threaten to interrupt the chain of relationship, and thus are counterbalanced and outweighed by considerations of responsibility. In the end, choice hinges on the determination of where "the greater responsibility lies," a determination based on an assessment of vulnerability, the relative estimate of who will be hurt more.

However, in relinquishing her "right to act as an independent party" and instead letting her "unselfishness take control," she has also suspended her own interpretation of a morality of responsibility. This feeling of suspension is then caught in her description of herself as "a little round jelly bean, sort of wandering around, picking up snow here and there, never really sinking with the weight of snow." Yet toward the end of the interview she indicates her wish to anchor herself more securely by becoming more "thoughtful" about her relationships, more concerned with knowing how she is "interacting with people" rather than just "letting it ride." Whereas previously she had been "kind of defensive and afraid" to think about what she was doing in relationships, she has come to see that "thinking about it has taken away that fear because when you think about what you are doing, you know what it is; if you don't know, you just kind of let it ride, you don't know what is going to come next."

This image of drifting along or riding it out recurred to denote the experience of women caught in the opposition between selfishness and responsibility. Describing a life lived in response, guided by the perception of others' needs, they could see no way of exercising control without risking an assertion that seemed selfish and hence morally dangerous. Like the heroine of *The Waterfall* who begins the novel by saying, "If I were drowning I couldn't reach out a hand to save myself, so unwilling am I to set myself up against fate," without even thinking "that is might be the truth," these women were drawn unthinkingly by the image of passivity, the appeal of avoiding responsibility by sinking, like Jane, into "an ice age of inactivity . . . [so that] providence could deal with her without her own assistance."

But the image of drifting along while seeming to offer safety from the onus of responsibility carries with it the danger of landing instead in a more painful confrontation with choice, as in the stark alternatives of an abortion decision or, as Maggie Tulliver found, in the realization that one had unwittingly come to do the one thing one most had feared. Then in the recognition of consequence the issue of responsibility returns, bringing with it added questions pertaining to matters of choice and of truth.

Maggie, giving in to her feelings for Stephen by momentarily ceasing her resistance to him,

> felt that she was being led down the garden among the roses, being helped with firm tender care into the boat, having the cushion and cloak arranged for her feet and her parasol opened for her (which she had forgotten)—all by this stronger presence that seemed to bear her along without any act of her own will. (Eliot, 1860/1965, pp. 486–487)

But when she realized how far they had gone, "a terrible alarm took possession of her," and her "yearning after that belief that the tide was doing it all" quickly gave way first to "feelings of angry resistance toward Stephen" whom she accused of having wanted to deprive her of choice and having taken advantage of her thoughtlessness, and then to the recognition of her own responsibility. No longer "paralyzed," she realized that "the feelings of a few short weeks had hurried her into the sins that her nature had most recoiled from: breach of faith and cruel selfishness." Then Maggie, "longing after perfect goodness" chose "to be true to [her] calmer affections and live without the joy of love."

However, while Maggie longs for goodness, her counterpart Jane searches for truth. Discovering in her desire for James "such depths of selfishness" that she considers drowning herself "in an effort to reclaim lost renunciations like Maggie Tulliver," she chooses instead to question the renunciations and, in the end, to "identify [herself] with love." Observing that while "Maggie Tulliver never slept with her man, she did all the damage there was to be done, to Lucy, to herself, to the two men who loved her, and then, like a woman of another age she refrained," Jane confronts "an event seen from angles where there used to be one event and one way only of enduring it," and "wonders, in this age, what is to be done?"

Thus the moral distinction between selfish and selfless behavior that became increasingly clear to Maggie, becomes for Jane increasingly blurred. Having "sought virtue" only to find that she "could not ascend by the steps that others seemed to take," she had then sought innocence

> in abnegation, in denial, in renunciation . . . [thinking] that if I could deny myself enough I would achieve some kind of innocence, despite those intermittent nightmare promptings of my true nature. I thought I could negate myself and wipe myself out. (Drabble, 1969, p. 52)

Yet she discovers that, no matter which way she tells the story, in the end she confronts the truth that, despite all the renunciations, she had "drowned in a willing sea."

It is against the pull of such renunciations, the vision of an innocence attained by the denial of self, that women begin to search for the truth of their own experience and to talk of taking control.

> [Thinking back over the past year, what stands out for you?] Taking control of my life.

Thus a recent Radcliffe graduate begins to tell of her struggle to overcome the opposition between selfishness and responsibility and to take control of her life. The struggle erupted in her senior year over her attempt to enact a decision to leave a varsity team in order to do "other things that were important to me." In contemplating the radical act of saying no to the "unquestioned past priority" of sports in her life, she found herself "kind of paralyzed in a way" and unable to make a decision:

> I just was having a hard time; the decision was very difficult. It was like I couldn't make it, was just stuck, and I would try to think about it, and it was just like coming up against a wall, even trying to figure out why it was so difficult and why I was having such a hard time. So, finally, it turned into a little bit of a crisis situation in that the coach said to me, look, you have to decide, one way or the other, and I just didn't feel like I could decide. Things had gotten really messy in terms of emotions and everything. So, for the first time, significantly that I can think of, I admitted that I was having big troubles.

Her troubles stemmed from the fact that in saying no she was challenging a "whole ethic" that previously had been unquestioned. Having grown up thinking of the world view represented to her by her father ("succeeding in whatever you do and the sports ethic") as "the only legitimate one," she now realized "how basic a thing it had become in terms of being an attitude I lived by." Thus in saying that "there were other things that were more important to me," she had posed "a real threat or a real challenge to one of the root assumptions that I had been living by for a long time," an assumption that had been an anchor of her identity and a bond between her and her father.

Seeing herself previously as having "floated" through school with "such a nonexistent sense of what I wanted to do that I kind of went the path of least resistance," she has taken control by starting "more and more doing what I want to do and less and less what I thought I should be doing or was supposed to be doing." Becoming "more embedded in where I am," she has come to recognize the legitimacy of different world views and to rely more on her own interpretations. Thus the process of taking control, of coming "to a more defined sense of what I wanted to do and what options are available and what kinds of paths make sense," was a process of

> coming into myself a little bit, and so becoming more confident in my own judgment, because I had something to base my judgments on, feeling stronger in myself and so relying more on myself . . . to make decisions and to evaluate situations and not accepting my parents' judgments or Harvard's judgments. And finding myself in situations where I was taking one position and someone else was taking another position and both positions seemed legitimate and neither was *the* right one, and learning how to accept that. And trying to figure out why that was, but being able to accept that, or starting to, or starting to question that whole idea that one person is more right than the other or doing it better than the other.

In starting to question the idea that there was a single right way to live and that differences were always a matter of better and worse, she begins to see conflict in a new way, as a part of rather than a threat to relationships. Contrasting her current thinking about morality with her previous belief that "there were right answers," she refers to a course on moral development which she had taken with Kohlberg in her sophomore year. Then

> the idea that at the highest level of moral reasoning, you get a group of people together on a problem and ideally, they should all agree made sense to me. It was amazing to me, although it was very confusing. . . . It was so clean; it is so clean, that idea that there are right answers, that everyone will reach the right answers.

Since the notion of agreement was premised on the concept of rights, it tied in with her understanding of feminism at that time ("legitimizing a lot of the grumblings and dissatisfactions that I had for what I felt were women's choices"), and the equation of morality with respect for rights offered a justification for the freedom of choice she sought, placing bounds on responsibility by limiting duty to the reciprocity of noninterference. Now, however, she sees the limitation of the "individually centered" approach of balancing rights and claims in its failure to take into account the reality of relationships which she sees as "a whole other dimension to human experience." By seeing individual lives as connected and embedded in a social context of relationship, her moral perspective has expanded to encompass a notion of "collective life" so that responsibility includes both self and other, seen as different but connected rather than as separate and opposed. Thus a cognizance of interdependence rather than a concern with reciprocity informs her belief that "we all do to some extent have responsibilities to look out for each other."

Since moral problems arise in situations of conflict where "either way I go, something or someone will not be served . . . [their resolution] is not just a simple yes or no decision, it is worse." Given her image of a world that extends through an elaborate network of interrelationship, the recognition that someone will be hurt affects everyone who is involved, complicating the morality of any decision and removing the possibility of a clear or simple solution. Thus morality, rather than being opposed to integrity or tied to an ideal of agreement, instead is aligned with "the kind of integrity" that comes from "making decisions after working through everything you think is involved and important in the situation," and taking responsibility for choice. In the end, then, morality is a matter of care,

> [of] taking the time and energy to consider everything . . . to decide carelessly or quickly or on the basis of one or two factors when you know that there are other things that are important and that will be affected, that's immoral. The moral way to make decisions is by considering as much as you possibly can, as much as you know.

Describing herself as "a strong person," though acknowledging that she does not feel strong all the time, she sees herself as "thoughtful and careful," as "painfully starting to learn how to express myself and be more open," rather than taking, as before, "a very stoic attitude." While her participation in sports had led her to "take [herself] seriously physically," her involvement in feminism led her to take her ideas and her feelings seriously as well. More responsive now to herself and more directly responsive to others, she describes a morality based not on the logic of reciprocity but on an emerging understanding of life. Seeing life not as "a path" but "a web [where] you can choose different paths at any particular time, so it's not like there is just one way," she realizes that there will always be conflict and that "no factor is absolute." Instead, the "real constant is the process" of making decisions with care, on the basis of what you know, and taking responsibility for choice while seeing the possible legitimacy of other solutions.

By equating responsibility with caring rather than with not hurting ("We do have responsibilities to each other in terms of helping other people—I don't know how far"), she recognizes the problem of limitation, that while inclusion is the goal of moral consciousness, exclusion may be a necessity of life. The people whom she admires are "people who are really connected to the concrete situations in their lives," whose knowledge comes not from detachment but from living in connection with themselves and with others, from being embedded in the conditions of life.

In one sense, then, not much has changed. George Eliot, observing that "we have no master-key that will fit all cases" of moral decision, returns to the causists in whose "perverted spirit of minute discrimination" she sees

> the shadow of a truth to which eyes and hearts are too often fatally sealed— the truth that moral judgments must remain false and hollow unless they are checked and enlightened by a perpetual reference to the special circumstances that mark the individual lot. (Eliot, 1860/1965, p. 521)

Thus she considers that moral judgment must be informed by "growing insight and sympathy," tempered by the knowledge gained through experience that

> general rules . . . [will not] lead to justice by a ready-made patent method, without the trouble of exerting patience, discrimination, impartiality, without any care to assure whether [one has] the insight that comes from a hardly-earned estimate of temptation or from a life vivid and intense enough to have created a wide, fellow-feeling with all that is human (p. 521)

And yet for Eliot, at least in this novel, the moral problem remains one of renunciation, a question of "whether the moment has come in which a man has fallen below the possibility of a renunciation that will carry any efficacy and must accept the sway of a passion against which he had struggled as a trespass." The opposition of passion and duty thus binds morality to an ideal of selflessness, the "perfect goodness" toward which Maggie Tulliver aspired.

Both this opposition and this ideal are called into question by the concept of rights, by the underlying assumption of justice as fairness that self and other are equal. In the 1970s the concept of rights entered into the thinking of Radcliffe students to challenge the premises of a morality of self-sacrifice and self-abnegation. Questioning the stoicism of self-denial and replacing the illusion of innocence with an awareness of choice, they struggled to grasp the essential notion of rights, that the interests of the self could be considered legitimate. In this sense the concept of rights changed women's conceptions of self, allowing them to see themselves as stronger and to consider directly their own needs. As assertion no longer seemed dangerous, the concept of relationships changed from bonds of continuing dependence to a dynamic of interdependence. Then the understanding of care could expand from the paralyzing injunction not to hurt others to the activity that sustains relationships in a world of interdependence. A consciousness of the dynamics of human relationships then becomes central to moral understanding, joining the heart and the eye in an ethic that ties the activity of thought to the activity of care.

Thus changes in women's rights change women's moral judgments, seasoning mercy with justice so that women consider it moral to include themselves in the universe of people for whom it is responsible to care. As the concern with not hurting extends to an ideal of nonviolence in human relationships, women begin to see their understanding of relationships as a source of moral strength. But the concept of rights also changes women's moral judgments by adding a second perspective to the consideration of moral problems with the result that judgment becomes more tolerant and less absolute.

As selfishness and self-sacrifice become a matter of interpretation and responsibilities live in tension with rights, moral truth is complicated by psychological truth and the matter of judgment becomes more complex. Drabble's heroine who had sought to write "a poem as round and hard as a stone" only to find that words and thoughts obtrude, concluded that "a poem so round and smooth would say nothing" and set out to describe the variegated edges of an event seen from all angles, finding in the end no unified truth. Instead, through a shift in perspective, she relegates her suspicions to "that removed third person," and no longer fending off the accusation of selfishness, identifies herself with the first-person voice.

References

Belenky, M. Conflict and development: A longitudinal study of the impact of abortion decisions on moral judgments of adolescent and adult women (Doctoral dissertation, Harvard University, 1978).
Block, J. H. *Sex differences in cognitive functioning, personality characteristics and socialization experiences: Implications for educational policy.* Unpublished report prepared for the Presidents of Smith, Wellesley, and Mount Holyoke Colleges, 1977.
Chodorow, N. Family structure and feminine personality. In M. Rosaldo & L. Lamphere (Eds.), *Women, culture and society.* Stanford, Calif.: Stanford University Press, 1974.
Drabble, M. *The waterfall.* Hammondsworth, England: Penguin Books, 1969.
Eliot, G. *The mill on the floss.* New York: New American Library, 1965. (Originally published, 1860).

Freud, S. Some psychical consequences of the anatomical distinction between the sexes. In J. Strachey (Ed.), *The standard edition of the complete psychological works of Sigmund Freud* (Vol. 19). London: Hogarth Press, 1961. (Originally published, 1925).

Gilligan, C. In a different voice: Women's conceptions of self and morality. *Harvard Educational Review*, 1977, *47*, 481–518.

Gilligan, C. *In a different voice: Psychological theory and women's development.* Cambridge: Harvard University Press, 1982.

Gilligan, C. & Belenky, M. A naturalistic study of abortion decisions. In R. Selman & R. Yando (Eds.), *Clinical-developmental psychology*. San Francisco: Jossey-Bass, 1980.

Gilligan, C., Langdale, S., Lyons, N., and Murphy, M. The contribution of women's thought to developmental theory: The elimination of sex-bias in moral development research and education. Final Report to the National Institute of Education, 1982.

Gilligan, C. & Murphy, J. M. Development from adolescence to adulthood: The philosopher and the "dilemma of the fact." In D. Kuhn (Ed.), *Intellectual development beyond childhood*. San Francisco: Jossey-Bass, 1979.

Guttman, D. Women and the conception of ego strength. *Merrill-Palmer Quarterly*, 1965, *11*, 240.

Kohlberg, L. & Kramer, R. Continuities and discontinuities in childhood and adult moral development. *Human Development*, 1969, *12*, 93–120.

McCarthy, M. *Memories of a Catholic girlhood*. New York: Harcourt Brace, 1946.

McClelland, D. *Power: The inner experience*. New York: Irvington, 1975.

Miller, J. B. *Toward a new psychology of women*. Boston: Beacon Press, 1976.

Murphy, J. M., & Gilligan, C. Moral development in late adolescence and adulthood: A critique and reconstruction of Kohlberg's theory. *Human Development*, 1980, *23*, 77–104.

Piaget, J. *The moral judgment of the child*. New York: The Free Press, 1965. (Originally published, 1932).

Witkin, H. Socialization, culture and ecology in the development of group and sex differences in cognitive style. *Human Development*, 1979, *22*, 358–372.

Chapter 4

Emerging Patterns of Female Leadership in Formal Organizations
Must the Female Leader Go Formal?

Jean Lipman-Blumen

From Machiavelli to modern times, the conundrum of leadership has tantalized the human intellect. Philosophers and researchers have approached the leadership question from varied perspectives, often reaching discrepant conclusions. Despite its generally elusive character, two qualities of effective organizational leadership emerge with considerable consistency:[1] task orientation and people orientation.

Although traditional organizations primarily reward task orientation, several studies of organizational leadership suggest that effective leaders combine task and people orientations (Blake & Mouton, 1968; Couch & Carter, 1952; Gibb, 1954; Halpin & Winer, 1957; Vroom & Yetton, 1973). The exact balance between these two orientations and their relationship to other leadership and organizational conditions remain somewhat uncertain.

If the general issue of leadership is problematical, it is hardly surprising that the conditions of female leadership are even more ambiguous (particularly since most leadership studies have focused on male subjects). As with other poorly understood phenomena, female leadership, too, is overgrown with mythology. Accepted myths and some

---

[1]Although we recognize that leadership and management are distinguishable phenomena, here we shall use the terms somewhat interchangeably.

Jean Lipman-Blumen, Ph.D. • LBS International, Bethesda, Maryland 20814. This paper was written when the author was a fellow at the Center for Advanced Study in the Behavioral Sciences, Palo Alto, California, with partial funding from the Spencer Foundation and the National Endowment for the Humanities.

research findings (when these two are even distinguishable) suggest that women make poor leaders. In recognition of this "fact," subordinates allegedly dislike working for them (Bass, Krusell, & Alexander, 1971; Bowman, Worthy, & Greyser, 1965; Ellman, 1963).[2] That women have not had a major share in leadership roles is seen as further proof of their shortcomings—another case of "blaming the victim." Moreover, the few acknowledged women leaders, in a peculiar combination of denigration and praise, are perceived as masculine. The first prime minister of Israel, Ben-Gurion, reportedly described Golda Meir as the "only real man" in his cabinet.

These myths are difficult to shatter, particularly since the small ratio of women leaders in both public and private sectors is marshalled as confirming "evidence." Despite recent harbingers of change, the last two centuries have been a virtual wasteland for potential women leaders in the arena of American public life.[3] Even in the 1970s, within the private sector women were rarely found in key leadership positions.[4] But the winds of change slowly began to shift.[5] The emergence of groups specifically promoting female leadership presaged rising concern about female leaders in both private and public sectors. In the late '70s, industry, government and academia felt growing pressure to bring women into leadership positions.

More recently, economic rentrenchment and slackening government vigilance has dampened the urgency of the '70s. Nonetheless,

---

[2]More recent evidence (Handley & Sedlacek,1977) suggests that women who worked for a female supervisor were more likely to report greater job satisfaction and less sex bias than women working for male managers.

[3]During the 200 years between 1776 and 1976 the federal government has included 11 women vs. 1,715 men in the U.S.Senate, 87 women vs. 9,591 men in the U.S. House of Representatives, no women and 101 men on the Supreme Court, and 5 women vs. 507 men in thePresident's Cabinet..At the present time,there is one woman Supreme Court Justice, two women serve in the U.S. Senate, and 21 in the U.S. House of Representatives.

[4]Among 1,350 U.S. companies surveyed by Heidrick and Struggles (1982), only 3 (0.2%) have women as chief executive officers. Women constitute only 0.9% of the presidents of 106 national unions. Among approximately 2,800 two-and four-year accredited institutions of higher learning, 8.75% (n = 245) have women presidents.

[5]In state legislatures 991 women have won election (13% of the total 7,482 seats) a 5% gain (from 8% to 13%) in the seven-year period 1975–1982. While women are gaining in areas of elective office, their record in appointed managerial or administrative roles is somewhat more vigorous. By January, 1983, women comprised 32% (n = 10, 697,000) managerial and administrative workers. The number of women applying to and graduating from law and business schools is on the rise (Randour, Strasbourg, and Lipman-Blumen, 1982). The percentage of women seeking ordination degrees in divinity schools has increased 180.9% between 1970 and 1978, offering some slight basis for optimism about their future corner on the divine leadership market.

women than ever before are seeking high level leadership positions in formal organizations, and many more are in the "pipelines" of law, medical, business, and public administration graduate schools. These conditions suggest that a reconsideration of female leadership within the context of formal organizations is a timely endeavor. This chapter, therefore, addresses this critical question.

The purpose here is *not* to present a systematic review of leadership theories, achievement literature, or even female leadership and achievement research. Rather, the aim is to examine several ideas related to female leadership, most of which, we shall argue, have contributed to its current condition. To that end, we shall consider (1) female and male leadership in mixed-gender groups; (2) communication as authority and homosociality of the informal structure; (3) male–female socialization structures and formal organizations; (4) the informal structure as a re-source-allocation mechanism; (5) male–female predilections for different achieving styles; and finally (6) possibilities for change. This effort undoubtedly is overly ambitious; however, these are concepts whose links beg at least a modest exploration.

FEMALE AND MALE LEADERSHIP IN MIXED-GENDER GROUPS

The growing literature on leadership behavior in mixed-sex groups has distilled three major generalizations about differences between male and female behavior (Hall, 1972; Lockheed, 1976; Lockheed & Hall, 1976):

First, *men talk more than women;* that is, they "initiate more verbal acts" (Lockheed & Hall, 1976). Studies of jury deliberations (Strodtbeck & Mann, 1956; Strodtbeck, James, & Hawkins, 1957), as well as those of classroom discussions (Lockheed, 1977; Zander & Van Egmond, 1958); and dating, engaged, and married couples' verbal interaction (Heiss, 1962; Shaw & Sadler, 1965) support this finding. The Zander and Van Egmond (1958) research suggests that as early as second grade little boys, confronting problems to be solved through discussion, talk significantly more often than girls. This suggests an inaccuracy in the mythology that tells us women talk more than men. Talking or communicating, as we shall argue later, is an important leadership dimension, and women, in the company of men, are apparently often inhibited from talking.

Negative attitudes toward female communication have not changed much since Aristotle wrote, ". . . a woman would be thought loquacious if she imposed no more restraint on her conversation than a good man" (Jowett, 1943, p. 294). Nonetheless, more recent work by Askinas (1971) suggests that women's inhibitions against talking in mixed-gender groups are not immutable. In friendship groups *without* a task orientation, Askinas (1971) found that women college freshmen talked more than men.

Other research on activity levels and perceived leadership indicates that the most active group members are more likely to be perceived as leaders by group members (Lana, Vaughan, & McGinnies, 1960; Marak, 1964; Morris & Hackman, 1969; Zdep, 1969; Zdep & Oakes, 1967). Women clearly face a "Catch-22" situation in terms of group activity, particularly verbal activity, and leadership.

The second generalization emanating from the research on leadership in mixed-gender groups is that *men's opinions are more likely than women's to influence the opinions of both male and female group members.* Testing for the extent to which subjects would acquiesce to a distorted norm, Tuddenham, MacBride, and Zahn (1958) found that in mixed-gender groups men were less likely to do so in all-male groups, while women tended to acquiesce more than they had in all-female groups. Whittaker's (1965) experiments with judgments about autokinetic lights revealed that male opinion leaders were more readily followed by both male and female subjects, and that female opinion leaders evoked considerable resistance from subjects of both genders. Again, the works of Strodtbeck *et al.* (1957), Kenkel (1957), and Zander and Van Egmond (1958) all seem to offer supportive evidence. Resistance to women's analyses and presentations creates serious obstacles to female organizational leadership.

The third generalization centers around Parson's (1955) formulation that *males are more task oriented, while females are more socioemotionally oriented.* According to Borgatta and Stimson (1963), as well as Strodtbeck and Mann (1956) and Heiss (1962), men more frequently than women offer task-related suggestions in group decision-making situations, while women more often provide encouragement and support to other group members.

Other work by Lockheed and Hall (1976) suggests that men are not necessarily more active and task oriented than women. They indicate that maleness *per se* represents a more highly valued status characteristic translatable into increased opportunities for action (and therefore leadership) within a group setting. Their research suggests that intervention techniques—such as training and demonstrating competence specific to the task at hand—may offset initial group leadership advantages accorded males, based simply on gender.

To confound matters, Bartol and Wortman (1975) present data that question the degree to which the leader's gender influences either subordinates' perception of that leader's behavior or subordinates' own job satisfaction. Their findings highlight the power of *subordinates'* gender in predicting subordinates' satisfaction levels. Male subordinates are more likely than females to express lower levels of satisfaction, regardless of leader's gender.

Although additional research is needed to resolve these conflicting results, important insights may emerge from the juxtaposition of these findings:

If, in mixed-gender situations (as in day-to-day organizational life),

- the more active members are seen as leaders;
- men are given more opportunities to talk and act;
- men actually do talk more than women;
- men's opinions tend to evoke positive group reactions, while women's opinions spark negative or resistant responses; ·
- male, more often than female, subordinates express dissatisfaction with their leader, regardless of the leader's gender; and
- the most powerful informal group consists of men (as we shall discuss below);

then the current structure of organizations serves as a serious barrier to the acceptance of female leadership.

COMMUNICATION AS AUTHORITY AND HOMOSOCIALITY OF THE INFORMAL STRUCTURE

The Bartol and Wortman (1975) study is important because it extends the focus beyond the behavior and characteristics of women leaders. Much recent leadership and management research has disproportionately emphasized the leader's personal characteristics and behavior (Bayes & Newton, 1978; Hennig & Jardim, 1977). Earlier, Max Weber (1922/1947) distinguished between the charismatic leadership of the individual possessing a gift of grace (*mana*) and the routinization of charisma through a bureaucratized structure, replete with statuses and authority. In the late 1930s, Barnard (1968) also differentiated between authority of the individual and authority associated with a position. Other organizational literature considers the importance of symbols (i.e., corner offices, chauffeured limousines) that authenticate authority of positions most commonly held by men.

More important, perhaps, is Barnard's insight that "authority is the character of a communication in a formal organization by virtue of which it is accepted by a member as governing the action which [the member] contributes to the organization" (Barnard, 1968). According to Barnard, the decision that an act of leadership has authority "lies with the persons to whom it is addressed and does not reside in 'persons of authority' or those who issue these orders" (p. 163).

The analysis of female leadership (or nonleadership) therefore should consider its acceptance or legitimation by those to whom it is directed. This is not to deny that the character of the communication (to which we shall return later) carries weight, but more to emphasize the importance of subordinates' attitudes. If (1) authority is, indeed, a characteristic of communication and "rests upon the acceptance or consent" (Barnard, 1968, p. 164) of those to whom it is addressed, and (2) the subordinate group has a high proportion of men, then women who attempt leadership (or, more modestly, managerial) roles in male-dominated organizations are in serious trouble.

First, if we recall the research finding that women talk less than men in mixed-gender groups, it is clear that establishing communication, and thereby authority, is more problematical for women. One function of the women's loquaciousness myth becomes apparent: it serves as a control mechanism,[6] reducing women's communications in men's presence by embarrassing women about behavior defined as negative (for women only). This mechanism whereby women limit their own communication in men's presence conveniently reduces the amount and quality of leadership that women exercise in mixed-gender groups.

Second, mixed-group research tells us that even when women do talk, their opinions often negatively affect group opinion. Michels (1937) notes, "Whether authority is of personal or institutional origin, it is created and maintained by public opinion, which in its turn is conditioned by sentiment, affection, reverence or fatalism" (Vol. 2, p. 319). The formal and (perhaps even more important) the informal systems separately generate public opinion which maintains authority. Women's exclusion from the most influential informal system presumably keeps them from building a positive public opinion base which would make their opinions more acceptable to the group.

Within each sphere, the individual builds a credibility base on somewhat different grounds: official rank in the formal system, sentiment and personal ties in the informal system. Personal credibility generated in the informal system influences authority in the formal structure, and often vice-versa. More specifically, organizational leaders inherit credibility levels linked to their rank or position in the formal system. That rank-related credibility, however, receives increments or decrements depending on the personal regard, affection, and sentiment the individual creates in the informal system.

From a slightly different vantage point, the leader who also happens to be a member of the informal system (i.e., "the old-boy net-

[6]For an extensive analysis on the impact of this and other control myths on the power relationships between women and men, see J. Lipman-Blumen, Sex/gender roles. In A. Inkeles (Ed.), *Foundations of Modern Sociology*. Englewood Cliffs, N.J.: Prentice-Hall Publishers (forthcoming.)

work") is allowed an extra margin of credibility. *Ceteris paribus,* that leader's co-workers are prepared to be receptive to his (rarely her) ideas. (Compare this to the common experience of high-level organizational women, excluded from the informal male system, who complain that their comments in official situations are often ignored altogether or attributed to a male group member.)

To add to the complexity of organizational life, high credibility associated with formal rank marks the individual as a desirable recruit for the informal structure. Individuals with high formal rank increase the status and desirability of the informal system. Moreover, the bonds they build in the informal system enhance their possibilities in the formal system. The Catch-22 circularity is apparent in the connections between the formal and informal bases of credibility: if you're "in" in one system, you're likely to be "in" in the other system, which in turn makes you more "in" in the first. It also follows that if you're "out" in one, you're more likely to be "out" in the other, and so on. Thus, for the formal and informal bases of credibility to potentiate one another, the individual must have access to both structures, the formal and informal.

External pressures in the 1970s created opening wedges for women in formal organizational structures.[7] Nonetheless women leaders still confront serious difficulty in entering the informal structure, the greenhouse milieu for growing sentiment and affection so critical to public opinion, as well as decisions and transactions that ultimately move the formal structure.

Beyond building supportive sentiment and affection within the informal structure, a leader sharpens communication by an accurate assessment of events, conditions, and people. Again, there is a troublesome circularity to the information process. To be credible, information from leaders to followers must be informed by the culture and currency of those led. Leaders gain credibility when they seem to know "everything and more" than their followers. Leaders who transmit information subordinates perceive as naïve soon lose credibility. Intelligence that flows from the informal network augments formal information. Such intelligence itself is a valuable resource.

Of course, women in leadership positions receive the usual official information through formal channels, such as staff meetings, briefings, memoranda, and the like. But important "insider's" knowledge—communicated through the informal system—is not readily available to women. This informally transmitted knowledge, offering the insider

---

[7]For example, the National Women's Political Caucus was formed to assist women political candidates, and a presidential task force was appointed to consider the factors inhibiting women business owners.

strategic advantages, is not readily accessible to women who are barred from executive-level, all-male formal groups.

Women's exclusion from the informal male network prevents them from developing an "intelligence or communication base," which could spread a mantle of authority over their communications in the formal structure. The resulting handicap activates a vicious cycle which women managers or leaders rarely have the resources to break. Parallel all-female informal networks ordinarily do not transmit executive- and policy-level information. This flows partly from the sex segregation of formal organizations (Blaxall & Reagan, 1976) and partly from the companion tendency for women to be confined within the lowest strata of such structures. Rarely do sufficient numbers of executive-level women within any single formal organization exist who might constitute an informal network.[8] Only recently have women begun to offset this information barrier through interorganizational networks.

Although informal networks are commonly sex segregated, heterosocial relationships are often conduits for resource exchange between the informal male and female structures. For example, the secretary–executive relationship historically has been the channel through which male executives tapped into the female informal network, thereby acquiring valuable information about their male co-workers. Similarly, females in organizational settings have often had to rely on their individual relationships with male co-workers for important organizational resources, including information.

MALE–FEMALE SOCIALIZATION STRUCTURES AND FORMAL ORGANIZATIONS

Male homosociality[9] has been described elsewhere as a powerful factor in the sex segregation of American social institutions (Lipman-

---

[8]Some recent exceptions have emerged in the world of women's issues within the public and private sectors, where strong informal networks have developed. Since women's programs commonly involve small, all-female staffs within larger, mostly male (except for support staff) organizations, the feminist networks that have developed often cross organizational lines. These informal structures serve as avenues for policy-level and other information, support, decision-making, and strategy development across organizational boundaries. Thus, women managers in unrelated subdivisions of a large-scale organization, in separate but similar private institutions, and within different agencies in government have created effective feminist homosocial networks. These networks have involved coalitions not only among "insiders" in different divisions, but also between "insiders" and "outsiders." Partly because professionals are segregated within their own organizations, they still have difficulty penetrating the informal male homosocial structures within their parent organizations.

[9]Homosociality is defined as "seeking, enjoyment, and/or preference for the company of the same gender" (Lipman-Blumen, 1976).

Blumen, 1976; forthcoming). Here, we would suggest that both the formal and more critical segments of the informal structures of organizations reflect the early homosocial structures in which young boys are socialized. As other researchers (Hennig & Jardim, 1977; Safilios-Rothschild, 1975, 1979) note, early male socialization within highly structured teams is iterated in the formal and informal structures of men's adult occupational lives.

The male homosocial ethic focuses on competition and winning. It operates within a context replete with complex role networks and clearly articulated hierarchies. Coordinated roles within teams are designed for successful task completion, for winning. They are based on universalistic, rather than particularistic, criteria (Parsons, 1949).[10] Each role is important to the completion of the team's task, and a role candidate's competence in specific skills is the overriding criterion for selection. Formal coordination among roles is based on rules designed for successful task completion.

The team, with its formal structure of interlocking, task-oriented roles, is a depersonalized world. Specialized, task-oriented skill is the primary, if not the only, criterion for entry into team roles; feelings, sensitivities, understanding, and other interpersonal skills are far less relevant. For example, no soccer team is complete without a goalie. The goalie position, however, is filled by the candidate most adept at defending the goal, without regard to that individual's interpersonal skills.

Males learn early on that winning the game often means playing with unlikeable teammates. Team spirit may be interpreted as recognition of the superordinate importance of the group over the individual. Team spirit, esprit de corps, homosociality—all are the very fabric of the winning process. As noted earlier, personal relationships among role occupants become the domain of the informal, not the formal structure. The informal structure provides a necessary cushion against the formal structure's (i.e., the team's) impersonality and arises in its service.

The informal structure fulfills personal needs frustrated by the formal structure. In his autobiography, Roethlisberger (1977), the dean of the early human relations movement in management, lucidly underscores this distinction:

> These relations of interconnectedness among persons . . . I call the strong, close, and warm relationships. They make the cheese more binding. The

---

[10]Parsons (1949) has distinguished between universalistic and particularistic standards in the following manner: "The standards and criteria which are independent of the particular social relationship to a particular person may be called universalistic, those which apply by virtue of such a relationship on the other hand are particularistic" (p. 192). (The relevance of the universalistic/particularistic dichotomy to the role/person differentiation was suggested to me by Prof. Mathilda W. Riley.)

[formal] ones in contrast are weak, distant, and cold. . . . It seemed to me that in most organizations the employees found these informal relationships rewarding. Whenever and wherever it is possible, they generated them like crazy. . . . The two kinds of relations were in sharp contrast. Among members of [formal] relations, there were few interactions, few close friendships and seldom any small, warm, cozy groups. There was sometimes "respect" but quite often distrust, apprehension, and suspicion. Interaction was limited to what the task required. It looked as if the logic of rational management generated weak, distant, and cold relations, whereas the employees as persons generated strong, close, and warm relations. The outcome, which was often conflict, was not because anyone was deliberately trying to throw a monkey wrench in the machinery. The logic of management could do only what it was supposed to do, its business, so to speak. It could only produce those relations in which rational order existed. To ask it to produce strong, close, cozy and comfortable relations would be like asking an icicle to produce warmth for man. However, that man as man sought for these warm relations was also not being just ornery. He also was doing what his nature as man and the itch–ouch balance compelled him to do. (p. 165–66)

Given the offsetting warmth and personal interaction of the informal structure, team members can more readily tolerate the formal structure's coolness and impersonality. The early articulated coordination among formal roles can then be accepted as more crucial than the personalities who happen to occupy the roles. This formal-informal counterpoint provides the context of male socialization. Hence, in early childhood males learn to distinguish and move easily between formal and informal structures.

Females grow up mostly outside the world of large, complexly structured teams. They are socialized in small play groups of two or three individuals (Maccoby & Jacklin, 1974) in which the formal is undifferentiated from the informal structure. The focus is on individual personalities and relationships among them. Winning is not highly emphasized; relating is.

Adult females, whose early socialization has not been marked by the complex, universalistic role structures of teams, feel the difference. They are typically less experienced in moving within the context of formally coordinated roles, particularly when these roles take priority over personalities. The early female social world's greater structural simplicity (i.e., its tendency to be configured in dyads or triads rather than larger role networks) and its particularistic emphasis lead to a merger of formal and informal structures. When two children relate as playmates, the functional playmate role and the expressive friend role merge. In larger, formal structures, informal structures arise more easily. In small, formal structures, there is insufficient surplus role material from which informal structures may be fashioned.

Socialized from an early age within structures of less complexity and greater particularism, females often see the formal and informal worlds as one and treat informally even formal roles. Given the emotionally positive aspects of the informal structure, as Roethlisberger describes, the choice is a natural one, one that men, too, probably would make if the structure of their world permitted.

Women's inexperience in separating the formal and informal structures, nonetheless, is a liability. This liability is obvious when, as adults, women seek to enter leadership roles in organizations whose complex role networks necessitate separate but related formal and informal structures. But it is more than a question of inexperience. Women learn to *value* personal relationships, to rank their importance above simple task orientation and winning. The more adept females become in interpersonal relationships, the more they value this *modus vivendi,* and the more likely they are to incorporate this value in their managerial style (Reif, Newstrom, & Monczka, 1975).

Raphaela Best's (1983) ethnographic study of third-graders at play describes how little girls happily let their girl friends win the race in the name of friendship. Because young females' play structures are mostly dyadic or triadic, the individuals in these roles are not depersonalized. Personality counts. The person and the role more easily become one, but it is the individual, not the role, who has salience. An individual lacking certain personal characteristics will not be accepted in the playmate role, even if the role must remain vacant. Emphasis is on people as personalities and on relationships, rather than on the structure and coordination of goal-oriented roles. The relationship is the goal, the external task may even be the means. The focus in on relating, not on winning.

If it is important to females to like people in impinging roles, it is equally (perhaps too) critical for them to feel that *they* are liked.[11] In fact the early achievement studies of McClelland, Atkinson, Clark, and Lowell (1953) suggested that social acceptability cues were the only significant stimuli for females' need for achievement. This need to be liked may impede women in organizational situations requiring group participation where competence and task orientation, unalloyed with personal popularity, are required. The priority females assign to personal popularity may inhibit competitive and other task-oriented behavior essential to leadership roles.

Cooperation, rather than competition, tends to characterize young girls' relationships. Even when vying for male attention, females' competition is veiled, indirect, and subtle compared to the open, direct, and all-out quality of male competition. Females are taught that overt com-

---

[11]The reciprocal need to be liked was suggested to me in personal communication by Prof. Constantina Safilios-Rothschild (1978).

petition is masculine—another control myth—and that contributing, helpful behavior is more appropriately female. As we shall see, this conditioning casts a wide net. Hennig and Jardim's (1977) former tomboys recalled high levels of adolescent frustration in their struggles with parental admonitions to forgo the aggressive and open competition of boys' team sports for more traditional female pastimes. More recent research on achieving styles (Lipman-Blumen et al., 1983) suggests that women, even women in highly "competitive" occupations, are less competitive than their male counterparts.

THE HOMOSOCIAL INFORMAL STRUCTURE AS A RESOURCE MECHANISM

Analogous to the formal structure, the informal structure is composed of numerous, segmented, and unequal parts. It reflects, but is not strictly isomorphic with, the hierarchy and sex segregation of the formal structure. Most often, sex segregation of the informal structure is more severe than that of the formal structure. Although the informal structure may be replete with heterosexual activity (commonly of a dyadic nature), large and usually important segments are limited to a single-gender or homosocial group.

Earlier, we discussed the information and bonding functions of the informal network. The informal structure that arises in a large formal system has still another related critical function: it serves as a resource-allocation mechanism. The homosociality characterizing the informal structure facilitates and is reinforced by its control and distribution of resources. Again, those segments of the informal structure which control high-level political, professional, organizational, even financial resources are more accessible to men than to women.

Both tangible and intangible resources flow along the tributaries of the informal network. Thus, autonomy and extra degrees of freedom are dispersed through the informal network. That is, the ordinary bureaucratic controls are not applied very rigidly to the "inner circle" members of the informal network. A related commodity—time—is another vital resource allocated through informal channels. Hence, personal time as well as official time (e.g., deadlines) gain a measure of flexibility through the informal system. For example, members of the informal group are less likely to have their comings and goings carefully scrutinized. Their organizational tether is longer, providing greater latitude for action before being called to account. In this way, time and autonomy, as well as personal and organizational freedom of the "old-boy network" are enlarged.

These important resources, allocated by the informal system, enable leaders to fashion their own organizational worlds. These resources are building blocks of power which create leverage in the formal system. Leaders who accrue autonomy and time are able to offer these resources to staff, clients, and colleagues, thereby augmenting the leaders' power in the formal system. The assets which enable leaders to provide special treatment for staff, colleagues, and clients eventually yield loyalty, reciprocal help, profits, and promotions.

The informal structure as a resource-allocation device also distributes loopholes, "ways around" the formal requirements of the system. Special perquisites are distributed as well. For example, when budgetary constraint periods presumably restrict all travel funds, favored members of the informal network, nonetheless, often manage to commandeer travel monies.

Still another resource available through the informal network is accessibility to people and services. While a certain formal accessibility to co-workers and services is a legitimate part of every organizational role, that accessibility is enhanced or inhibited by the informal system. Thus, while division managers have some legitimate claim on the time and help of their supervisors, that claim is processed quickly or lackadaisically according to the manager's informal standing. Members of the informal group do not "cool their heels" waiting for an appointment. Both the quality and quantity of accessibility and service are influenced by the informal system. Even official resources such as staff and budget are influenced by the informal structure. Any seasoned organizational observer knows that favored members of the informal system somehow manage to secure staff and budget allotments beyond official allocation levels.

Political, financial, legal, professional, and other extraorganizational help are still other resources that flow along the informal tributaries. The easy accessibility of the informal group allows insiders to develop a "sixth organizational sense." Insiders know one another well enough to sense the appropriate moment for requesting or offering help. Easy access to one another provides the context within which implicit understandings about goals, values, and sentiments develop. This intimate knowledge decreases the probability of serious political or interpersonal errors that could jeopardize leadership. All these valuable resources—autonomy, freedom, time, loopholes, perquisites, accessibility to people and services, political, professional, financial, and legal help—(not to mention valuable "insider's" information discussed earlier)—are distributed by the all-male executive informal system.

Female homosocial enclaves within the informal structure also exist, serving control and distribution functions; however, resources flowing along the female homosocial network channels are more likely to be interpersonal or relational in nature. Women's access to crucial organizational resources is more limited; therefore, the benefits they may disperse to other women are rarely keyed to organizational or individual professional goals. Lacking adequate alternatives, the solo executive women is pushed to offer her organizational help to male colleagues, whose potential reciprocity is desired but rarely won.

Because their access to the informal male structure is barred, women commonly lack the resources necessary for negotiating their way through higher levels of the formal structure. They rarely participate in transactions and decisions allocating vital organizational resources. The result: Less access to executive power and organizational maneuverability.

Women who enter formal organizations with their own resources (i.e., family fortunes and linked organizational positions, as well as sociopolitical networks) may more efficiently counteract the informal male homosocial context. If such women can maintain their resources *within* the organization, their authority ultimately may be sustained and acknowledged by male colleagues and subordinates. But authority, as suggested earlier, is an aspect of communication. And women's more general exclusion from the informal byways reduces their access to other critical resources—information and a communication network (plus still other resources which can be exchanged for intelligence and dissemination). In this way, women's leadership opportunities are constrained.

Occasionally women with male mentors who are "plugged in" to the male informal network vicariously receive information and other key resources from the informal system. Mentors with "lines" to the organization's power centers can confer upon their protégés impressive resource arrays, including status and support. Young, ambitious men in organizations rather easily attach themselves to successful male mentors. For women, association with a male mentor is a process commonly fraught with sexual overtones (Rowe, 1977; Shapiro, Haseltine, & Rowe, 1978) and potential pitfalls for mentor and protégée alike, as in the much-publicized Bendix fiasco.

MALE–FEMALE PREDILECTIONS FOR DIFFERENT ACHIEVING STYLES

The attention organizational goals and structure have garnered in the literature has tended to eclipse an equally important area: styles of achieving. While the nature of goals and the structures within which one seeks goals are undeniably important, how one goes about attaining those goals is equally crucial. Both men and women develop characteristic ways of achieving whatever goals they set for themselves. The more adept individuals become at certain achieving "orientations" or "styles," the more likely they are to continue using them (Lipman-Blumen, Leavitt, Patterson, Beis, and Handley-Isaksen, 1980).

Males raised in the world of competitive teams easily focus on the nature of the task and ways of winning. The context of the early male world encourages pitting oneself against the environment, acting directly on one's own behalf, achieving through one's own efforts all aspects of direct achieving styles.

Another aspect of early male socialization contributes to the development of a direct achieving style: expectations that adult males will support themselves and possibly others. Males are expected to act on their own behalf. For adult males there is no escape from responsibility for direct action. Only demonstrated failure to perform or, conversely, a substantial history of successful direct achieving performance lets men off the hook. (Females, by contrast, must prove they can perform before being admitted to adult task-oriented organizations.) In fact, institutionalized loopholes—including marriage—channel females away from front-line responsibility. The difference between male and female socialization is great on this point. Little boys traditionally are asked what they want to *be* when they grow up; little girls, *whom* they want to marry. Major differences in mind set are natural sequelae. From early socialization, males expect to protect and support women. Women traditionally have been socialized to accept male protection and support, without recognizing that this arrangement is tantamount to control.

As we have suggested earlier, the female world emphasizes relationships, which ultimately become conduits to goals. Hoffman's (1972) review of the affiliation and achievement literature emphasizes the importance of affiliation in female achievement. And Bernard's (1981) work on female cultures provides additional insight into this phenomenon. For women, the relationship itself often becomes the goal, as noted above. To this end, acts contributing to the establishment and/or maintenance of relationships become valued means of achieving. Female socialization inclines women away from direct achieving styles and roles embodying these characteristics. The focus on relationships encourages what we have described elsewhere (Leavitt & Lipman-Blumen, 1980; Lipman-Blumen & Leavitt, 1976, 1978a; Lipman-Blumen et al. 1980, 1983) as relational achievement.[12] Relational achievement is measured not by one's own success but by the success of another individual to whom one relates, with whom one identifies, and to whose success one may have contributed.[13] Relational achieving styles are translated into

---

[12]For a description of the three achieving style domains—direct, instrumental, and relational—and the nine subsumed individual styles, see Lipman-Blumen et al. (1979, 1983) and Leavitt & Lipman-Blumen (1979).

[13]Contribution to the success of another is carried out with the explicit recognition by both actors that the activity and the reward for success are essentially the property of the other achiever. The relational achiever satisfies his or her own achievement needs by contributing to the success of the other achiever.

certain occupational roles. Service or helping roles are good examples. While traditional "feminine" occupations such as teaching, social work, and nursing may be described as "relational," coaching and managerial roles combine aspects of relational, instrumental, and direct achieving styles. Here we begin to see the importance of relational roles for organizations (Leavitt & Lipman-Blumen, 1980).

An interesting phenomenon of formal organizations involves rewarding competence in nonsupervisory roles by promotion to supervisory positions. Supervisory or managerial roles subsume large relational components, in which the individual is expected to contribute to the achievement of subordinates. Adjustment to managerial roles may be particularly stressful for direct achievers, who experience difficulty in relinquishing long-standing habits of "doing it themselves." Moreover, acquiring supporting and coaching skills required in supervisory roles compounds the stress. It is precisely in this area that women have developed the greatest skills. But present organizational reward structures frustrate the match of women to managerial or leadership roles.

Even when leadership roles actually involve considerable attention to relationships,[14] organizational reward structures in Western society rarely openly applaud relational achieving styles. Nonetheless, it is clear that technical expertise without interpersonal skill rarely sends one to the head of the leadership line.[15]

POSSIBILITIES FOR CHANGE

One consensus point in the vast social-change literature is the difficulty of changing individuals, organizations, or society. The organizational problems women leaders confront require changes in all three areas. While many efforts to ease these problems are possible, few are simple, inexpensive, and feasible. Nor can the "remedies" be discharged with a few paragraphs of cavalier advice. Nonetheless, some first steps are worth considering.

Change agents know that success is dependent on the size, profundity, complexity, pervasiveness, and duration of the change intended. These factors interact not simply with one another, but with many aspects of the society, organizations, and/or people concerned. Some changes we shall suggest are small, rather simple first steps designed to

[14]Numerous studies indicate that the chief executive officers of many large companies spend a large proportion of their time dealing with interpersonal (i.e., relational) problems.

[15]Japanese organizational structures assign higher priority to interpersonal or relational skills than to technical expertise (Abegglen, 1958; Johnson & Ouchi, 1974; Lipman-Blumen & Leavitt, 1978b; Okamoto, n.d.; Vogel, 1968).

promote easy success and prepare the way for later, more complex changes. Other changes we shall propose are greater, more complicated, and more difficult to achieve. How difficult or easy a specific strategy is depends in part on the condition of the soil in which the seeds of change are planted.

We take a problem-oriented approach to change, starting with the major problems discussed in earlier sections of this chapter: the general problems of leadership roles, credibility in the formal and informal structures, separating the formal and informal systems, relational achieving styles, homosocial networks, and so forth. Some solutions we shall suggest involve changing the structure of organizations, the people, the task, even the technology (Leavitt, 1964)—changes that inevitably will meet resistance. Some solutions demand organizational initiatives; others, individual efforts by women in leadership roles. Other recommendations require steps by both the organization (including male workers) and the individual woman leader. And still others call for changes—particularly value changes—in the larger society.

Given the growing disenchantment with current organizational structures (Argyris, 1960; Leavitt, 1975) and the quality of work life (Kerr & Rosow, 1979), solutions that attempt both organizational and human change seem worth the try. Our proposals are directed at the entire organization and represent strategies to make men's, as well as women's, lives more productive, satisfying, and humane. As the organizational literature insists, creating positive changes for people ultimately produces better organizations—organizations whose goals are met, as well as organizations whose people are satisfied and committed.

GENERAL LEADERSHIP PROBLEMS

Our earliest discussion of leadership roles dealt with the hazards and difficulties leaders face, the general problems that leadership itself generates. Changing leadership roles in various ways is one starting point in dealing with these problems. Several *structural* changes could limit the disadvantages, as well as the importance, of leadership roles tied to specific individuals.

Rotating leadership positions. Rotating responsibility among members of the group ensures that no one individual is the permanent leader whose authority and power tend to build resentment, jealousy, and resistance. When leadership is rotated among group members, the temporary leader knows he or she eventually will return to regular group membership. This knowledge is conducive to judicious exercise of leadership.

Having recently risen from the follower's ranks, the leader is more cognizant of problems as they appear from that end of the telescope. Rotated leadership becomes a responsibility more than a privilege, and the burdens of leadership are more appreciated by subordinates. Leadership rotation functions most easily within a peer group context, where members are nearly interchangeable and the leader is seen as "first among equals." The advantages of rotation are evident in academia where rotating departmental chairs have reduced certain abuses and burdens of leadership. In some settings, however, leadership rotation faces serious obstacles.

Decreasing the Size of Work Groups Directly Responsible to the Leader. Smaller groups enable the formal and the informal systems to remain fairly isometric, a condition beneficial to female leadership. Personal bonds, which benefit both women and men, have improved growth potential in smaller work units.

Minimizing the Number of Organizational Levels. Fewer organizational levels reduce the sharpness, depersonalization, and alienation often found in the rigid hierarchies of megaorganizations. Flattened hierarchies, combined with smaller units, provide a step toward closer personal relationships and commitment. Encouragement for this strategy comes from recent research suggesting that flatter organizational hierarchies can boost worker satisfaction (Tannenbaum, Kavcic, Rosner, Vianello, & Welser, 1974).

Decentralization. This fourth structural possibility can increase (1) the autonomy of leaders and (2) the interpersonal bonds among peers, as well as between leaders and their staffs. Reporting to individuals whom one sees daily and knows personally increases the likelihood of a satisfied and loyal work group.

Reexamining Entry Criteria for Leadership Roles. Leaders are frequently chosen for their potential contributions to goal attainment (defined in terms of task completion). Despite ample evidence that organizational leadership requires both a task and people orientation, leaders more often than not are chosen without regard to their interpersonal skills. Reexamining criteria for entry into leadership roles and explicitly recognizing the contribution of interpersonal skills to goal attainment is a structural strategy worth trying.

Reevaluation of Organizational Reward Systems. Organizational reward systems need reevaluation, possibly redesign, to ensure that people orientation, and not simply task orientation, is rewarded meaningfully. Women's carefully learned relational skills should be harnessed to managerial roles. Mechanisms tying relational skills to organizational power centers should be developed. Promotions and access to organizational resources should be based on evidence of a leader's ability to integrate direct and relational achieving styles. This strategy presupposes that top management is convinced (or convincible) that relational ties are important organizational "glue," deserving system resources and rewards.

Recognizing New Leadership Potential. The emergence of new leadership in crisis periods is a lesson repeatedly taught by history. Organizations could take advantage of this process by recognizing emergent leadership potential in individuals not previously in leadership roles. In addition, periods of social, organizational, or personal crisis offer individuals locked into direct achievement roles opportunities to shift to relational achievement roles, and vice-versa (Lipman-Blumen, 1973a, 1975, 1977, 1979). Organizational sensitivity to the potential of crisis states could encourage the assumption of new leadership roles, as well as personal achieving style changes, during episodes of societal, organizational, and/or individual transition. Crisis periods commonly create adult socialization or learning experiences enabling individuals to enter previously avoided or inaccessible roles. Moreover, crisis experience can create organizational conditions conducive to the perpetuation of crisis-induced role change.

CREDIBILITY IN THE FORMAL AND INFORMAL STRUCTURES

Level and Domain of Organizational Entry. Credibility in the formal structure, we noted, is a major problem for female leaders, a problem partially amenable to structural solution. First, women leaders must enter the organization at high enough levels so their positions carry adequate and unequivocal formal credibility. Unlike men, women have special difficulty in establishing credibility when they enter at the lower ranks. The domains women leaders supervise must be more central to the goals of the organization. In addition, women leaders should be given all the *symbols of power,* as well as the *reality of resources.* Corner offices and large budgets will lend reality to women leaders' clout, just as they always have to men's. Adequate resources and the symbols of clout will encourage male co-workers to seek the help, even the sponsorship, of women leaders.

Entering or Creating Informal Groups. As noted earlier, credibility in the formal group partially depends on sentiment and personal ties in the informal group. Formal credibility is strengthened by critical information created and distributed in the informal group. Two obvious possibilities exist: women must create their own informal groups, or they must find ways of entering men's. The former may be easier than the latter. If cadres of high-level women are brought into organizational positions that reduce potential competition among them, they can serve as their own informal network, providing executive-level informational and other resources, as well as interpersonal support. Where there are not enough top-level women in a single organization, women leaders should seek out and construct an interorganizational informal network composed of top-level women in analogous positions in similar organizations. Academic women have set an example by developing inter-university informal networks which act as support groups and resource-allocation devices.

Entering male informal networks is a complicated problem; however, some initial steps may be possible. One-to-one professional relationships with male co-workers who are members of the male homosocial informal system offer an obvious partial solution. The personal regard created in one or several individual relationships can have a positive impact on the woman leader's subsequent credibility in the formal group. This is not to deny the hazards of this approach, noted above.

Access to an existing male informal network may be more difficult than building a new informal mixed-gender network based on mutual interests outside of work. For example, an informal group (often including spouses) that regularly attends or engages in cultural, community, and athletic activities can offer possibilities for low-threat, mixed-gender informal networks.

Ties to Co-Workers. Even if the woman leader cannot enter as a *bona fide* member of the male informal network, she may still develop access to information transmitted through the informal system. Not only will individual professional ties to one or more members of the male informal network help, but particular male co-workers may be more helpful than others. For example, a male member of the informal system to whom the woman leader reports in the formal structure is a critical linchpin to the informal structure. The organization can help here by making it the male supervisor's quasi-legitimate responsibility to keep the female leader "posted." This can sustain the woman leader's information level (and, therefore, her credibility in the formal group). Obviously, this strategy must be implemented judiciously to avoid jeopardizing the male informant's trustworthiness in the informal group.

The recent plethora of work on the importance of *mentors* in individual careers makes elaboration redundant. Nonetheless, the male supervisor just mentioned is one possible mentor. Other high-status males, both in and outside of the organization, are additional mentor candidates for women leaders.

Composition of Groups. Gender and status composition of the groups women lead offer other structural possibilities for enhancing women's leadership credibility. If, indeed, male subordinates more often than female subordinates express dissatisfaction with group leaders, regardless of the leader's gender, then women leaders initially should direct groups where women outnumber men. Once their reputations and confidence as leaders are established in preponderantly female groups, women leaders can increase the male ratio among their subordinates or move to groups with larger proportions of men. Moreover, the presence of a supportive high-status male group member can help a woman new to the leadership game. The group should be structured to enhance the perception and the reality that the high-status male is her *ally*, rather than her competitor or puppet.

Kinds of Group Participation. Credibility in groups, we have seen, is promoted by active participation. Organizations should place women in (and women should seek) organizational roles offering possibilities for active contribution to group tasks. Roles such as team leader, team expert on a given issue, and liaison to other important groups offer structured possibilities for unequivocal contribution to goals. Individuals contributing to group tasks, rather than to the socioemotional climate of the group, are more likely to be perceived as leaders within the current value system. Women group leaders, at least initially, should downplay nurturance, emotional support, and encouragement. Instead, they should concentrate on task-related directions and advice. The reciprocal of this strategy is to train males (1) to listen when women talk and (2) to offer emotional and social support to other group members.

Training women for exclusive expertise in an important task is one method for simultaneously building credibility in the group and encouraging women to focus on tasks rather than on people. Training women as *specialists* in short-term tasks can improve the group's appreciation of their contribution to goal attainment. For example, a consulting group planning to enter a new substantive area could offer a woman leader special "crash" training in that subject to ensure her claim to unique leadership eligibility.

A variation on this strategy: Assign women already trained as specialists to be the sole experts in their field in a given work group. For example, when the female lawyer is the only group member with a legal background, her unique expertise brings credibility, almost by default.

An important caveat: Specialist roles often prove to be dead-end positions. If women enter organizations in specialist roles, they should be offered the training possibilities and promotional opportunities allowing them to rise to the *"generalist"* ranks of leadership. Urging women to enter organizations as specialists runs counter to the current trend in leading business schools, where managers are advised to become "generalists." Nonetheless, entrée as a specialist is a useful short-term strategy for establishing women's leadership credibility before moving to generalist roles.

Speaking Up. Although women's comments are often ignored in group discussions, research findings suggest that leadership is attributed to those group members who talk the most. Structural opportunities for women to *talk* more in groups should be devised by organizations that wish to develop more women leaders. For example, women should have frequent opportunities to make oral presentations and should receive additional preparation and coaching if necessary. Roles that require much talking, such as team leader, presenter, or discussion leader, offer structural opportunities for women to talk. Moreover, if men's subsequent performance depends on information gleaned specifically from a woman leader's presentation, this "structured talking" by women could be a valuable way of encouraging male workers to attend to women's verbal contributions ("structured listening").

"Anointed analysis," where a woman's opinions are validated by the explicit approval of the high-status male leader, motivates women to talk and men to listen. In official meetings, the top executive can solicit the woman executive's opinion, then listen deferentially, seriously, and attentively, thus setting the example for the other males.

Although these structural changes represent primarily organizational initiatives, in most cases there are parallel individual approaches. For instance, women can offer to make oral presentations. They can volunteer to be or become group experts in new areas, and, when offered a choice, they can select staffs where the male/female ratio is in their leadership favor. In such ways, individual women can facilitate structural leadership opportunities.

SEPARATING THE FORMAL AND INFORMAL SYSTEMS

Earlier, we examined the greater difficulty women seem to encounter in separating formal from informal structures. We related this predilection to young girls' early dyadic and triadic play groups and their relative inexperience in larger, coordinated teams. One presumed outcome of these early socialization experiences is that women seem less willing than men to work with people whom they do not like and more likely than men to be concerned with personal popularity.

Executive Development Programs. Popular with many organizations, such programs could train women that performance counts heavily, and personal feelings should aid, not hinder, performance. Such development programs could help women to focus more on tasks, rather than relationships. Training should involve quick and clear feedback, confirming that evaluations were based on task completion, not popularity or emotional support. Demonstrating that personal popularity is less relevant than competence, both for themselves and others, may be an important consciousness-raising point for women. Exploring how task-oriented competence leads to popularity and respect may draw women away from the safety zone of previously acquired interpersonal skills. At the same time, men should be sensitized to recognize that being liked and liking co-workers can be beneficial both to one's individual self-image and to organizational goal attainment. In essence, balance between task- and people-orientation is a valuable lesson for female and male leaders, alike.

Recreational and Work-Related Teams. Within recreational and work teams, women can practice separating formal and informal structures. These skills can be learned in executive development programs. The early team experience of males offers them important advantages in adult organizations; educators designing curricula for young girls should take this into account. Long before entering large-scale work organizations, girls can gain experience in teamwork in sports, as well as other projects that require teams of varying size and complexity. Males, on the other hand, should be given additional opportunities to work in small groups, where the formal and informal are easily merged, in order to experience the benefits of close personal/work ties.

Collaborating Team Roles. Women should be assigned (as well as seek) collaborating, not supporting, team roles. Women should avoid functioning as group recorder or arrangements facilitator. As noted earlier, women should concentrate their activity on core group tasks. In teams that require supportive roles, either those roles should be rotated among men and women, or technological alternatives (e.g., tape recorders) should be utilized. If service roles are functionally unavoidable, then workers occupying formal service or support roles (i.e., stenographers, waiters) should be recruited to provide these service functions.

FLEXIBILITY IN ACHIEVING STYLES

Both male and female leaders would benefit from learning flexibility in moving between different achieving styles. Training programs in direct achieving skills, including the use of competition and power, should be available to more women; relational achieving training should be offered to more men. Organizations should be sensitized to the value of the special relational skills women have learned. When organizations officially recognize the importance of these skills to system goals by tying such expertise to reward structures, personal satisfaction, and self-esteem, male acceptance and practice of relational skills will grow.

We are *not* urging women to become pseudo-men and men pseudo-women; rather, we are stressing a need for greater balance and freedom for *both* genders. Gender-role stereotypes of active, demanding males and passive, helpful females contribute to the rigid perpetuation of sex-segregated organizational roles.

While changing these stereotypes in the larger society admittedly is a longer, more complex, and arduous process, altering values and perceptions within organizations is a somewhat more attainable goal. The linkages among competition, aggression, and masculinity must be loosened. Women must be able to work aggressively and compete without feeling or being perceived as "defeminized." And men must feel freer to be noncompetitive and supportive without fearing "demasculinization."

Separating masculinity from competition and aggressiveness on the one hand, and femininity from helpfulness and passivity on the other, is a challenging task for the entire society, but one which organizations can begin to address right now. Thoughtful changes in sex-role socialization are necessary in the larger society, and they imply serious reassessment of our entire value system. Nonetheless, wide-scale value reassessment is a growing phenomenon in the wake of the Vietnam War, the civil rights movement, Watergate, and the environmentalist, consumer, and feminist movements.

The predilection for direct achieving styles may be linked to the recognition that individuals are responsible for themselves. Males are raised with societal expectations that they will support themselves and possibly others. They learn to act as agents on their own behalf. Females are socialized to the expectation that they will not be directly responsible for themselves. They are taught that by helping others achieve, by providing encouragement and emotional support, women can achieve vicariously (Lipman-Blumen, 1973b). Thus, women traditionally have been channeled into "helping" occupations, person-oriented occupations that call for qualitative, rather than quantitative skills.

Closing some of the "escape hatches" for women, including their socially approved avoidance of mathematics and science (Aiken, 1970, 1976; Fennema, 1976; Sells, 1973; Tobias, 1978), will help women develop direct achieving styles. As more women recognize the inevitability of labor force participation, they will value the capacity to use direct achieving styles when appropriate. The linked importance of quantitative skills and direct achieving styles will become more apparent.

At the same time that we close some of the traditional female escape hatches, we should think about opening a few for men. Offering men opportunities for less rigid career paths, for greater freedom to enter and leave the labor force at different career points, as well as for non-traditional roles, will ease some of the current tensions in men's occupational lives. Developing male flexibility to shift from direct to relational achieving styles will be a decided asset in this process.

HOMOSOCIAL NETWORKS AND HETEROSOCIAL RELATIONSHIPS[16]

Earlier in this chapter we stressed the difficulties women face in trying to enter formal male homosocial groups. Individual heterosocial relationships were suggested as links between the gender-segregated informal networks in organizations. However, the feminist movement has begun to question traditional forms of female–male interaction, giving rise to ambiguities on both sides.

As the norms for female–male interaction change, men seem increasingly uncertain about what constitutes "nonsexist" behavior toward women, particularly professional women. And the issue of sexual relationships with colleagues raises additional problems (Bradford, Sargent, & Sprague, 1975). Since women have been the prime movers in changing the boundaries of female/male interaction, it is perhaps easier for them to indicate to men where the new boundary lines are drawn.

As the situation requires, women can offer simple, matter-of-fact guideposts to nonsexist communication (e.g., language and topics), manners (e.g., cigarette lighting, door holding), and economics (e.g., who pays for what) that pave the way for relaxed professional interaction between the genders. Although the creation of interpersonal comfort is not solely a female responsibility, during the current transition period women should feel free to set the tone, as well as the limits, without self-deprecation.

Indicating the new boundaries of acceptable female–male interaction initially may require women to trade off their priorities, holding fast on nonnegotiable and central issues and disregarding more trivial points. Since sexism is an historically engrained perspective, realism suggests that all vestiges of sexism will not be obliterated in a single stroke. In the pursuit of individual and organizational goals, women leaders will have to set priorities, deciding which issues temporarily can wait. Perhaps the best advice here is consistency and steady encroachment on the boundaries of sexism, coupled with a nondefensive posture.

Nonetheless, the barriers to entering the male homosocial network have been remarkably impervious. What, if any, strategies might be useful? Incorporating new members into homogeneous groups usually presents difficulties, particularly when potential members differ in sig-

---

[16]This section has benefited from discussion with Prof. David Bradford.

nificant ways from the group. If would-be members are sufficiently similar to the group on key dimensions, other less important differences may become operationally meaningless. Differences that are irrelevant to the task or social network of the group are the least disruptive.

Increasing similarities between women and men on contributions and orientation to group tasks and goals is possible through several approaches: selection of people who are already similar to the group members, training new members to be more like group members in certain ways, and training group members to be more like the new entrants. Promoting the entry of women who are similar to the male homosocial group in terms of education, political outlook, and professional interests is another possibility. But it is clear that these approaches also have serious limitations: (1) they downplay the important special skills, qualities, and orientations that women can bring to organizations; (2) they limit the potential strength and richness that diversity brings to any group; and (3) they ignore the equitable imperatives of affirmative action.

Until women do enter male homosocial networks in organizations, what alternatives exist to offer them the advantages of informal structures, particularly support and resources? A totally different approach would be a "divide and conquer" strategy, in which what are being divided and conquered are not people but support and resources. More simply, women should be urged to distinguish between support groups and resource-allocating groups and to seek them from different sources.

Earlier we suggested that women could develop their own interorganizational support groups; they also might create cross-level support groups (professional to nonprofessional) among the women of their own organization. Additional alternative routes to resources should be developed. As more top-level women enter organizations, the resources associated with their position, as well as the personal and professional resources they bring with them, will be available for allocation to their own homosocial informal networks.

Negotiating resources at the time of entry into the organization is a strategy men have long employed and which women are learning rapidly. Those resources, judiciously used, can proliferate. Establishing individual links to other resource holders, both male and female, and demonstrating legitimate official need for resources (as well as the ultimate advantages to the organization) should help women leaders open alternative resource veins.

The challenge of change, as this volume testifies, is enormous. The approaches to change delineated in this section represent a limited range of possibilities—small, large, short term, long term, individual, organizational, and societal. Implementation of change is the subject of an impressive literature (Leavitt & Webb, 1978) whose distillation is not possible in a few paragraphs. And clearly the vast societal changes called for are beyond the scope of this chapter. Nonetheless, a few last cautionary words might be useful.

When changes are inevitable, reducing the costs as much as possible for those most affected facilitates acceptance. If initial changes impose limited and reasonably equitable costs for *all* involved, there is greater likelihood of receptivity. If the most affected groups or individuals play a significant role in the planning stage, implementation presumably will be accomplished more smoothly. Organizational opinion leaders' unambivalent endorsements also facilitate change. The tendency to dramatize change often creates unnecessary problems, while open and free discussion of the costs and benefits of proposed innovations helps reduce many difficulties, real and illusory. In these closing lines, we do not presume to capture the wisdom of the vast literature on implementing social change. That is the subject for another essay.

Acknowledgments

This chapter has benefited from the insightful suggestion of Professor Harold J. Leavitt, who reviewed an earlier draft.

REFERENCES

Abegglen, J. G. *The Japanese factory*. Glencoe, Ill.: The Free Press, 1958.
Aiken, L. R. Attitudes toward mathematics. *Review of Educational Research*, 1970, *40*, 551–596.
Aiken, L. R. Update on attitudes and other affective variables in learning mathematics. *Review of Educational Research*, 1976, *46*, 293–311.
Argyris, C. *Understanding organizational behavior*. Homewood, Ill.: Dorsey Press, 1960.
Askinas, B. E. The impact of coeducational living on peer interaction (Doctoral dissertation, Stanford University, 1971). *Dissertation Abstracts International*, 1971, *32*, 1634–A.
Barnard, C. I. *Functions of the executive*. Cambridge, Mass.: Harvard University Press, 1968.
Bartol, K. M., & Wortman, M. S., Jr., Male versus female leaders: Effects on perceived leader behavior and satisfaction in a hospital. *Personnel Psychology*, 1975, *28*, 533–547.
Bass, B. M., Krusell, J., & Alexander, R. A. Male managers' attitudes toward working women. *American Behavioral Scientist*, 1971, *15*, 221–236.
Bayes, M., & Newton, P. M. Women in authority: A sociopsychological analysis. *Journal of Applied Behavioral Science*, 1978, *14*(1), 7–25.
Bernard, J. *The female world*. New York: The Free Press, 1981.
Best, R. *We've all got scars: What boys and girls learn in elementary school*. Bloomington: University of Indiana Press, 1983.
Blake, R. R., & Mouton, J. S. *Grid organization development*. Houston: Gulf Publishing, 1968.
Blaxall, M., & Reagan, B. (Eds.), *Women and the workplace: The implications of occupational segregation*. Chicago: University of Chicago Press, 1976.
Borgatta, E. F., & Stimson, J. Sex differences in interaction characteristics. *Journal of Social Psychology*, 1963, *60*, 89–100.

Bowman, C. W., Worthy, N. B., & Greyser, S. A. Are women executives people? *Harvard Business Review*, July-August 1965, *43*, 14–17.

Bradford, D. L., Sargent, A. C., Sprague, M. S. The executive man and woman: The issue of sexuality. Chapter 3 in F. E. Gordon & M. H. Strober (Eds.), *Bringing women into management*. New York: McGraw-Hill, 1975, pp. 39–58.

Couch, A. S., & Carter, L. A factorial study of the rated behavior of group members. Paper presented at Eastern Psychological Association meeting, Atlantic City, April 1952.

Ellman, E. S. *Managing women in business*. Waterford, Conn.: Prentice-Hall, 1963.

Estler, S., & Davis, C. *Women in decision-making*. Stanford University Center for Research on Women, April 1977.

Fennema, E. *Influences of selected cognitive, affective and educational variables in sex-related differences in mathematics learning and studying*. National Institute of Education, Office of Education Grants, Grant No. P–76–0274, 1976.

Gibb, C. A. Leadership. Chapter 24 in G. Lindzey (Ed.), *Handbook of social psychology*.(Vol. 2). Reading, Mass.: Addison-Wesley, 1954, pp. 877–920.

Hall, K. P. Sex differences in initiation and influence in decision-making among prospective teachers. (Doctoral dissertation, Stanford University, 1972.) *Dissertation Abstracts International*, 1972, *33*(8), 3952–A.

Halpin, A. W., & Winer, B. J. A factorial study in the leader-behavior descriptions. In R. M. Stogdill & A. E. Coons (Eds.), *Leader behavior: Its description and measurement*. Columbus: Ohio State University, Bureau of Business Research, Research Monograph #88, 1957, pp. 39–51.

Handley, A., & Sedlacek, W. Characteristics and work attitudes of women working on campus. *Journal of the National Association of Women Deans, Administrators, and Counselors*, 1977, *40*(4): 128–134.

Heidrick, A., and Struggles, B. *Women in the corporate environment*. Chicago: University of Chicago Press, 1982.

Heiss, J. Degree of intimacy and male–female interaction. *Sociometry*, 1962, *25*, 197–208.

Hennig, M., & Jardim, A. *The managerial woman*. Garden City, N.Y.: Anchor Press, Doubleday, 1977.

Hoffman, L. W. Early childhood experiences and women's achievement motives. *Journal of Social Issues*, 1972, *28*(2), 129–155.

Johnson, R. T., & Ouchi, W. G. Made in America (under Japanese management). *Harvard Business Review*, Sept.-Oct. 1974, pp. 61–69.

Jowett, B. (Trans.). *Aristotle's politics*. New York: Modern Library, 1943.

Kenkel, W. F. Differentiation in family decision making. *Sociology and Social Research*, 1957, *42*, 18–25.

Kerr, C., & Rosow, J. M. (Eds.). *Work in America*. New York: Van Nostrand Reinhold, 1979.

Lana, R. E., Vaughan, W., & McGinnies, E. Leadership and friendship status as factors in discussion group interaction. *Journal of Social Psychology*, 1960, *52*, 127–134.

Leavitt, H. J. Applied organization change in industry: Structural, technical, and human approaches. Chapter 4 in W. W. Cooper, H. J. Leavitt, & M. W. Shelly (Eds.), *New perspectives in organization research*. New York: Wiley 1964, pp. 55–71.

Leavitt, H. J. Beyond the analytic manager. *California Management Review*, 1975, *17*(3), 5–12, and *17*(4), 11–21.

Leavitt, H. J., & Lipman-Blumen, J. A case for the relational manager. *Organizational Dynamics*, Summer 1980, pp. 27–41.

Leavitt, H. J., & Webb, E. Implementing: Two approaches. Research Paper #440. (Research Paper Series) (Stanford, Calif.: Graduate School of Business, Stanford University, May 1978.)

Lipman-Blumen, J. Role de-differentiation as a system response to crisis: Occupational and political roles or women. *Sociological Inquiry*, 1973a, *43*(2), 105–129.

Lipman-Blumen, J. The vicarious achievement ethic and nontraditional occupational roles for women. Paper presented at the Eastern Sociological Association annual meeting, New York, April 1973.

Lipman-Blumen, J. A crisis framework applied to macro-sociological family changes: Marriage, divorce, and occupational trends associated with World War II. *Journal of Marriage and the Family*, November 1975, pp. 889–902.

Lipman-Blumen, J. Toward a homosocial theory of sex roles: An explanation of the sex segregation of social institutions. *Signs*, 1976, *1*(3), part 2, pp. 15–31. (Reprinted in M. Blaxall & B. Reagan (Eds.), *Women and the workplace* [Chicago: University of Chicago Press, 1976].)

Lipman-Blumen, J. A crisis perspective on divorce and role change. Chapter 10 in J. R. Chapman & M. Gates (Eds.), *Women into wives: The legal and economic impact of marriage* (Sage Yearbooks in Women's Policy Studies), Vol. 2 (Beverly Hills, Calif.: Sage Publications, 1977).

Lipman-Blumen, J. A paradigm for the entrance of women into new occupational roles. In B. Cummings & V. Schuck (Eds.), *Women organizing* (Garden City, N.Y.: Adelphi University Press, 1979).

Lipman-Blumen, J. *Sex/gender roles*. In A. Inkeles (Eds.), *Foundations of modern sociology*. Englewood Cliffs: Prentice-Hall, forthcoming.

Lipman-Blumen, J., & Leavitt, H. J. Vicarious and direct achievement patterns in adulthood. *Counseling Psychologist*, 1976, *6*(1), 26–32. (Reprinted in L. S. Hansen & R. S. Rapoza-Blocher [Eds.], *Career development and counseling of women*. Springfield, Ill.: Charles C Thomas, 1977.)

Lipman-Blumen, J., & Leavitt, H. J. Sexual behavior as an expression of achievement orientation. In H. Katchadourian (Ed.), *Human sexual development: Alternative perspectives*. Berkeley: University of California Press, 1978a.

Lipman-Blumen, J., & Leavitt, H. J. Socialization and achievement patterns in cross-cultural perspective: Japanese and American family and work roles. Paper presented at the Ninth World Congress of Sociology, Uppsala, Sweden, August 14–19, 1978b.

Lipman-Blumen, J., Leavitt, H. J., Patterson, K., Beis, R., Handley-Isaksen, A. A model of direct and relational achieving styles. In L. Fyans (Ed.), *Achievement motivation: Recent trends in theory and research*. New York: Plenum, 1980.

Lipman-Blumen, J., Handley-Isaksen, A., & Leavitt, H. J. Achieving styles: A model, an instrument, and some findings. In J. Spence (Ed.), *Achievement and achievement motives: Psychological and sociological approaches*. San Francisco: W. H. Freeman, 1983, pp. 91–126.

Lockheed, M. E. *The modification of female leadership behavior in the presence of males*. Educational Testing Service, Princeton, N. J., N.I.E. Grant No. NE–G–00–3–0130, October 1976.

Lockheed, M. E. Cognitive style effects on sex status in student work groups. *Journal of Educational Psychology*, 1977, *69*(2), 158–165.

Lockheed, M. E., & Hall, K. P. Conceptualizing sex as a status characteristic: Applications to leadership training strategies. *Journal of Social Issues*, 1976, *32*(3) 111–123.

Maccoby, E. M., & Jacklin, C. N. *The psychology of sex differences*. Stanford, Calif.: Stanford University Press, 1974.

Marak, G. E. The evolution of leadership structure. *Sociometry*, 1964, *27*, 174–182.

McClelland, D. C., Atkinson, J. W., Clark, R. A., & Lowell, E. L. *The achievement motive*. New York: Appleton-Century-Crofts, 1953.

Michels, R. Authority. In R. A. Seligman & A. Johnson (Eds.), *The encyclopedia of the social sciences* (Vol. 2). New York: Macmillan, 1937, pp. 319–321.

Morris, C. G., & Hackman, J. R. Behavioral correlates of perceived leadership. *Journal of Personality and Social Psychology*, 1969, *13*, 350–361.

Okamoto, Y. Japanese business behavior and the management based on groupism. (Mimeographed manuscript) (Tokyo: Faculty of Economics, University of Tokyo, no date.)

Parsons, T. *Essays in sociological theory pure and applied.* Glencoe, Ill.: The Free Press, 1949.

Parsons, T. Family structure and the socialization of the child. In T. Parsons & R. F. Bales, *Family, socialization and interaction process.* Glencoe, Ill.: The Free Press, 1955.

Reif, W. E., Newstrom, J. W., & Monczka, R. M. Exploding some myths about women managers. *California Management Review,* 1975, 7(4), 72–79.

Roethlisberger, F. J. *The elusive phenomena: An autobiographical account of my work in the field of organizational behavior at the Harvard Business School* (G. F. F. Lombard, Ed.). Boston: Division of Research, Graduate School of Business Administration, Harvard University, 1977.

Rowe, M. P. Go hire yourself a mentor. In *Proceedings of the conference on women's leadership and authority in the health professions,* University of California at Santa Cruz, June 19–21, 1977 (sponsored by the Program for Women in the Health Sciences, University of California at San Francisco), pp. 40–42.

Safilios-Rothschild, C. Sex role socialization patterns in selected societies. Paper presented at the American Educational Research Association Annual Meeting, Washington, D.C., April 2, 1975.

Safilios-Rothschild, C. *Sex role socialization and sex discrimination: A synthesis and critique of the literature.* Washington, D.C.: National Institute of Education, October, 1979.

Sells, L. High school mathematics as the critical filter in the job market. In *Developing opportunities for minorities in graduate education* (Proceedings of the Conference on Minority Graduate Education at the University of California, Berkeley, May 1973), pp. 47–59.

Shapiro, E., Haseltine, F., & Rowe, M. P. Moving up: Role models, mentors, and the "Patron System." *Sloan Management Review,* 1978, 19, 51–58.

Shavlik, D. & Touchton, J., *Women Chief Executive Officers in Colleges and Universities,* Table 8, Washington, D.C.: Office of Women in Higher Education, ACE, December, 1982.

Shaw, M. E., & Sadler, O. W. Interaction patterns in heterosexual dyads varying in degree of intimacy. *Journal of Social Psychology,* 1965, 66, 345–351.

Strodtbeck, F. L., & Mann, R. D. Sex role differentiation in jury deliberations. *Sociometry,* 1956, 19, 3–11.

Strodtbeck, F. L., James, R. M., & Hawkins, C. Social status in jury deliberations. *American Sociological Review,* 1957, 22, 713–719.

Tannenbaum, A., Kavcic, B., Rosner, M., Vianello, M., & Wieser, G. *Hierarchy in organizations: An international comparison.* San Francisco: Jossey-Bass, 1974.

Tobias, S. *Overcoming math anxiety* (lst ed.). New York: W. W. Norton, 1978.

Tuddenham, R. D., MacBride, P., & Zahn, V. The influence of the sex composition of a group upon yielding to a distorted group norm. *Journal of Psychology,* 1958, 46, 243–251.

U.S. Department of Labor, Bureau of Labor Statistics. *The employment situation: January, 1983.* Washington, D.C.: U.S. Government Printing Office, 1983, USDL News Release No. 83-60.

U.S. Department of Labor, Women's Bureau. *1975 Handbook on women workers.* Washington, D.C.: U.S. Government Printing Office, 1975, Bulletin 297.

Vogel, E. F. *Japan's new middle class: The salary man and his family in a Tokyo suburb.* Berkeley: University of California Press, 1968.

Vroom, V., & Yetton, P. W. *Leadership and decision-making.* Pittsburgh: University of Pittsburgh Press, 1973.

Weber, Max. *The theory of social and economic organization.* (A. M. Henderson & T. Parsons, trans.). Glencoe, Ill.: The Free Press, 1947. (Originally published, 1922).

Whittaker, J. O. Sex differences and susceptibility to interpersonal persuasion. *Journal of Social Psychology,* 1965, *66,* 91–92.

Zander, A., & Van Egmond, E. Relationship of intelligence and social power to the interpersonal behavior of children. *Journal of Educational Psychology,* 1958, *49,* 257–268.

Zdep, S. M. Intragroup reinforcement and its effects on leadership behavior. *Organizational Behavior and Human Performance,* 1969, 4:284–98.

Zdep, S. M., & Oakes, W. F. Reinforcement of leadership behavior in group discussion. *Journal of Experimental Social Psychology,* 1967, 3:310–20.

PART II

Families and Work

The increased need to make decisions about the expenditure of time and energy and to set priorities among claims on one's commitment and affiliation is an important theme of this book. The two spheres in the lives of adults which most reflect the need for such "trade-off" decisions are the family and the workplace.

One of the recent substantial changes in patterns of family life—the increase in the number of working mothers with young children—has aroused concern about the effects of a mother's work on children and family life. The debate about women's working has revived many old prejudices, stimulated some new simplistic assertions, and caused a good deal of confusion that is in part due to the complexity of the issue, the many variables involved, and the shifting focus of much of the argument.

At this time only a tiny proportion of American families fit the traditional model of two parents, with the husband working and the wife caring for children at home. Approximately half of all women 16 years old or older are in the work force or are actively seeking employment. Some 41% of these women have children under 18 years of age, and 31% of children under 6 have working mothers. The number of women in the work force has increased by 60% since 1972.

The "traditional" pattern itself, with a full-time mother at home, was actually traditional for only one or two generations. It is a product of modern historical development, including industrialization and relative affluence. In the past, women who were in the lower economic classes had always filled many roles and shared the burden of work outside the home in order to sustain their families.

Responses to the changing role of women have varied. There are those who herald a new era of freedom while others cite mothers who are out of the home as the cause of divorce, teenage pregnancy, delinquency, violence, and other problems of society. This second view reflects both anxiety about change and inability to assess its impact realistically, while the first view itself does not adequately take into account many of the complex trade-offs involved.

The cry is often heard that the rising divorce rate and the declining birthrate, coupled with the increased acceptance of unmarried couples' living together and married couples' infidelity, signify the decline and fall of the American family. Yet we also find that, while norms for marriage and parenthood have indeed changed dramatically, the way in which people actually view their marriages and children—the importance they attach to family ties, the gratifications they derive from marriage and parenthood, and the centrality of family roles in self-definitions and support networks—have not changed nearly as much nor as dramatically as so many would believe.

The chapters by Jessie Bernard, Joseph Veroff, Mary Jo Bane, and Elizabeth Douvan serve to counter some of the prevailing fears that marriage and the family are on the brink of collapse.

Jessie Bernard details the undeniable change in the "ground rules" for the life, careers, and marital roles of men and women in the last century. She describes the time when woman's place was in the home, marriage was forever, and childrearing was the major function of women's lives in marriage. While the new roles occupied by women have clearly let them join men outside the home, Bernard shows that equality of status within the household is not yet achieved. She points to the shift in values evident between, on the one hand, young unmarried couples for whom exclusivity in the relationship takes precedence over permanence as a desired goal, and on the other, older married couples for whom tolerance of infidelity is seemingly the price to be paid for the longevity of the relationship.

Joseph Veroff's chapter, "Psychological Orientations to the Work Role," complements the works on patterns of family life and roles with his data on changing attitudes toward the work role in the two decades 1957–1976. While more men and women choose and find employment, the personal impact of work has, ironically, diminished in importance. As the women's movement has reshaped the meaning of work for both sexes, a task-oriented sense of accomplishment has been replaced by an individual sense of achievement. With increasingly unreachable goals in work, leisure has come to replace work as a sphere for accomplishment. Veroff finds, not surprisingly, that with more individuated searches for achievement and power, men and women are finding both increased satisfactions and increased dissatisfactions in their work roles.

Mary Jo Bane, in her chapter, further documents the extent to which marriage and family continue to be critical to personal satisfaction; ironically, she does so through the study of rising divorce rates. She concludes that the increased incidence of divorce may signify decreases both in long-term separations and in marital unhappiness. While individual marriages are less likely to last forever, innumerable research reports indicate that remarriage is eagerly sought.

Elizabeth Douvan, writing on family roles, demonstrates that, despite an increased recognition of problems and conflict in marriage, there is evidence of an overall increase in marital satisfaction over the last two decades. She also finds that for both men and women the quality of their performance in the roles of spouse and parent remains more important to them than does their performance at work.

Chapter 5

Ground Rules for Marriage
Perspectives on the Pattern of an Era

JESSIE BERNARD

PREAMBLE: IS THE GLASS HALF EMPTY OR IS IT HALF FULL?

"What, if anything, has changed in the last century?" The implication of this question is sometimes "Has anything really changed?" Do we merely have a situation in which, despite efforts to improve marriage and family, "plus ça change, le plus c'est la même chose"? It is a question that receives quite opposite answers from different observers. Using exactly the same data, some conclude that marriage, and hence family, have changed for the worse and are now suffering severe and perhaps even irremediable disintegration. Others label such a point of view as mere myth. The general academic "line" seems to be that, yes, there have been some changes and as a result some things are clearly wrong about the current situation of marriage and family, but in the overall perspective it remains essentially strong; the evidence actually shows marriage and the family better in some ways than in the past. Most of the research on which these conflicting conclusions are based is statistical. In and of themselves, statistics can tell us only about trends or prevalence or incidence. What looks like a lasting change to one observer may seem a mere short-term change to another. What seems like a widespread, even revolutionary, change to one observer may be minimized by another because its incidence is relatively low. In the present discussion the research data themselves are secondary to what are called "ground rules." It is clear that these ground rules have indeed changed

JESSIE BERNARD, PH.D. • The Pennsylvania State University, University Park, Pennsylvania 16802.

in the last century. Whether these changes show the glass half empty or half full is difficult to discern. Whether it is under our power to fill—or empty—it is not all clear to me. The glass may be fuller now for one member of the marriage or family but emptier for another; fuller for women in some classes, emptier for those in other classes.

THE VICTORIAN ERA AS A BENCHMARK

Stanley Coben (1975) dates the Victorian age as encompassing the years from about the 1820s to about 1890. Scholars, he tells us, believe that

> the essentially middle class Victorian culture [of those years] in both Great Britain and the United States . . . unified all but the very top and bottom of society.

During this period in both countries

> a shifting consensus prevailed among the middle class on almost every matter of importance to that group. The years 1830–1890, with a height of influence in the United States around 1870 [thus] serve as plausible points in time for explanation of this [Victorian] culture.

Victorian culture was an essentially middle-class creation made possible by the wealth industrialization was producing. It was the culture, Coben reminds us, reflected in the work of Max Weber and Sigmund Freud, a culture, as Tawney, Sombart, and Marx have shown, that developed personality and character traits "well suited to promote rapid industrial and commercial expansion." Although a large part of the thinking and research on these years has dealt with industrialization, with the marketplace, with what happened to work, to careers, to bureaucracy, to technology, the real focus of Victorians, as Coben reminds us, "lay within the family." The Victorian family was the basic, essential counterpart to industrialization.

The Victorian model for marriage and family was quite different from the model that preceded it and from the one now in the process of emerging. Nancy Cott (1977) has illuminated the conditions that ushered in the Victorian era and came increasingly to characterize it:

> the period between 1780 and 1830 was a time of wide and deep-ranging transformation, including the beginning of rapid intensive economic growth, especially in foreign commerce, agricultural productivity, and the fiscal and banking system; the start of sustained urbanization; demographic transition toward modern fertility patterns; marked change toward social stratification by wealth and growing inequality in the distribution of wealth; rapid pragmatic adaptation in the law; shifts from unitary to pluralistic networks in personal association; unprecedented expansion in primary education; democratization in the political process; invention of a new language of political

and social thought; and—not least—with respect to family life, the appearance of "domesticity." (p. 3)

The operative word is "domesticity." For in the Victorian model the
husband went forth each day to grapple with the cruel, cold—social
Darwinian—world and the wife remained the "heart" of the home,
generating sweetness and light to bind the wounds inflicted on the
husband and to serve in general as a hovering angel. Roles were defined
in conformity with that model. "To an extent never true before or
since," Coben (1975) tells us, "Children learned," at least in theory,
"the lessons necessary for success in their society. Within the home,
ideally, an aggressive 'masculine' father stood between his family and a
harsh economic world, a passive, nourishing 'feminine' mother kept
alive in the higher values of Christian morality."

It was taken for granted that the family, like the school and church,
was preparing boys for participation in the industrial enterprise and
girls for marriage and motherhood, teaching them respect for authority,
the virtue inherent in hard work, and other tenets of *Poor Richard's
Almanac*. Not until the 1960s were young men and women to challenge
this model. Only then did young men protest being trained—as it
looked to them—to help corporations make more money and young
women the socialization that presupposed no future beyond marriage
and motherhood for them.

The life span of Victorian culture in its pristine form was little more
than a century. After the 1870s it began slowly to recede. Coben (1975)
finds it still surviving today, more or less intact, in some segments of the
population, especially among the older and among the nonurban, but
he also notes especially two periods in which, though it survived, it was
nevertheless seriously challenged, namely in the post–World War I
1920s and again in the 1960s. In the 1920s, he says, "Victorianism suffered irremediable damage . . . before discouragement . . . forced discontent back into quieter channels." Since the 1960s the challenge has
been even more insistent.

Coben attributes great importance to social scientists in undermining crucial Victorian tenets after World War I, including especially Ruth
Benedict and Margaret Mead, the Lynds, literary intellectuals like Sin-
clair Lewis, and Theodore Dreiser, F. Scott Fitzgerald, and, later, the
several ethnic and racial groups. These assaults were directed at several
facets of Victorian culture but "probably the most devastating . . . have
been delivered at that culture's most vital point: 'the home.'" For some,
these assaults called forth loud hurrahs. But, Coben continues,

Those who valued that basic unit of Victorian society watched with despair
as Americans tore it apart. Parents who placed personal fulfillment above

devotion to spouse and children; the consequent skyrocketing divorce rate; the rapid rise of women's proportion in the work force; children who felt closer to their peers than to their parents—all delivered shattering blows to the primary Victorian haven against the world's vicissitudes. The process was hastened by feminists . . . and by intellectuals with critiques like the Lynds' and Mead's.

This same kind of despair is echoed today.

Without minimizing the importance of the work of the social scientists and literary intellectuals in the decline of Victorian culture, recognition must be paid to other underlying forces at work. For although Coben tells us that future historians may view Victorian culture "as the first fairly successful attempt to create a cohesive industrial civilization," there was an intrinsic contradiction within its ethos between, for example, the strong work ethic which had undergirded it and belief in deferred gratification on one side and the slowly recognized need for wide consumption of the goods being produced, on the other. As Coben himself notes, the very process

of economic modernization or post-modernization . . . contributed to undermining of Victorianism . . . by creating social conditions which outmoded the very culture and personality types that had most encouraged rapid modernization.

The personality and character suitable for an economy of scarcity were not suitable for an economy that was coming—one based on affluence. Thus "confidence in Victorianism eroded." It was, of course, the social critics who first made clear to us the contradictions implicit in the Victorian ethos and the actual state of affairs. Their

insidious criticism of the Victorian ethos diminished the conviction with which its formidable superstructure of institutions and behavior patterns were regarded and kept and left them more vulnerable to onslaughts by minority groups . . . most obviously among college students and middle class feminists.

This, in abbreviated form, is one historian's perspective on the rise and decline of the patterns of one era—the Victorian—as they waxed, crested, and waned. Now we stand at the point where many of the components of that era's culture have all but disintegrated if not wholly dissolved. Or at least seem to some observers to have suffered severe attrition, leaving us rudderless. Or in any event, less in certitude.

Against this overview as backdrop, the present discussion dealing with several trends in Victorian marriage takes place. The general procedure to be followed is straightforward. Several ground rules of Victorian marriage are examined from the heyday of the Victorian era about a century ago up to the present in an attempt to determine "what, if anything, has changed and to assess these changing social indicators from a prospective as well as retrospective point of view," as the charge to the authors of this volume was framed.

The ground rules examined here may be encapsulated as follows:

1. Woman's place is in the home.
2. The husband is head of the household.
3. The marital bond is permanent.
4. Lifelong fidelity, or sexual exclusivity, is enjoined.
5. Parenthood is a major component of marriage.

There was an almost inexhaustible literature of sermons, polemics, etiquette books, didactic treatises, and tracts extending, elaborating, and interpreting these ground rules as well as a considerable corpus of novels showing them in operation, and interminable exegesis on all of this work. Together the rules constituted a coherent, consistent entity. For a while they seemed to work.

GROUND RULE NUMBER ONE: WOMAN'S PLACE IS IN THE HOME

The term "woman's place" is almost a code word encompassing a whole sex-role ideology, the very essence of marriage in Victorian culture. In fact it might be said to include all the other ground rules as corollaries. It prescribed both the correct or proper division of labor between the sexes and the correct or proper specialization of functions between them. It implied separate, even segregated, worlds for the two sexes. There is a growing literature on the resulting "women's sphere" and "the cult of domesticity" and "the cult of true womanhood" which describes and analyzes women's place in Victorian culture (Cott, 1977; Kraditor, 1968; Sklar, 1973) and some of its concomitants and consequences, among them the economic dependency on husbands it involved. For the corollary or counterpart to woman's place in the home was the husbands' place in the work force. He was obligated to support her.

Although ground rule number one said woman's place was in the home, it did not say that it was exclusively in the home, that she was to be restricted within a kind of purdah. In practice it meant in effect primarily that she was to keep out of the labor force. She was not to "work." There were in fact quite a lot of acceptable places for a married woman provided she did not aspire to independence. So long as married women did not challenge husbands or deprive them of their services, they were permitted a tether not quite so short as the code word implied. For purely alliterative purposes, married women's permitted places can be encapsulated as the five Cs: church, community, charity, consumption, and culture. A sixth C—career—is not included because if women chose a career the ground rule precluded marriage altogether. The first two Cs—church and community—do not call for much discussion. Even the reactionary Germans included *Kirche* as well as *Kinder* and *Küchen* and Victorians recognized the local neighborhood also as suitable places for married women. More interesting among women's places—and ultimately more dysfunctional for them—was the consumer market. For toward the end of the 19th century a new phenomenon was beginning to attract the attention of social observers, namely, the emergence of a class of women who had "no duties to discharge in providing for themselves or their children" (Thwing & Thwing, 1887, p. 120). Woman's place in the home was, as Charlotte Perkins Gilman (1898/1966) put it, becoming increasingly to "wait upon" the bric-a-brac with which she had surrounded herself (p. 257), for as technology relieved married women from much of the hard manual physical work of the household, many chose to elaborate their living standards rather than save their energies (Folsom, 1934). As Veblen (1899/1953) noted, "conspicuous" consumption was one of the functions of middle- and upper-class married women. Arthur Schlesinger has (1946) traced the trend toward this consumer role back to the burst of affluence that followed the Civil War when the families of the newly created class of millionaires began to import European standards of elegance. Gradually the patterns filtered down to the middle and even the working classes (Schlesinger, 1946, p. 30). Finally the role of wife even among the least affluent came to include a large component of conspicuous consumption (Myrdal & Klein, 1956). There was considerable lip-clicking among those who believed that "when those who can ill afford [even] alpaca persist in arraying themselves in silk . . . the matter is a sad one" (Schlesinger, 1946, p. 40).

Sad in more ways than one. For though economists might view such emphasis on consumption as performing an important societal function (Galbraith, 1973), it had deteriorating effects on married women themselves. They were ensconced in "gilded cages" which greatly increased their dependency. Charlotte Perkins Gilman (1898/1966) was not the only one to point this out. The Thwings, for example, in 1887 did so also.

> By one of those strange paradoxes so common in society, the idea of the subordination of women, which once made her the drudge and slave of man, now makes her the petted object of his labor and care. She is his, but not to work for him, but to be worked for. Even language shows the disposition to convert the woman and wife into the lady. We no longer have the housewife. She has been lost in the lady of the house. . . . Under conditions of equality

the woman whose husband labors will not expect to be supported without labor. The large (and increasingly large) class of wives, childless, and with no home but a boardinghouse, who contribute nothing of material, intellectual, or moral wealth either in society or the family will be forced by public opinion to justify their existence. (pp. 120–121)

In 1887 this was a radical challenge to ground rule number one. Married women were being challenged to contribute something material, intellectual, or moral to society or to their families.

If conspicuous consumption could have deleterious effects on married women, vicarious leisures—Veblen's other conceptualized function—could have positive ones. Since husbands were themselves too busy making money—as even Tocqueville (1840) had noted—to engage in leisure-class activities, wives did it for them (Cohn, 1943). European observers came to view affluent women in the United States as the only remaining leisure class (Cohn, 1943). Among working-class women, just remaining at home was enough; such leisure at least validated her husband's ability to provide for his family (Myrdal & Klein, 1956, pp. 5–6). But vicarious leisure could also be performed outside the home, and it did in fact become a way of extending married women's place beyond the walls of the household.

Although the women's culture-club movement in the late 19th century became almost a craze (Harland & Van de Water, 1905), it did create for married women an autonomous place outside the home. In some cases there was even a physical clubhouse which served as a haven for members, where women could supply support for one another in a way acceptable to their society but without violating ground rule number one. And more important, unlike the first three Cs this one had implications for autonomy. For practice in organizing made it possible for some of them—and increasingly—to move beyond the cultural toward even broader goals, to expand women's place further. Such practice could have an impact on the larger world, ultimately even on the political world.

The fifth C—charity—was also an outgrowth of the vicarious leisure made possible for married women by affluence. They had time to serve on boards of community charitable agencies (Berg, 1978) as well as of such cultural institutions as orchestras, art galleries, museums, and the like. Less affluent women could perform vicarious leisure functions as volunteers in community service agencies. Still others could show the world that their husbands could support them by giving time to humbler charitable activities through church organizations. It was to take a long time until women learned that these activities had marketable value.

Ground rule number one had two quite contradictory aspects. On one side it came to make for serious mental health difficulties in women in the home, but on the other it also permitted women to be more humane in their opinions and attitudes outside the home. There is research support for both of these aspects. In the late 19th century there was already beginning to be discussion of the deteriorating effect which affluence was having on women. In the 1920s the "nervous housewife" was already a topic of concern (Meyerson, 1929). As late as 1963 Betty Friedan had spoken of the malaise she found in suburban housewives, a problem that had no name. In the 1970s researchers were beginning to pinpoint the factors involved in the housewife's poor mental health (Bernard, 1972). Building on Seligman's (1974) theory of learned helplessness and the work of Lenore Radloff (1975), Marcia Guttentag concluded that the greater vulnerability to depression among women as compared to men had a dependency-related basis (Guttentag, 1976, p. 43). A considerable component in the helplessness and powerlessness of housewives was related to their economic dependence. On the other hand the fact that women in the Victorian model were supported by their husbands put them in effect "above the battle." The voting records of women in political positions and public opinion polls do show that women have tended to be on the more humane side of most social issues (Constantini & Craik, 1972; Fritchey, 1977; Harris Poll, 1972; McCormack, 1975).

It was not until the second quarter of the 20th century that ground rule number one, the very keystone of the Victorian model, buckled. During the Depression of the 1930s married women could often get jobs more easily than their husbands; during World War II they were actively recruited into the labor force; during inflationary times their incomes were needed by the family. The ramifications for marriage are widespread. Although the labor force is now recognized as a legitimate place for a married woman, her place still remains in the home as well, in the sense that she is still responsible for its operation. And the hundreds of thousands of women who wish to remain in the home, sheltered, protected, and taken care of, protest against the low status of the housewife; some feel threatened and deprived of their security.

In urban studies it has been found that when a certain proportion of the houses of a given area are taken over by an incoming group, it tends to "tip" in their direction. Analogously, when half of a population accepts a given norm, we might also speak of "tipping." Such a tipping was reached with respect to the first ground rule by the 1980s when more than half of all women living with their husbands were in the labor force. Now it was the nonemployed wives who became the nonconformists. The impact of wives' employment on husbands, wives, and children was great enough to warrant calling the resulting change a qualitative as well as a quantitative one. It had widely ramifying consequences. When the husband had been the sole breadwinner it had seemed logical that he should make the family decisions. Since he paid the piper he should call the tune. But when wives were also helping to pay the piper it seemed only logical that they have some say in calling the tune.

GROUND RULE NUMBER TWO: HEADSHIP OF THE HUSBAND

The "cult of domesticity" referred to above was to have other fateful implications for women than those sketched above. It implied female dependency, a theme that irradiated all the ground rules of marriage. The economic interdependence which had characterized husband–wife relationships in colonial and pre-Victorian times—and which was to continue to prevail in rural life long thereafter—began to suffer attrition in Victorian culture as affluence relieved women of more and more productive activities in and around the household. As a market economy increasingly replaced a subsistence economy and as monetary transactions came to loom larger and larger, the market expanded, and the relationship between spouses became less one of economic interdependency and more one of economic dependency on the part of the wife. Though she was still contributing services, they were not, like garden produce, eggs, or textiles, saleable in the local or expanding market. Victorian marriage cannot be understood without recognition of the ramifying effects of the economic dependency of married women.

In a book on *Courtship and Marriage* in 1746, far in advance of its time, Benjamin Franklin challenged the accepted view on the inequality of the sexes. He blamed men for the inadequacies attributed to women, and Schlesinger tells us, he counseled that "the husband should rule the roost only if he were the more sensible of the two" (Schlesinger, 1946, pp. 8–9). Avant garde as the book was, it went through three more editions in 13 years, and in Edinburgh yet another. The more usual position in colonial times was, however, acceptance of the ground rule that gentlewomen were to render unquestioning obedience to their husbands (Schlesinger, 1946, p. 7). They were also to evince that "consciousness of *inferiority*, which, for the sake of *order*, the all-wise author of nature manifestly intended" (Schlesinger, 1946, p. 7; emphasis in the original). The ground rule was unequivocal: the husband was indisputably the head of the household. The wife owed him obedience, submission, subordination. And according to Tocqueville (1840) in the first half of the century, she submitted not only willingly but even pridefully.

Catherine Beecher (1841) borrowed her apologia for the subservient status of women from Tocqueville; status differences were intrinsic in the social order and it was better to base them on sex than on class.

Scanzoni (1979) has shown the transformations of this ground rule from the early owner–property form to the head–complement form and then to the senior partner–junior partner form, each in turn mollifying the impact on women. In Victorian marriage it was perhaps in the head–complement form but, at least theoretically, not too far beyond owner–property ideas. Thwing and Thwing (1887), citing James Schouler (1921), encapsulate the law of domestic relations current in the late 19th century:

> The husband as the head of the household has the right to dictate the policy of the family. The wife is expected to conform to his habits, tastes, even to his eccentricities, provided her health be not seriously endangered by so doing. The husband may even restrict his wife's calling list, or forbid her from visiting her relations. The courts also sustain him in preventing her from attending the church of which she is a member. (pp. 122–123)

A vast structure of religion and law, church and state, shored up this ground rule. The apostle Paul had admonished women to subordinate themselves to their husbands; the common law viewed the wife as swallowed up in her husband. Until relatively recently the bride still promised in the marital vow to obey her husband.

What husbands and wives really did in marriage was of course often quite different. In fact the Thwings found this ground rule already anachronistic almost a century ago. It was not even then enforceable by public opinion.

> The man who should attempt to put in practice the theory of compelling or even demanding, obedience, would find little sympathy; while the wife who refused obedience would probably be fully sustained by society, if not by the courts. While preserving the form of the time-honored belief in wifely subjection, the substance has passed away. (p. 112)

Women, to be sure, still promised to obey, but they shrugged "their shoulders with a careless laugh at the possibility of ever being asked to fulfill their promise" (p. 119). This ground rule was honored as much in the breach as in the practice.

The Thwings favored legal and institutional change in this ground rule to conform to the times. They saw women's flouting of it as both cause and consequence of the "present chaotic state of the family" (p. 112). They argued for change in the direction of equality, not in the direction of taking away the privileges of women but by adding to their responsibilities. As things were the power of women was "conceded as a compliment, as an act of chivalry, and not as a right" (p. 120). They had more rights granted as favors than society held them responsible for. But if women were granted power not as a personal concession but as a right, they could be held accountable and duties commensurate with their authority could be demanded of them (p. 120). The Thwings argued, therefore, that the structure of marriage be rebuilt "upon the complete equality of the husband and wife in the domestic relations" (p. 112). They justified their position on the basis of scriptures, justice, and expediency.

Having then argued the case for marital equality, the authors proceeded to lay down the ground rules for implementing it. For questions related to common matters they arrived essentially at Franklin's conclusion: "experience must decide to whom the decision may be more safely committed" (Thwing & Thwing, 1887, p. 122). But enlightened though they might be, the Thwings were still captive of the current conceptualization of marital roles. So "in affairs regarding the relation of the family to the outside world" they arrived at the same conclusion as did Talcott Parsons and Robert Bales (1955) many decades later. The Thwings concluded that "the peculiar training of the man fits him to be the safer guide" (p. 122). But within the household such concerns "as the selection and furnishing of the house, the oversight of servants, the training of the children, the house-mother is the natural leader" (p. 122). In personal matters each should have complete freedom. Neither should dictate what friends the other may visit, what habits he or she may indulge, what private expenses each may incur. Each should control his or her own property. The wife should have complete control of her own body. Thus the theory of equality proved in effect to result in a practical validation of the status quo.

Family power relationships 100 years later are still equivocal. The actual situation that prevails today is not easy to determine. Sociologists had engaged in an orgy of research on the subject of power in the family and produced a ballooning literature dealing with it before Safilios-Rothschild (1970) punctured it and left it in considerable disarray. The ground rule still specifies at least lip service to the theory of equality but it recognizes that bona fide power may be achieved in practice by a bargaining process in which men have greater resources (Scanzoni, 1979).

Much of the research on power in marriage and family has been done in connection with the quality of the relationships and here the story is equivocal, even regressive, in the last generation. An examination, that is, of the research on the relation, if any, between marital structure and criteria of well-being, however defined, shows a remarkable difference between the older and the more recent work. Thus a study of rural families published in 1930 concluded that families which in all aspects of family life exercised joint control showed up better than those in which the husband tended to dominate in most aspects of family life. Two other studies, one by Paul Popenoe (1933) and one by E. W. Burgess and Leonard Cottrell (1939), however, found that marriages in which the husband held a slight edge over the wives were more likely to be successful than others. But Terman (1938), on the other hand, found just the reverse. He found that

> contrary to popular opinion, the wife's dominance score correlates positively instead of negatively with her husband's happiness whereas . . . dominance in the husband correlates slightly positively with his own happiness, but not with his wife's. (p. 22–23)

He found no relation between difference in dominance in husband and wife and the success of the marriage.

In this earlier work when there was a balance on the side of superior power in husbands, it was only slight; in the rural families, joint control was most favorable; and in Terman's sample, dominance by the wives. In the studies of the 1960s, however, there was hardly anything worse than a family in which there was a strong mother and a weak father. Almost every psychological pathology was traceable to such a family pattern. Lip service might be paid to the variability of possible combinations in marriage but there was often an implicit—and sometimes explicit—lesson that the best pattern was one in which there was a superordinate husband and a subordinate wife (Westley & Epstein, 1969).

With the increase in two-earner families, the support of male family headship that rested to a large extent on the husband's economic contribution eroded. The official demise of this ground rule was finally recognized April 1, 1980, when the U.S. Census Bureau substituted the term "householder" for "head of household" which it had until then automatically assigned to the husband. From now on the household itself will determine who is the householder. No doubt the designated householder in many households will continue to be a male for some time to come. Still, we seem to be moving in the direction Benjamin Franklin advocated: let the one best equipped make the decisions. When young people formulate the marriage commitment in contract form they usually specify egalitarian relationships (Weitzman, 1981) and polls report an increase in such a preference in the general public (Roper, 1980).

GROUND RULE NUMBER THREE: PERMANENCE

Marriage in the Victorian model was for keeps. The marital vows specified "till death do us part." People assumed the roles of husband and wife with both a religious and a legal commitment to permanence.

Thwing and Thwing (1887) state the ideal situation with respect to divorce as specified in the Victorian ambience as follows:

> The nature of the marriage state does not admit of its being the subject of experimental and temporary arrangements and fleeting partnerships. The union is, and should be, for life. It is so equally in reason, in the common sentiments of mankind, and in the teachings of religion. No married partner should desert the other, commit adultery, beat or otherwise abuse the other, or forbear to do all that is possible for the sustenance and happiness of the other and of the entire family. Figuratively speaking, the two should walk hand in hand up the steps of life and down its declivities and green slopes, then lay themselves together for the final sleep at the foot of the hill. Consequently, there should be no divorce, no divorce courts, no books on the law of divorce (p. 153)

Still, though the ground rule forbade divorce, provisions for it were made and already, then as now, there were cries of alarm about the rising divorce rate which was awakening "great apprehension for the perpetuity of important social institutions" (Thwing & Thwing, 1887, p. 153). In New Hampshire in 1860, for example, there were 107 divorces; in 1882, 314, thus almost tripling in 22 years. In Vermont there was 1 divorce to every 23 marriage licenses granted; by 1878, 1 in every 14. In Maine in 1880, 1 to almost 10. In Connecticut the annual average rate for the 15 years after 1863 was 1 divorce to just over 10 marriages. In Massachusetts the number more than doubled between 1860 and 1878. Nor was the situation any better outside of New England. Indiana had 1 divorce for every 12 marriages in 1884; Michigan, 1 to every 13. In Cook County, Illinois, the annual rate for six years was 1 divorce to 9 marriages. In San Francisco, a divorce was reported for every 8 marriages; in 29 other counties of California a divorce was granted for every 7 licenses in 1882. Then there was Marin County:

> One county in California deserves perhaps to be called the banner divorce section of the United States. It bears the name of Marin, and has as its capital San Rafael, a snug and acceptable retreat, under the shadow of great cities, easy to flee to for the concealment or dispatch of the unseemly business. This county "reports 57 licenses, and 27 divorces"; or one divorce for every two and eleven-hundredths marriages. (Thwing & Thwing, 1887, p. 155)

Whatever the actual divorce rate may be at any particular time, it always seems to be soaring. Actually in the 40 years between 1920 and 1960, with the exception of the 1946 dissolution of wartime marriages, the increase had been fairly moderate, even reaching a relatively low point in 1958.

The discussion of the causes of this shocking rise in divorce almost 100 years ago seems to validate the old cliché, "plus ça change, plus c'est la même chose."

> The last fifty years have apparently changed the marriage relations from a
> permanent and lifelong state to a union existing during the pleasure of the
> parties. The change thus swiftly wrought is so revolutionary, involving the
> very foundations of human society, that we must believe it to be the result
> not of any temporary conditions, but of causes which have been long and
> silently at work. (Thwing & Thwing, 1887, p. 158)

Equally familiar is the Thwings' analysis of the causes: the growth of
individualism; the reduction of marriage by secularization from status to
a mere contract terminable at either party's pleasure or convenience; the
attrition of the sacred or religious nature of marriage; the loosening of
divorce laws; social mobility; affluence (Thwing & Thwing, 1887, pp.
159–162). And of course, the changing status of women.

The rise in the number of divorces vis-à-vis the number of marriage
licenses granted called for serious consideration. It challenged the very
keystone of Victorian marriage, ground rule number one, which defined
woman's place. It forced a reconsideration of the nature of the "ties that
bind." The question for some became not why people leave a marriage
but why they remain in it. What *are* the ties that bind: law, religion,
conscience, love, duty, social sanctions, habit? Or in the case of women,
need for economic support? For the current scene there is strong research evidence favoring the last answer. Cherlin (1979), for example,
finds that "wives whose potential wage compared favorably with the
wage of their husbands had a greater probability of dissolution" (p. 164).
The increased labor force participation of women may indeed thus be a
significant factor in rising divorce rates. Essentially the same conclusion
was being reached almost a century ago:

> Her [a woman's] sphere of activities has broadened in every direction. In
> nearly every business, trade, and profession, women now appear as the
> competitors of men. Fifty years ago, the household and the school house
> marked the boundaries of the sphere of women's work. The industries in
> which she now engages are numbered by the hundreds. Such a radical
> change, made in so short a time, cannot fail to exercise disturbing effects on
> the family." (Thwing & Thwing, 1887, pp. 162–163)

The potential independence then becoming available to women was
making them less willing to remain in an unsatisfactory marriage; for if a
woman

> fails to find happiness, justice, and recognition of her personality in her
> position as wife and mother, a woman is now independent of this position,
> so far as the supply of her needs is concerned. Means of a decent livelihood
> for a competent woman opens on every side. (Thwing & Thwing, 1887, p.
> 163)

So what reason was there for a woman to remain in an unsatisfactory
marriage?

Education had also played into the hands of women, making them less dependent on men.

> The educational advantages for women have kept pace with their enlarged opportunities. The education of the average American woman, so far as it pertains to a knowledge of books, is undoubtedly superior to that of the average man. Especially is this true in the middle class, a class among which the rate of divorce is by far the highest. Among this class in the older groups the intellectual superiority of the wife to the husband is plain to even a casual observer. (Thwing & Thwing, 1887, p. 163)

The women's colleges no doubt contributed to the "intellectual superiority" of wives.

The expanded rights accorded to women were also a contributing factor in the high divorce rates. They had been enlarged without any corresponding recognition of accompanying duties.

> As an individual the rights of women are now fully recognized before the law. While her political disabilities have not been removed, save in two Territories, her rights to acquire and hold property, to carry on business, or to be a party to a suit are fully granted. (Thwing & Thwing, 1887, p. 162)

But the women have not risen to these challenges:

> We thus find a class of irresponsible women, who, while jealous of all rights, neither hold themselves, nor are held by society, to a strict performance of duties commensurate with their rights. (Thwing & Thwing, 1887, p. 165)

The authors thus conclude that

> the enlargement of woman's rights has increased the number of divorces; and it may have already also proved a cause of dissoluteness, and have tended to disintegrate the conserving forces of the republic. (Thwing & Thwing, 1887, p. 168)

The remedy? Clearly women could not be denied access to jobs, nor could their education be abridged, nor could their rights be withdrawn, nor their independence revoked. What was needed was greater emphasis by women on the duties and responsibilities imposed by their independence (Thwing & Thwing, 1887, p. 169).

Some 40 years later, during the recession of the Victorian ethos in the 1920s referred to by Coben (1975), a feminist interpretation of the same kinds of facts was viewing divorce not as the destruction of marriage and family but as a redress for women. Divorce was a measure not of societal breakdown but of the status of women, the higher the rate the higher their status:

> In all of these circumstances in which we are confronted with divorce as essentially a mode of redress for women, we are dealing with one partner who for the first time in history is not bound hand and foot in her situation. This is one of the interesting fruits of the fact that her serious economic value

as a worker finds expression outside of rather than within the home. Work is
no longer deeply identified with the tie of sex in woman's case, but is largely
independent of it. This opens a door which does not necessarily imperil the
bond of love and the integrity of the marriage contract but it does put it to the
test, in that it must hold henceforth largely on its genuine merit. If it is
spurious and not real it is no longer supported and indefinitely continued by
the old economic organization. (Messer, 1928, p. 332)

Instead of seeing divorce as a negative phenomenon, this woman saw it
as a positive force. "The new order, as economically organized enables
woman's 'taste in sex to remain noble' (to borrow the fine German
phrase)" (Messer, 1928, p. 332). It makes for purifying and perfecting
domestic life as well as for disrupting it. A similar point with respect to
the selective effect of divorce was made in my paper on success in
marriage (Bernard, 1934), and by Veroff, Douvan, and Kulka in 1981:
"In a number of ways . . . the modern institution of divorce may be a
force not weakening but strengthening marriage in American Society"
(p. 163). It thus also raises the status of women. The fact, then, was that
a woman's "serious economic value as a worker" released her from the
psychology of serfdom, from the status of a pet bred for incompetence.
Liberated now from

all these states in which the old home actually found much of its security and
basis, she sets up a requirement befitting a human being. And in the process
she is likely to avail herself of all the help the law affords. (Messer, 1928, p.
333)

Including, of course, the law of divorce.

It is interesting to note how frequently divorce is discussed in connection with the position of women. Although it is true that most divorce suits are brought by women, some of them, W. J. Goode (1956)
has told us, are the result of what he calls the "strategy of divorce" by
which husbands manipulate wives to bring action. Actually a considerable corpus of research shows that marital dissolutions are economically
bad for a large number of women, for the erosion of the general rule of
permanence in marriage ramifies widely, especially among those left
stranded by divorce, desertion, or abandonment after years of marriage
and also among their children. Lois B. Shaw (1978) found, for example,
that a fourth of white families and half of black families became poor
after marital disruption.

Although the economic costs of divorce are greater for women than
for men, the reverse may be true for emotional and psychological costs.
Commitments to psychiatric hospitals tend to be substantially higher for
divorced/separated men than for divorced/separated women (Bloom,
White, & Asher, 1979, p. 186). But household surveys of noninstitu-
tionalized populations show psychiatric impairment slightly higher

among divorced women (42.1%) than among divorced men (40.0%) (Bloom *et al.*, 1979, p. 187).

We are, as a society, still wrestling with the kinds of ground rules to apply when permanence ceases to be recognized at all. How much emphasis, if any, should be placed on permanence and just how the partners, especially wives and children, can best be protected in nonpermanent relationships still waits on further research for answers. The hope is that the phenomenon of "displaced housewives" will eventually die out by attrition. It is hoped, that is, that in the training of girls it will be made clear to them that they cannot count on "being taken care of" all their lives, that the chances are not insignificant that they will be left on their own some time or other in their lives so that the "trained helplessness" which crippled so many women reared under the old ground rules will not be their fate. And also that the care of children as well as their support can be as much expected from fathers as from mothers. These goals of course presuppose the elimination of discrimination in other roles as well, at the work site as well as at home.

Whether we accept the Thwings' evaluation or Messer's, whether, that is, we see the modification in the ground rule of permanence as evidenced by divorce as bad or good, as constituting a step toward societal disintegration or a giant step forward for women, it is clear from the trends in divorce that permanence is no longer a major ground rule in marriage. Norton and Glick (1979) estimate that 4 out of every 10 marriages entered into by women born between 1945 and 1949 would eventually terminate in divorce. This is considerably higher than the estimated 3 out of 10 for women born a decade earlier (Norton & Glick, 1979, p. 9). The same rate of increase would lead to an expectation that half or more of marriages contracted by women born in the 1950s would end in divorce. Thus although most marriages now as in the past still conform to the ground rule prescribing permanence, enough do not as to challenge its viability. Divorce now outstrips death as the cause for marital disruption. In 1860 only 4.1% of all marital disruptions had been by divorce; in 1900, 12.5%; by 1950 the proportion had reached 36.2% (Jacobson, 1959, Table 70). By 1973–1974 for the first time in our history the proportion was more than half (Glick, n.d.). Just as changes in ground rules one and two reverberated in ground rule number three, so also do changes in the ground rule of permanence have impact on ground rule number four, fidelity.

A generation ago the term "serial monogamy" was coined to refer to the situation in which men and women went from one monogamous relationship to another (Landis, 1950). It was pointed out that in our country there was as much polygamy in terms of the proportion of people who engaged in it sequentially if not concomitantly as there was in societies that officially permitted it. The trend has continued until now a new marital status—"transitional"—is coming to be recognized (Ross & Sawhill, 1975). Such sequential or serial polygamy is related to another ground rule which characterized Victorian marriage, namely, the rule of sexual exclusivity.

GROUND RULE NUMBER FOUR: FIDELITY

The ground rules of the Victorian family specified not only monogamy but also exclusivity. Not only one wife or husband throughout one's life but also only one sex partner ever, before or after marriage. Virginity before and chastity after marriage were enjoined, theoretically for both partners but both theoretically and actually for women. Monogamy was undergirded by law, exclusivity by both law and the marital vow. Adultery, a legal concept, was forbidden by both legal and religious norms. Thus engaging in sexual relations with anyone other than a spouse was both a crime and a sin. It is still universally accepted as grounds for divorce wherever divorce is granted. Infidelity, as distinguished from adultery, was violation of a promise made at marriage to "forsake all others." But the precise nature of what these promises included became murkier and murkier.

A relatively superficial examination of the literature on infidelity suggests at least seven kinds of infidelity of varying levels of seriousness: (1) coquetry and flirtation; (2) fly-by-night sex; (3) "the matinée" or playful relationship among working men and women; (4) cocktail-lounge relationships; (5) monogamous and permanent relationships outside of marriage; (6) fantasied infidelity; and (7) noncoital, nonfantasy relationships which involve intimate sharing of the self (Bernard, 1972). Perhaps there should also be added the recently advocated forms of technical infidelity exemplified by such relationships as "open marriage," group marriage, some kinds of communal relationships, and swinging.

Another straw which shows which way the wind is blowing with respect to the ground rule of fidelity is the phenomenal increase in so-called swing clubs in the 1960s, 1970s, and 1980s (Bernard, 1968, 1972, 1982b). "Swinging," or organized spouse-sharing, has been called one of the fastest growing forms of—commercialized—recreation or entertainment in the country.[1]

---

[1]On a television program early in 1982, the president of the National Association of Swing Clubs, Robert McGinley, a counseling psychologist, estimated that there were 200 "swing clubs" in the country and perhaps 5,000,000 swingers. (transcript of interview, "Phil Donahue Show," January 19, 1982).

That the ground rule of exclusivity is changing may be inferred by several straws in the wind. There is, for example, increasing emphasis on the positive aspects of extramarital relationships by researchers and counselors as well as by some ethicists. There is not only tolerance but even advocacy on the part of some (Sapirstein, 1948). The increasing frequency of infidelity among women is further evidence of the attrition in the rule of fidelity. The trends in divorce also suggest that fidelity is no longer conceived of as intrinsic to marriage. Despite the documented frequency of adultery, the grounds alleged for divorce have changed dramatically from a frequent use of adultery to a frequent use of cruelty. In 1938 a *Ladies Home Journal* survey reported by H. F. Pringle found that three-fourths of the respondents did not think a single act of adultery by either spouse should necessarily lead to divorce. And with the introduction of the no-fault concept of divorce, fidelity is no longer intrinsic to marriage. A person who engages in extramarital relationships but does not want a divorce cannot necessarily be divorced for this alone. Unless there are those who wish to prosecute for the crime of adultery, it will for all intents and purposes disappear as a legal entity.

A question has been raised with respect to the relationship between the ground rule of exclusivity and the ground rule of permanence. There may be an implicit conflict between the two. That is, they may be incompatible. We may have to choose between them. If we insist on permanence, exclusivity may be harder to enforce; if we insist on exclusivity, we may be endangering permanence. Exclusivity meant one thing when a marriage lasted only, let us say, about 25 years; it is another when it may last twice that long. A comparison of Kinsey's (Kinsey, Pomeroy, Martin, & Gebhard, 1953) findings and findings on young couples living together outside of marriage suggests that exclusivity is more important to the young people but permanence more important to the older couples.

> The trend . . . seems to be in the direction of exclusivity at the expense of permanence in the younger years but permanence at the expense of exclusivity in the later years. (Bernard, 1972, pp. 113–115)

There has been only a moderate amount of exegesis on fidelity. But of considerable interest was the conclusion of two commentators that fidelity did not condone jealousy of innocent friendships. In Victorian marriage such friendships were common among women (Smith-Rosenberg, 1975). But women's "place" did not foster them with men. Now that there are so many places for women outside the home, the opportunity for friendships between the sexes increases. There is an almost unlimited literature on the joy of sex. But with the increasing opportunity for contacts between men and women in a variety of settings, new kinds of "joy" become possible which are not dependent on genital relationships, such, for example, as the "joy of gender," the kind of pleasure men and women sometimes achieve in the interplay of personality, erotic perhaps but not necessarily genital. In a London play some years ago the wife was justifiably more concerned about the Platonic intimacy between her husband and another woman than she would have been about a coital relationship. For

> the kind of relationship which can develop between men and women who work together as a team over a period of time sometimes assumes an emotional interdependence outweighing the marital bonds of either one without supplanting them. These may be among the innocent relationship . . . not forbidden by the marital vows. (Bernard, 1972, p. 107)

There is as yet little research on this kind of relationship and it is only now beginning to attract attention as the potential reaction of wives to having their husbands work closely with female professional colleagues becomes a factor in women's careers.

Both exclusivity and permanence as ground rules for marriage have been subjected to a considerable research scrutiny in the recent past, especially vis-à-vis the so-called sexual revolution and alternate lifestyles. Many marriages still conform at least moderately well to both rules. But increasing numbers seem not to be conforming to either one. A vast body of experience is being accumulated related to nonconformity to both of them. Precisely what is the degree of exclusivity that should be incorporated in the ground rules of marriage to produce, overall, the least amount of suffering and the most benefit to both partners is something we will only know as more definitive research is available.

GROUND RULE NUMBER FIVE: BEAR CHILDREN

Because it introduces a totally different realm of discourse—the demographic—only a bow is made here in the direction of another, quasi-ground rule of Victorian marriage: bear children. It is qualified by the term "quasi" because although there was no ground rule more basic, more unchallenged, more taken-for-granted, compliance was not always possible. A couple might be pitied if they could not conform but they could not be sanctioned. This rule had scriptural foundations so unequivocal that legal support was not necessary except in the form of prohibiting contraception and punishment for abortion. It seemed to have been laid down by Nature herself in the form of a maternal instinct or at least of mother love. Still, Nature was not wholly relied upon; powerful pressures were invoked, just in case Nature did not succeed (Bernard, 1974, Chapter 3). But in recent years the whole environmental and ecological movement has counteracted these pressures with negative ones. Thus in a Gallup poll in 1975 1 parent in 10 said that if they had it to do over again they would have no children, a 10-fold increase over the results of a similar poll 10 years earlier (McLaughlin, 1975). And an increasing—though admittedly still small—number of young couples do indeed report that they plan to have no children at all (Veevers, 1979). The creation of a National Organization for Optional Parenthood with chapters all over the country highlights the revolutionary change in this ground rule. The proportion of women who say they want no children remains small, although it may be increasing. It was 1.3% among those 18–24 in 1967 and 3.9% four years later (Bernard, 1974, p. 43). In two surveys, 1957 and 1976, it was found that there had been "a 5 percent rise in childlessness for the youngest age group who were married at one time or another" but this did not necessarily imply a "new norm against having children" (Veroff, et al., 1981, p. 198).

A corollary in Victorian marriage to the ground rule to bear children was the rule that child care was the sole responsibility of women. Here too change is in process. Thus rearing children is becoming the first choice of a smaller and smaller proportion of women. A Louis Harris Survey in 1975, for example, found that

> the percentage of women who believe that "taking care of home and raising children is more rewarding for women than having a job" has declined from 71% to 51% in the past five years.

Child care may prove to be the most intractable aspect of marriage to find new consensual ground rules (Bernard, 1976a).

WHITHER BOUND?

This retrospective sketch shows that in answer to the question raised earlier, a great many things about marriage and family have indeed changed since the founding of Radcliffe College a century ago. Although the "place" of women is still in the home, it is not the only place for them; there are a great many other places for women. Although equality of status within the household is not yet achieved, some headway, especially among the young, seems to be in process. Although most marriages—some 60%—are still lifelong in duration, and although permanence may be the dream of young lovers, it is no longer taken for granted. Lifelong fidelity, like permanence, may also be the dream of young lovers, but no more than permanence is it taken for granted. Pressures to have children still remain strong, but support for those who choose not to is also becoming strong.

It is far easier to point to past forms that are disintegrating than it is to discern prospectively the new forms in process of emerging. Or to delineate the new forms to aim for. Or to be sure how to create them. Or just how much we can actually control them. There is a perennial controversy in the literature of jurisprudence and sociology with respect to the limits of change that can be achieved by way of law. Those who have looked on the ground rules of marriage as established by Divinity or by Natural Law and as supported by reason and human nature or by "biogrammer," find that law and legislation can do little to change them. In the 19th century this was a commonly expressed view; it still is today. Thus some students doubt whether "changing attitudes and even laws will induce people to act in ways that contravene, contradict, or distort what may be natural mammalian patterns" (Tiger & Shepher, 1975, pp. 12–13). If we knew what were the "natural mammalian patterns" that neither attitudes nor laws can change, it would greatly help us in planning for the future.

Sometimes collective behavior changes and law belatedly catches up with it; more rarely law changes and collective behavior changes to conform (Bernard, 1942, 1976b). In the case of marriage the first pattern seems to be more common. Thus, for example, divorce by collusion was being granted long before no-fault divorce laws rendered it unnecessary. Or the law is nullified in effect by not imposing sanctions for violation. The crime of adultery, for example, is almost never prosecuted and is rarely anymore even a ground for divorce. The legal obligation of husbands and fathers to support their families is flouted by thousands of men without enforcement by the courts. The spread of alternative styles of relationships which involve technical adultery or extramarital relationships is not stopped by the enforcement of the law against them.

The problem is even more complicated when we turn to the indirect effect of law on marriage, such as the effect of laws dealing with property rights, with taxes, with credit, and the like. It usually takes a considerable amount of research to tease out all the indirect effects of any legislation. Tax laws, for example, may encourage marriage or discourage it, may help or hinder labor force participation by wives and mothers, may encourage or discourage having the extra child. Welfare laws may encourage men to desert their families (Moles, 1979). So aware are we becoming of these indirect effects of legislation on marital roles that "family impact" statements are being asked for to accompany all federal programs, just as an environmental impact statement is asked for in other kinds of legislation.

Law will be involved in a host of changes now being proposed. Contractual marriages, for example, will have to be sanctioned by law if they are put to the test. Marriage between homosexuals will also call for legal validation. In almost all the viable alternative lifestyles where property is seriously involved there will have to be legal support. The most controversial interface between marital relations and the law has to do with constitutional guarantees of equality. If such equality could be incorporated in the Constitution, the effect would be to codify the emerging ground rules of marriage and bring old ones up to date. It would not, in and of itself, change them, but it would help us in clarifying them. No demand could be legitimized for one sex that was not also legitimized for the other. The actual implementation of the ground rules would still have to be worked out between the marital partners. Such guaranteed legal equalization could not change the fact that there are a variety of functions that have to be performed in any social system—that people have to be fed, for example, and children cared for—but the arbitrary assignment in all cases of any specific function to any individual solely on the basis of sex would not be shored up by law.

These then were the ground rules for marriage when Radcliffe began its first century. And these were the events which transformed them during that century. What they will be at the second centennial is not at all clear at this moment. But it is certain that Radcliffe, through the research it fosters, through the standards it projects, through the women scholars it nurtures, will have a great deal to do with the form they will take.

REFERENCES

Beecher, C. *Treatise on political economy.* New York: Harper, 1841.
Berg, B. J. *The remembered gate, origins of American feminism: The women and the city, 1800–1860.* New York: Oxford University Press, 1978.
Bernard, J. Factors in the distribution of success in marriage. *American Journal of Sociology* 1934, 40, 49–60.
Bernard, J. *American family behavior.* New York: Harper, 1942.
Bernard, J. Present demographic trends and structural outcomes in family life today. In J. A. Peterson (Ed.), *Marriage and family counseling.* New York: Association Press, 1968.
Bernard, J. Infidelity: Some moral and social issues. In J. W. Masserman (Ed.), *Science and psychoanalysis* (Vol. 16). New York: Grune and Stratton, 1972.
Bernard, J. *The future of motherhood.* New York: Dial Press, 1974.
Bernard, J. *Women, wives, mothers.* Chicago: Aldine, 1976a.
Bernard, J. Change and stability in sex-role norms and behavior. *Journal of Social Issues,* 1976b, 32, 207–223.
Bernard, J. *The future of marriage* (Offset Ed.). New Haven: Yale University Press, 1982.
Bishop, J. P. *New commentaries on marriage, divorce, and separation.* Chicago: T. H. Flood, 1891.
Bloom, B. L., White, S. W., & Asher, S. J. Marital disruption as a stressful life event. In G. Levinger & O. Moles (Eds.), *Divorce and separation, context, causes and consequences.* New York: Basic Books, 1979.
Burgess, E. W., & Cottrell, L. S. *Predicting success or failure in marriage.* New York: Prentice-Hall, 1939.
Cherlin, A. Work life and marital dissolution. In G. Levinger & O. Moles (Eds.), *Divorce and separation, context, causes and consequences.* New York: Basic Books, 1979.

Coben, S. The assault on American Victorian culture. New York: Oxford University Press, 1983.

Cohn, D. L. *Love in America*. New York: Simon and Schuster, 1943.

Costantini, E., & Craik, K. H. Women as Politicians: The social background, personality, and political careers of female party leaders. In M. Shuch-Mednick & S. Schwartz-Tangri (Eds.), New Perspectives on Women. *Journal of Social Issues.* 1972, *28*, 217–236.

Cott, N. *The bonds of womanhood*. New Haven: Yale University Press, 1977.

Folsom, J. K. *The family and democratic society*. New York: Wiley, 1934.

Franklin, B. *Courtship and marriage*, 1746.

Friedan, B. *The feminine mystique*. New York: W. W. Norton, 1963.

Fritchey, C. The true champions of family life. *Washington Post*, Dec. 3, 1977.

Galbraith, J. K. Economics of the American housewife. *Atlantic Monthly*, 1973, *232*, 78–83.

Gallup Poll, 1975.

Gilman, C. P. *Women and economics*. New York: Harper Torchbooks, 1966. (Originally published, 1898).

Glick, P. C. Remarriage: Some recent changes and variations. Unpublished manuscript, no date. (Available from author.)

Goode, W. J. *After divorce*. New York: Free Press, 1956.

Guttentag, M., Salasin, S., Sex differences in the utilization of public supported health facilities: The puzzle of depression. Unpublished manuscript, Harvard University, 1976.

Harland, M., & Van de Water, V. *Everyday etiquette*. Indianapolis: Bobbs-Merrill, 1905.

Harris Poll, 1972.

Harris Survey. *Washington Post*, Dec. 14, 1975.

Jacobs, A. C., & Angell, R. *A research in family law*. (No publisher given), 1930.

Jacobson, P. H. *American marriage and divorce*. New York: Rinehart, 1959.

Kinsey, A. C., Pomeroy, W. B., Martin, C. E., & Gebhard, P. H. *Sexual behavior in the human female*. Philadelphia: W. B. Saunders, 1953.

Kraditor, A. S. (Ed.). *Up from the pedestal*. Chicago: Quadrangle, 1968.

Landis, P. Sequential marriage. *Journal of Home Economics*, 1950, *42*.

McCormack, T. Toward a nonsexist perspective on social and political change. In M. Millman & R. Hanter (Eds.). *Another voice: Feminist perspectives on social life and social science*. New York: Anchor, 1975.

McLaughlin, M. Parents who wouldn't do it again. *McCall's* 1975, *103*(2), 37–38.

Messer, M. B. *The family in the making*. New York: Putnam, 1928.

Meyerson, A. *The nervous housewife*. New York: Little, Brown, 1929.

Moles, O. Marital dissolution and public assistance payments. In G. Levinger & O. Moles (Eds.). *Divorce and separation, context, causes and consequences*. New York: Basic Books, 1979.

Myrdal, A., & Klein, V. *Women's two roles*. London: Routledge and Kegan Paul, 1956.

Norton, A. J., & Glick, P. C. Marital instability in America: Past, present and future. In G. Levinger & O. Moles (Eds.). *Divorce and separation, context, causes and consequences*. New York: Basic Books, 1979.

Parsons, T., & Bales, R. *Family, socialization, and social process*. New York: Free Press, 1955.

Popenoe, P. Can the family have two heads? *Sociology and Social Research*, Sept.-Oct. 1933, *18*, QS GS

Pringle, H. F. What do the women of America think? *Ladies Home Journal*, February 1938.

Radloff, L. Sex differences in depression: The effects of occupation and marital status. *Sex Roles*, 1975, *1*, 249–265.

Radloff, L. Demographic groups by average CES-D (depression) score: All . . .whites only. Unpublished manuscript, July 1976 (Available from author).

Roper Organization. *The 1980 Virginia Slims American women's opinion poll*, 1980.

Ross, H., & Sawhill, I. *Time of transition*. Washington, D.C.: Urban Institute, 1975.

Rossi, A. A biosocial perspective on parenting. *Daedalus*, 1977, *106*(2), 1–31.

Safilios-Rothschild, C. The study of family power structure: A review 1960–1969. *Journal of Marriage and the Family*, 1970, *32*: 539–552.

Sapirstein, M. R. *Emotional security*. New York: Crown, 1948.

Scanzoni, J. An historical perspective on husband-wife bargaining power and marital dissolution. In G. Levinger & O. Moles (Eds.). *Divorce and separation, conditions, causes and consequences*. New York: Basic Books, 1979.

Schlesinger, A. M. Learning how to behave. In *A historical study of American etiquette books*. New York: Macmillan, 1946.

Schouler, J. *A treatise on the law of marriage, divorce, separation and domestic relations*. Cited in *Domestic relations* (Vol. 1). Albany: M. Bender, 1921, pp. 122–123.

Seligman, M. E. P. Depression and learned helplessness. In R. J. Friedman & M. M. Katz (Eds.). *The psychology of depression: Contemporary theory and research*. Washington, D.C.: Winston and Sons, 1974.

Shaw, L. B. Economic consequences of marital disruption. Unpublished manuscript, 1978.

Sklar, K. K. *Catherine Beecher: A study of American domesticity*. New Haven: Yale University Press, 1973.

Smith-Rosenberg, C. The female world of love and ritual: Relations between women in nineteenth century America. *Signs*, 1975, 1, 1975, pp. 1–30.

Thwing, C. F., & Thwing, C. F. B. *The family, an historical and social study*. Boston: Lee and Shepard, 1887.

Tiger, L., & Shepher, J. *Women in the kibbutz*. New York: Harcourt Brace Jovanovich, 1975.

Tocqueville, A. de, *Democracy in America*. Part Two *The social influence of democracy*. New York: Langley, 1840.

Terman, L. *Psychological factors in marital happiness*. New York: McGraw-Hill, 1938.

Veblen, T. *The theory of the leisure class*. New York: New American Library, 1953. (Originally published, 1899).

Veevers, J. E. Voluntary childlessness: A review of issues and evidence. *Journal of Marriage and the Family*, 1979, *2*(2), 1–26.

Veroff, J., Douvan, E., Kulka, R. A. *The inner American, a self-portrait from 1957 to 1976*. New York: Basic Books, 1981.

Weitzman, L. J. *The marriage contract, spouses, lovers, and the law*. New York: Free Press, 1981.

Westley, W. A., & Epstein, N. B. *Silent majority*. San Francisco: Jossey-Bass, 1969.

Chapter 6

Psychological Orientations to the Work Role: 1957–1976

Joseph Veroff

Work in America, a report of a special task force to the Secretary of Health, Education and Welfare in 1973, presented a gloomy picture of the life of the American worker in the 1970s. That report summarized the research observations and social speculations about the nature of work in the 20th century that have filled the social scientific journals and college classrooms for many years. It was an excellent integrative survey, well balanced with both theory and empirical information, and it offered some ameliorative proposals for the sorry state of our work life. No group seemed to be exempt from its pessimistic view: blue- and white-collar workers, managers, young and old people, women in the labor force, those who are full-time housewives—all were diagnosed to have similar chronic and debilitating problems within their lives stemming from difficulties in the meaning or lack of meaning of work.

Such statements are captured more directly in popular accounts of working life found in Studs Terkel's (1973) snapshots of Chicago workers in various occupations and in Lilian Rubin's (1976) interviews of the personal lives of working families in California in the early '70s. Two themes are consistent: the jobs we are asked to do for the most part do not offer gratification for men's and women's desires for personal impact, and the demands of the work setting usually make people feel

Joseph Veroff, Ph.D. • Survey Research Center, Institute for Social Research, University of Michigan, Ann Arbor, Michigan 48109. Research reported in this chapter was largely supported by a grant from NIMH (MH 26006). Further support was made possible through an NIMH training program in Mental Health and Social Roles (MH 14613). In addition to the trainees involved in that program, the author wishes to thank Elizabeth Douvan and Richard Kulka for their valuable advice in pursuing the analyses in this paper.

alienated in each of the many senses of the word: alienated from the product, alienated from the organization which produces the product, alienated from the people with whom they are working, and alienated from themselves as people holding a meaningless position in this society.

Are these observations accurate? If so, we are in a bad way. We should be doing everything in our power to turn our institutions into more viable places to work or to produce "something of value for others," in the words of *Work in America*. I have no doubt that many of these observations are true. Surveys done at the Institute for Social Research have shown that working in the United States in the 1970s has many dimensions of discontent for many different strata of workers in our society (see Quinn, Mangione, & Baldi de Mandilovitch, 1973). But as the authors of *Work in America* suggest, some of this discontent might very well be from a rising level of expectation for what the work setting should be. As our working population has become more educated, as more young people have made up the majority of the work force in the United States, many more people are expecting work to provide them with all sorts of challenges. As we socialize our young people to want more out of a job than good pay, good working conditions, a place to congregate with peers, and a way to structure the hours of a day, many young people will be expressing discontent if the quality of jobs do not keep pace with these expectations. To get some perspective on whether or not the rising sense of discontent with work that seems to prevail in American society stems mostly from overextended aspirations set by our young people or from a rapid disintegration of the nature of work in American life, we have to take an historical perspective that examines possible changes in the working life. What were working conditions like in mid-century compared to now? What did people, especially young people, want from a job then as compared to now? If we are able to answer such questions, then perhaps we can judge how much changes in work aspirations and/or changes in the workplace have affected our sense of well-being. An historical perspective then will enable us to be more clearly prognostic of what the future meaning of work in the 1980s and 1990s might be.

In this chapter I would like to present some exciting data that may provide this kind of historical perspective. In 1957 Gurin, Veroff, and Feld (1960) collected data from a national survey of adult men and women asking about their general well-being, their symptoms of distress, their feelings of satisfaction and discontent in three major life roles—marriage, parenthood, and work—and how they cope with problems they encounter. Some major results from the survey were reported in *Americans View Their Mental Health* (Gurin, Veroff, and Feld, 1960) and in

Marriage and Work in America (Veroff & Feld, 1970). In 1976 my colleagues Elizabeth Douvan, Richard Kulka, and I had the opportunity to redo, in major outline, this same survey in a different national population. The same questions were used in the majority of instances. Thus we can compare the reactions of the American population in 1957 to a question about job satisfaction with the reactions of the American population in 1976 to the same question. We also asked some additional questions in 1976 to amplify aspects of the life roles we were examining.

This chapter will examine the work role, primarily looking at the 1957 data compared to the 1976 data.[1] We will examine whether there have been any major changes in the way people react to the work role: the general salience of work, and the quality of their experience in working. By looking at which reactions remain constant and which reactions change, we can get some sense of how Americans' expectations may have changed, and indirectly we can get some information about the impact of changes in the structure of working conditions. I will be sharing a great deal of data with you in this chapter, including some results about the 1976 sample for which there is no comparative 1957 data but which are too provocative to leave out of a report on work. Indeed I view these data as the major contribution that I can make to the celebration of Radcliffe's 100th birthday, for they will provide some basic information about the changes in people's reactions to their work over 20 years. Such information can be grist for many mills as we think about the meaning of various life roles in our society today and for the future. Hidden within the many tables will be pieces of information that can be used in a variety of contexts for thinking about men's and women's lives today in contrast to a generation ago. I will be emphasizing only a few possible integrative themes in my interpretations of the data.

Before the results are presented, I will spell out the major ideas that structured our thinking about these issues. Some derive from the work of other people in reviewing the meaning of work in America and some derive from our own thinking about the analyses of the initial survey.

---

[1] A few words about the specifics of these two surveys. The total samples were 2,460 (1975) and 2,264 (1976). Each was representative of adults (21 and over) living in households in the United States. Each sample was derived by stratified random block sampling. The Survey Research Center's interviewing staff followed their research doorstep-interviewing procedure. The response rate in 1957 was considerably higher (80%) than the rate in 1957 (71%), although the latter is acceptable. The general context given for the survey was to assess reactions to modern living. Coding procedures for open-ended questions were identical in both years. The replications studies have been reported in two volumes: *The Inner American* (Veroff, Douvan, and Kulka, 1981) and *Mental Health in America* (Veroff, Kulka, and Douvan, 1981).

THEORETICAL PROPOSITIONS CONSIDERED IN CONTRASTING THE
MEANING OF WORK IN 1957 AND 1976

1. *Personal Impact in Work Has Diminished.* The authors of *Work in America* propose that the major difficulty with work in this country today is that men and women feel out of personal control in their work settings. In general they do not feel they have a role in the decision processes in an organization whether it be blue or white collar, nor do they feel that their talents and interests are utilized in work. Both of these feelings are presumed in *Work in America* to be important underpinnings for the sense of identity in a work structure. Any organization that undermines these feelings is likely headed for trouble because people within such organizations are likely to be extremely discontented. The authors of *Work in America* pay particular attention to young people whose level of education has been dramatically upgraded in the past generation. They argue that young people's perceived qualifications for upgraded work are much higher than their comparable cohorts in previous generations but they are without jobs to fulfill these upgraded expectations. Thus young people today are likely to experience an alienation from work as a major commitment for life. Jobs commensurate with one's ability should be provided, they would argue, or we will have in our midst a generation of people who are no longer committed to the larger structure of the society. This general hypothesis makes us look in our data for the degree to which people have or have not found satisfactions in their accomplishments or in their feeling of power in the work setting.

2. *Increased Achievement Motivation in the New Generation May Mean That Achievement Goals in Work Have Become Increasingly Insatiable.* Related to the idea that personal individuation in work has diminished is an idea that Sheila Feld and I developed in *Marriage and Work in America* (Veroff & Feld, 1970): with higher achievement motivation people in the new generation should set higher and higher challenges for accomplishment and work. What we found in *Marriage and Work in America* was that men with high achievement motives as measured through thematic apperception in the 1957 national survey were those most likely to express dissatisfaction with work, not only in lower status jobs but also in higher status jobs. We expected those with high achievement motives in undemanding jobs to be those who would be dissatisfied, following the ideas that were promoted in *Work in America*. We were not expecting those with high achievement motives in professional jobs to express more discontent than those with low achievement motives. And it was for this reason that we entertained the hypothesis that high achievement motives egg people on to set higher and higher goals

for accomplishment at work. Discontent comes from unfulfilled aspirations that sometimes emerge from the person's own heavy demands on his or her environment.

3. *Leisure Has More and More Come to Replace Work as an Arena for Accomplishment.* A third idea that shaped some of our analyses was to search out the connection between leisure and work as best we could. We have been impressed with the contradictory theories that seem to exist about the relationship of work and leisure. Seligman (1965) brilliantly pieces together the problem by recognizing that leisure and free time can become as meaningless as work if they fall prey to the consumer orientation of an industrial society. If leisure can *generalize* the orientation that different work environments instill, so can it also *compensate* for the alienation from work. If there has been a turning away from the work role as a source of major identity fulfillment, as many social observers have indicated, then it could very well be that leisure has taken over as a means of fulfilling some of our more self-actualizing interests. We found little evidence in the 1957 survey for any compensatory connection between motives (especially the achievement motive) and engaging in particular kinds of leisure activities. Contradictory evidence has come forward on compensation. Meissner (1971) has shown that people are more likely to engage in active organized leisure pursuits if they have more actualizing jobs. Young and Willmott (1973) clearly show that English urban lower class with high-status achievement-satisfying jobs have a greater range of activities in their leisure than those with low-status jobs. Some studies have shown, however, evidence for compensation in leisure for lack of gratification at work. Hagerdorn and Labovitz (1968) show more social community participation among people whose jobs are isolating. Spreitzer and Synder (1974) have shown a greater involvement with leisure for self-identity among people who find their work not very intrinsically challenging. Thus it remains an open question as to whether or not there is a compensatory relationship between leisure and work.

4. *Occupational Communities Have Slowly Been Eroded.* A fourth idea that we considered in our research comes from the sociological thinking about how occupations structure one's social life outside of the work world. The most interesting set of ideas for that relationship has come from a book by Salaman (1974) called *Community and Occupation,* in which a concept of *occupational community* is explored. Salaman's idea is that if people are *involved* with their work, then that occupational class becomes a major frame of reference for defining a set of relationships in the outside world. Salaman examines two occupational groups very thoroughly—middle-class architects and working-class railwaymen— and in both he discovers the concept of occupational community very

useful in understanding their patterns of leisure and social relations outside the job. Salaman is quick to note that if people are not involved with their work, then their occupation does not define a community for them. He refers to a study by Goldthorpe and colleagues (Goldthorpe, Lochwood, Bachofer, & Platt, 1968) which shows that affluent industrial workers, very discontented with the meaning of their work in the industrial setting, rarely make friendship choices among their own fellow workers. Such phenomena may be rampant. Thus we see that a very important aspect of our analysis might be to examine workers' problems in maintaining and enjoying the company of their peers at work.

Affiliative connections through work reflect an active involvement, even if at times they might represent banding together out of misery. In fact a disregard for the affiliative nature of work might represent an extreme form of alienation from work.

5. *Specialization in the Work Setting May Interfere with Affiliativeness at Work.* One of the major ideas that Shelia Feld and I developed in *Marriage and Work in America* (1970) was that people can easily attain affiliative satisfactions at work if there are many people doing *parallel* activity. Under such conditions people band together, see themselves in either their pleasures or discontents as having a common fate, and therefore have the means of communication for establishing affiliative ties. We saw such phenomena most clearly in the case of men working as operatives in the industrial setting. In a later paper (Veroff, 1977b) I found a similar phenomenon occurring in the case of women clerical workers. Solidarity in experiencing a common fate can thus become an important source of emotional gratification.

Has the nature of the work setting changed in this respect over the past generation? One possible hypothesis is that increased specialization in the work setting has decreased solidarity. The more people separate functions in an organization, the less they see common fate. Affiliative discontent may be rampant.

6. *The Women's Movement Has Reshaped the Meaning and Salience of Work for Both Men and Women.* Since 1957 women have become more eager to participate equally in work and not to be glibly relegated to the role of housewife. The values attached to women's working in the past decade can have enormous repercussions on the nature of family and work roles, not only for women but also for men. If feminist values have become popular with more than the avant garde, one might expect a lowering of satisfactions that women can derive from the housewife role and an increase in the sense of oppression among women who do not work. Furthermore one can entertain the widely held hypothesis that by going into the labor market as wage earners, women have increased their resources in the family setting, especially with the feminist ideol-

ogy to support them. To be a married working mother in 1976 should be politically different from such a role set in 1957. To be a full-time housewife also means something different in 1976 from what it did in 1957. Women might be more defensive about the choice of being a housewife if they have recently gone through an educational institution.

7. *Over the Generation There Has Been a Shift Away from a More Task-Oriented Sense of Achievement to a More Individuated Sense of Achievement.* A final framework that I used in approaching these data is one that I developed in the context of thinking about achievement motivation generally (Veroff, 1977a). The idea that the nature of achievement motivation is a unitary phenomenon is now open to serious question. Different sources of gratification for accomplishment can underlie achievement incentives. An important distinction that can be made is whether or not a person needs to focus on his or her own self-expressiveness in accomplishment. Having personal impact on an accomplishment is a special focus for achievement that seems to typify male reactions to achievement more than female. Another style of achievement incentives is one which focuses on the process of achievement, or an involvement with a task or a job for its own sake, a sense of participation in a more collective enterprise. These ideas can be important in thinking about the meaning of work. If the focus for achievement incentives in our society has shifted from a task to a more individuated sense of accomplishment, then the whole structure of the work organization that depends on collective involvements with work goals can be in jeopardy. If accomplishment is evaluated very specifically by individualized efforts more than by collective products, then different styles of achievement motivation may be differentially gratified. Increased specialization in the work setting, for example, could have positive consequences on people who are deriving more individuated achievement gratification from their efforts. Increased specialization, however, could have a detrimental effect on people whose achievement styles are more collective or task-oriented.

These then were some of the general ideas that influenced our approach. None of them offers us very explicit deductions that we feel comfortable in laying out ahead of time. They do give us a way of orienting to the set of data that we are about to present. We will return to a number of these themes as this chapter progresses. Enough speculation. Let us move to the data.

Before we begin our comparisons, we have to note important sets of facts about demographic shifts over the generation.

The 1957 adult American working population was different from the 1976 work force in a number of ways. Table 1 shows that the 1976

Table 1. Age and Education Comparison of 1957 and 1976 Working Samples (by sex)

	Males		Females	
	1957	1976	1957	1976
Age				
21–34	32%	42%	32%	45%
35–44	26%	22%	28%	19%
45–54	22%	15%	24%	18%
55+	20%	21%	16%	18%
	100%	100%	100%	100%
	N = (922)	(753)	(453)	(598)
Education				
Grade school	31%	9%	26%	8%
High school	46%	46%	55%	57%
College	23%	45%	19%	35%
	100%	100%	100%	100%
	N = (919)	(752)	(453)	(599)

work force is considerably younger and much better educated. Although these differences have to be considered in any changes reported, gross sample differences are still meaningful to the extent that they give us a positive understanding of the meaning of work in the country over the two years. Another way to look at the same phenomenon is to ask what being of a certain age means about working in 1957 and 1976. Table 2 shows the work status of men and women of different ages. The 1957 survey had fewer retired men and women at any age. In 1976 there were clearly more working women at each age level. These demographic shifts should be kept in mind as we approach the substantive results.

We will be examining two major topics: changes in the *salience* of work in people's lives; and changes in *reactions to jobs*. In the first topic we are asking whether or not the impact of the work role on various *other* aspects of people's lives has shifted or not. We are asking such questions as: Has the general importance of work in people's lives changed over the generation, or its relationship to other roles, or its general contribution to overall satisfactions? Within the second topic we will focus on how people have reacted specifically to their jobs: their satisfactions, commitments, and problems and feelings about adequacy at work. This is an arbitrary division for our analysis. Obviously the reactions people have had to their work will have an impact on what meaning work has for other aspects of their lives. And the place of work in the hierarchy of people's other roles should influence how a person reacts to his or her particular job. There is a dynamic interaction between

Table 2. Relationship of Age to Employment Status (by sex and year)

	Age							
	21–34		35–54		55–64		65+	
Employment status	1957	1976	1957	1976	1957	1976	1957	1976
Males								
Working	92%	91%	99%	90%	87%	75%	36%	26%
Retired	0%	0%	—	5%	6%	22%	62%	73%
Unemployed	2%	6%	1%	4%	7%	3%	2%	1%
Student	6%	3%	0%	1%	0%	0%	0%	0%
	100%	100%	100%	100%	100%	100%	100%	100%
	N = (317)	(346)	(450)	(312)	(146)	(160)	(161)	(142)
Females								
Working	33%	58%	42%	57%	34%	41%	6%	12%
Housewife	66%	32%	56%	36%	64%	42%	79%	52%
Retired	0%	0%	0%	3%	2%	14%	14%	34%
Unemployed	1%	8%	2%	4%	—[a]	3%	1%	2%
Student	—[a]	2%	0%	0%	0%	0%	0%	0%
	100%	100%	100%	100%	100%	100%	100%	100%
	N = (442)	(468)	(557)	(386)	(183)	(193)	(192)	(255)

[a] < 1%.

the overall salience of work to individuals and their reactions to their particular jobs. People are adaptive: if they are in bad situations, they may come to minimize the importance that role has for them; if they are in good situations, they may come to get more involved in that role as a way of defining themselves. In spite of this dynamic interaction we are going to treat these two topics separately. Perhaps at some future date we can examine how they interact.

CHANGES IN THE SALIENCE OF WORK FROM 1957 TO 1976

We approached the topic of finding or looking for changes or stability in the salience of work in America from 1957 to 1976 in a number of different ways. These approaches can be grouped under a series of five questions:

1. Has one's job contributed more or less to one's consciousness of well-being?
2. Does job satisfaction or dissatisfaction relate to other measures of adjustment to life outside of the job in 1976?

3. Are the people who work psychologically different from people
who do not work in 1976 compared to 1957?

4. Has there been a change in the significance of a life role that is
intimately connected with the meaning of work—the housewife
role?

5. Has the salience of leisure as an arena for challenge changed over
the generation?

We will discuss each of these topics separately in the sections below. In a concluding section we will present some exciting data only
available from the 1976 survey in which we asked people to compare the
potential of various life roles for fulfilling basic personal values. These
comparisons enable us to assess the salience of these life roles directly
for the 1976 population. These more direct data may give us some perspective on the changes that we might discover from the preceding
indirect comparisons of work salience in 1957 and 1976.

HAS THE JOB CHANGED IN ITS IMPACT ON PEOPLE'S CONSCIOUSNESS
OF WELL-BEING? In both 1957 and 1976 we asked each sample to tell us
what it is they were worried about and what sorts of things make them
happy or unhappy. The specific questions used in the surveys are listed
in Appendix B.[2] These questions were coded for various sources of
worries, happiness, and unhappiness, including a category identified as
job related. If a person mentioned not having enough money, his or her
response was not coded as a job worry or unhappiness but rather as a
financial concern. Only responses directly related to one's job were
coded as sources of job worries, happiness, or unhappiness. The details
of the code also appear in Appendix B, as they do for all questions used
in analyses in this report. In Tables 3 (for men) and 4 (for women) we
can see that over the generation mentioning one's job as a source of
worry has increased among men, especially among the more educated,
and that unhappiness about one's job has increased quite a bit among
employed women, especially young women. Furthermore reporting aspects about one's job as a source of happiness has not increased or
decreased over the generation. These data alone would suggest that the
general consciousness of work has somewhat shifted, with one's job
becoming more figural as a source of discontent but no more figural as a
source of happiness.

How deep-rooted is this shift in the meaning of one's job as a
negative feature of one's life? In another part of the questionnaire we

[2]All other questions to be analyzed in this report will appear in one of these appendices:
Appendix A—job-related questions used in both surveys; Appendix B—non-job-related
questions used in both surveys; Appendix C—questions used only in the 1976 survey.

Table 3. Mentioning One's Job as a Source of Happiness, Unhappiness, and Worries: 1957–1976 Working Men Compared (by age and education)

Education	Age	N 1957	N 1976	Job as source of happiness 1957	Job as source of happiness 1976	Job as source of unhappiness 1957	Job as source of unhappiness 1976	Job as source of worries 1957	Job as source of worries 1976
Grade school	21–34	(42)	(13)	7%	15%	19%	23%	24%	23%
	35–54	(133)	(23)	6%	13%	17%	9%	16%	22%
	55+	(98)	(35)	6%	6%	13%	14%	21%	14%
	Total	(273)	(71)	6%	10%	16%	14%	19%	18%
High school	21–34	(160)	(138)	10%	8%	29%	30%	18%	29%
	35–54	(212)	(134)	11%	8%	26%	26%	21%	13%
	55+	(51)	(74)	10%	5%	26%	15%	20%	23%
	Total	(423)	(346)	11%	8%	27%	25%	20%	22%
College	21–34	(87)	(164)	25%	24%	33%	38%	26%	39%
	35–54	(99)	(124)	22%	15%	27%	32%	24%	33%
	55+	(28)	(47)	14%	19%	21%	28%	11%	23%
	Total	(214)	(335)	22%	20%	29%	34%	23%	35%
Total		(910)	(752)	12%	13%	24%	28%	20%	27%

Table 4. Mentioning One's Job as a Source of Happiness, Unhappiness, and Worries: 1957–1976 Working Women Compared (by age and education)

Education	Age	N 1957	N 1976	Job as source of happiness 1957	Job as source of happiness 1976	Job as source of unhappiness 1957	Job as source of unhappiness 1976	Job as source of worries 1957	Job as source of worries 1976
Grade school	21–34	(21)	(6)	5%	0%	10%	17%	14%	17%
	35–54	(58)	(17)	14%	6%	9%	6%	10%	6%
	55+	(34)	(25)	9%	16%	6%	0%	12%	20%
	Total	(113)	(48)	10%	10%	8%	4%	17%	15%
High school	21–34	(95)	(140)	10%	8%	17%	30%	12%	18%
	35–54	(128)	(144)	9%	6%	16%	22%	6%	8%
	55+	(23)	(56)	22%	5%	9%	10%	9%	16%
	Total	(246)	(340)	11%	7%	10%	24%	8%	14%
College	21–34	(28)	(123)	25%	28%	32%	34%	14%	23%
	35–54	(45)	(59)	18%	15%	7%	34%	13%	10%
	55+	(13)	(28)	15%	18%	8%	11%	15%	4%
	Total	(86)	(200)	20%	23%	15%	31%	15%	17%
Total		(445)	(588)	12%	13%	14%	25%	10%	15%

asked all the respondents how they would like a son or daughter to be different from themselves. In 1957, 16% of the working men and 7% of the working women mentioned a different life's work as a desired difference for a child. In 1976 only 12% of the working men and 6% of the working women mentioned such a response. If anything, feeling negative about one's job as a source of identity has decreased in the population. One might therefore conclude that in spite of the increased mention of one's job as a source of unhappiness or worry, this change has not been accompanied by an increased rejection of one's occupational identity.

DOES JOB SATISFACTION OR DISSATISFACTION RELATE TO OTHER MEASURES OF ADJUSTMENT TO LIFE OUTSIDE OF THE JOB MORE OR LESS IN 1976? In the national survey we had an opportunity to ask many questions about feelings of well-being in areas of life outside of the work situation. We accumulated a number of these measures of adjustment and well-being to see whether they were correlated with our major measure of job adjustment—job satisfaction. Although the concept of job satisfaction has been questioned as a major measure of reactions to work by a number of people (see Nord, 1977), it still remains one of the most important assessments we have of how people are reacting to their jobs. The measure that was used in the national surveys in 1957 and 1976 simply read: Taking into consideration all things about your job, how satisfied or dissatisfied are you with it? We coded the response to this question along a 5-point scale, including: very satisfied, satisfied, neutral, ambivalent, and dissatisfied. (A full description of the code for the job satisfaction measure appears in Appendix A of this chapter.) To what aspects of life adjustment does the measure of job satisfaction relate in 1976 compared to 1957?

The different assessments of life adjustment used for this analysis of the salience of the work role include the following: general feelings of happiness; marital happiness; symptoms of psychological anxiety,[3] immobilization,[3] ill-health,[3] drinking; feelings of nervous breakdown; spending one's leisure in challenge. (All of these measures are described in detail in Appendix B.) The measure of marital happiness asks people to judge how happy their marriage is on a scale. The measures of symptoms derive from a symptom checklist. The symptoms of psychological anxiety reflect a person's feelings of nervousness. The symptoms of

[3]Each of these symptom scales is a sum of items which clearly and consistently defined a factor in repeatedly emerging factor analyses performed on the intercorrelation matrices of a checklist of psychological and physical symptoms. Separate factor analyses of these data (1957 females, 1957 males, 1976 females, and 1976 males) produced remarkably parallel results.

immobilization reflect a person's inability to take action. The symptoms of ill-health reflect a person's evaluation of his or her state of physical health. The drinking symptom refers to the responses to a single item: "Do you sometimes drink too much?" Feelings of nervous breakdown reflect the reponses to a simple question: "Have you ever felt you were going to have a nervous breakdown?" Spending one's time in challenging leisure is a tally of whether a person, in response to an open-ended question about how he/she spends his/her time, mentions an activity judged to be challenging, such as sports, hobbies, crafts, and the like. The happiness measure is a simple 3-point scale asking people to judge their overall happiness.

Table 5 reports the correlations between the measure of job satisfaction and the above indices of well-being. An overall scan of the table would suggest that our measure of job satisfaction does not bear a great deal of relationship to other measures of adjustment either in other life roles or in general feelings of well-being. There is very little correlation between job satisfaction, leisure spent in challenge, or in marital happiness in either survey. There was a significant positive relationship between feelings of happiness and job satisfaction for both sexes in each generation. Futhermore there seems to be some consistent trend for job satisfaction to be related to lack of symptoms across the generations although the patterns change somewhat from 1957 to 1976.

Table 5. Relationship (r) of Job Satisfaction to Other Nonjob Measures of Well-Being and Distress (by sex and year)

Measure of well-being/distress	Males		Females	
	1952 (N = 925)	1976 (N = 761)	1952 (N = 457)	1976 (N = 612)
Happiness	.16****	.14***	.15**	.11**
Marital happiness	.09*	.02	.07	.06
	(N = 813)	(N = 578)	(N = 262)	(N = 323)
Symptoms				
Psychological anxiety	−.12***	−.08*	−.21****	−.08*
Immobilization	−.15****	−.09**	−.03	−.14***
Ill-health	−.08*	−.11**	−.19****	.02
Drinking	−.06	−.09*	−.11*	−.05
Nervous breakdown feeling	−.07*	−.10**	−.13**	−.08
Leisure spent in challenge	.02	.06	.05	.00

$*p < .05$ $**p < .01$ $***p < .001$ $****p < .0001$.

Table 6. Relationship (r) of Job Satisfaction to Symptoms of Distress (by year, sex, and age)

			Symptoms			
Age	Year	N	Psychological anxiety	Immobilization	Ill-health	Drinking
Males						
21–34	1957	(291)	−.17**	−.16**	−.13*	.04
	1976	(318)	−.07	−.16**	−.13*	−.14**
35–54	1957	(413)	−.14**	−.11*	−.10*	−.09*
	1976	(282)	−.10	−.01	−.04	−.03
55+	1957	(185)	−.02	−.04	−.11	−.08
	1976	(154)	−.07	.04	−.27***	−.03
Females						
21–34	1957	(144)	−.18*	.04	−.08	−.04
	1976	(276)	−.10	−.11	.03	−.10
35–54	1957	(235)	−.18**	−.04	−.20**	−.15*
	1976	(220)	−.04	−.03	−.08	.07
55+	1957	(74)	−.31**	−.21	−.30**	−.30**
	1976	(111)	.05	−.24*	.00	.04

*$p < .05$ **$p < .01$ ***$p < .001$.

Table 6 further amplifies the results about symptoms by presenting a control by age for men and women in each of the years. What we find in that analysis is that in 1976 more young men are drinking if dissatisfied with their jobs than were their counterparts in 1957. Mangione and Quinn (1975) have found parallel results about drug use at work. In 1976 we also had a measure of whether one takes drugs to relieve tension. Indeed young men who were job-dissatisfied in 1976 were also more likely to say they took drugs to relive tension. Thus among the young men in 1976 job dissatisfaction is associated with retreating kinds of symptoms. The more they express disgruntlement with their work, the more they are involved in both drinking and in using drugs, both of which may be interpreted as passive coping mechanisms. These results are descriptive of young men at each of the educational levels when we instituted that control.

In Table 6 we can also see that older women in 1976 were not reporting ill-health or drinking as much when dissatisfied with their jobs as did their counterparts in 1957. The same trends exist for middle-aged women. Perhaps these data can be understood by a demographic analysis of the 1957 and 1976 older work force. In addition a more psychological interpretation of this change is provocative to consider. To be job-dissatisfied may not be as disruptive to a sense of personal well-being for middle-aged or older "career women" in 1976 as it was in 1957. Job dissatisfaction among women may now be openly expressed as a political *collective* problem for women. There may have been much more self-attribution for difficulties experienced at work in 1957 than there is now, the kind of attribution which could affect women's perceived health and might even drive them to drink. Career women today undoubtedly have personally benefited from the articulation of women's special problems in the sexist world of work.

Special attention should be drawn to the lack of correlation between job satisfaction and whether or not reported leisure activities are spent in challenging ways. If the hypothesis that leisure can compensate for job dissatisfaction is accurate, one might have expected a negative correlation. The fact that it was not suggests that the relationship between job adjustment and how one spends one's leisure time is not a simple one.

We did one special analysis for testing the compensatory hypothesis about the work–leisure relationship and found an important pattern of results, reported in Table 7. We asked the following: "If people who are dissatisfied with their job spend their time in challenging leisure activity, does this compensate enough to increase their overall sense of happiness?" We find some evidence for that to be so. We separately divided men and women into those who expressed job satisfaction and those who expressed some job dissatisfaction. Then within each of those two groups we broke them into two subgroups: those whose leisure included challenging activities or those whose leisure did not. We looked at the reported level of happiness for each of the four groups of men and women. What we found is that job satisfaction seems to be the critical variable in relating to overall happiness *whether or not* one spends one's leisure time in challenging ways. For men and women, the two groups who are job-satisfied are the ones who report the highest degree of happiness. However, if people are job-dissatisfied and spend time in challenging leisure activities, then they report a higher level of happiness than those who do not spend time in challenging leisure activities. It is almost as if leisure is a buffer between job dissatisfaction and overall feelings of discontent. Although people may be unhappy if they are not satisfied with their jobs, what they do in their leisure time can keep them from falling into low depths of discontent. In these analyses, however, we have no evidence that this buffering effect of leisure is any stronger in 1976 than it was in 1957.

ARE PEOPLE WHO WORK PSYCHOLOGICALLY DIFFERENT FROM PEOPLE WHO DO NOT? Another approach to assessing the salience of work in American society in 1957 and 1976 was to analyze the comparative adjustments of people who were working compared to those who were not

Table 7. Interaction of Job Satisfaction and Leisure Spent in Challenge to Overall Happiness (by year and sex)

			Patterns of job satisfaction/leisure spent in challenge			
Year	Sex	Happiness	Job satisfaction high/leisure spent in challenge	Job satisfaction high/leisure not spent in challenge	Job satisfaction low/leisure spent in challenge	Job satisfaction low/leisure not spent in challenge
1957	Males (N = 787) (χ^2 = 24.21, p < .001, 6 df)	Very happy	38%	45%	28%	12%
		Pretty happy	56%	50%	65%	72%
		Not too happy	6%	5%	7%	16%
			100% (N = 503)	100% (N = 76)	100% (N = 156)	100% (N = 49)
	Females (N = 376) (χ^2 = 24.98, p < .001, 6 df)	Very happy	40%	41%	32%	18%
		Pretty happy	50%	43%	57%	44%
		Not too happy	10%	16%	11%	38%
			100% (N = 230)	100% (N = 58)	100% (N = 54)	100% (N = 34)
1976	Males (N = 658) (χ^2 = 22.15, p < .001, 6 df)	Very happy	35%	40%	24%	18%
		Pretty happy	60%	53%	66%	61%
		Not too happy	5%	7%	10%	20%
			100% (N = 434)	100% (N = 43)	100% (N = 132)	100% (N = 49)
	Females (N = 511) (χ^2 = 15.00, p < .02, 6 df)	Very happy	36%	38%	32%	18%
		Pretty happy	58%	53%	56%	60%
		Not too happy	7%	9%	12%	22%
			100% (N = 290)	100% (N = 58)	100% (N = 114)	100% (N = 49)

working. For men this generally meant contrasting working men with those who retired. When we set up tables to analyze these differences, we soon realized that there was a big difference between retired men and working men at the various ages on their reported ill-health symptoms, and when we controlled for ill-health there was too little variance left in other measures for those who retired to test any differences between working and nonworking men. (One digression should be mentioned in our attempts to get an analysis of working and nonworking men. We found that there was a large increase in the number of retired men in the age bracket 35–55 in 1976 compared to 1957. There were nearly seven times as many retired men in that bracket in 1976 compared to 1957. These retired men were nearly all men who reported some kind of physical health trouble. It might very well be that the increased potential for getting medical disabilities and workmen's compensation from companies might increase the tendency for men in that age group to withdraw from the work setting by attending to both serious and minor physical complaints. This might have been further enhanced in 1976 if retirement as a general life status has become more attractive, if for no other reason than that there are many more men in that status now than a generation ago. If this line of reasoning is accurate, there is a strong possibility that men who find the work role at all distasteful can more easily fall into conscious or unconscious ploys for early retirement than did comparable men in 1957.)

Generational changes in the comparison between working women and full-time housewives were explored using the same set of variables that we used to correlate with job satisfaction in prior tables. In these explorations we found little difference between working women and full-time housewives both in 1957 and in 1976 on a variety of indices of adjustment, except for their differential reactions to marriage and their differential report of physical symptoms.

We did find a consistent difference between the reported marital happiness of working women versus housewives in 1957 contrasted to 1976. These results are reported in Table 8, where we contrast working and nonworking women of each year, controlling on age. We find that working women in 1976 seemed to be consistently happier in their marriage than working women in 1957. When controlling for age we find that the younger working wives in 1976 report their marriages as being "average" or "not too happy" quite a bit less often than did the working women of 1957. In the older age groups working women in 1976 report "very happy" marriages more often than do working women in 1957. These differences are confirmed when the additional control of education is introduced. Although the housewives in both 1957 and 1976

Table 8. Relationship of Reported Happiness in Marriage by Working versus Nonworking Women in 1957 and 1976 (by age)

				Reported happiness in marriage		
Age	Year	Working status	(N)	Very happy	Happier than average	Average; not too happy
21–34	1957	Working	(89)	45%	10%	45%[a]
		Nonworking	(279)	50%	22%	28%
	1976	Working	(151)	49%	32%	19%[a]
		Nonworking	(152)	57%	21%	22%
35–54	1957	Working	(151)	44%[a]	24%	32%
		Nonworking	(283)	46%	20%	34%
	1976	Working	(134)	54%[a]	24%	22%
		Nonworking	(139)	45%	26%	29%
55–64	1957	Working	(19)	32%[a]	26%	42%
		Nonworking	(85)	35%	17%	48%
	1976	Working	(23)	61%[a]	17%	22%
		Nonworking	(63)	48%	33%	19%

[a]Differences consistent across all educational levels except for middle-aged, grade-school-educated women.

show some similar differences, none represents consistent differences at all educational levels.

What do these results add up to? We would suggest that being a working woman in 1976 has more positive implications for her marital role than it did in 1957. It does not necessarily mean that she will have a happier marriage than a woman who does not work in 1976, but it does mean that if she chooses to work in 1976 she has less personal concern about what that will do to her marriage than she had in 1957. This all suggests that, compared to a generation ago, being a working wife now gives a woman a greater sense of being a resource for her marriage. It may be that more women in 1957 were worried that their working raised questions about their husband's competence or masculinity.

The other results worth noting in the contrast of working and non-working women is that working women at all ages were lower in their reported ill-health than nonworking women. This seems like a trivial result, but it does bear on an important issue in research on sex differences. Many studies have puzzled over the result that we also find in our sample: women on the average report a much higher incidence of physical complaints than men. Some of the general hypotheses that have been offered for this result are:

off

1. Men's greater involvement in being primary wage earners makes them deny or not attend to physical symptoms that might signify their incapacity to work.
2. Housewives' work never being done, women experience more overall strain from their assigned role than wage earners who focus their responsibilities in their specific hours of employment.
3. Housewives are in a role that permits them to focus their attention on matters other than their ongoing activities; it permits them to think about the state of their health more than most men do.

The previously stated explanations for sex differences in incidence of physical symptoms may also be used to explain why working women report a lower incidence of ill-health than do housewives. Working may encourage women to deny symptoms in order to preserve their wage-earning capacity. Working may relieve the strain of having incessant household responsibilities. Working may shift women's focus away from their own concerns, including their physical state. Using any of these interpretations to help us account for why working women are lower in ill-health than housewives, and predicting that the number of women becoming wage earners will continue to grow, we might foresee some reversals in the differential mortality rates customarily found between men and women. While women report more symptoms than do men, they also live longer. If there is any connection between attending to symptoms and living longer, and if women, when they become wage earners, attend to symptoms less, then one might expect women's lifespan to narrow relative to men's. On the other hand if working actually reduces the strain of the housewife role, then we might predict that women's lifespan will increase relative to men's. Perhaps both expectations may be true, one for one group of men and women and another for a different group.

Summary. We have no definitive data to explicate what "not working" means to Americans in 1957 and 1976. All we know about men who are not working is that they are not physically healthy. Perhaps because of the widening of coverage of medical disabilities and workmen's compensation we may have many more men who retreat into perceiving themselves as being physically unhealthy as a way to pull out of work roles that are satisfying. In contrast we have some evidence that working may preserve women's perception of their own health, both in 1957 and 1976. The most provocative result, however, was the increased sense of marital happiness found in working married women in 1976 compared to their counterparts in 1957. The impact of women's working on marriage has evidently shifted for the whole society; it does make working a much more viable alternative for women today than it did a generation ago.

Has There Been a Change in the Salience of the Housewife Role for Full-Time Housewives? The increased viability of working for marital happiness found in the 1976 working women's reactions raises an interesting question about the comparative salience of housework for women in our society. In both years we asked full-time housewives how much satisfaction they got out of housework aside from taking care of children (see Appendix B). In Table 9 we present the percentage of housewives in each year who expressed a liking for housework. It seemed important to us in this particular analysis to pay particular attention to the simultaneous controls for education and age. This table is very impressive in showing the general increased dissatisfaction with full-time housework for full-time housewives from 1957 to 1976. Overall there has been a 13% drop in expressed satisfaction from housework from 69% to 56%. Moreover when education is controlled we can note that the drop is particularly striking for college-educated women at each age level. There are similar trends for high school–educated women, but no difference in expressed satisfaction from housework for grade

Table 9. Percentages of Full-Time Housewives Expressing Liking for Housework (by education, age, and year)

		1957		1976	
Educational level	Age	% expressing liking for housework	(N)	% expressing liking for housework	(N)
Grade school	21–34	69	(32)	83	(6)
	35–54	78	(89)	83	(18)
	55+	75	(161)	75	(92)
	Total	75	(282)	76	(116)
High school	21–34	62	(211)	46	(94)
	35–54	66	(167)	53	(91)
	55+	77	(78)	67	(84)
	Total	66	(456)	55	(269)
College	21–34	63	(49)	32	(50)
	35–54	65	(52)	40	(30)
	55+	81	(16)	52	(33)
	Total	67	(117)	40	(113)
Across all educational levels:	21–34	63	(292)	43	(150)
	35–54	69	(308)	54	(139)
	55+	76	(255)	68	(209)
	Total	69	(855)	56	(498)

school–educated women interviewed at these different times. Therefore the general increased dissatisfaction with housework seems to be the result of the increased education of women in the adult population. Associated with higher education in women seems to be an increased discontent with maintaining a full-time housewife role. Although it is difficult to do a cohort analysis of full-time housewives because those women who are full-time housewives in the younger ages in 1957 are not necessarily going to be the same who were full-time housewives at a later period, we can approximate one. Let us assume that the youngest group in 1957 corresponds more or less to the middle-aged group in 1976, and the middle-aged group in 1957 corresponds more or less to the older age group in 1976. Looking at these across-time comparisons, one can see that there has not been so much of a shift from 1957 to 1976 in the liking of housework *within* a cohort. The shift seems to be primarily in the younger generation of 1976 women, who are relatively discontended with housework. The older generation of women in both years are very content with the housewife role. They perhaps remain the women most committed to housework because they saw or actually had so few other options for their time. Among young women, especially in 1976, however, not only has housework become a less valued way of defining one's work in the society, but becoming a wage earner has become a more valid one.

HAS THE SALIENCE OF LEISURE AS AN ARENA FOR CHALLENGE CHANGED? Another way to think about the shift in the meaning of work is to examine the shift in the capacity of leisure to engage Americans' sense of challenge. In Table 10 we present the comparisons of men's and women's mentioning challenging leisure time activities in response to an open question about how they spend their time (see Appendix B for a full description of that measure). In that table we also control for age and education simultaneously. In these analyses we are only looking at people who are employed. What is remarkable about this table is the general lack of change there seems to be in whether workers spend their leisure in challenging activities. There are two groups that appear to show some trends for change. One group is older men, who show some increase in use of leisure for challenging activities. We found that true for all older men, regardless of their educational level. The other group is younger women, who are spending more time in challenging leisure activities than their counterparts in 1957. When we control for education within the younger group of women, we find this particularly true for high school–educated women. College-educated women by and large were high in the use of challenge in leisure activities in both 1957 and 1976. Thus the group that was showing change was high school–educated women.

Table 10. 1957–1976 Comparisons of Percentages of Working People Participating in Challenging Leisure Activities (by sex, age, and education)

	1957		1976	
	(N)	%	%	(N)
By sex				
Males	(924)	73	76	(753)
Females	(457)	63	67	(599)
By sex and education				
Males				
Grade school	(282)	66	62	(71)
High school	(423)	77	78	(346)
College	(214)	73	77	(335)
Females				
Grade school	(117)	55	52	(48)
High school	(249)	61	65	(341)
College	(87)	80	74	(210)
By sex and age				
Males				
21–34	(292)	82	74	(315)
35–44	(237)	70	78	(165)
45–54	(208)	69	75	(116)
55+	(185)	66	76	(157)
Females				
21–34	(144)	58	76	(269)
35–44	(127)	66	58	(111)
45–54	(108)	65	67	(109)
55+	(74)	62	57	(109)

The results for older men are quite interesting in that they probably demonstrate that working men are preparing for retirement more in 1976 than they were in 1957. Perhaps older working men can anticipate retirement better and realize that they have to be spending their leisure time activities *before* retirement doing challenging things so that the transition to retirement will go smoothly. It is as if they were taking seriously Simone de Beauvoir's (1972) main message in *Coming of Age*.

The results for the younger women are also interesting, and perhaps speak of a growing awareness within the young at lower levels of educational attainment that leisure may be their route for fulfillment of achievement aspirations. Young men were high in uses of leisure for challenge in both years, but showed a consistent decline in each of the educational levels. As a result one might suggest that high school—

educated women are catching up with their male counterparts in pursuing leisure as a means of fulfilling self-mastery interests.

In both years men report doing more challenging things in their leisure than women do. Although college men and women are generally similar in reported leisure spent in challenging activities, men at the lower educational levels clearly report more challenging activities in their leisure than women. This general sex difference in the use of leisure time for challenging activities is corroborated in our 1976 data by a question that we asked men and women: How much free time do you spend doing challenging things? (See Appendix C.) We found that 42% of working men said that they spend "most" or "a lot" of their free time doing challenging things while only 31% of working women say they spend their time that way (see Table 11). Furthermore, it is interesting to explore how working women and full-time housewives compare on their feelings of spending their free time in challenging ways. More employed women than full-time housewives see their free time as spent in challenging ways: 32% of working women report that they spend their free time in challenging ways "most" or "a lot" of the time; 23% of full-time housewives report that they spend their free time that way. Controls for marital status and age did not appreciably affect this contrast. For women, a job may enable them to demarcate their "free time" more clearly than full-time housewives. Full-time housewives' use of the day in what they see as their "responsibilities" may merge a great deal with what they think their "free time" is. As a result they probably see less of their free time as spent in activities that they consider challenging but more of it in activities they see as responsibilities incurred by their

Table 11. Percentage of Men and Women in 1976 Who Report Spending "Most" or "A Lot" of Their Free Time Doing Challenging Things (by various marital and employment statuses, 1976 only)

	Men		Women	
	(N)	%	(N)	%
Working				
Married	(574)	42	(315)	31
Single	(95)	50	(84)	33
Housewives (married)	—	—	(361)	23
Retired				
Married	(101)	27	(34)	18
Single	(15)	13	(14)	36

household role. There was very little difference between working women and full-time housewives in how much of their leisure time they *actually* said they spent in so-called challenging activities. As a result the differences in perceived experience of challenge in leisure represents critical differences in how working women and housewives orient themselves to what they are experiencing as "free time."

THE SALIENCE OF VARIOUS LIFE ROLES FOR FULFILLING LIFE VALUES. When Shelia Feld and I were writing *Marriage and Work in America* (1970) and were contrasting people's reactions to marriage, work, and parenthood, we constantly regretted that we had not asked men and women to tell us directly what the relevant salience of these life roles was for them. In the 1976 survey we did introduce such questions and they produced some interesting results for the 1976 data. Unfortunately we cannot contrast these data to parallel responses in the 1957 sample. Nevertheless I think it would be instructive to introduce these data in our discussions of the changing salience of work role even if they only describe the 1976 sample. These data summarize how the 1976 population evaluates the potential of each of their life roles for fulfilling major life values.

We first asked our respondents in 1976 to pick a critical life value from their list of 10 values: sense of belonging, excitement, warm relations with others, self-fulfillment, being well respected, fun and enjoyment in life, security, self-respect, and sense of accomplishment (see Appendix C). Some of these life values were selected from Rokeach's work on the study of values (Rokeach, 1973). Our criterion for selecting these values was that they be general enough so that they could be seen as relevant to any life role and not just one or two. We used this criterion because we then asked each respondent to judge how much each of five life roles (leisure, work around the house, job, marriage, parenthood) fulfilled the major value that they selected (see Appendix C). For those not currently in a given role (e.g., widows/widowers or single people, with respect to marriage) we asked either how *did* or how *would* that role fulfill their value. For each analysis we combined some of the values into a more general value position. Thus we ended up with five primary values that our respondents could be identified with: sociability (sense of belonging and warm relations with others); hedonism (excitement, and fun and enjoyment in life); self-actualization (self-fulfillment, and sense of accomplishment); moral respect (being well-respected and self-respect); and security. In this chapter we are interested in how people perceive work in contrast to other life roles as fulfilling their values.

Tables 12, 13, 14, and 15 permit us to answer questions about how respondents perceive life roles as fulfilling major values differentiating people according to which primary value they selected. Tables 12 and 13

Table 12. Married Working Fathers' Evaluation of How Much Five Life Roles Lead to Fulfillment of Primary Value Orientation[a] (by age and value orientation)

				Role			
Primary value	Age	N	Leisure	Work in house	Job	Marriage	Parenthood
Sociability	21–39	(42)	19%	17%	29%	48%	60%
	40+	(43)	28%	28%	40%	58%	60%
Hedonism	21–39	(20)	30%	10%	30%	50%	60%
	40+	(8)	25%	12%	50%	88%	87%
Self-actualization	21–39	(64)	17%	25%	41%	41%	52%
	40+	(59)	33%	28%	56%	25%	67%
Moral respect	21–39	(55)	22%	11%	44%	47%	47%
	40+	(102)	18%	13%	50%	51%	55%
Security	21–39	(54)	7%	9%	52%	46%	48%
	40+	(50)	18%	10%	60%	44%	36%
Total (across values)	21–39	(235)	17%	15%	41%	46%	53%
	40+	(263)	23%	18%	52%	57%	56%

[a]Percent of people of a given value orientation who report that a given life role leads to that value orientation "a great deal."

Table 13. Married Working Mothers' Evaluations of How Much Five Life Roles Lead to Fulfillment of Primary Value Orientation[a] (by age and value orientation)

				Role			
Primary value	Age	N	Leisure	Work in house	Job	Marriage	Parenthood
Sociability	21–39	(40)	25%	25%	20%	68%	70%
	40+	(32)	22%	9%	3%	62%	75%
Hedonism	21–39	(4)	0%	0%	0%	25%	25%
	40+	(2)	0%	0%	0%	50%	100%
Self-actualization	21–39	(25)	16%	8%	24%	52%	52%
	40+	(19)	37%	42%	47%	79%	84%
Moral respect	21–39	(35)	23%	20%	29%	51%	65%
	40+	(43)	23%	16%	30%	51%	51%
Security	21–39	(25)	4%	12%	24%	48%	64%
	40+	(29)	3%	21%	38%	52%	48%
Total (across values)	21–39	(129)	18%	17%	23%	55%	63%
	40+	(125)	20%	19%	34%	58%	62%

[a]Percent of people of a given value orientation who report that a given life role leads to that value orientation "a great deal."

Table 14. Men's Evaluation of How Much Five Life Roles Lead to Fulfillment of Primary Value Orientation[a] (by value orientation and age)

| | | All men | | | | All workers (Job) | | All married people (Marriage) | | All parents (Parenthood) | |
| | | (Leisure) | | (Work in house) | | | | | | | |
Primary value	Age	N	%	N	%	N	%	N	%	N	%
Sociability	21–39	86	22	86	15	79	24	55	45	52	60
	40+	90	31	90	24	57	37	70	57	77	62
Hedonism	21–39	44	39	44	14	36	22	34	53	27	52
	40+	21	29	21	19	11	36	15	73	17	65
Self-actualization	21–39	139	17	139	19	127	33	85	38	73	47
	40+	86	34	86	28	68	54	70	74	75	67
Moral respect	21–39	95	20	95	10	90	38	69	45	62	45
	40+	190	22	190	17	135	51	150	50	165	56
Security	21–39	83	10	83	7	75	49	62	45	65	48
	40+	111	14	111	16	69	55	78	51	87	38
Total (across values)	21–39	447	20	447	14	407	34	305	44	279	50
	40+	498	24	498	25	340	31	383	57	421	56

[a]Percent of people of a given value orientation who report that a given life role leads to that value orientation "a great deal."

Table 15. Women's Evaluations of How Much Five Life Roles Lead to Fulfillment of Primary Value Orientation[a] (by value orientation and age)

| Primary value | Age | All women | | | | All workers (Job) | | All married people (Marriage) | | All parents (Parenthood) | |
| | | (Leisure) | | (Work in house) | | | | | | | |
		N	%	N	%	N	%	N	%	N	%
Sociability	21–39	154	21	154	18	85	26	113	61	111	67
	40+	203	31	203	19	67	27	111	60	173	75
Hedonism	21–39	24	33	24	4	16	6	16	56	11	46
	40+	11	29	1	0	4	0	8	38	11	91
Self-actualization	21–39	157	19	157	12	89	35	96	43	90	58
	40+	84	34	84	26	40	55	51	49	70	70
Moral respect	21–39	129	24	129	16	80	34	92	46	95	57
	40+	153	22	252	22	92	41	123	50	221	57
Security	21–39	95	7	95	16	55	34	56	61	74	57
	40+	171	14	171	21	66	38	72	58	144	50
Total (across values)	21–39	559	20	559	15	325	31	363	53	381	58
	40+	722	24	722	21	269	38	365	54	619	62

[a]Percent of people of a given value orientation who report that a given life role leads to that value orientation "a great deal."

include only respondents who are in all three roles of marriage, parenthood, and work; Table 12 is for married working fathers and Table 13 for married working mothers. Tables 14 and 15 look at a larger set of respondents. In Table 14 we used as sample bases: all men's evaluation of the leisure role and work around the house; all working men's evaluation of the job role; all married men's evaluation of marriage; and all fathers' evaluation of the parent role. Table 15 is a parallel table for women. In all of these tables we introduced age as a control and in addition computed how each of the life roles is perceived to fulfill life values regardless of the specific value orientation. These tables can be used for many many comparisons; for this chapter we are only interested in the fate of work in these contexts.

For people in all three roles, work seems much more salient for men in fulfilling life values than it does for women. Indeed the job role is perceived as leading to people's primary value almost as much as marriage and parenthood do for most men. The only men for whom a job does not come close to these other roles are those who identify sociability or hedonism as their primary life values. It is clear that for men who hold all three roles, their jobs are much more critical than their leisure in fulfilling their life values. It is also clear that older men in 1976 perceived their jobs as fulfilling their values much more than did younger men. This age contrast is also true of other roles. It is impossible to ascertain whether this is a generational or a developmental change in the perceived value of roles. Our guess is that it is a developmental shift from seeing value fulfillment in more personalized terms when one is young to seeing it in more social terms when old. But personalism has been a style of life presumably more characteristic of the new generation of young people in the 1960s and 1970s. It will be instructive to pursue these different interpretations of this age difference in other analyses in the future.

What about women? Married working mothers evaluate their jobs as contributing to life values a little more than their leisure or work around the house, but certainly a lot less than their marriages and their parent role. And again, older women perceive their job role as fulfilling their life values more than younger women.

When we move on to Tables 14 and 15 to explore the larger set of people who are in each of those roles, there are some interesting new trends in the results. One finding is that the job fulfills the value of security for men much more clearly than any other value. Indeed those who select security as a major life value find that the job fulfills that value just as much as marriage and parenthood do. A second trend occurs in older men: their job fulfills the value of moral respect as much as marriage and parenthood do. A third trend is that the larger group of employed women, represented in Table 15 under the job role, evaluate the job role much more highly for fulfilling primary values than do working women who are also married mothers (Table 13). This is true regardless of which value is selected by these women. This result suggests that as women experience the explicitly feminine roles of wife and mother, they are less likely to see the work role as *the* one that fulfills their major life value. The exact opposite tended to be true when we contrasted men who were in all three roles with all men working. That is, men who were in all three roles tended to rate the job more highly in fulfilling primary values than the larger group of men who were employed. One might conclude that being married and having children accentuated the importance of work in fulfilling life values. Perhaps married fathers look at their work as having more significance for other people in their lives, and thus they view work with greater value generally. As more and more married working mothers work as a means to keep their family incomes at a level that is acceptable for a moderate standard of living, then they too might begin to see stronger connection of their jobs to their values.

This analysis tends to corroborate a generalization we have been drawing from previous analyses in this section, and that is that the work role is still relatively salient for men and women in 1976, especially in contrast to the leisure role. Work is clearly not as important as family roles for both men and women. This generalization has to be tempered by two factors: men with values on security and moral respect tend to evaluate their job role very highly; men who are married fathers especially tend to value the role. These facts suggest that to the degree to which men see their job role as enhancing their validity for a family (giving security and maintaining moral respect), the job remains a very salient role for men in our society.

In contrast, women who are working as an adjunct to their family roles do not see their jobs as being as important as do working women who are either not married or do not have children or who are neither married nor have children. One might suggest that in the future the job role will become a particularly salient role for women who explicitly take nontraditional choices about marriage and raising children. More important will be further analyses with these data to see whether we can separate married mothers who work out of perceived necessity from those who have explicitly selected the work role as a desired role. The salience of work for fulfilling values could be different for these two groups. Married women who work out of financial necessity could come to value work as fulfilling primary values just because it is a *necessary* family activity. Furthermore, women who do not work out of financial necessity could be defensive about their choice to work in the shadows of dominant family roles and might tend to minimize the value of work for primary values.

SUMMARY OF CHANGES IN THE SALIENCE OF WORK: 1957–1976. What significance should we attach to all these different ways of viewing the salience of work in America in 1976 contrasted to 1957? Overall, it would be hard to say that the meaning of work has drastically changed. Job satisfaction in 1976 correlates with happiness and lack of symptoms of distress in about the same way that the measure did in 1957. Job satisfaction seems to have little to do with marital happiness in both years. Further, involvement with leisure has not changed much, although in both years it seems to be a compensatory arena for achievement for some people who are dissatisfied with work. Just holding a job seems to be a state of being that has changed in meaning in certain groups. Older men in 1976 seem to be preparing for their leisure through retirement more than they did in 1957 as if the critical necessity of holding the job has lost its force for them as they see more people successfully retire and use their leisure effectively. Younger men in 1976 seem more likely to use passive styles of defenses for coping with job difficulties (drinking and use of drugs) than their counterparts did in 1957. Thus we have some hints of withdrawal from work as a focus of active struggle for young men. Perhaps this is so because work has become an arena of more negative involvement (worries) without becoming an arena of increased fulfillment (happiness).

Contrariwise, many women seem to be getting some positive general benefits from work, more so in 1976 than in 1957. Working now seems less correlated with their sense of disrupted marriages; being dissatisfied with a job seems less correlated with women's reports of ill-health and drinking in 1976 than in 1957. Perhaps women over the generation have learned to be actively involved with the meaning of work in their lives. Young women these days are more likely to mention jobs as a source of worries than did comparable groups in 1957. This increased involvement with work dovetails with what seems to be a clear disenchantment with being a housewife. As housework has lost its appeal, there has not only been a greater interest in work for one's self-gratification but also a greater involvement in leisure time for seeking challenges.

Work in 1976 has not become a bed of roses for women. With their increased involvement there has come an increased tendency for women to mention work as a source of unhappiness, and, like men, no increased tendency to mention work as a source of happiness. As the work role has become a more deliberate choice for more women, at a time of sex-role transition, the negative features of working perhaps become better articulated than the positive features.

Men who are involved in all three roles—marriage, work, and parenthood—seem to place a special emphasis on the work role. The work role seems to be pivotal for them in their coordination with their other roles. For women who are in all three roles, work seems less salient than for women who are not experiencing all three roles simultaneously. It is as though women who work and who are simultaneously mothers and wives have a slightly different perspective on the meaning of work. For those who are missing at least one of the family roles, work evidently takes on greater significance. Nevertheless it is important to bear in mind that for all men and women, family roles seem much more salient, work roles a poor second, with leisure and work-around-the-house roles holding up the rear. How we wished we had parallel data in 1957 to discover whether this hierarchy of role salience had shifted over the generation.

CHANGES IN REACTIONS TO JOBS: 1957–1976

In both years we asked working people a series of questions that examined their reactions to the particular jobs they were in. In this series we tried to get at different facets of how people react to their work: the extent of job satisfaction, types of satisfactions and dissatisfactions experienced, perceived adequacy in one's work, perceived requirements of one's job, the nature of any experienced work problems, whether workers would prefer another job, and how committed they were to working if they did not need the money. The types of measures we evolved, the specific questions that we used as the basis for these measures, and the codes we developed are reported in Appendix A. Needless to say, for some of the qualitative codes that we used, theoretical assumptions about the significance of work are involved. Some of the variables thus represent a distillation of discussions in our research group about the meaning of certain responses. For example, a typical response to the questions of what people like about their work is "it's interesting." A question about coding this response arises: Should we say that this response signifies involvement with achievement or with some more general intrinsic interest in work? The linkage between curiosity and achievement-based incentives in work has not been clearly established. We therefore decided to keep such responses separate from responses which had a clearer achievement connotation (e.g., "I get a sense of accomplishment"). This differentiation became important in our analysis of change, as it turns out. I have presented this example as a reminder to the reader that many subtle distinctions about how to categorize responses were involved in our behind-the-scenes work. Our analyses therefore summarize many implicit theroretical ideas.

Table 16 presents the comparison of the 1957 and 1976 working

Table 16. Job Reactions in 1957 and 1976 Compared (by sex)

Job reaction	Males 1957	Males 1976	Females 1957	Females 1976
Satisfaction				
Very satisfied	28%	27%	37%	30%
Satisfied	48%	47%	41%	42%
Neutral	5%	5%	5%	4%
Ambivalent	9%	8%	8%	10%
Dissatisfied	8%	12%	8%	13%
NA	2%	1%	1%	1%
	100%	100%	100%	100%
	N = (925)	(761)	(457)	(611)
Types of job satisfaction				
Economic	17%	14%	13%	12%
Extrinsic—noneconomic	26%	20%	18%	20%
Achievement-related	17%	30%	11%	22%
Affiliation-related (general)	18%	22%	34%	38%
Specific people	16%	12%	26%	22%
Power-related	14%	22%	9%	10%
Interesting work	33%	22%	29%	20%
	N = (925)	(761)	(457)	(611)
Type of job dissatisfaction				
Economic	18%	14%	10%	11%
Extrinsic—noneconomic	31%	28%	29%	22%
General: hard work	12%	13%	12%	13%
Lack of achievement potential	6%	8%	4%	9%
Affiliative lack or problem	10%	19%	12%	20%
Lack of power at work	4%	10%	4%	5%
	N = (925)	(761)	(457)	(611)
Prefer other job?				
Percentage yes	38%	49%	44%	48%
	N = (924)	(763)	(300)	(612)
Work commitment				
Achievement commitment	4%	12%	1%	10%
Affiliative commitment	2%	3%	8%	10%
"Work as habit" commitment	2%	3%	2%	2%
Moralistic commitment	9%	8%	3%	4%
Time use commitment	55%	43%	27%	24%
Escape from home commitment	1%	1%	3%	8%

(*continued*)

Table 16.   (*Continued*)

Job reaction	Males		Females	
	1957	1976	1957	1976
General liking				
commitment	10%	9%	8%	13%
No commitment to work	15%	16%	42%	23%
	N = (924)	(763)	(301)	(612)
Perceived job requirement				
A lot (of ability)	39%	54%	—[a]	44%
Some, little, not much,				
none	35%	32%	—[a]	36%
NA, DK	26%	14%	—[a]	20%
	100%	100%	—[a]	100%
	N = (313)	(763)	—[a]	(612)
Feelings of job adequacy				
Very good	55%	64%	—[a]	58%
> average	23%	16%	—[a]	30%
Average	16%	15%	—[a]	1%
Not very good	2%	2%	—[a]	<1%
NA	4%	3%	—[a]	<1%
	100%	100%	—[a]	100%
	N = (925)	(761)	—[a]	(611)
Work problem?				
No problem	73%	59%	—[a]	71%
Problem in self	11%	17%	—[a]	11%
Problem in relationship at				
work	3%	4%	—[a]	5%
Problem in situation, or				
other person	11%	14%	—[a]	10%
General problem	2%	6%	—[a]	3%
NA	<1%	<1%	—[a]	0%
	100%	100%	—[a]	100%
	N = (925)	(761)	—[a]	(611)

[a]Question was not asked of working women in 1957.

population's reactions to their jobs. In that table we compare women and men separately in the two generations and simply ask if there has been any shift in how men or women react to their jobs on the variables we have designated.[4] With such large sample sizes, small percentage

[4]As an aside, we should note that all comparisons are not possible for women since (I am embarrassed to say) as social researchers in 1957, we did not feel it important to examine the work role for women very intensively.

differences are significant.[5] Let us isolate the ones that seem important. In subsequent tables (Tables 17–20), we will examine only job reactions that do change, and try to estimate what effect the variables of a person's social status (educational level) and age have on understanding the changes that we emphasize. In future papers we will also control for psychological dimensions of the structure of one's job, as Kohn and Schooler (1973) so impressively did. Kohn and Schooler clearly show how certain dimensions of work (e.g., substantive complexity, frequency of time pressure, bureaucratization, risk of loss) have very clear impacts on psychological functioning.

What did we discover from examining Table 16? In what follows we will highlight our findings for each type of job reaction. Overall, the shifts that do occur seem to occur generally for both men and for women. There are some changes that seem clearer for one sex or the other, but the overall pattern seems to be descriptive of both male and female workers.

JOB SATISFACTION. While there are only some light shifts in overall evaluation of job satisfaction over the generation, with both men and women showing some slight tendency to be more dissatisfied in 1976 than they were in 1957, there are clear shifts in what qualities about working are mentioned as sources of satisfaction and dissatisfaction with work. Particularly, there seems to be a rise in how much people mentioned achievement types of satisfactions in work in 1976, compared to 1957. (Men also show an increase in reported power satisfactions from work.) Furthermore all workers seem to be reporting *fewer* satisfactions that reflect their feeling that they are doing "interesting work." Thus while workers as a whole are *increasing* their involvement with achievement satisfactions at work, they seem to be *decreasing* their involvement with the interest of work for its own sake.

When we follow up these results about satisfaction in Tables 17–20, where we can control for age and education within each sex, we find that the slight decrease in satisfaction among people over the generation is largely attributable to the growing dissatisfaction among *older* men and among the younger, more educated women in the current work force. The shift in reporting satisfaction at work from merely being interested in one's work to a more articulated achievement satisfaction is true for both sexes at all age levels and at all education levels, but it is most evident in both the college-educated men's and women's responses. Thus the more educated over the generation especially seem to

---

[5]We are about to apply log-linear analyses to all contingency tables to estimate significant effects of year, sex, and age (and their interactions), in addition to other independent variables like social status or occupational groupings.

Table 17. Selected 1957 versus 1976 Comparisons of Men's Job Reactions (by education)

Job reaction		Year	Grade school	High school	College
	(N)[a]	1957	(282)	(423)	(214)
		1976	(73)	(350)	(337)
Job satisfaction					
% Neutral,		1957	19%	27%	22%
Ambivalent, dissatisfied		1976	20%	27%	24%
Type of satisfaction					
Achievement-related		1957	10%	19%	26%
		1976	16%	24%	40%
Interesting work		1957	33%	31%	36%
		1976	25%	23%	20%
Type of dissatisfaction					
Lack of achievement		1957	3%	6%	12%
		1976	4%	5%	12%
Lack of affiliation		1957	8%	9%	13%
		1976	7%	15%	25%
Lack of power		1957	2%	5%	6%
		1976	4%	7%	16%
Prefer other job		1957	28%	43%	44%
% Yes		1976	38%	47%	55%
Work commitment					
Achievement commitment		1957	1%	2%	9%
		1976	3%	5%	23%
Time-use commitment		1957	47%	59%	58%
		1976	47%	50%	36%
No commitment		1957	16%	17%	11%
		1976	18%	17%	15%
Perceived job requirements					
	(N)[b]	1957	(100)	(137)	(74)
% a lot of ability required		1957	38%	37%	43%
		1976	40%	55%	56%
Feelings of job adequacy					
% very good		1957	31%	28%	35%
		1976	44%	47%	60%
Work problem?					
No problem		1957	79%	70%	63%
		1976	71%	62%	52%
Problem in self		1957	8%	11%	16%
		1976	12%	16%	20%

[a]Unless otherwise indicated, N refers to frequency for a given educational level for all cells.
[b]Frequencies for this measure are different.

Table 18. Selected 1957 versus 1976 Comparisons of Men's Job Reactions (by age)

Job reaction		Year	Age			
			21–34	35–44	45–54	55+
(N)[a]		1957	(292)	(237)	(208)	(185)
		1976	(319)	(168)	(116)	(158)
Job satisfaction						
Neutral, ambivalent,		1957	29%	26%	21%	13%
dissatisfied		1976	30%	24%	17%	22%
Type of satisfaction						
Achievement-related		1957	17%	17%	18%	18%
		1976	28%	30%	41%	27%
Interesting work		1957	32%	35%	36%	28%
		1976	21%	21%	22%	25%
Type of dissatisfaction						
Lack of achievement		1957	9%	6%	6%	3%
		1976	12%	7%	5%	4%
Lack of affiliation		1957	11%	15%	4%	7%
		1976	19%	22%	16%	16%
Lack of power		1957	4%	5%	5%	4%
		1976	12%	6%	15%	7%
Prefer other job?		1957	51%	43%	28%	25%
% Yes		1976	67%	57%	33%	24%
Work commitment						
Achievement commitment		1957	5%	3%	1%	4%
		1976	17%	12%	10%	7%
Time-use commitment		1957	59%	58%	50%	49%
		1976	40%	49%	46%	40%
No commitment		1957	15%	4%	18%	14%
		1976	17%	16%	12%	18%
Perceived job requirements						
(N)[a,b]		1957	(87)	(95)	(68)	(61)
% a lot of ability required		1957	36%	42%	44%	43%
		1976	52%	50%	59%	57%
Feelings of job adequacy						
% very good		1957	28%	30%	35%	31%
		1976	50%	54%	59%	51%
Work problem						
No problem		1957	62%	67%	77%	83%
		1976	50%	60%	62%	73%
Problem in self		1957	16%	12%	7%	7%
		1976	21%	15%	16%	15%

[a]Unless otherwise indicated, N refers to frequency for a given educational level for all cells.
[b]Frequencies for this measure are different.

Table 19. Selected 1957 versus 1976 Comparison of Women's Job Reaction (by education)

			Educational level		
Job reaction		Year	Grade school	High school	College
	$(N)^a$	1957	(117)	(249)	(87)
		1976	(50)	(350)	(212)
Job satisfaction					
% Neutral, ambivalent,		1957	25%	20%	15%
dissatisfied		1976	24%	28%	28%
Type of job satisfaction					
Achievement-related		1957	3%	13%	15%
		1976	8%	18%	34%
Interesting work		1957	21%	29%	37%
		1976	6%	19%	25%
Type of job dissatisfaction					
Lack of achievement		1957	0%	4%	6%
		1976	2%	6%	16%
Lack of affiliation		1957	6%	15%	13%
		1976	6%	20%	24%
Lack of power		1957	0%	6%	3%
		1976	0%	3%	9%
Work commitment					
	$(N)^b$	1957	(71)	(170)	(57)
Achievement commitment		1957	0%	1%	2%
		1976	6%	4%	22%
Time-use commitment		1957	28%	26%	28%
		1976	10%	26%	24%
Home avoidance commitment		1957	3%	4%	2%
		1976	4%	10%	5%
No commitment		1957	41%	45%	33%
		1976	40%	28%	10%

[a]Unless otherwise indicated, N refers to frequency for a given educational level for all cells.
[b]Frequencies for this measure are different.

obtain more achievement satisfaction from work, but at the expense of finding their own work "interesting."

Let us turn our attention to the changes in the reported dissatisfactions that men and women in 1976 expressed in comparison to their counterparts in 1957. Both men and women in 1976 report more affiliative dissatisfactions with their work than they did in 1957. Working men in 1976 report more power dissatisfactions than they did in 1957. Examining Table 20 we can see that the increase in reported affiliative dissatisfactions at work occurs in women of all age groups. However, in Table 19 we can also see that it is primarily the college-educated women who

Table 20. Selected 1957 versus 1976 Comparison of Women's Job Reaction (by age)

Job reaction		Year	Age 21–34	35–44	45–54	55+
	(N)[a]	1957	(144)	(127)	(108)	(74)
	(N)[a]	1976	(273)	(112)	(111)	(114)
Job satisfaction						
Neutral, ambivalent,		1957	18%	21%	20%	24%
dissatisfied		1976	35%	26%	19%	21%
Type of job satisfaction						
Achievement-related		1957	15%	9%	8%	8%
		1976	28%	20%	11%	22%
Interesting work		1957	29%	27%	30%	27%
		1976	23%	12%	17%	24%
Type of job dissatisfaction						
Lack of achievement		1957	3%	4%	7%	0%
		1976	15%	4%	4%	3%
Lack of affiliation		1957	15%	11%	9%	11%
		1976	25%	15%	19%	18%
Lack of power		1957	4%	6%	3%	3%
		1976	7%	4%	4%	4%
Work commitment						
	(N)[b]	1957	(103)	(78)	(74)	(42)
Achievement commitment		1957	1%	0%	0%	2%
		1976	18%	7%	10%	8%
Time-use commitment		1957	21%	22%	37%	31%
		1976	26%	27%	20%	24%
Home avoidance commitment		1957	5%	5%	2%	0%
		1976	10%	8%	5%	6%
No commitment		1957	49%	42%	43%	26%
		1976	19%	27%	26%	24%

[a]Unless otherwise indicated, N refers to frequency for a given educational level for all cells.
[b]Frequencies for this measure are different.

are responsible for this increased report of affiliative problems at work, although the trends are there for the high school-educated groups.

We see these results about the rising dissatisfactions with social factors of work to be among the most important findings from our comparisons of 1957 and 1976 data. There is evidence for an increased discontent with the nature of social relations at work, especially among the more educated men and women in our population. Thus while work settings permit increased satisfactions for achievement, they are beginning to disrupt people's sense of solidarity with their peers and associates at work. In future analyses we would like to piece out what particular types of work settings are responsible for the feeling or lack of affiliative satisfaction from work. Is it because we are becoming more embedded in bureaucratic structures? in overly challenging structures? in overly supervised structures? Such questions would be important to answer in the future. Nevertheless the phenomenon is noteworthy, perhaps because it seems even clearer than any increased feelings of discontent about achievement and power, which were the concern of the authors of *Work in America*. We did find some evidence for increased dissatisfaction about power in comparing men's reactions from 1957 to 1976, but this phenomenon seems largely relegated to the college-educated men contrasted across the generation. And we do have some evidence for increased dissatisfaction about achievement issues in our comparative samples. This phenomenon, however, seems largely found in the contrast of the young people in both generations. Younger women (ages 21–34) in 1976 were especially more likely to mention achievement dissatisfactions in their work environment than were their counterparts in 1957. This was true for both high school- and college-educated women in 1976. Three percent of high school–educated young women in 1957 mentioned achievement dissatisfactions at work; 9% of their counterparts in 1976 mentioned such dissatisfactions. The comparable figures for the college-educated young women are 4% in 1957 and 23% in 1976. Again, it will be important to gather more information about which particular jobs evoke these kinds of dissatisfactions in both men and women in each year. But is is also important simply to note that these increased reports of achievement dissatisfactions are occurring. These phenomena probably do reflect what many observers have noted: our educational institutions have taught young people to demand achievement gratifications from work and the jobs available do not meet their standards. We have upgraded aspirations but not jobs. We suggest this interpretation of these data very tentatively for we realize that there is a second interpretation: these changes may in fact reflect *lowered* achievement potential in jobs over the generations. People who have argued for the increased routinization and automation of both the blue-collar and white-collar settings are probably arguing from this second interpretation.

   Another set of findings from Table 16, however, suggests that workers in America today may not be experiencing diminuation of actual challenge from work. Let us turn to these analyses.

   PERCEIVED CHALLENGE OF ONE'S JOB. Changes in perceived difficulty of one's job can be estimated for men in our sample, since in both 1957 and 1976 we asked men how much ability is required in the kind of job they are doing (see Appendix A). Unfortunately we did not ask this question of the 1957 working women. For all ages and all educational levels, and for a set of analyses where we controlled education and age simultaneously, we find that working men today are much more likely to say that their jobs require a lot of ability. The only census occupational category which did not show this shift was low-level laborers. Thus we have *perceived* upgrading of jobs in American society today compared to a generation ago. Furthermore, we have an upgrading in the perceived adequacy that men feel about their ability in their jobs in 1976 compared to 1957. We asked people how good they thought they were at the kind of work they were doing (see Appendix A). This shift in increased perceived adequacy occurs at every age and educational level and at each age × educational level we looked at. The only census occupational category that did not show this change was "farmer."

This set of results further supports the interpretation made earlier that the increase in perceived dissatisfactions around achievement and power for men (and probably for women) is not a function of a change in absolute level of challenge in their work but a change in the discrepancy between aspirations and what the work offers. One might say that it is no longer sufficient to feel as if one is doing well at what one is required to do, even if the job is one that requires a lot of overall ability. In Table 21 we examine this contention directly. Here we plot the correlation between feelings of job adequacy and job satisfaction among those who feel that their job requires a lot of ability. We find that in 1957 this correlation between job satisfaction and perceived adequacy was relatively high for those men who felt the job required a lot of ability, but in 1976 the correlation drops to −.01. The comparable correlation for the 1976 women is also near zero. What the table suggests is that indeed it is not sufficient for overall good feelings about one's job to think one is doing adequately at something relatively demanding. Something else

Table 21. Correlation Between Feelings of Job Adequacy and Job Satisfaction among Those Who Feel Job Does and Does Not Require a Lot of Ability (by year and sex)

| | Males | | | | Females | | | |
| | 1957 | | 1976 | | 1957 | | 1976 | |
	r	(N)	r	(N)	r	(N)	r	(N)
Workers who think job requires a lot of ability	.26**	(117)	−.01	(405)	—[a]		.04	(269)
Workers who think job does not require a lot of ability	.05	(157)	.08	(315)	—[a]		.00	(297)

[a]Perceived ability and adequacy not assessed in 1957.
**$p < .01$.

must be at stake. My contention is that what is at stake for Americans' sense of achievement at work is a more differentiating experience of achievement, an awareness of success in comparison to other people. We have been taught that being better than someone else is the clearest sign of one's worth. As more and more people are trained for skilled jobs, a worker begins to feel like only "one of the crowd" performing competently. Achievements that *many* others share can be threatening to one's sense of achievement. I am reminded of remarks made by two young seniors at the University of Michigan who, reflecting on their college experience, spoke of how much they were disengaged from most classroom encounters with professors. They suggested that one of the reasons why they were turned off by their academic experience was that in their college classes they were just "one of many," while in high school they received special attention for having unique intellectual aspirations and insights. One of them said she became very disinterested in her class in the modern novel when she realized that all of the other people in the class were being turned on to Joyce and Faulkner at the same time. In high school she was the only person who was discovering the joys of English literature. Thus our socialization for achievement tends to train people for individualistic, unique senses of achievement, either to feel very differentiated from others or to feel that they excel in social comparison. When they are thrust into work settings where uniqueness and excellence by social comparison standards are more difficult, dissatisfaction can fester.

These findings about the increased dissatisfaction about achievement or power among people who see themselves with a lot of ability in challenging jobs might not be unrelated to the other set of findings we were discussing earlier: increased dissatisfaction about affiliation at work. To the degree that people are seeking individuation and competitive standards at work, they will also discourage affiliative contact. Academics know well about the individualistic atmospheres in many departments in our universities. Young and not-so-young professors are constantly comparing their productivity. This type of orientation to academic accomplishment does not make a community of scholars easy to achieve. Individualism interferes with affiliation.

COMMITMENT TO JOB AND TO WORK. In light of these results it is not too surprising to find among men an increased preference for another job over the generation. Eleven percent more men in 1976 say they would prefer another job to the one they are in (see Appendix A for the question). Among women there was no evidence for such change. Such increased preference for another job occurred in all types of occupations, but particularly among higher status blue-collar workers. Of those men who were categorized as craft workers in 1957 43% said they would prefer other work while 59% of those so categorized in 1976 said they preferred another job. Those categorized as operative showed a parallel change from 45% to 51%.

The question that more directly got at work commitment rather than job commitment was one that asked whether the person would go on working if he or she did not need the money. We coded this question not only for whether or not the person would go on working but also for what reason they gave to go on working (see Appendix A for the question and codes). While there was no overall change in men's commitment to work from 1957 to 1976, there seems to be a dramatic change in women's commitment to work as a way of life over these years (see Table 16). No more men in 1976 said they would quit work if they did not need the money, while many fewer women gave that response in 1976. For both men and women there is a shift in giving more achievement-related reasons for why they would go on working. This is especially clear in the college-educated groups in 1976 (see Tables 17 and 19). For almost all men, but especially for the college educated (Table 17) and the young groups (Table 18), there seems to be less involvement with work as just a means to use up time in 1976. For more educated women in 1976 (Table 19) there seems to be an increase in becoming committed to work as a means to avoid the time that they would spend at home cooped up in a house. Thus some of women's increased commitment to work occurring in 1976 may be a function of the decreased commitment to housework that we noticed earlier.

Although we found no changes in overall commitment to work among men, older men in 1976 seemed clearly less committed to work than older men in 1957. This is an important result because it suggests, as we have noted before, that the transition to retirement is probably somewhat easier now than it was in 1957, less feared, and perhaps even longed-for. As more people retire the role ambiguities for that status diminish. Disengagement by older men from the work role may now be much easier than it was a generation ago.

WORK PROBLEMS. At every age and educational level more men in 1976 are seeing themselves as having work problems and seeing themselves as the locus of the problem (see Tables 16–18). The questions asking about perceived problems directed people to consider *psychological* proglems of work—not "knowing what to do" or not being "able to get along at work" (see Appendix A). This more psychological approach to work problems has been explicitly taught in school settings during the 1950s and 1960s. We have perhaps socialized our young to be sensitive to school problems, and when they do perceive problems, to ask themselves what they have done to exacerbate the problem or what they can do to solve the problem. What is more, we have socialized our young to be so conscious of their *choice* of vocation that when they do experience tension at work, they may likely view it as their own fault for having chosen such a field. More open vocational choice incurs more responsibility. Maybe we have given our young that burden along with their increased freedom of movement.

A COHORT ANALYSIS. Before drawing conclusions about the change and stability of people's job reactions, I would like to present one other set of analyses which lends a slightly different perspective on what we have been examining. One could ask of a generational study such as ours: Has change or stability been *intracohort* (within the *same* cohort of people aging over time—e.g., 21- to 29-year-olds in 1957 who were 40–48 years old in 1976) or intercohort (between cohorts of the same age at different times—e.g., the 21- to 29-year-olds in 1976 contrasted to 21-to 29-year-olds in 1957)? An intracohort change implies a societal across-the-board change. An intercohort change without an intracohort change often implies that the young people of the new generation have been socialized differently from the preceding generation, and have come to replace some old-fashioned attitudes and values of the older people in the earlier generation. Both the inter- and intracohort changes can be occurring, one and not the other; or neither.

In Table 22 we examine such comparisons for men. We are assuming that we could effectively look at four age groups in both years— 21–29, 30–39, 40–49, and 50–59[6]—which would then allow us two intracohort comparisons: 21- to 29-year-olds in 1957 who are represented by the 40- to 49-year-olds in 1976; 30- to 39-year-olds in 1957 who are represented by the 50- to 59-year-olds in 1976. Lines connecting these groups have been drawn in Table 22 for an easy visual scan of intracohort effects. We examined these effects for men only, because women's age cohorts in the labor force are very variable—and hence make intracohort estimation very unreliable.

What we discover in Table 22 is that almost all of the effects we have been discussing as social changes in the meaning of jobs for men are apparent as both inter- and intracohort effects except two: overall job satisfaction and perceived difficulty with the self as the basis of one's problem with work. The change in job satisfaction for men actually applied only to those 55 and over in both years. We already knew that. This analysis dramatizes the effect, but the other finding which fails to show an intracohort effect gives us a new insight. The change in perceived problem in one's self as a source of a work problem seems to be the peculiar way that young people in 1976 view work problems. In other words, a really new perspective about work is occurring in young

---

[6]Groups older than 59 get us into retired groups.

Table 22. Selected Intra- or Intercohort Comparisons of Men's Job Reactions (1957 to 1976)

		1957		1976	
	Age	(N)	%	%	(N)
Job satisfaction					
Ambivalent, neutral, dissatisfied	21–29	(164)	29	34	(210)
	30–39	(245)	27	23	(202)
	40–49	(230)	22	19	(142)
	50–59	(107)	21	22	(118)
Perceived type of job satisfaction					
Achievement	21–29	(164)	18	23	(210)
	30–39	(245)	14	34	(202)
	40–49	(230)	18	32	(142)
	50–59	(167)	22	38	(118)
Interesting work	21–29	(164)	33	20	(210)
	30–39	(245)	34	21	(202)
	40–49	(230)	34	20	(142)
	50–59	(167)	34	23	(118)
Lack of achievement	21–29	(164)	8	11	(210)
	30–39	(245)	9	10	(202)
	40–49	(230)	6	6	(142)
	50–59	(167)	6	5	(118)
Lack of affiliation	21–29	(164)	10	22	(210)
	30–39	(245)	12	17	(202)
	40–49	(230)	10	20	(142)
	50–59	(167)	8	16	(118)
Lack of power	21–29	(164)	6	12	(210)
	30–39	(245)	3	9	(202)
	40–49	(230)	6	9	(142)
	50–59	(167)	4	10	(118)
Work commitment					
Achievement commitment	21–29	(164)	4	16	(210)
	30–39	(245)	5	14	(202)
	40–49	(230)	2	13	(142)
	50–59	(167)	4	8	(118)
Perceived job requirements					
% "a lot of ability" to do work	21–29	(164)	35	46	(210)
	30–39	(245)	37	58	(202)
	40–49	(230)	48	55	(142)
	50–59	(167)	36	58	(118)

(*continued*)

Table 22.   (Continued)

		1957		1976	
	Age	(N)	%	%	(N)
Feeling of job adequacy					
% very good	21–29	(164)	32	50	(210)
	30–39	(245)	26	51	(202)
	40–49	(230)	30	56	(142)
	50–59	(167)	38	58	(118)
Work problem?					
No problem	21–29	(164)	60	51	(210)
	30–39	(245)	67	54	(202)
	40–49	(230)	71	56	(142)
	50–59	(167)	80	70	(118)
Difficulty in self	21–29	(164)	20	20	(210)
	30–39	(245)	12	18	(202)
	40–49	(230)	10	19	(142)
	50–59	(167)	8	13	(118)

people—more young men today have evidently been taught to view work problems intrapsychically, a perspective relatively absent from the older generation in 1957.

SUMMARY. Men's and women's reaction to their job settings show some remarkable consistencies and some remarkable changes. The extent of satisfaction with work reported seems to be remaining relatively constant although there seems to be some shift in certain groups. Particularly important seems to be a growing tendency for women to own up to dissatisfaction in their work. However, the quality of satisfactions and dissatisfactions in work changed considerably. More and more men and women are seeing work as providing achievement satisfactions. This increased perception of achievement at work, however, seems to come at the expense of finding work gratifying just because it is interesting. Paradoxically, in 1976 more men are seeing work as having power dissatisfactions, and many more women are seeing work as having achievement dissatisfactions. Thus the more individuated searches for power and achievement in work seem to be providing both increased satisfactions and dissatisfactions in 1976 contrasted to 1957.

All of these results suggest that there is a greater involvement in the American working force in personalized accomplishment and work. This increased involvement with individuated impact at work seems to be coordinated with increased sense of dissatisfaction with the social relations in the work setting. Although it is hard to draw a direct causal connection between the two, my speculation is that indeed there is one.

As people become more and more concerned about unique, individualized performance in work settings where other people are equally competent and well trained, they will more and more learn to distrust the social relations that exist. As more and more people seek unique satisfactions for self-expression in the work setting, more and more people should find some problem in their relationships with other people at that setting. The more one attends to and wants differentiation of self from others, the more one weakens one's sense of similarity with others. To perceive and enjoy the sense of being similar to others is the essence of the affiliative incentive. Thus I am suggesting that the press for a sense of accomplishment at work has promoted our discomfort with our colleagues at work, and we may well be on the way to seeing our occupational communities eroded.

There are other factors that may contribute to this increased dissatisfaction with the affiliative nature of work. Some of this change may also be due to increased bureaucratization in the work setting, which instills and formalizes the hierarchical nature of organizations. Some of this change may also be due to the promotion of self-actualization as the supreme type of motivation. The theoretical hierarchy of motivation that Maslow (1948) proposed became very popular in the early 1960s and 1970s. In the large scheme of things, it is not clear why affiliative needs are any lower in a hierarchy of motives than a need like self-actualization. Educational institutions may well have fostered the press for self-actualization in work. Some of the change may be attributable to pure demographic shifts in the society from a less to a more educated population, and to one where the work force has become increasingly dominated by young people, all seeking success. To whatever cause this change in the affiliative fabric of the work setting is attributed, it is a change that we as social researchers of roles and motivation should attend to, and one we as educators should keep in mind as we restructure the messages about work that we want to give to the young people of the future.

REFERENCES

Beauvoir, S. de, *Coming of age*. New York: Putnam, 1972.
Goldthorpe, J. H., Lochwood, D., Bachofer, F., & Platt, J. *The affluent worker: Industrial attitudes and behavior* (Vol. 1). New York: Cambridge University Press, 1968.
Gurin, G., Veroff, J., & Feld, S. C. *Americans view their mental health*. New York: Basic Books, 1960.
Hagerdorn, R., & Labovitz, S. Participation in community association by occupation: A test of three theories. *American Sociological Review*, 1968, *33*, 272–287.
Kohn, M. L., & Schooler, C. Occupation experience and psychological functions: An assessment of reciprocal effects. *American Sociological Review*, 1973, *38*, 97–118.
Mangione, T. W., & Quinn, R. P. Job satisfaction, counterproductive behavior and drug use at work. *Journal of Applied Psychology*, 1975, *60*, 114–116.

Maslow, A. H. Some theoretical consequences of basic need gratification. *Journal of Personality*, 1948, *16*, 402–416.

Meissner, M. The long arm of the job: A study of work and leisure. *Industrial Relations*, 1971, *10*, 239–260.

Nord, W. R. Job satisfaction reconsidered. *American Psychologist*, 1977, *32*, 1026–1035.

Quinn, R. P., Mangione, T. W., Baldi de Mandilovitch, M. S. Evaluating working conditions in America. *Monthly Labor Review*, November, 1973, 32–31.

Rokeach, M. *The nature of human values*. New York: Free Press, 1973.

Rubin, L. B. *World of pain*. New York: Basic Books, 1976.

Salaman, G. *Community and occupation*. New York: Cambridge University Press, 1974.

Seligman, B. On work, alienation, and leisure. *American Journal of Economics and Sociology*, 1965, *24*, 337–260.

Spreitzer, E. A., & Synder, E. Work orientations meaning of leisure and mental health. *Journal of Leisure Research*, 1974, *6*, 207–219.

Terkel, S. *Working*. New York: Avon Books, 1974.

Veroff, J. Process vs. implicit in men's and women's achievement motivation. *Psychology of Women Quarterly*, 1977a, *1*, 283–292.

Veroff, J. *Women and work at home and away from home*. Unpublished manuscript, 1977b.

Veroff, J., Douvan, E., and Kulka, R. *The inner American*. New York: Basic Books, 1981.

Veroff, J., & Feld, S. C. *Marriage and work in America*. New York: Van Nostrand, 1970.

Veroff, J., Kulka, R., and Douvan, E. *Mental health in America*. New York: Basic Books, 1981.

Work in America, Cambridge, Mass.: MIT Press, 1973.

Young, M., & Willmott, P. *The symmetrical family*. New York: Pantheon, 1973.

APPENDIXES

Appendix A. Questions and Codes about the Work Role Used in National Surveys of 1957 and 1976

Job reaction title	Question	Code
Job satisfaction	Taking into consideration all things about your job, how satisfied or dissatisfied are you with it?	*Very Satisfied:* very good; real good; very happy; love my work; very well satisfied; couldn't be better
		Satisfied: good; pretty good; I like it; pretty well satisfied; basically satisfied
		Neutral: okay; all right, fair, average; so-so
		Ambivalent: mention both satisfaction and dissatisfaction; yes and no; good and bad; like it and don't
		Dissatisfied: not too good; not very well; unhappy; I don't like it; no good, terrible; I hate it
Perceived ability on job	How good would you say you are at doing this kind of work, would you say you were: *very good, a little better than average, just average, or not very good?*	As is
Prefer other job?	Regardless of how much you like your job, is there any other kind of work you'd rather be doing?	Yes No
Work commitment	If you don't have to work to make a living, do you think you would work anyway? (Women, 1957 only: If you didn't need the money that you get from working, do you think you would work anyway?) (If Yes: What would be your reasons for going on working?)	

(continued)

Appendix A. (Continued)

Job reaction title	Question	Code
Achievement commitment		Working gives feeling of accomplishment, makes you feel useful
Affiliative commitment		Likes chance to be with people, friendships, helping people
Work as habit		Only way of life R knows; easier to keep on what you're doing
Moralistic commitment		Work keeps you healthy, prevents feeling useless or immoral, "good to work"
Time-use commitment		Avoids boredom, upset if didn't work, go crazy if no work
Escape from home commitment		Better than housework, being with family, staying at home
General like		Like to work; like the work I'm doing
No commitment to work		Answer "no" to the first question
Type of job satisfaction	What things do you particularly like about the job?	Presence of:
Economic		—inadequacy of wages, money, salary —lack of job security
Extrinsic—noneconomic		—nice place to work —easy work —convenience —employee benefits —physical working conditions
Achievement-related		—responsibility —complexity —use of abilities —feelings of importance —recognition
Affiliation-related (general)		—contact with people —helping people
Specific people		—satisfaction with particular people

Appendix A. (Continued)

Job reaction title	Question	Code
		—nice people
		—friends
		—good boss
Power-related		—independence
		—no one pushes me around
		—leadership, teaching
		—prestige
Interesting work		—job, work is interesting
		—novelty
		—chance to learn
		—like kind of work it is
Type of job dissatisfaction	What things don't you like about the job?	Presence of:
Economic		—inadequacy of wages, money, salary
		—lack of job security
Extrinsic—noneconomic		—not a nice place
		—hard physical work
		—inconvenience
		—lack of employee benefits
		—hours
		—dirty place
General: hard work		—"hard work"
		—too much pressure
Lack of achievement		—lack of responsibility
		—excess of responsibility
		—work too complicated
		—work too simple
		—nonuse of abilities
		—feeling of incompetency
		—lack of recognition
Lack of affiliation		—no (little) contact with people
		—dissatisfied with particular people, superiors
Lack of power		—not enough independence
		—too much restraint

(continued)

Appendix A.   (Continued)

Job reaction title	Question	Code
Nothing		—not enough leadership —not enough prestige —R likes everything about work
Perceived job requirements	What does it take to do a really good job at the kind of work you do? Think it takes to do a really good job at the kind of work you do?	—a lot —some —little —not much —none

Appendix B. Questions and Codes about Nonjob Reactions in National Surveys of 1957 and 1976

Type of Reaction	Question	Code
Liking for housework	Different people feel differently about taking care of a home—I don't mean taking care of the children, but things like cooking and sewing and keeping house. Some women look on these things as just a job that has to be done—other women really enjoy them. How do you feel about this?	*Expresses liking:* —"I like it." —"I like it" and gives reasons. —"I like . . ." (mentions particular aspect). *Other:* —ambivalent —answer or expressed dislike
Marital happiness	Taking things all together, how would you describe your marriage—would you say your marriage was: *very happy, a little happier than average, just about average, not too happy?*	As is
Leisure challenging	How do you usually spend your time when your work is done—what kind of things do you do, both at home and away from home?	Leisure challenging if mentions any of the following: —gardens —construction —creative arts —homemaking hobby —collecting —fishing —sports —hobbies —political work —youth work
Happiness	Taking things all together, how would you say things are these days—would you say you're: *very happy, pretty happy,* or *not too happy* these days?	As is
Symptoms Psychological anxiety	How often have you had the following?	*Sum of:* All items coded and summed

(continued)

Appendix B.   *(Continued)*

Type of Reaction	Question	Code
	a. Do you ever have any trouble getting to sleep or staying asleep?	1—never 2—not very much 3—pretty often 4—nearly all the time
	b. Have you ever been bothered by nervousness, feeling fidgety and tense?	
	c. Are you ever troubled by headaches or pains in the head?	
	d. Do you have loss of appetite?	
	e. How often are you bothered by having an upset stomach?	
	(Response categories for all the above: nearly all the time, pretty often, not very much, never)	
Immobilization	How often have you had the following? a. Do you find it difficult to get up in the morning? (nearly all the time, pretty often, not very much, never) b. Are you troubled by your hands sweating so that you feel damp and clammy? (many times, sometimes, hardly ever, never)	*Sum of (a) and (b):* a. 1—never 2—not very much 3—pretty often 4—nearly all the time b. 1—never 2—hardly ever 3—sometimes 4—many times
Ill-health	Do you have any particular physical or health trouble?	*Sum of:* 2—No 4—Yes
	How often have you had the following:	*Sum of:*
	a. Has any ill-health affected the amount of work you do?	1—never 2—hardly ever 3—sometimes 4—nearly all the time
	b. Have you ever been bothered by shortness	1—never 2—hardly ever

Appendix B. (*Continued*)

Type of Reaction	Question	Code
	of breath when you were not exercising or working hard?	3—sometimes 4—nearly all the time
	c. Have you ever been bothered by your heart beating hard?	1—never 2—hardly ever 3—sometimes 4—nearly all the time
	(Response categories for all of the above: many times, sometimes, hardly ever, never)	
	Here are some more questions like those you've filled out. This time just answer "yes" or "no."	*Sum of:*
	a. Do you feel you are bothered by all sorts of pains and ailments in different parts of your body?	2—No 4—Yes
	b. For the most part, do you feel healthy enough to carry out the things that you would like to do?	2—No 4—Yes
Feelings of nervous breakdown	Have you ever felt you were going to have a nervous breakdown?	Yes No
Drinking	Do you ever drink more than you should?	1—Never 2—Hardly ever 3—Sometimes 4—Nearly all the time
Job sources of worries	Everyone has some things he worries about more or less. What kinds of things do you worry about?	—my job —my salary —time pressures at work —am I doing well at work? —success of my business
Job sources of happiness	Now I want you to think about your whole life— how things are now, how they were 10 years ago, how they were when you	

(*continued*)

Appendix B. (Continued)

Type of Reaction	Question	Code
	were a little (boy/girl). What do you think of as the happiest time of your life?	
	a. (If mentions present time as happiest or both the present and past times) Why is this a happy time—what are some of the things that you feel pretty happy about these days?	—good job —steady job —enjoy my job —success on my job
	b. (If mentions past time only as happiest) How about the way things are today—what are some of the things you feel pretty happy about these days?	
Job sources of unhappiness	Everyone has things about their life they are not completely happy about. What are some of the things that you are not too happy about these days?	—my job, my business —my salary; I'm not making enough money —physical work conditions —social work conditions —adequacy on the job —time pressures at work

Appendix C. Questions and Codes for Nonjob Reactions in 1976 National Survey Only

Reaction	Question	Code

Primary value orientation	Here is a list of things that many people look for or want out of life. Please study the list carefully, then tell me which *two* of these things are most important to you in *your* life.
	
	a. Of these two, which *one* is most important to you in your life?
	
	  1. Sense of belonging
	  2. Excitement
	  3. Warm relations with others
	  4. Being well-respected
	  5. Fun and enjoyment in life
	  6. Security
	  7. Self-respect
	  8. A sense of accomplishment	

Sociability		Choice of *either* in (a): —sense of belonging —warm relations with others
Hedonism		Choice of either in (a): —excitement —fun and enjoyment
Self-actualization		Choice of *either* in (a): —self-fulfilment —a sense of accomplishment
Moral respect		Choice of *either* in (a): —being well respected —self-respect
Security		Choice of "security" in (a)
Fulfillment of values through roles	Now I'd like to ask you how much various things in your life have led or would lead to (most important value chosen in primary value question).	As is

(*continued*)

Appendix C. *(Continued)*

Reaction	Question	Code
Leisure-value fulfillment	First, how much have the things you do in your *leisure* time led to (most important value) in your life—*very little, a little, some, a lot,* or *a great deal?*	As is
Work in house-value fulfillment	How much has the work you do in and around the house led to (most important value) in your life—*very little, a little, some, a lot,* or *a great deal?*	As is
Job value fulfillment	How much (has/would/did) *work at a job* (led/lead) to (most important value) in your life?	As is
Marriage-value fulfillment	How about being married? How much (had/would/did) *being married* (led/lead) to (most important value) in your life?	As is
Parenthood-value fulfillment	What about being a (father/mother)? How much (has/would) being a parent (led/lead) to (most important value) in your life?	As is
Perceived challenge of free time	How much of your free time do you spend doing things that challenge you? Would you say that you spend *most, a lot, some, a little* or *none* of your free time doing such things?	As is

Chapter 7

The American Divorce Rate
What Does It Mean? What Should We Worry About?

Mary Jo Bane

The Basic Facts

THE INDICATORS. The basic fact about the American divorce rate is that it is rising. The number of divorces per 1,000 married women has risen annually since 1960. Before that annual divorce rates fell somewhat during the late 1930s, rose to a sharp peak after World War II, and fell until the late 1950s. In 1977, the most recent year for which final divorce statistics have been published, 1,091,000 divorces were granted, 21.1 per 1,000 married women. Figure 1 charts the course of the annual divorce rate from 1930 to 1976.

Another way of looking at divorce shows a steadier increase over time, suggesting that some of the annual variations reflect changes in the timing of divorces rather than the incidence. This is the cohort divorce rate: the proportion of people born at a certain time whose marriages have ended or can be expected to end in divorce. Table 1 shows these rates by age cohort. It shows that the proportion of marriages expected to end in divorce has risen steadily, with the divorce rate expected for women born between 1945 and 1949 nearly triple that actually experienced by women born between 1900 and 1904. It is worth keeping in mind, however, that no cohort has yet experienced a divorce rate over 21.5% (that of women born between 1935 and 1939 who were

MARY JO BANE, PH.D. • John F. Kennedy School of Government, Harvard University, Cambridge, Massachusetts 02138. The research in this paper was supported in part by a grant from the National Institutes of Mental Health.

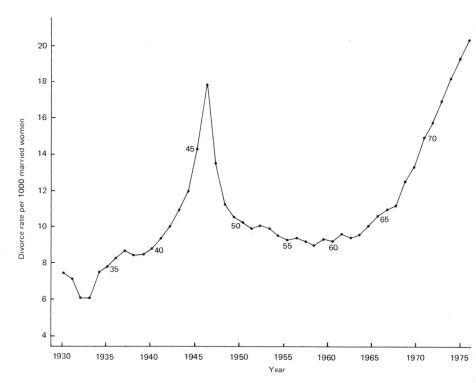

Figure 1. Divorce Rate per 1000 Married Women 1930–1975. Source: NCHS, 1977, 1979.

Table 1. Percent of Ever-Married Persons Whose First Marriage May Eventually End in Divorce (by year of birth and sex; June 1975)

Year of birth	Men ever married		Women ever married	
	% ended by 1975	% may end in divorce	% ended by 1975	% may end in divorce
1900–1904	13.3	13.3	12.8	12.8
1905–1909	14.9	15.2	14.9	15.1
1910–1914	16.7	17.2	15.8	16.2
1915–1919	17.4	18.4	16.4	17.2
1920–1924	18.4	20.4	18.0	19.5
1925–1929	18.1	21.8	21.0	23.8
1930–1934	18.4	24.0	20.6	26.2
1935–1939	20.1	29.5	21.5	30.7
1940–1944	16.9	31.5	19.9	34.4
1945–1949	13.1	34.1	17.2	38.3

SOURCE: U.S. Bureau of the Census, 1977b, Table H.

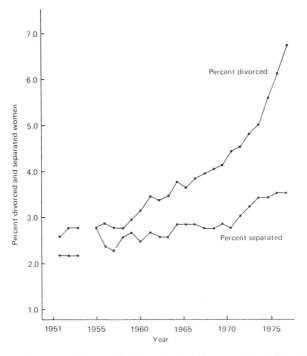

Figure 2. Percent Divorced and Separated of Ever-Married Men Ages 14 and Over, 1951–1953 and 1955–1976. Source: Current Population Reports, Series P–20, "Marital Status and Living Arrangements," years from 1951 to 1953 and 1955 to 1976.

age 36–40 when these data were collected). The higher figures are projections made by extrapolating the age-specific rates of older cohorts.
Actual figures may turn out to be higher or lower.

A third indicator of divorce is the proportion of the population
divorced. This is obviously a "net" number, added to in any given year
by people who become divorced and subtracted from by those who
leave the divorced state. Figures 2 and 3 show the changes since 1951 in
the proportions divorced among men and women who have ever been
married. The rise in the proportion of divorced men and women mirrors
the divorce rate, suggesting that the annual remarriage rate (the proportion of divorced men and women who remarry each year) has not risen
at the same rate as the divorce rate. The remarriage rate of divorced men
and women, however, is and has been high: over half of divorced wom-
en remarry within five years of their divorce; about three-quarters seem
to remarry eventually.

TOTAL MARITAL DISRUPTIONS. In discussing marital disruption as a
social phenomenon, one should consider trends in desertion and long-
term separation in addition to trends in divorce and annulment. Because

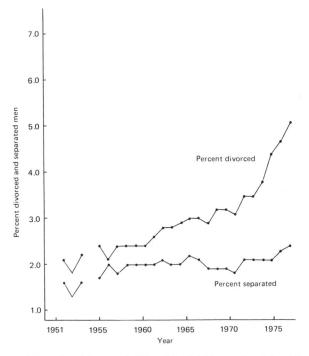

*Figure 3. Percent Divorced and Separated of Ever-Married Women Ages 14 and Over 1951–1953
and 1955–1976. Source: Same as for Figure 2.*

Table 2. Percent Black Women by Marital Status and Age, 1970

Age	All	Ever divorced	Divorced	Separated
20–24	11.4	8.5	10.9	34.2
25–29	11.2	9.7	14.3	44.0
30–34	11.7	12.4	17.7	49.1
35–39	11.4	13.7	17.6	49.5
40–44	10.7	14.2	16.2	47.4

SOURCE: U.S. Bureau of the Census, 1972, Tables 1 and 4.

desertions and long-term separations are not recorded, it is, however, impossible to calculate these rates and thus impossible to determine the extent to which the rise in the divorce rate is accounted for by an increased tendency to formalize disruptions.

There is some evidence that the rate of marital disruption is indeed higher than the divorce rate. This evidence comes from examining the characteristics of those who report their marital status as "separated." If all separations led to divorce or reconciliation, the characteristics of those who are separated should be similar to the rest of the married and divorced population. Tables 2–4 show that this is not the case: separated women are more likely than other groups to be poor, black, and poorly educated—the ones less likely to be able to afford formal divorce or to see the benefit in formalizing their status.

It is not possible to calculate the long-term separation rate with existing data. A maximum current rate can, however, be estimated from the number of separated persons. If half of the separated women in 1976 were long-term rather than predivorce or short-term separated (half

Table 3. Mean Years of School Completed, Women by Marital Status, Race, and Age, 1970

Age	All	Ever divorced	Divorced	Separated
White women				
20–24	12.7	12.2	12.3	12.1
25–35	12.5	12.2	12.4	12.1
35–44	12.3	12.1	12.3	11.7
Black women				
20–24	12.3	12.1	12.2	11.6
25–34	12.1	12.1	12.2	11.3
35–44	11.1	11.3	11.7	10.4

SOURCE: U.S. Bureau of the Census, 1972, Tables 1 and 4.

Table 4. Percent without Income and Median Income for Those with Income in 1969
(women by marital status, race, and age)

Race/age	% without income		Median income	
	Divorced	Separated	Divorced	Separated
White women				
25–34	6.0	14.0	$4,447	$3,282
35–44	5.7	11.9	5,396	3,771
Black women				
25–34	7.1	10.3	3,760	2,942
35–44	6.2	9.5	3,794	2,954

SOURCE: U.S. Bureau of the Census, 1972, Table 7.

would seem to be a maximum), and if the average duration of a long-term separation was five years, then the number of separated women in 1976 suggests an average annual rate of about 3 or 4 long-term separations per 1,000 married women, less than one-quarter of the divorce rate over the same period.[1] If this is correct, then the total rate of marital disruption (excluding short-term separations which end in reconciliation) is about 125% of the divorce rate.

That the long-term separation rate may have been decreasing as the divorce rate has been increasing is suggested by comparing the proportions of men and women separated and divorces, as in Figures 2 and 3.[2]

The proportion of separated among ever-married men and women has been nearly steady since the early 1950s in contrast to the proportion of divorced persons and the divorce rate, both of which have risen sharply since 1960. This suggests that either the duration of predivorce separations has been decreasing, the rate of short-term separations has been declining, the rate of long-term separations has been declining, or some combination of the three has been occurring. The possibility that part of the increase in divorce can be explained by a decrease in long-term separation cannot be ruled out.

[1] A comparison of the number of separated women in one year with the number of divorces the following year shows that there are about twice as many separated women as divorces. A year seems a minimum estimate of predivorce separations; 1969 data from the National Center for Health Statistics (NCHS, 1973) suggest an average duration closer to 1.5 or 2 years. Five years as a duration for long-term separation is obviously a very low estimate.
[2] These figures also illustrate one of the enduring puzzles about separation: about twice as many women as men report themselves as separated. This suggests overreporting by women, underreporting by men, or both. Speculative explanations are numerous and often imaginative; facts are not available to settle the issue.

TOTAL MARITAL UNHAPPINESS. To place the divorce rate in proper perspective, it would be useful to have still another (also unavailable) time series: a valid, reliable measure of marital unhappiness. In the absence of such a measure it is impossible to tell whether the rising divorce rate reflects increasing marital unhappiness or an increasing tendency to dissolve unhappy marriages—the former an increase in overall unhappiness, the latter presumably a decrease. Needless to say, no time-series data on marital happiness exist, and this issue too must remain a matter for speculation.

SO WHAT?

The basic facts of American divorce, like any other facts, do not speak for themselves. Are they indeed cause for the alarm which so often accompanies their publication? And if so, precisely what is alarming? These questions are not usually asked; the assumption that something bad is going on is not usually questioned. Trying to answer the questions seems to me, however, an absolutely necessary preliminary to thinking about what, if anything, ought to be done on a governmental level about rising divorce rates.

Some Americans seem to find the rising divorce rate alarming in and of itself: they believe that divorce is sinful or morally wrong and thus deplorable under any circumstances. Most, however, worry about divorce because of its perceived harmful consequences. These consequences can be of three types: increased claims upon the resources of the society (welfare, for example), personal hurts to the individuals involved; and threats to the integration of society. All of these consequences do seem to me to be legitimate matters of public concern, and so it is important to examine carefully what evidence there is on the actual effects of divorce. Three kinds of consequences will be taken up, in turn, before questions are raised about public policy.

CLAIMS ON PUBLIC RESOURCES. One reason that some people worry about rising rates of marital disruption is that marital disruptions and the single-adult families which result generate increased claims on public resources. As separated and divorced people have become a political force, claiming rights to cash assistance and demanding increased services, they have placed severe pressure on public resources. In addition many Americans worry that public programs themselves contribute to marital disruption: that families split in order to go on welfare. Thus divorce is seen as both a cause and a symptom of an increased reliance on public transfers. It is a problem from one point of view because it represents a widespread character defect (shirking work and taking advantage of public generosity), from another because it may bankrupt the treasury, and from a third because it represents a failure of the society to provide nonwelfare earnings opportunities for many people.

It is indeed the case that total welfare benefits and numbers of welfare recipients have risen dramatically over the same time period which saw a sharp rise in the divorce rate.[3] It is also true that about a quarter of single-parent families receive at least some income from welfare at some time (Rein & Rainwater, 1977). Moreover, single-parent families make up a large and increasing proportion of those with incomes below the official poverty line. In 1976, 32% of divorced or separated women and 12% of divorced or separated men were living in poverty (compared with 10.3% of all persons). Some 36% of the poor in 1976 were in female-headed families of all types (including families of widows and never-married women), up from 18% in 1959 (U.S. Bureau of the Census, 1978).

Divorce and separation are indeed accompanied by increased reliance on public welfare. The availability of welfare, however, does not actually seem to cause divorce or separation, despite the perverse programs in many states that exclude two-parent families from eligibility for AFDC. Studies are inconclusive and somewhat contradictory, but none shows more than a trivial relationship between welfare availability or the level of benefits and either increased separation or decreased remarriage.[4] Nor does the poverty of single-parent families reflect unwillingness to work. Some 77% of divorced women and 54% of separated women with children participated in the labor force in 1976, and many of the rest expressed a desire to work if the opportunity became available (Haygbe, 1978). Few single-parent families are dependent on welfare as their main income source for long periods of time, only about a quarter of those who ever receive welfare. Most apparently use welfare as supplemental or tide-over income (Rein & Rainwater, 1977).

[3]For example, the number of AFDC recipients grew from 3.1 million in 1960 to 11.2 million in 1976. Total payments under AFDC grew from $1.1 billion in 1960 to $9.9 billion in 1976 (U.S. Bureau of the Census, 1977a, Tables 543 and 544).
[4]The two best studies both use data from the Panel Study of Income Dynamics, a five-year, longitudinal study of 5,000 American families. They estimate the probability of marital disruption during a seven-year period as a function of background characteristics, economic status, and the level of welfare benefits available in the state. The two studies use different variable specifications and analysis methods. They come to different conclusions. Sawhill et al. conclude that AFDC benefit levels have no effect on the probability of remarriage (Sawhill, Peabody, Jones, & Caldwell, 1975). Hoffman and Holmes (1976) conclude that AFDC benefit levels have a small positive effect on the probability of disruption and no effect on remarriage. (See also Moles, 1978). Some surprising results from the negative income tax experiments, suggesting that experimental families were more likely than controls to break up, are reported in Hannan, Tuma, and Groenveld (1978).

Why then are so many divorced and separated women poor and thus legitimate claimants of public transfers? There are several possible explanations. First, families may have been poor before the disruption, which may have contributed to marital tension and eventual disruption, and certainly contributes to postdisruption poverty.[5] This is especially true of the separated, who are more likely to be poor than the divorced. Second, two households are more expensive to maintain than one, and the loss of economies of scale may push marginal families into poverty.[6] Third, women's job and earnings opportunities are limited by labor market discrimination, occupational segregation, and the problem of child care. Fourth, men tend to remarry faster than women (U.S. Bureau of the Census, 1977b), often taking on responsibilities for new families and eliminating or reducing the contributions they make to their first families. Fifth, men may not contribute their fair share to the support of their children for other reasons—because they are not forced to, or not inclined to, or whatever (Hill & Hoffman, 1976).

All these factors seem to contribute to high poverty and welfare dependence rates among single-parent families. Only the loss of economies of scale, however, follows inexorably from marital disruption. The others come either from a general failure of the economy and of the labor market, especially toward women and young minority men, or from a failure in the arrangements through which men are expected to continue financial support of their children. Thus the harmful consequences of divorce vis-à-vis public resources could be alleviated by correcting a variety of problems.

PERSONAL HURTS. A different reason for worrying about marital disruption is that people are hurt by it, not only the adults but also the children whose parents break up. Presumably this is only a legitimate worry if people are hurt more by a disruption than they would have been had the marriage continued. Whether this is indeed the case— whether the sum total of human happiness would be greater if there were fewer divorces—is obviously a controversial matter.

[5] Both the level and the source of family income appear to affect the probability of marital separation. Simple cross tabulations show an inverse relationship between income and divorce (for example, Carter & Glick, 1970). More sophisticated studies, for example Sawhill et al. (1975), suggest that stability of the family head's employment decreases the probability of divorce, with level of income less important. However, higher levels of wives' earnings relative to husbands' appear to increase the probability of disruption. Economists label these "income effects" and "independence effects," and hypothesize that they have opposite effects.
[6] I calculated from Census Bureau poverty figures that in 1973 the ratio of the low-income level for broken families to intact families ranged from 1.5 for families with one child to 1.12 for families with five children.

The trend over time cannot, of course, be known. There are no time-series data, not even untrustworthy data, on marital unhappiness. Thus there is no way of knowing whether the increased divorce rate reflects increased happiness through the dissolution of misery-producing relationships and their replacement with more livable alternatives or whether it reflects decreased happiness. That divorce has in fact increased suggests that more and more people perceive the divorced state as preferable to being married. In retrospect this judgment may or may not be accurate, and if accurate may reflect either a deterioration in marital happiness or increasingly available—because of changes in public attitudes and opportunities for women, presumably—tolerable alternatives. The trend itself tells us nothing about the dynamics of change.

The relationship of a person's well-being after divorce to his or her well-being had the marriage continued presumably depends on a variety of personal and situational characteristics, including sex, the duration of the marriage, and whether that person is one of the partners or a child in the family, as well as the emotional, social, and economic qualities of the two situations. Table 5 shows the distribution of divorces in divorce registration states in 1973 by duration of the marriage and number of children involved. Table 6 shows changes over time in the duration of marriage before divorce, the percent of divorces involving children, and the average number of children per decree. The data show that the majority of divorces, now and in the past, do involve children. They also show a concentration of divorces in the first years of marriage but also many divorces later in marriages.

In looking at the hurts of divorce, it is important to look at both adults and children, and at both long and short predivorce marriages. There is by now quite a large body of literature on the effects of divorce,

Table 5. Divorces by Duration of Marriage and Number of Children (percent of divorces in divorce registration area with information on both items, 1973)

Duration of marriage (total)	All (100.00%)	0 (40.5%)	1 (25.5%)	2 (19.0%)	3+ (14.9%)
under 1 year	4.7	4.1	0.3	0.1	0.1
1–2 years	17.3	12.0	4.4	0.4	0.1
3–4 years	17.3	8.1	6.7	2.1	0.3
5–9 years	26.0	7.3	8.0	7.8	3.1
10–14 years	13.2	2.1	2.0	4.5	4.0
15+ years	21.4	6.9	4.0	4.1	6.4

SOURCE: NCHS, 1977, Table 2–18.

Table 6. *Statistics on Marriage and Children of Divorced Couples: Selected Years, 1955–1976*

Year	Number of divorces	Divorces per 1,000 married women	Average duration of marriage before divorce (years)	% of divorces involving children[a]	Mean number of children per decree[b]	Total children involved in divorce[b]	Children involved per 1,000 children[b]
1955	377,000	9.3	6.4	48.1	0.92	347,000	6.3
1960	393,000	9.2	7.2	56.7	1.18	463,000	7.2
1965	479,000	10.6	7.2	59.8	1.32	630,000	8.9
1970	708,000	14.9	6.7	59.9	1.22	870,000	12.5
1971	773,000	15.8	6.7	59.9	1.22	946,000	13.6
1972	845,000	17.0	6.7	60.1	1.20	1,021,000	14.8
1973	915,000	18.2	6.6	59.5	1.17	1,079,000	15.9
1974	977,000	19.3	6.5	58.0	1.12	1,099,000	16.4
1975	1,036,000	20.3	6.5	57.1	1.08	1,123,000	17.0
1976	1,083,000	21.1	6.5	57.3	1.03	1,117,000	17.1

SOURCE: NCHS, 1979.
[a]Data from Divorce Registration Area (29 states).
[b]Estimated from sample data from Divorce Registration Area states.

and it will not be reviewed here in any systematic way. Instead I will present some findings which may be relevant to the question of what is worrisome about divorce.

EFFECTS ON ADULTS. A number of surveys have asked about perceived well-being, using questions of various sorts (e.g., lists of feeling states, such as being bored, depressed, etc.; or general questions of the sort "How would you say things are for you these days—are you very happy, pretty happy, or not too happy?"). The surveys almost all find large differences in perceived well-being by marital status, with married people the happiest and divorced or separated people less happy. Divorced and separated adults also seem to have higher death, illness, and institutionalization rates than those who are married (Campell, Converse, & Rodgers, 1976).

None of the surveys is longitudinal and thus cannot compare well-being before the disruption with well-being immediately and several years after. Indeed the surveys have not been analyzed either by duration of marriage before divorce or by time since divorce. One can argue that disruptions of long-term marriages should be more socially and emotionally disturbing than breakups after short marriages, but this is not necessarily the case. There is evidence from small-scale studies that the period immediately after divorce is the hardest, followed by gradual adaptation, but this has not been taken into consideration by the surveys.[7]

In short there is ample evidence that getting a divorce is hard on adults, but no evidence on how hard for how long, or how hard relative to continuing the marriage.

EFFECTS ON CHILDREN. Since children are considered the innocent victims of divorce, effects of marital breakup on children are of more concern to the public generally than effects, however serious, on adults. The sheer number of children involved makes the problem a serious one: estimates suggest that 35%–40% of American children born in the 1970s will experience a parental breakup sometime before they reach age 18 (Bane, 1976).

Early research seemed to show that parental breakups led to increased delinquency, emotional problems, and low achievement among children. More sophisticated recent studies, however, suggest that the situation is much more complicated. Most studies now seem to find that when economic status and other variables are adequately controlled, parental breakup per se has no important long-term effects on children's development. One study found that children in one-parent families

---

[7]Robert Weiss's *Marital separation* (1975) is an excellent presentation of the clinical literature.

were better off than children in unhappy two-parent families. Other studies suggest that when children are harmed, the harm is often caused not by the divorce but by subsequent economic deprivation or lack of adult attention (Zill, 1978).[8]

Many clinicians have reported on the adjustment problems of children after a parental breakup, and these difficulties are not denied by studies which find few long-term effects. Nonetheless the hurt done the children by disruption may have been exaggerated, especially when compared with the available alternatives.

SOCIAL INTEGRATION. The most difficult arguments to assess objectively are those which claim that divorce causes, or represents, a failure of social integration or a diminution of social responsibility. Since these are potentially the most compelling reasons for concern about divorce, it is especially troubling that they are so hard to get a handle on.

At the simplest level social integration arguments can be examined and largely dismissed. One can look, for example, at the relationships between divorce, delinquency among children, and criminality among adults. Such relationships do exist, but they are small and probably explained by other deprivations—like poverty—common to both broken homes and criminality. Thus the spectre of divorces leading to a lawless society is probably just that.

More complicated arguments see in divorce indications of a breakdown in the institutions of marriage and family life, which leads in turn to dramatic changes, probably for the worse, in the social fabric. What level of divorce represents a fundamental change in marriage and family life is, of course, a question: some in the early 1930s predicted the breakdown of family life from 5 or 6 divorces per 1,000 married women of that time.

Neither that divorce rate nor America's current rate seems to me to signal widespread rejection of marriage. While 40% of first marriages are expected to end in divorce, 60% are expected to last until the death of one party. Most divorced people remarry, indicating (perhaps) the rejection of a particular partner but a commitment to the institution. Few people marry more than twice, and the average marriage lasts quite a long time, even if it is a second marriage. These facts lead me to conclude that long-term marriages, with their strong mutual commitments, are still an important feature of our society.

One can imagine, however, a level of divorce which would signal that fundamental changes were taking place. This would be a divorce rate near 100% for both first and second marriages; however, we should not dismiss as completely silly those who consider the current rate al-

[8]An excellent review of earlier literature can be found in Longfellow (1978).

ready alarmingly high. We must seriously consider the possibility that the character of marriage as we have known it may be changing. Then we must consider the potential consequences of that change for society.

Emile Durkheim, in *Suicide*, used the divorce rate as an indicator of social disintegration and offered a powerful analysis of its potential consequences (Durkheim, 1975). More recently Christopher Lasch has argued that the changed character of family relationships is creating a new kind of person, incapable of strong emotions, unable to achieve genuine, binding intimacy, and unable to assume responsibility for others (Lasch, 1977). These are disturbing possibilities, and at present we have no way of assessing the extent to which they describe contemporary reality. And of course if the social and character changes Durkheim and Lasch suggest are occurring at the societal level, we shall never to able to assess them, since we shall have no reference group against which to judge ourselves.

Worry about the affect of divorce on the social fabric does not seem unreasonable to me, even though it may be impossible to document actual chains of effects. In the absence of evidence, however, and in the absence of agreement on what rates are "too high" and what changes "too harmful," it would probably be unreasonable to do more than worry.

WHAT IS TO BE DONE?

Analyses of social problems usually conclude with recommendations for public policy, and this chapter is no exception. The task is made more difficult by the absence of clear evidence on what the consequences of divorce in fact are. Nor is it helped by the fact, common to all policy analysis, that the statement of a problem, however clear, does not imply that a policy response is necessarily appropriate, much less what the response should be. Nonetheless some policy responses to the various categories of consequences do seem reasonable.

SOCIAL INTEGRATION. If the consequences of divorce for social integration are potentially the most worrisome, they are also the least amenable to amelioration through public policy. One possible cure, forbidding divorces or making them much more difficult to obtain, is clearly worse than the disease. It not only impinges on the personal freedoms which Americans have come to cherish, but it would probably also bring about increased misery, increased evasion of the law, and differential treatment of rich and poor—all the ills, in short, that have finally persuaded all the states to liberalize their divorce laws.

Cures that would somehow strengthen marriage and family life without impinging on personal freedoms are not easily found. Good social policy generally—full employment, income maintenance, and so on—may relieve some of the pressures on families and thus increase marital stability; but there is no guarantee that this will happen. More equal employment opportunities for women may in fact lead to increased disruption: there is some evidence that this is now happening (Hannon et al., 1978; Hoffman & Holmes, 1976; Moles, 1978; Ross & Sawhill, 1975; Sawhill et al., 1975). The effect of income maintenance on family stability is equally difficult to predict, as the Seattle and Denver income maintenance experiment have shown (Hannon et al., 1978; Hoffman & Holmes, 1976; Moles, 1978; Ross & Sawhill, 1975; Sawhill et al., 1975). There are obviously lots of good reasons for advocating full employment and income maintenance, but it is not clear that family stability is one of them. Surely, good social policy will not solve whatever problems divorce may pose for the quality of social life.

Solutions other than changing laws and making social policy more progressive elude me. Exhortation does not seem to work very well in any area, and it is difficult to be optimistic about formal educational programs' changing either attitudes or behavior toward marriage and family responsibility. Perhaps the alleged religious revival can have some effect, or a secular moral counterpart, but these are clearly private rather than governmental possibilities.

PERSONAL HURTS. Humane policies that lessened the frequency of divorce, if such could be found, might mitigate the personal hurt as well as the social integration consequences of divorce. In addition, however, public policy can help alleviate hurtful consequences of marital disruption.

The basic, pressing problem of poverty can be attacked through a variety of public programs, from job creation and welfare reform, already on the public agenda, to children's allowances, guaranteed maintenance allowances, and tax credits. Many European countries already have such programs and have demonstrated their feasibility. The arguments for income maintenance seem to me compelling: while income maintenance may not slow the incidence of divorces, it could certainly dissolve the link between divorce and abject poverty.

The social and emotional problems that follow marital disruption are less amenable to public solution. This is probably just as well, since most people see these as private problems and do not relish governmental intrusion. However, some simple social services could possibly relieve some of the pressures on single-parent families and thus increase their chances of coping successfully with their situations. These services include child care, especially emergency child care, short-term homemaker services (for times when the demands of job and children on the single parent are simply too much), and hotlines. In addition it may not be out of place for public service agencies to provide some counseling for adults and children or to encourage the formation of self-help groups on the model of Parents Without Partners. Public agencies might also provide information and assistance to those who deal with single-parent families in other settings—schools, Head Start programs, welfare agencies, and so on.

The most important social and emotional supports for men, women, and children after divorce obviously come from themselves, their families, and their friends. Public agencies can allow and encourage the development of this support, and can provide supplemental services in special cases.

PUBLIC RESOURCES. Income maintenance and social service programs obviously raise the issue of resources. The issue has two parts: general claims on public resources and special claims resulting from marital disruption. It seems that one special claim may be legitimate, a claim that requires the government to guarantee a maintenance allowance for single parents with children and that uses the resources of government to collect support payments from parents not living with their children. This recommendation recognizes the obligation of parents to support children but removes the burden of collecting support from the parent and places it on the government. It also guarantees continuous support, a kind of loan program that should not prove unreasonably expensive.

Only when the parents are too poor to provide adequate support must the government allocate additional resources. In those cases, however, claims are based on poverty rather than on single-parent status. Programs for jobs and income would presumably apply to the population, or the population with children, on the basis of income rather than marital status. Single parents would share in the benefits of such programs, but the programs would not be designed for single parents alone. That our present welfare system should be reformed so as to remove distinctions based on marital status has long been recognized. It is probably not wise, and it is certainly not fair, to maintain such distinctions.

The same line of argument suggests that social service programs should also be designed for use by all families in need. Two-parent families also experience tension and stress and occasionally need support services. If these services are to be made available, they should be available to all. They are a legitimate use of public funds and would be well worth their cost.

CONCLUSION

In summary, it seems that there is no pressing reason to despair about the rising divorce rate, nor to take strong public steps to turn it around. The consequences of the current level of divorce are not so bad, and can in any case be alleviated by the kinds of social policy we ought to advocate independent of the divorce rate. The institutions of marriage and family are not yet seriously threatened; and even if they were, it is not clear that there is anything to be done which would not create a situation even worse than the present one. We need social policy to make the society a more just and tolerable place for all sorts of families, but in any case we must let the divorce rate run its own course.

I have been described as the Pollyanna of American sociology for an earlier book, and perhaps these conclusions simply confirm that judgment. Other interpretations of the evidence and issues will, no doubt, come forth.

REFERENCES

Bane, M. J. Marital separation and the lives of children. *Journal of Social Issues,* 1976, *32,* 103–117.

Campbell, A., Converse, P. E., & Rodgers, W. L. *The quality of American life.* New York: Russell Sage, 1976.

Carter, H., & Glick, P. C. *Marriage and divorce: A social and economic study.* Cambridge, Mass.: Harvard University Press, 1970.

Durkheim, E. *Suicide.* New York: Free Press, 1975.

Hannon, M. T., Tuma, N. B., & Groenveld, L. P. Income and marital events: Evidence from an income maintenance experiment. *American Journal of Sociology,* 1978, *82,* 1186–1211.

Haygbe, H. Marital and family characteristics of workers, March 1977. *Monthly Labor Review,* 1978, *101*(2), pp. 51–54.

Hill, D. & Hoffman, S. Husbands and wives. In G. J. Duncan & J. N. Morgan (Eds.), *Five thousand American families* (Vol. 5). Ann Arbor: Institute for Social Research, 1977.

Hoffman, S. & Holmes, J. Husbands, wives and divorce. In G. J. Duncan & J. N. Morgan (Eds.), *Five thousand American families* (Vol. 4). Ann Arbor: Institute for Social Research, 1976.

Lasch, C. *Haven in a heartless world.* New York: Basic Books, 1977.

Longfellow, C. Divorce in context: Its impact on children. In G. Levinger & O. Moles (Eds.), *Divorce and separation.* New York: Basic Books, 1978.

Moles, O. Marital dissolution and public assistance payments. In G. Levinger & O. Moles (Eds.), *Divorce and separation* New York: Basic Books, 1978.

National Center for Health Statistics. *Divorces: Analysis of changes.* Vital and Health Statistics, Series 21, No. 22, 1973.

National Center for Health Statistics. *Vital statistics of the United States 1973* (Vol. 3: *Marriage and divorce).* Washington, D.C.: U.S. Government Printing Office, 1977.

National Center for Health Statistics. *Monthly Vital Statistics Report* (Advance report, "Final divorce statistic, 1977"), May 16, 1979, *28*(2), Supplement.

Rein, M. & Rainwater, L. Patterns of welfare use. Working paper #47, Joint Center for Urban Studies of the Massachusetts Institute of Technology and Harvard University, 1977.

Ross, H., & Sawhill, I. *Time of transition.* Washington, D.C.: Urban Institute, 1975.

Sawhill, I., Peabody, G. E., Jones, C. A., & Caldwell, S. B. *Income transfers and family structure.* Washington, D.C.: Urban Institute, 1975.

U.S. Bureau of the Census. *Census of population: 1970, marital status* (Final report PC (2)–4C). Washington, D.C.: U.S. Government Printing Office, 1972.

U.S. Bureau of the Census. *Statistical abstract of the United States 1977.* Washington, D.C.: U.S. Government Printing Office, 1977a.

U.S. Bureau of the Census. Marriage, divorce, widowhood and remarriage by family characteristics: June 1975. *Current Population Reports* (Series P–20, No. 312). Washington, D.C.: U.S. Government Printing Office, 1977b.

U.S. Bureau of the Census. Marital status and living arrangements, 1976. *Current Population Reports* (Series P–20, No. 306). Washington, D.C.: U.S. Government Printing Office, 1977c.

U.S. Bureau of the Census. Characteristics of the population below the poverty level: 1976. *Current Population Reports* (Series P–60, No. 115). Washington, D.C.: U.S. Government Printing Office, 1978.

Weiss, R. *Marital separation.* New York: Basic Books, 1975.

Zill, N. Divorce, marital happiness and the mental health of children: Findings from the FCD national survey of children. Paper prepared for the NIMH workshop on Divorce and Children, Bethesda, Maryland, 1978.

Chapter 8

Family Roles in a 20-Year Perspective

Elizabeth Douvan

Of the many remarkable insights which have come our way as a legacy
bestowed on the intellectual arena by the women's movement, two have
been most impressive: Matina Horner's (1970) pointing to the complexity of women's motives regarding achievement, and the demonstration
by Louise Tilly and her students (Moch, 1976; Tilly & Scott, 1978) that
industrialization not only failed to destroy the family, but actually
strengthened family bonds in certain ways for certain people.

The two chapters in this volume from the national replication
study[1] touch and explore these insights. Joseph Veroff presents data on
the work role. Among other issues, he is critically concerned in this
analysis with the way in which work and achievement are integrated
into women's lives, and the ways in which that integration has changed
over the last generation (see Chapter 6). This chapter presents early
analyses of family roles—how they figure in the life space of American
adults, the normative structure which surrounds marriage and parenthood, how family roles are performed, the part they play in people's
self-definitions. The extent to which changes have occurred in these
critical life roles over the last 20 years will be explored.

We approach the topic with a conservative bias, which may be
evident from my allusion to Louise Tilly's research. Tilly and her colleagues have shown that forces associated with industrial develop-

---

[1]In 1976 Joseph Veroff, Richard Kulka, and I conducted a national interview study (2,264
adult respondents chosen to represent the adult population residing in households)
which repeated a study done in 1957 by Gurin, Veroff, and Feld (1960). The replication is
reported in two vols.: *The inner American*, and *Mental health in America*, New York: Basic
Books, 1981.

Elizabeth Douvan, Ph.D. • Survey Research Center, Institute for Social Research, University of Michigan, Ann Arbor, Michigan 48106.

ment—the move from country to city, the dilution of ascribed statuses and palpable functions of peasant family organization, the isolation and alienation of factory work—led at least some members of society to value primary relationships and marriage more highly than they might have under the presumptive and nonreflective conditions of peasant family life. Young women isolated in the city and factory were likely to view marriage as an attractive alternative. Youngsters alone in America cultivated their attachments to and sentiments for their families in Europe with a steadfastness which they might not have shown had they stayed at home where they could have taken their families for granted or even tripped over their filial loyalties in the normal course of seeking their own autonomy, their own space.

What is particularly striking about this work is not simply the demonstration that family bonds withstood the centripetal force of industrial development, but the convincing argument that, paradoxically, this very force set up counterforces within individuals and families which resisted the destruction of family life.

If industrialization could not destroy the family—and obviously it did not, no matter how much pain and devastation it caused in some individual families—then it seems clear that the pill will not do it either, that people will find a way, bumpy and circuitous though that way may be during the transition, to reconstitute and reassert the legitimacy and value of family relations. The world historical event of birth control technology will affect relationships and ideology, but it will not ultimately destroy the family or supplant its role in the lives and self-definitions of most people.

Often in the past, events which the media, politicians, and social analysts declared were occurring and were pervasive, our national data did not uncover in anything approaching pervasiveness in the national consciousness. "The American people will not stand by and allow Red China admission to the United Nations" said the politicians. But national surveys at the moment these declarations were made showed quite clearly that "the American people" were in actuality apathetic about mainland China. The generation gap was touted but data revealed that the overwhelming majority of parents and children accommodated to each other because they were very similar in their values and views on most issues. A famous anthropologist advised us to include questions about horseback riding in our studies of adolescents because "adolescent girls are crazy about riding and horses," but we could not find 1% of the population of girls who had any interest in or experience with horses.

So now when we hear that the pill and the new sexual morality or women entering the labor force or impossible adolescents or the women's movement has destroyed family cohesion and has the family on the skids, we are more than mildly skeptical and immediately turn to the data. Our assumption has always been that most people know wherein important human meaning lies, and it seems doubtful that they yield that meaning casually.

And what do the data show? In brief we have in our analysis so far found clear evidence for the following assertions:

1. Norms about marriage and parenthood have indeed changed dramatically over the last 20 years. That is, attitudes about the necessity of marrying and having children and assumptions about people who do not choose to assume these roles have softened and loosened strikingly.

2. People's performance of these roles—the way they look at their own marriages and children, the importance they attach to family ties, the gratifications they derive from marriage and parenthood, the problems they encounter, the centrality of family roles in self-definitions and in support networks—have changed somewhat and in certain subgroups, but not nearly as much or as broadly as the futurists and our alarmist folklore would predict.

3. There has increased in the population a relational model for conceiving and discussing family roles, as well as other aspects of life. This seems to be part of the general secular trend in our culture. Individual guilt and blame are less prominent in people's discussion of problems or in attributions around particular choices and lifestyles. The space between people—the relationship itself—is more dominant in conceptions of both the values and hazards of family roles than was true 20 years age.

What is our evidence for these generalizations?

Norms

On the issue of normative change the evidence is rich and remarkably consistent. In both the 1957 and 1976 national studies all respondents were asked "Suppose all you knew about a man/woman—(same sex as respondent) was that he/she didn't want to get married. What would you guess he/she was like?" In 1957 four-fifths of all respondents gave answers which indicated that they thought such a choice bad—the person was seen as either sick or immoral, too selfish or too neurotic to marry. About one-fifth gave reasons that were relatively neutral. In 1976 these figures shifted to one-third negative and two-

Table 1. Year Comparisons of Attitudes toward Experience of Marriage for Men, Women, and the Total Sample

	Year	% men	% women	% total sample
	1957	N = (1,077)	(1,383)	(2,460)
Item	1976	N = (960)	(1,304)	(2,264)
1. Opinion of young person who refuses marriage				
Negative	1957	85	84	84
	1976	39	31	34
Neutral	1957	11	14	13
	1976	45	55	51
Positive	1957	4	3	3
	1976	16	14	14
2. Attitude toward marriage				
Very positive	1957	6	6	6
	1976	3	2	3
Positive	1957	42	34	36
	1976	29	27	26
Neutral	1957	32	35	33
	1976	41	42	41
Ambivalent, negative	1957	20	26	22
	1976	27	29	28
3. Restrictiveness of marriage				
No restriction	1957	23	21	21
	1976	14	16	14
Some restriction	1957	34	33	32
	1976	27	27	25
All restriction	1957	43	46	43
	1976	60	58	56
	Year	% men	% women	% total sample
	1957	N = (944)	(960)	(1,904)
	1976	N = (686)	(732)	(1,418)
4. Marital problem in past				
Yes	1957	38	49	47
	1976	58	62	62
5. Marital happiness				
Very happy	1957	48	45	46
	1976	55	51	52
Above average	1957	23	20	21
	1976	27	27	27

Table 1. (Continued)

	Year	% men	% women	% total sample
	1957	N = (944)	(960)	(1,904)
Item	1976	N = (686)	(732)	(1,418)
Average, not too happy	1957	28	35	32
	1976	18	22	20
6. Marital inadequacy				
A lot	1957	12	12	11
	1976	11	12	11
Sometimes	1957	41	43	41
	1976	41	44	41
Rarely, never	1957	47	45	45
	1976	48	45	45

thirds neutral or positive. That is, less than 35% of the population now thinks that a person who chooses not to marry must be sick or morally flawed. The weight of public opinion is now clearly on the side of neutrality. There is even a small minority of respondents in 1976 who view the choice positively (see Table 1).

Two other pieces of evidence about norms: In 1957 the large majority of respondents took this sanctioning attitude toward the refusal to marry *irrespective of their own marital status* (see Table 2). That is, even people who had themselves not married and respondents who had had bad marriages which ended in divorce (who might reasonably be expected to take a jaundiced view of the institution) overwhelmingly evaluated the choice not to marry negatively. The smallest proportion of any marital status group giving a negative evaluation occurs among single men, and here it is 74%; 80% of single and divorced women and 92% of divorced men answered the question in ways indicating a negative view of people who do not marry. The uniformity of response across groups is probably evidence of imposing societal norms.

The last bit of evidence requires skipping ahead of the data presentation a little, but it is such a compelling and poignant reflection of the moral force of pro-marriage norms in 1957 that it seems appropriate here. Many will remember that Jessie Bernard used the 1957 data as evidence for one of her inimitable, provocative generalizations: to wit, that marriage was good for men but bad for women (Bernard, 1972). She based the assertion on symptom data and general life-satisfaction which

Table 2. Selected Marital Attitudes and Mental Health Indices by Marital Status and Year

		Men				Women			
Item	Year	% married (N) =	% single	% divorced	% widowed	% married	% single	% divorced	% widowed
	1957	(889)	(80)	(39)	(47)	(948)	(73)	(109)	(225)
	1976	(657)	(123)	(79)	(40)	(710)	(115)	(168)	(234)
1. Opinion, refusal to marry									
Negative	1957	86	74	92	96	85	80	80	83
	1976	42	26	33	38	31	14	30	39
Neutral	1957	11	14	5	2	13	18	15	16
	1976	45	50	42	38	56	68	55	46
Positive	1957	4	13	3	2	3	3	6	1
	1976	13	24	25	25	13	18	16	15
2. Attitude toward marriage									
Positive	1957	59	26	45	68	40	46	30	43
	1976	36	14	25	39	28	17	24	42
Negative	1957	16	29	28	5	23	19	31	16
	1976	18	32	28	14	20	32	33	18
3. How restrictive marriage									
No restriction	1957	22	11	26	46	19	37	23	26
	1976	14	9	15	16	16	5	11	24
Some restriction	1957	35	26	27	29	33	27	26	33
	1976	29	23	13	28	27	23	23	25

All restriction	1957	42	63	47	25	47	36	51	41
	1976	57	68	72	56	57	72	65	51
Mental Health Measures									
4. Overall life happiness									
Very happy	1957	36	11	22	13	43	27	18	19
	1976	34	26	15	14	40	27	13	20
Not too happy	1957	8	12	20	40	7	11	27	24
	1976	8	11	19	21	6	14	20	19
5. Anxiety									
Low	1957	34	14	43	39	25	27	24	23
	1976	24	35	17	26	14	20	10	18
High	1957	13	25	13	24	24	15	28	36
	1976	10	5	16	11	25	25	33	29
6. Nervous breakdown									
Yes	1957	11	13	15	11	25	17	28	22
	1976	12	19	23	22	25	24	37	21
7. Immobilization									
Low	1957	50	36	53	75	45	55	49	75
	1976	36	26	24	55	40	33	38	61
High	1957	14	20	28	7	18	19	24	7
	1976	18	34	24	7	18	23	21	8

indicated that single men had more negative mental health symptoms
than married men, but that in general single women were more symp-
tom-free than married women. Because there was an age bias in these
findings (that is, single men are largely young men, and young men
were particularly high on the "immobilization" factor in the symptoms
on which Bernard's observation was based) we decided to look at attitudes toward marriage by marital status to see whether married women
were more negative in their attitudes than married men or single wom-
en. We found that indeed they were, but the findings were particularly
striking about single women. In every marital status in which people
had experienced the married state—that is, among the married, widowed, divorced, and separated—women were always more negative
about marriage than men were. Only among those who had never been
married were women more positive than men (see Table 2), and they
were extraordinarily positive—more so than married women and more
so than any group except widowed men. By 1976 their positive evaluation of the married state had dropped more dramatically than any other
group.

We read these findings as a reflection of the normative climate of
1957, in which marriage was defined as the only legitimate status for a
woman. While married women knew that marriage was no miraculous
solution to life's problems and had its own share of burdens and re-
strictions, women who were not married tended to think of marriage as
a blissful, desirable state. By 1976 much fresh air and openness had been
injected into discussions of marriage, and single women's idealization of
marriage had disappeared. Two factors may have contributed to the
earlier idealization: on the one hand if marriage is the only status valued
by a society (particularly for women) and refusal to marry is thought to
reflect on one's good sense or morality, then obviously unmarried people will want to marry. But some women who in fact preferred the single
state might also be reluctant to admit their preference or reveal in any
way that they reject the idea of marriage. In 1957 women were certainly
under intense normative pressure to marry in order to realize legitimate
femininity, and women who were not married idealized the married
state because they wanted very much to achieve it. Once normative
pressure relaxed, they could look at marriage as one possible course but
not the only or ideal way to live.

In a smaller sample used for pretesting we also asked people
whether a young person could have a happy life remaining single. Over
two-thirds of these respondents said yes. When we gave these same
respondents a list of reasons a young person might have for not marrying, the ones most often seen as good reasons were "not in love" (75%)
and "needs a lot of freedom" (50%). Women more often thought love

was crucial; men more often alluded to freedom (see Table 2). Another reason thought valid by about half the respondents was "it's hard to think of living with one person for your whole life." Women more often thought this reason made sense (see Table 3). It is an interesting response, and in all likelihood a modern response. A hundred years ago people married, had children, and raised them. By that time a large proportion of wives died. Couples often did not go through the "empty nest" period or retirement because the partners did not both survive together that long.

One other indication that the norms for marriage are neither as strong nor as absolute as they once were is seen in responses to a question which asked "Is divorce ever a good solution to marital problems?" Some 20% of respondents said that divorce was never a good solution—that is apparently believed that marriage is an absolute and indissoluble commitment. But 80% think that, at least under some conditions, divorce is the best path. Men are somewhat more likely to reject the idea of divorce than women are (30% compared to 15%). In the pretest sample men were more likely also to say that, all in all, married

Table 3. Pretest Questions (Local Sample, 1976) about Marriage by Sex

Item	% men (N) = (47)	% women (42)
1. How much bothered by the idea of a young friend deciding never to marry		
Not at all	66	47
2. How much bothered by young friend not to have a valued work		
Not at all	27	33
3. Could young person have good life remaining single?		
Yes	71	85
4. Good reason for remaining single?		
Not in love	78	83
Needs freedom	56	49
Hard to think of living whole life with one person	39	55
Knows too many bad marriages	11	11
5. Which choice has more advantages: marriage or remaining single?		
Being married	70	56
6. Divorce ever a good solution?		
Never	30	15

life has more advantages than being single (70% of males, 56% of females).

Evidence indicates that pro-natal norms have also declined, that people in a national sample are now essentially neutral in their response to a young couple who decide never to have children. They are not as likely to see childlessness as either neurotic or morally reprehensible as people did in earlier studies.

Lest we begin to think that Americans have simply become more tolerant of any behavior—a fact which might testify to growing norm-lessness in our society—we should say that in the area of work we do not find the same neutrality. We asked pretest respondents to think about a young woman or man who had decided not to have an impor-tant work life, not to invest the self in work but to work only as much as she or he needed to to survive. The answers were very different and much less neutral. Over two-thirds of the respondents (both men and women) said that this would bother them somewhat or a lot—much more, in other words, than they are bothered by a person who decides not to marry. A great deal may have changed, but the Protestant work ethic has survived!

So family norms have softened. And all in all that is probably a good thing, reflecting a growth in tolerance toward varied life paths. But we must remember that norms tell us about people's expectations of the behavior of others; they are abstract. When we look at people's own behavior, we find that most people do marry and have children, and that they value these choices they make.

One derivation and series of findings ought to be added to the data on norms: if norms soften and people are more tolerant toward a variety of lifestyles, one might expect that the negative effect of choosing a deviant (i.e., nonnormative) lifestyle would also diminish. The evidence we have indicates, however, that this is not so. In 1957 two groups in the population showed notable symptoms of stress: divorced women and single men. We had thought some of this stress—any part attributable to a sense of deviance and normative pressure—might have ameliorated with a change in norms. But in fact our data reveal that in 1976 single men and divorced women are still exceptionally stressed. Either a time lag is required for changed norms to translate to the particularity of the individual's psychological state or—more likely—the stress of these positions comes from forces other than social norms. The divorced woman—particularly if she is raising children alone—faces realities like poverty and role overload which are so oppressive that they make social stigma pale by comparison.

The unmarried male in our culture has still not experienced a social-ization which prepares him with adequate social and interpersonal skills to create and maintain a reasonably integrated and satisfying life with people on his own—that is, without a wife to initiate and maintain friendships and kinship ties.

CENTRALITY AND PERFORMANCE OF FAMILY ROLES

Aside from questions having to do with norms and a generalized view of marriage and its meaning, there is notable stability in the structure of family attitudes. Unlike the area of work where relationships among attitudes show some remarkable variations from 1957 to 1976, the relationships among marital happiness, marital problems, and the sense of adequacy in the spouse role remain essentially the same over the generation. Relationships between these attitudes and demographic factors like age and education change little in direction even when the magnitude of the relationship changes. We interpret this stability as a reflection of salience. Presumably attitudes are more coherently structured around objects, goals, and values which are more important to one's adaptation and life, and stability of structure reflects this same importance.

But we have other indications of the centrality of family roles. In the data Veroff presents (Chapter 6, Tables 12–15), where values were chosen by respondents and they were then asked how much each of the critical life roles and leisure and housework contributed to the realization of their highest value, family roles almost uniformly rate higher in value production than the job role does. There are one or two exceptions—for example, older women say that the job allows them a lot of self-actualization, more so than marriage. And it is partly the rareness of this ordering which lends it a certain weight. But even in this case parenting yields more self-actualization than the job; and when the same analysis is restricted to people who occupy all three roles, women never rate the job more fulfilling than family roles and men (only older men) do so only for self-actualization and security. In most cases the job rates only half or two-thirds as high as one or the other of the family roles.

Another series of questions asked respondents to choose between two fixed alternatives: "Which of these would you rather overhear someone say about you?"

She/he is a fine mother/father	OR	She/he is excellent at her/his work
She/he is a good wife/husband	OR	She/he is excellent at her/his work
She/he is a good wife/husband	OR	She/he is a fine mother/father

ELIZABETH DOUVAN

Either family role pitted against work yields a ratio in favor of family
larger than 3:1 (see Table 4). The salience of family roles is the same for
males and females. When the spouse role is compared to the parent role,
the spouse role dominates in a ratio of 3:2 for men and slightly less for
women. This series seems to touch very close to the core sense of self—
that aspect which carries central significance or meaning. Clearly for
both men and women such significance attaches to family more than to
work.

The fact that people value their family attachments and hold them
central to self-definition does not mean that marriage and parenthood
are without problems and conflicts. We know from divorce statistics that
problems abound. And in 1976 our findings reveal a significant increase
in people's awareness of marital stress and of the fact that family roles
involve problems and burdens as well as satisfactions. Respondents
were asked "How is a man's (woman's) life changed by being married?"
In 1957 some 42% of the national sample gave answers which indicated a
view of marriage as enlarging the individual, opening new oppor-

Table 4. Sex Comparisons on Questions Asked Only in 1976

Item	% men N = (960)	% women (1,304)	% total (2,460)
1. Is divorce ever a good solution?			
Often	13	11	12
Sometimes	47	62	54
Rarely	24	17	21
Never	13	8	10
2. Rather overhear			
Good parent	74	73	74
Good worker	22	23	23
Fine parent	33	38	36
Fine spouse	54	50	52
Fine spouse	68	69	69
Good worker	26	28	27
3. Most important value			
Sense of belonging	6	10	8
Excitement	—[a]	—[a]	—[a]
Warm relationships with others	13	18	16
Self-fulfillment	9	10	10
Being well-respected	8	9	9
Fun and enjoyment in life	7	3	4
Security	20	21	20
Self-respect	21	20	21
A sense of accomplishment	14	9	11

[a]Less than one-half of 1%.

tunities (e.g., "makes a person more mature," "gives a person a goal in life"). In 1976 the proportion of such answers had dropped to 29%—a 13% decrease in this enlarging conception, and the proportion of people who saw marriage only as restrictive or burdensome increased by 13% (see Table 1).

When, however, we look at questions about happiness in marriage and the sense of adequacy in the marital role ("Almost all men/women feel that they are not as good husbands/wives as they would like to be. Have you ever felt this way?"), we find that there has been no decrease in people's feelings of adequacy, and a rather strong trend toward increased happiness in marriage. One might immediately think that the increase in marital happiness is an artifact of the higher divorce rate in 1976—that the people who are unhappy in marriages are less likely to stay in those marriages today than they were 20 years ago. But an analysis of first and later marriages does not support this interpretation—the increase occurs equally in each kind of marriage from 1957 to 1976.

In Table 2 we note certain variations in response to marriage across marital status categories. While all groups change in the direction of increased skepticism (one might say realism) about the positive outcomes of marriage, the largest changes have occurred among single women and divorced and widowed men. Overall, men have changed more than women, except for the category of unmarried women. Unmarried men have changed little, but they seem to have been unusually negative toward marriage even in 1957. In 1957 unmarried women were exceptionally positive about the married state, and in 1976 they have become essentially indistinguishable from unmarried men in their awareness of the negative and burdensome features of marriage. They also shift dramatically in their attitude toward parenting, becoming the most negative of any group in this analysis.

In discussing norms, we interpreted these findings about the attitudes of unmarried women—particularly what seemed to be an idealization of marriage in 1957—as revealing something about the stringency of pro-marriage norms in our society at that time. It seems important to note, however, that if unmarried women are by and large young women, the changes in their attitudes toward marriage and children could have major significance for social change in the future. That is, one might say that young unmarried women were traditionally idealistic about marriage and mothering and that it was this idealism which ensured that they *would* marry and have children in sufficient numbers to ensure societal continuity. It could be especially critical that the *young* women were turning away from traditional institutions. And while our data indicate that the young were always somewhat less positive toward marriage and parenting than older people (a dissonance phenomenon?), the gap does seem to have grown.

Why should divorced and widowed men have changed their views of marriage? We would suggest that the widowed men held a highly idealized view of marriage in 1957. In part their shift may be attributable simply to the fact that they had farther to shift. And divorced men in 1957 may have come out of marriage and divorce relatively unscathed compared to men in the same situation today. In 1957 divorce was likely to be sought by men and men could relatively easily move into other marriages, leaving the first wife to rear the children and bear the resentment. In 1976, on the other hand, women may be instituting a larger number of divorces, and more fathers are sharing custody of dependent children or taking full custody—an arrangement virtually unheard of in the 1950s. Men then may well be suffering a larger share of the problems created by divorce, and reacting more negatively to the idea of marriage as a consequence.

Among people who are currently married the question which drew the largest difference over time asks: "Even in cases where married people are happy there have often been times in the past when they weren't too happy—when they had problems getting along with each other. Has this ever been true for you?" The difference here is that respondents in 1976 are more likely to say that they have at some point had problems in their marriage. The shift is larger for men than for women (from 38% to 58% for men, from 49% to 62% for women), although women give the response more often than men do in both years.

Now this finding—that respondents, and particularly men, are more likely to say in 1976 they have experienced problems in their marriages—might mean several things. It might indicate that males have come to be more open—with themselves and with interviewers—about negative feelings, complaints, and problems. In general we know from our own studies and from other research about health and mental health that women are more aware of the internal world, of the reality of feelings and fantasy. Yet the increase in men's report of marriage problems stands out: they do not show the same large increase in either parenting or work. It seems, in other words, to be a real finding which reflects real stress.

Along with increased recognition of problems in marriage we find increased happiness in marriage. This is not necessarily contradictory, and indeed throughout the earlier study awareness of problems and gratification in a role tended to be associated, as though recognition of problems reflected in part a more articulated and larger set of expectations in various roles—as though holding more demanding criteria also implied a larger capacity for gratification in the role. If all you want from

Table 5. Use of Informal Support and Readiness for Referral to Formal Sources, by Sex

Item	Year (N)		% men	% women	% total
	(1976)	N =	(960)	(1,309)	(2,264)
1. Number of friends/relatives can talk about problems with[a]	(1976)				
Many			16	21	19
Several			21	25	23
A few			53	48	51
None			9	5	7
2. How often talk to friends/relatives about problems, worries[a]					
Very often			5	13	10
Often			10	19	15
Sometimes			30	35	33
Rarely			40	26	32
Never			15	7	11
	(1957 N)		(1,077)	(1,383)	(2,460)
3. Readiness for referral					
Have used help	1957		11	16	14
	1976		22	29	26
Could have used	1957		8	11	9
	1976		10	11	11
Might use	1957		27	27	27
	1976		22	22	22
Self-help	1975		37	32	34
	1976		33	27	29
Strong self-help	1957		12	9	10
	1976		8	6	7
4. Source of help					
Marriage counselor	1957		4	3	3
	1976		10	7	8
Other mental health specialist	1957		8	10	10
	1976		17	19	18
Social service	1957		2	4	3
	1976		5	3	4
5. How handle worries					
Nothing, do nothing	1957		13	9	10
	1976		11	8	9
Denial, displacement	1957		21	16	18
	1976		15	10	12

(*continued*)

Table 5. (Continued)

Item	Year (N)	% men	% women	% total
Action-individual	1957	21	9	14
	1976	22	13	17
Informal help	1957	23	30	25
	1976	31	40	35
Formal help	1957	3	3	3
	1976	2	3	3
Pray	1957	8	23	16
	1976	9	18	14
6. How handle unhappiness				
Nothing	1957	9	6	7
	1976	8	4	6
Denial, displacement	1957	17	14	15
	1976	15	14	15
Individual action	1957	10	5	7
	1976	11	5	8
Informal help	1957	21	23	22
	1976	31	35	33
Formal help	1957	2	2	2
	1976	1	2	2
Pray	1957	22	41	33
	1976	17	29	24

[a]The questions about use of friends as informal support were asked only in 1976.

a marriage is lack of conflict, a bland, smooth interaction, you can of course have this by reducing interaction to a minimum.

What do people do with the stress they experience in marriage? Do they, having admitted problems, do something about them? Do they talk the problem through with someone, either their spouses or friends? Are men in particular more likely than they were in 1957 to seek professional help?

The answers to these questions are complex and we have not by any means done all of the controlled analysis we need to do to answer definitively. We know already that across the board people's willingness or readiness to seek help from mental health and other professionals (doctors and ministers) has increased (from 15% to 27%, depending on the particular help source). But women are more likely to seek help than men, and if anything, women's readiness has increased more than men's. Men are also considerably less likely than women to say that they have informal supports—friends or relatives—they can talk to (see Table 5).

In the parent role we find no striking changes in reports of satisfaction, feelings of adequacy, or problems among parents, nothing as large or consistent as changes in the report of marriage problems. To the general question asked of everyone (whether they had children or not) we find an increase in the proportion of people viewing parenthood entirely as restricting or burdensome (13%) but the satisfaction and adequacy expressed by parents—the fact that they do not consistently report more problems than 1957 parents—makes it look like it is the childless who are expressing negative conceptions of parenthood (see Table 6).

Table 6. Parenting Attitudes by Sex and Year

	Year		% men	% women	% total
Item	1957	N = (1,077)		(1,382)	(2,459)
	1976	N = (960)		(1,304)	(2,264)
1. Attitude toward parenthood					
Positive	1957		59	52	55
	1976		45	39	37
Neutral	1957		22	18	19
	1976		30	24	26
Ambivalent, negative	1957		14	25	20
	1976		18	32	26
2. How restrictive parenting?					
No restriction	1957		38	34	36
	1976		24	19	21
Some restriction	1957		34	34	34
	1976		32	36	34
All restriction	1957		29	32	30
	1976		45	45	45
3. Problem raising children?					
Yes	1957		25	16	20
	1976		28	20	23
4. Inadequacy as parent?					
A lot	1957		14	18	16
	1976		15	17	16
Sometimes	1957		28	34	31
	1976		36	39	37
Rarely, never	1957		59	47	51
	1976		48	44	46

The Diffusion of a Relationship Model

In discussing family roles, respondents in 1976 seem to have a new model in which prescribed aspects of the role are less salient and relational elements have gained currency. The data here are not completely consistent, but in describing how marriage changes a person's life, the best parts of their own marriages, and the best things about parenthood, 1976 respondents more often than those in 1957 phrase answers in the vocabulary of relationships. These findings are consistent with other findings from the study about the willingness and ability of people to conceive personal problems in a psychological frame rather than either situationally or individually determined. Together, they argue for an increasingly differentiated and sophisticated conception of relationships.

On the other hand when people are asked to talk specifically about the problems they have had in marriage or in raising their children, relationship allusions do not increase from 1957 to 1976. In fact they decrease slightly. It may be that discussing problems provokes concepts of guilt and blame whereas discussing "changes brought by marriage" or "the nicest things about your marriage" is more susceptible to interpretation as an aspect of the relationship. That is, when a situation is good or neutral it may more readily be cast as a product of interaction. When it is negative it calls forth more primitive evaluative attributions which are easiest to locate in an individual or a hostile environment (see Table 7).

Table 7. Allusion to Relationship in 1957 and 1976 for Men, Women, and Total Sample

Item	Year	% men	% women	% total
	(1957) N =	(889)	(948)	(1,837)
	(1976) N =	(657)	(710)	(1,367)
1. Allude to relationship in describing	1957	24	33	28
changes marriage brings	1976	31	47	40
2. Allude to relationship as "nicest	1957	40	44	43
thing about marriage"	1976	51	60	57
3. Allude to some aspect of relationship	1957	32	37	35
as "nicest thing about having	1976	38	41	40
children"				
4. Allude to some aspect of relationship	1957	12	14	13
as "least nice" about marriage	1976	21	24	23
5. Allude to relationship as source of	1957	26	28	27
own inadequacy as spouse	1976	31	27	28
6. Allude to relationship as source of	1957	32	31	31
marriage problem	1976	29	29	29

There is some hint in the data that the increase in allusion to relational aspects of marriage may represent a diffusion of this orientation from the most highly educated group in the population (college or over) to those with less education (particularly those with high school education). That is, in discussing marriage in general and the positive aspects of their own marriages, the high school group showed a larger relative increase in relational responses than did the college educated.

One might also speculate that a relational stance might have increased relatively more among males than females, but this is clearly not the case. Men do show quite large shifts, but women shift more. The socioemotional and relationship arenas are still sex linked. We find strong evidence of this fact in many places in the study. In the selection of a most important value, for example, women in 1976 choose the values of warm human relationships and love more than men do, and men choose hedonism and self-actualization more than women. But young women are closer to young men in the choice of the work-related "self-actualization" than they are to older women (see Table 4).

REFERENCES

Bernard, J. *The future of marriage.* New York: Bantam, 1972.
Gurin, G., Veroff, J., & Feld, S. *Americans view their mental health.* New York: Basic Books, 1960.
Horner, M. Femininity and successful achievement: A basic inconsistency. In J. Bardwick *et al., Feminine personality and conflict.* Belmont, Calif.: Brooks/ Cole, 1970.
Moch, L. D. Domestic servants in London and Paris, 1890 to 1914. In D. McGuigan (Ed.), *New research on women and sex roles.* Ann Arbor: University of Michigan, Center for Continuing Education of Women, 1976.
Tilly, L. A. & Scott, J. W. *Women, work, and family.* New York: Holt, Rinehart and Winston, 1978.
Veroff, J., Douvan, E., and Kulka, R. *The inner American.* New York: Basic Books, 1981.
Veroff, J., Kulka, R., and Douvan, E. *Mental health in America.* New York: Basic Books, 1981.

PART III

Options, Obstacles, and Opportunities

The consensus in this country is that the American educational system has played a critical role in shaping the goals and expectations that men and women have for themselves and those around them. The educational level of women has proved to be a very important determinant and predictor of some of our most basic social indicators, such as fertility rate and family size, employment patterns, and the level of satisfaction felt with lifestyle and employment status.

For all these reasons, many believe that the extent of participation of women at various levels of the educational system is a sensitive index of the position and value that women have in the society. Women's position in the educational system, it is argued, is very closely associated with the expectations held for and ultimately by them, and reflects accurately the roles they are called upon to play in the home, in the family, in the political arena, in the paid and unpaid work force, and in the community. If this argument is true, then women interested in expanding their roles have little cause for rejoicing. Despite the fact that women have had consistently better academic records than men at each level of the educational system, at each step of the way a decreasing proportion of women go on to the next higher level.

Although the fraction of undergraduates in America who are women has exceeded the 50% mark, up substantially from 30 years ago, we find that attitudes and beliefs about women's education still bear the stamp of an earlier era when it was assumed by most that women could not withstand the rigors of advanced education.

Even though a virtual revolution in thought has occurred since those 19th-century days when women were not assumed to be educable in the same sense as men, the old fears about physical and moral deterioration have in many instances been replaced by new fears about the impact of education for women on the economy, on the workplace, and especially on marriage and the family.

Until recently, higher education for women still had to be justified on the grounds that it would make women better homemakers, better mothers, and more intelligent companions for their husbands. And although education in its own right has become an acceptable goal for women today, we have only recently recognized through research the pervasiveness of sex-based inequalities in higher education, as well as the persistence of negative attitudes and habits that greatly inhibit efforts to provide women with equal educational opportunity. The need for a searching look at discrepancies between stereotypes and reality and for a significant reformation and refinement of existing stereotypic assumptions and expectations about women and higher education has been established.

The chapter by Valory Mitchell and Jeanne Block, "Assessing Personal and Social Change in Two Generations," discusses the study the authors undertook to follow the student generation of the 1960s and their parents. They found that those who were adolescents in the 1960s were occupied in adulthood with prototypical tasks of the adult developmental stage. They found too that these students and their parents held common attitudes and styles, although they disagreed on methods of implementation. The developmental paths of both students and parents were in sharp contrast to the patterns of conservative families whose young people and parents did not deviate from convention or tradition. The authors suggest the need for additional study of the ways in which changes in the meanings of socially noticeable behavior affect future personal and social change.

Joseph Katz, in his chapter "The Past and Future of the Undergraduate Woman," describes some of the favoring conditions in the last 20 years which stimulated the large-scale attitude changes concerning women's place in higher education. He reviews many of the advances that have occurred in undergraduate education for women in the last decade, and concludes with some sound recommendations for policy and structural changes within institutions which might lend aid to the movement for equality of opportunity and quality in women's education.

Abigail Stewart and Patricia Salt, in their chapter "Changing Sex Roles," suggest that the pattern of role differences between the sexes changed between 1964 and 1978. Focusing on the concept of androgyny, they discuss the integration of traditionally male instrumental roles with traditionally female expressive roles and personalities. They conclude that female activities have become more instrumental and more like those engaged in by men in the past, but that male activities have not become substantially more expressive. In their attitudes, however, men show increasingly expressive concerns, even as women show increasingly instrumental concerns. This evidence supporting the concept of androgyny defines a task for the educator: to prepare both men and women students to assume both expressive and instrumental roles.

Jacqueline Fleming discusses the theory of black matriarchy, which has been prominent in social science literature and in popular beliefs about black family structure. She cites evidence to dispute the theory of the absent father and dominant mother; reviews evidence comparing the relative status of black men and women; and describes a study investigating different aspects of educational and occupational goals among black men and women, in which no sex differences were found in respect to many choices, and unexpected differences were discovered in respect to others.

Finally, Rhona and Robert Rapoport, in a concluding and summarizing statement, trace many common themes introduced through the preceding chapters. They consider changes in the roles of men and women in the family, in the work force, and in society. They discuss the linkages that individuals make outside their families, the value and the complex changes and conflicts surrounding these, and the consequences that derive from the trends and patterns described by each contributor.

Chapter 9

Assessing Personal and Social Change in Two Generations

VALORY MITCHELL AND JEANNE H. BLOCK

As we look back on the student generation of the 1960s we see that the university environment was characterized by unprecedented unrest. Many young people were developing their own values and lifestyles in a milieu marked by conflict between the value system they perceived in their families and those of significant others outside the family context. The substantive focal concerns were civil rights, humanitarian goals and ethical consistency, outrage against the war in Vietnam, and disillusionment with the university. Seeking to develop perspective about the impact of a decade of social unrest on the personological characteristics, value orientations, and goal definitions of persons in proximity to this foment is an irresistable temptation.

We began our study—a 10-year follow-up of students who were on the Berkeley campus in 1967, and their parents—within a theroretical context which we explore briefly here. We were attempting to view the response to unrest from the perspective of Piaget's (1954) notions about disequilibrium as a necessary condition for the elaboration and change in cognitive structures, Lewin's (1935) concept of restructuring as an adaptive response to destructuring of the environment, James Mark Baldwin's (1906) "dialectic of personal growth" which emphasizes the increasing ability to integrate and synthesize polarities as development proceeds, and Werner's (1948) orthogenetic principle. All these concepts

VALORY MITCHELL, PH.D. • Institute of Personality Assessment, University of California at Berkeley, Berkeley, California 94720. JEANNE H. BLOCK, PH.D. • Formerly with the Institute for Human Development, University of California at Berkeley, Berkeley, California 94720. This chapter was prepared with assistance from the Radcliffe Data Resource and Research Center.

share the notion of conflict-induced growth—the organismic view that development proceeds according to a process of successive differentiations, restructuring of earlier understandings, and hierarchical integrations of experience.

For many students the campus environment of the 1960s was a personally disequilibrating experience. For some parents too, having a child at the university during that era may have prompted an unsettling of assumptions regarding generational continuity of ideologies and values, with a range of intrapersonal and interpersonal consequences in the ensuing decade. From this perspective, then, the student movement of the 1960s could be viewed as an "intervention study in nature," and the varying responses to disequilibration and stress explored and related to characteristics of the personal-social-familial environments.

A second orientation prompted us to expand our study to include the parents of the young people who had been on the Berkeley campus during that period. While conjectures about the impact of the tumultuous decade of the 1960s have been focused almost exclusively on the students who were on the campus at that time, we sought in this study to begin to explore signs of influence on the parents of these young people—inverting the direction of effects which has been presumed to obtain in most studies of developmental psychology.

THE ORIGINAL STUDY

In the original study, 322 students enrolled at the University of California at Berkeley were selected randomly from the total student body and were interviewed by graduate students in sociology, under the supervision of Dr. Robert H. Somers. The interview was standardized and precoded questions were used almost exclusively. The bulk of the interview was concerned with assessing student attitudes on a variety of social issues and developing information about the nature and degree of their involvement in protest activities on campus as well as eliciting a history of their experiences with drugs (Wood, 1974). The parents of these students were sent questionnaires by mail that closely paralleled the student interviews. Additionally, parents were asked separately to describe their childrearing values and orientations using a standardized 91-item Q-sort (Block, 1965). Responses were obtained from 66% of the parents.

Different methods were used to categorize the students according to their participation in the student movement, and according to the degree of continuity in the value systems of the students and their parents (Block, 1972). Additionally, student drug use was also employed as a stratifying variable ranging from no drug use through experimentation, infrequent use of marijuana, more frequent use of marijuana and occasional use of other drugs, to weekly use of marijuana combined with the use of other drugs (i.e., amphetamines, hashish, LSD, barbiturates, etc.).

THE CURRENT STUDY

Because of our nagging questions about the fates of the students studied earlier and our increasing interest in the responses of adults to dramatic social change, a modest follow-up study was proposed. With support from the Radcliffe Data Resource and Research Center, we mailed materials to the participants in the original study. The data that we will report here have been obtained from analyses of a 24-page questionnaire returned by former students, and a 10-page questionnaire completed by their parents. (In addition, students and their parents completed the Loevinger Sentence Completion Test which assesses ego development, and the students received a 63-item Q-sort which allows comparisons between individuals' self-descriptions of personality. These data are not reported here.)

Our data archive has been set up to reflect the three-member family (mother, father, and student) as the unit of analysis. Accordingly we have limited our use of 1969 data to those families (mother and/or father and/or student) for whom we have both 1969 and 1979 data. Our maximum number of cases then is 65.

The 1969 data include 36 attitude and value scales for each parent, and 12 attitude and value scales for students. The 1979 data include over 100 variables for each individual, and assess attitudes toward social issues, goal priorities, objective life circumstances, intrafamily relations, involvement with current social movements, and subjective views of current and past life domains (work, marriage, children, lifestyle, etc.).

Included in both forms of the questionnaire are items that have been used by previous investigators (Hoffman, personal communication, 1977; Stewart, personal communication, 1977) as well as a number of questions used in various Gallup polls. The inclusion of these "marker variables" provides the potential opportunity to compare the responses of persons in our samples with those obtained by other investigators using different samples. These "marker variables" also can permit us to describe the political and social attitudes expressed by persons in our sample relative to the responses obtained in large national surveys.

A CAVEAT. Before sharing our findings with you we would like to emphasize some of the hazards in conducting studies such as this one, and in interpreting the data issuing from follow-up investigations generally.

Research designs for follow-up studies are often necessarily guided by strategies of convenience and feasibility. For comparative purposes one is limited by the data earlier collected. Even the most visionary researcher cannot anticipate questions and issues that may assume salience at a later time. So it is inevitable that follow-up studies will be less neat, elegant, esthetic, and informative than one might wish.

We speak of the 1960s in an undifferentiated way, whereas it is important to recognize the change which marked the early, middle, and later years of that decade. The nature of issues salient for students during this time changed; the response to student protests by institutions and law enforcement agencies became increasingly punitive; the anger of the students, frustrated by society's lack of responsiveness to their exertions and exhortations for change, was expressed in increasingly unruly demonstrations; and the difference in response to student protests among universities and across communities contributes to diversity within the cohort and complicates comparative attempts.

A cohort is defined by the interaction of *Zeitgeist* and life stage. War and the social press to experiment with new lifestyles are likely to have varying effects on different cohorts. Whether these social conditions of the 1960s have had lasting effects on the lives of young people as they move into adulthood, or on adults as they move through mid-life, is a central empirical question for a study such as ours and one raison d'être for the cohort follow-up approach. At the same time it is not possible for our study to make any definitive statements with regard to the lasting impact of social forces of the 1960s, or of the potentially mitigating fact that the students whose well-publicized behavior was seen as a harbinger of change enacted those behaviors during their late adolescence—a period reputed to permit experimentation both tentatively and with relative impunity as regards future consequences.

Finally, the mobility and extent of changing circumstances which characterizes our society creates serious practical difficulties for researchers engaging in follow-up studies which attempt to span a period as lengthy as the 10 years which have elapsed since our first investigation of a population which then united in occupation (student) and locale (Berkeley). Because the 1967–1968 student responses contained highly sensitive material, we initiated elaborate procedures to safeguard the anonymity of participants. Since we had not maintained lists of student names, we had to rely on parents' names and addresses that the students provided us 10 years ago. Necessarily, materials for the parents included stamped packets containing the materials for their grown children who had earlier participated in our study, along with an explanation to the parents asking them to address and forward the packets. In the 10-year interim some parents were deceased and a very large number had moved. With the new regulations limiting the period of time that even first-class mail can be forwarded, we simply could not contact about 40% of the original sample. Therefore we have only a small number of cases. The available data may disproportionately represent certain outcomes, and the ways in which the data are no longer representative of a random sample cannot be well determined. For this reason the findings which we report here must be viewed as no more than suggestive of the cohort we have studied.

Having stated these caveats, let us summarize some of our findings to date.

RESEARCH QUESTIONS. The data we will report here pertain to three general questions.

The first of these is whether, in this sample, there are enduring differences in attitudes, values, life circumstances, and family relations which distinguish the political activists of the 1960s from those who, 10 years ago, were less politically involved. As a corollary we will examine whether the parents of these activist young people differ now from the parents of the contrasting student group.

Similarly, we have sought evidence of enduring differences related to more- and less-frequent drug use during the college years.

Finally, using two scale scores of personal values obtained from all family members in 1969, we will examine the patterns of correlations which appear to cohere conceptually now and in the preceding decade. We will explore whether the espousal of the personal values of open-mindedness, or espousal of faith in the power of the individual voice, are related to attitudes, values, life circumstances, or relationships within the individual or within that individual's family unit. We anticipated that the espousal of particular personal values would be related to specific attitudes and goals and, superordinately, to different patterns of influence among family members.

RESULTS

STUDENT ACTIVISTS AND THEIR FAMILIES

Results of Analyses. Using the reduced sample for whom we had both 1969 and 1979 data, we found that in 1969 the activists differed significantly from other students on 8 of our 12 attitude and personal value scales. They reported greater support for a spectrum of liberal issues, and were more likely to espouse openmindedness and individual development as personal values than were other students (N = 17, 38).

In 1979 many of the expected differences between the groups failed to reach significance. Two possible trends, shown in Table 1, are worthy of note, however. First, where differences appear in our sample with regard to support for current social movements (population control, health food, consumer activism), the former activists are now *less* intense than the contrast group in their support for these causes. On the other hand the former activists are more supportive of the hippie movement, have been more personally affected by spiritual growth movements, and are more likely to have changed some aspects of their thinking and attitudes about marriage and children.

Second, the former activists in our sample report greater current disagreement with their mothers on a variety of personal and social issues, although our data do not yield significant differences between them and other former students in closeness of relationship with mothers, in desire to see mother, or in willingness to confide in her in a crisis (N = 17, 21).

In 1969 mothers of activists differed significantly from other mothers on only 2 of 36 scales. These two reflect a greater liberality toward student protests and a stronger opposition to the war in Vietnam.

Fathers of activists, however, different from other fathers on 7 of the 36 scales in 1969. These differences indicate the fathers' greater liberality on social issues (the Vietnam War, civil rights, black power, civil disobedience), but at the same time also reveal greater disagreement between them and their children on these same issues.

In 1979 the parents of activists differed only slightly from other parents. The differences which reach significance suggest a greater disenchantment among these parents with the political domain. Both mothers and fathers are less interested now in being politically effective. Mothers of activists are less likely than other mothers to believe that people like them can have a voice in affairs in Washington, and these mothers have become less interested in being politically informed (N = 17, 37).

While in 1969 fathers of activists were more likely to disagree with their children, in 1979 mothers of activists report significantly greater disagreement with their children than other mothers, and they are less likely than other mothers to feel that their grown children have fulfilled their aspirations.

Discussion of Analyses. The few significant differences between former activists and the complement may be looked at in a number of ways. First, we ought not overlook the possibility that as our sample size

Table 1. t-*Test Differences between Activists and Nonactivists and Their Families*

Student data—1969	F	Significance
Activist favored the hippie movement more than nonactivist	1.92	.06
Student favored social change more than nonactivist	2.73	.009
Student opposed the Vietnam situation more than nonactivist	2.06	.05
Student opposed war more than nonactivist	1.90	.03
Student favored black power movement more than nonactivist	2.72	.009
Student valued openmindedness more than nonactivist	3.48	.001
Student valued individual development more than nonactivist	1.89	.07
Student had more positive attitude toward marijuana use than nonactivist	2.24	.03

Student data—1979		
Student had more specific vocational goals in college than nonactivist	1.78	.09
Former activists have a more positive attitude toward the hippie movement than former nonactivists	1.99	.06
Former activists are more personally affected by spiritual growth movements	1.78	.09
Former activists report more frequent use of marijuana now	2.11	.05
Former activists have more often changed their attitudes about marriage and children	1.99	.06
Former activists believe they disagree with their mothers more than do other students regarding religion	2.23	.04
Former activists believe they disagree with their mothers more than do other students regarding political party	2.15	.04
Former activists believe they disagree with their mothers more than other students do regarding choice of friends	1.73	.10
Former activists believe they disagree with their mothers more than other students do regarding general lifestyle	2.33	.03
Students who were not activists have a more positive attitude toward zero population growth	−1.76	.09
Consumer activism is more personally important to students who were *not* activists in 1969	−1.99	.06
Students who were *not* activists have a more positive attitude toward the gay liberation movement	−2.96	.007
Students who were *not* activists have a more positive attitude toward health food/nutrition	−3.04	.005
Students who were *not* activists support the Equal Rights Amendment more strongly than former activists	−2.48	.02

Mothers of activists (vs. mothers of nonactivists)—1969 data		
Had more positive attitude toward student demonstrations	3.30	.004
Were more opposed to the Vietnam situation	1.94	.06

(*continued*)

Table 1. (Continued)

	F	Significance
Mothers of former activists (versus mothers of former nonactivists)—1979 data		
Were less likely to believe that an individual's voice would be heard in Washington, D.C.	−2.47	.02
Oppose the death penalty for murder more strongly	2.43	.02
Are less supportive of state-run child care	−2.55	.01
Believe that they agree less with their children regarding student demonstrations than other mothers do	−1.89	.07
Believe that they agree less with their children regarding the child's choice of friends than other mothers do	−2.52	.02
Believe that their child is further from fulfilling her own aspirations than do mothers of nonactivists	−2.01	.05
It is less important to them than to other mothers to be socially at ease	2.12	.04
It is less important to them than to other mothers to be important in the community	1.81	.08
It has become less important to them *than it was* to:		
Be good at sports	1.93	.06
Be politically effective	2.26	.03
Feel at ease socially	1.65	.10
Be politically informed	1.92	.06
Fathers of activists (versus fathers of nonactivists)—1969 data		
Were less likely than fathers of nonactivists to agree with their children regarding the value of protests	−2.05	.05
Were less likely than fathers of nonactivists to agree with their children regarding premarital sex	−2.35	.03
Were less likely than other fathers to agree with their children regarding prosocial/social issues	−2.09	.04
Were *more* likely than fathers of nonactivists to have a positive view of civil disobedience	1.66	.10
Were more likely than fathers of nonactivists to oppose the war	1.70	.10
Were more likely than fathers of nonactivists to favor civil rights issues	1.91	.06
Fathers of former activists (vs. fathers of former nonactivists)—1979 data		
Were more likely than fathers of nonactivists to support the black power movement	2.30	.03
Were more in favor of legalizing marijuana	1.89	.07
Are less concerned than other fathers with being politically effective	1.77	.09

decreased the power of our study was simply insufficient to allow differences that might obtain in fact to become statistically manifest.

Perhaps, though, we ought to question also whether political activism in the 1960s is likely to be a salient indicator of patterned differences in this group of current adults. The prominent issues of 1979—women's liberation, inflation, and the crisis of energy sources—are issues which are not elective political concerns for this cohort; rather they affect all members of the culture, albeit in less public but perhaps more personal ways. In addition many of the changes wrought by the hippie movement—in personal appearance, music, art, decor, drug use, and relational style—have become fashionable, perhaps in a somewhat palliated or stereotypic form, throughout much of urban American culture. Other issues—the Vietnam War and the movement for civil rights—no longer present a unifying rallying cry to unite subgroups of people. In some ways one might be tempted to surmise a minor radicalization of the entire cohort as these changes, along with the leadership crisis in the country and the change in national policy toward the Vietnam situation, have become accepted. At the same time the growing complexity of present social issues may pull for a more diversified response pattern to these issues among all adult age groups today, in contrast to the more unified stance toward a spectrum of social issues addressed in the 1960s.

Then, too, the developmental press of the "social clock" (Neugarten, 1976) may lead the young adults of our sample to a current focus on establishing viable occupations and families of their own. These tasks are time- and energy-consuming ones, and may limit variability in the domains we sampled, at least at this particular point in the adult lives of this cohort. Such a view would support the finding that differences, when they do appear, show the activists to be somewhat more unconventional and experimental in their personal lifestyles, while nonetheless differing little from the complement in marital or work status, satisfaction with these aspects of their lives, or with regard to involvement in and attitudes toward current social issues.

The greater disagreement between former activists and their parents across the last decade may also be viewed from several perspectives. First, it may well be that the less conventional and therefore more noticeable behavior of the activist young people, both in 1969 and 1979, may disturb parents and thus lead to dissension in the family.

If, however, we look at the absolute levels of disagreement, the intrafamilial picture may take on a somewhat different cast. While parents of former activists report less absolute agreement with their children on a variety of topics, they nonetheless agree substantially with their childrens' choices, and are more satisfied with them than not. The relative differences between these and other parents then may be a

function of the activists' parents' willingness to acknowledge slight disagreements and dissatisfactions more than other parents want to do. If
so, their responses may be viewed as less defensive (Block, 1972), or
alternatively as one indicator of a tendency to note and express dissatisfactions, disagreements, or disappointments. Our data cannot discrimi-
nate whether, or to what extent, this reported dissension is a function of
the grown child's behavior, the parents' evaluative tendencies, or an
interaction. The number, type, and degree of parental aspirations for
their children may vary, and the specificity and clarity with which these
aspirations are perceived by the grown child or by the parents themselves may also add to the variance.

In addition, our more global measures of closeness of relationship
between parents and their grown children have not provided us a description of the content of these relationships. Some parent–child relationships may be characterized by substantial information flow about
the grown child's attitudes, behavior, and social milieu. Other relationships, viewed by the participants as equally close, may be limited in
practice to relatively little personal disclosure but no less a heartfelt
bond. If so, some parents and grown children may base their evaluations on specific interpersonal information, while others' reports of
agreement and satisfaction may be essentially a response bias generated
by the accomplishment of minimal role-related aspirations and interactions.

Additional data, presented below, bear on a number of these speculations. Accordingly, we will return to them after the larger body of
findings has been presented.

DRUG USE IN THE 1960s

Results of Analyses. The reduced sample for whom we had data at
the two time periods was divided according to more and less frequent
drug use. Less frequent drug use was defined as smoking marijuana less
than once a week and/or use of any other drug less than twice a year.
More frequent drug use was defined by smoking marijuana once a week
or more and using other drugs twice a year or more. While today this
criterion might not define high drug use, it is perhaps a comment on the
fluidity of contemporary standards in this area over the past decade to
note that when the original data were collected in the 1960s, no discrimi-
nations were coded to further differentiate the high end of the drug use
spectrum.

In the 1960s frequent drug users differed from other students on 4
of the 12 attitude and value scales. Not surprisingly, they held a more
positive view of marijuana. Additionally, they were more opposed to

the Vietnam War, more positive toward the hippie movement, and espoused the personal value of openmindedness to a greater extent (N =
14, 44).

In 1979 drug use history yielded few significant differences between
the groups of former students. Some intriguing contrasts are extant in
the data, however (see Table 2). Young people who engaged in frequent
drug use in college are less likely to feel that their experience has shown
college education to be important, even though these young people are
equally likely to have gone to graduate school and/or to have obtained
professional employment. They report less interest in their college
courses, yet believe that professors encouraged their interests more.

The more frequent drug users are more likely to have changed some
aspect of their attitudes about marriage and children, but are no less
likely to have married or become parents. They report being less religious than the comparison group, but are more likely to be personally
affected by spiritual growth movements. They indicate less supportive
attitudes than the complement toward women's liberation, population
control, and ecology movements (N = 8, 22).

No significant differences were obtained among the former students on intrafamily relations, frequency of current marijuana use, attitudes about marijuana, or with regard to current social issues.

In 1969 mothers of more frequent drug users differed from other
mothers in holding a more positive view of civil disobedience and student demonstrations, yet these mothers disagreed with their children on
these and other issues more than other mothers did.

As they look back on their goal priorities in the 1960s, mothers of
more frequent drug users recall that they gave more importance to helping others and to being good at arts than did other mothers. They gave
less importance to feeling at ease socially, and to being important in
their communities in the 1960s, and they continue to differ from the
comparison mothers in giving lower priorities to these goals. In 1979
they are more liberal than other mothers on a number of social issues.

Mothers of frequent drug users report four shifts in goal priorities
over the past 10 years that differ from the goal shifts reported by comparison mothers. Career has become more important to these mothers,
while accomplishment in arts and cooking, and the priority of giving
help to others has decreased in salience over the past decade (N = 16,
43).

Fathers of more frequent drug users differed significantly from
other fathers in 1969 only in their more positive view of marijuana and of
the black power movement. When asked to recall their goal priorities in
that period, fathers of frequent drug users differed in being less invested
in career goals than was the contrast group.

Table 2. t-*Test Differences between More and Less Frequent Drug Users and Their Families*

Student data—1969	F	Significance
More frequent drug users had a more positive attitude toward the hippie movement than less frequent drug users	2.20	.03
More frequent drug users were more opposed to the Vietnam situation than less frequent drug users	1.76	.08
More frequent drug users valued openmindedness more than less frequent drug users	1.68	.10
More frequent drug users had a more positive attitude toward the use of marijuana than less frequent drug users	2.46	.02

Student data—1979		
Former frequent drug users were *less* likely to believe that a college education is important for a person than were former infrequent drug users	−2.43	.02
Former frequent drug users recall being less interested in their courses at U.C. Berkeley than do former infrequent drug users	−1.85	.08
Former frequent drug users recall that professors encouraged their intellectual interests *more* than do former infrequent drug users	2.37	.03
Former frequent drug users feel that high income is a *more* important criterion in their job choice than do former infrequent drug users	2.09	.05
Former frequent drug users are now less religious than former infrequent drug users	−2.15	.04
Former frequent drug users have a less pro-ecology attitude than former infrequent drug users	−2.31	.03
Former frequent drug users have a more positive attitude about zero population growth than former infrequent drug users	1.97	.06
Former frequent drug users are less personally affected by women's liberation than former infrequent drug users	−2.27	.03
Former frequent drug users have a less positive attitude toward women's liberation than former infrequent drug users	−3.28	.003
Former frequent drug users have been less affected personally by spiritual growth movements than former infrequent drug users	−1.91	.07
Former frequent drug users are more likely to have changed their attitudes about marriage and children than former infrequent drug users	2.09	.05

Mothers of more frequent drug users (versus mothers of less frequent drug users)—1969 data		
Disagreed with their children more on her/his attitudes about premarital sex	3.38	.002

Table 2.   *(Continued)*

	F	Significance
Disagreed with their children more about the dangers of marijuana	3.17	.003
In general, disagreed more with the attitudes and values of their children	2.06	.04
Were less likely to endorse punitive measures instituted by the university against unruly students	−2.46	.02
Had a more favorable attitude toward student demonstrations	2.14	.04
Had a more positive view of the value of civil disobedience	2.41	.02
Mothers of former frequent drug users (versus mothers of former infrequent drug users)—1979 data		
Believe the individual has less chance to have a voice in the affairs of government in Washington	−2.54	.01
Oppose the death penalty	2.76	.01
Favor unconditional amnesty for Vietnam deserters	2.58	.01
Favor the Equal Rights Amendment	2.09	.04
Consider it less important that they feel socially at ease	−2.20	.03
It was, they recall, less important 10 years ago for them to feel socially at ease	−1.84	.07
Consider it less important that they be important in the community	−3.56	.001
Recall that it was less important to them to be important in the community 10 years ago	2.29	.03
Giving and helping others was a more important goal for them than for other mothers 10 years ago	1.73	.09
It was more important to them to be good at arts 10 years ago	2.57	.01
Feel it is less important to them now to be a good cook as compared with their view 10 years ago	−1.95	.05
It is *more* important to them now to be good in a career than it was 10 years ago	1.97	.05
It is less important to them now to give and help others where their recollection of their goals 10 years ago ranked this as a more important goal for them than for other mothers	−1.79	.08
It is less important to them now to be good at arts than it was 10 years ago	−2.05	.05
Fathers of more frequent drug users (versus fathers of less frequent drug users)—1969 data		
Had more favorable attitude toward the black power movement	2.43	.02
Had more favorable attitude toward marijuana than other fathers	1.72	.09

(continued)

Table 2. (*Continued*)

	F	Significance
Fathers of former frequent drug users (versus fathers of former infrequent drug users)—1979 data		
Are more likely to work for social change on the personal rather than the organized level	2.06	.05
Are likely to support a more liberal/left party	1.73	.09
Are more likely to favor legalization of marijuana	1.77	.09
Consider it less important to be an important member of the community	−1.77	.09
Consider it less important to be good in career	−2.21	.04
Recall that it was less important to them 10 years ago to be good in career	−2.21	.04
Consider it less important now than it was 10 years ago to be good at sports	−2.04	.05
Consider it less important now than it was 10 years ago to be well liked, popular	−2.14	.04

In 1979 these fathers are likely to be more liberal in political affiliation, and to favor the legalization of marijuana. Career goals and importance in the community are less important to them than to other fathers. In the past 10 years, these fathers report, they have become less concerned with being popular, well liked, and good at sports, where fathers of the contrast group do not (N = 9, 21).

Parents of students who had greater frequency of drug use in the 1960s did not differ from other parents in perceived closeness of relationship with their grown children, in amount of perceived present agreement with their children, or in the extent to which their child has satisfied their aspirations for her or him.

Discussion of Analyses. As with student activism, the variable of drug-use history has not fulfilled the expectation which may have been held for it as a marker of diverging developmental paths among the late adolescents of this sample. Again this may be due to the lack of statistical power which has resulted from the small size of our present sample.

Alternatively, at least in urban environments such as ours, marijuana use has lost much of its impact as a symbolic gesture. Where in the 1960s it may have been viewed as a sign of rebellion, a dabbling in extralegal activity, or "turning on" as precursor to "dropping out," weekly marijuana use among many young adults is now no more profound a behavior than the consumption of alcohol at a cocktail party. That history of marijuana use in the 1960s fails to distinguish frequency of use in the 1970s may indicate too that for the more conventional adolescents of our early sample, the destigmatization of marijuana and decline of publicity and legal sanctions surrounding it may have gradually eased the salience of prohibitions against occasional use.

Similarly, parents may no longer regard marijuana use by their grown children as an indicator of deviance; intergenerational disagreement which centered upon this behavior may have dissipated over the years as society has redirected its attention to other markers of success or difficulty in adjusting to adult conventions.

Any contrasts which appear in the data reported here must be viewed as no more than trends awaiting verification through a larger data base. A few such trends may, however, be worthy of comment.

First, the differences we have noted between more and less frequent drug users and their families reveal among the more frequent marijuana users families that were and have remained politically somewhat more liberal than the complement. Fathers of this group are less oriented toward the personal primacy of masculine status markers than are other fathers. Mothers, formerly distinguished by an interest in art and helping others, have allowed their priorities to shift to accommodate a growing concern with career, as their children reach adulthood. Both parents indicate less concern than the complement with reinforcement of esteem by others, eschewing the priorities of popularity, social ease, and importance in the local community for the preeminence of more private accomplishments. In sum, then, these parents portray themselves as being less concerned with meeting sex-role traditions, and less concerned with the approval and ease of the generalized other.

While more open to some of the unconventional behavior of young people in the 1960s, it is intriguing that the mothers report more disagreement with their children at that time. Perhaps these women, themselves in a process of change from the more sex-traditional priorities toward the more "agentic" concerns of a career (Bakan, 1966) may have been both open to their adolescent children's breaking with convention and at the same time more disturbed about these activities and their potential personal consequences.

Among the students, the differences which reach significance seem to indicate an alienation from academic life in the college years, and a disaffiliation from social movements of the 1970s. In the absence of other distinguishing characteristics, our data may reflect a continuity between parents and their grown children in some subtle felt distance from the wholehearted pursuit of conventional role-related values and goals which mark the prototypical college student, political liberal, homemaker, or breadwinner in contemporary American society. If so, the failure to detect signs of intergenerational dissension among this group may be partially explained by this superordinate continuity. Of course such speculations are generated to support null findings which may be explained more parsimoniously by our small sample size.

Correlates of Personal Values

Up to now we have used past participation in certain kinds of activities as the criterion to contrast groups of former students and their families. In the process we detected differing orientations toward more abstract personal values which also tend to differentiate between groups. If we assume that behavior is guided at least in part by the attempt to act in accord with one's values, then the espousal of different values may be a more useful anchor variable for patterns of attitudes and behaviors, both across time and across individuals within a family.

We will report here the intrafamily correlates of espousing two personal values: openmindedness, and faith in the power of the individual voice. As we will show, the espousal of openmindedness is related to liberal and nonpunitive attitudes toward political-social issues of the 1960s, while espousal of faith in the power of the individual voice is associated with more conservative and less permissive views at that time. The two value scales are not significantly related, however. (See Table 3.)

While value espousal by one individual in a family unit tends to predict similar value espousal and political-social attitudes in other family members, this coherence is relative rather than absolute. The patterns of correlation are based on relationships with each family member's 1969 scale score. The data are based on a maximal number of 65 family units for which data are available at both time periods. The mean of each value scale for mothers, fathers, and students of the current subsample does not differ significantly from the mean of the original sample; thus the pattern of relationships described here does not disproportionately reflect one segment of value espousal over another. Although these value scales temporally precede by 10 years some of the variables to

Table 3. Intrafamily Correlation Matrix of Espousal of Personal Values

	OM[a]						FPIV[b]					
	Mothers		Fathers		Children		Mothers		Fathers		Children	
	r	p	r	p	r	p	r	p	r	p	r	p
Mothers OM[a]			.23	.10	.29	.02	.04	n.s.	.14	n.s.	−.14	n.s.
Fathers OM[a]					−.01	n.s.	−.05	n.s.	−.18	n.s.	−.01	n.s.
Child OM[a]							.22	n.s.	.17	n.s.	−.13	n.s.
Mothers FPIV[b]									.32	.05	−.10	n.s.
Fathers FPIV[b]											.22	n.s.
Child FPIV[b]												

[a]Openmindedness has been abbreviated to OM.
[b]Faith in the power of the individual voice has been abbreviated to FPIV.

which they relate, we would emphasize that this analysis is intended to be descriptive and not causal. The patterns of relationships are complex, and perhaps most succinctly and clearly conveyed in table form. Accordingly, we confine our comments to summary and interpretation.

ESPOUSAL OF PERSONAL VALUE OF OPENMINDEDNESS

In 1969 the extent of each family member's espoused openmindedness was measured by a 26-item scale of self-report items. Respondents reported extent of agreement on a 4-point Likert-type scale to such items as: "It makes me very uncomfortable to leave the really important questions undecided," or "It's more important to see the other person's point of view then it is to convince him of yours," or "If you start trying to change things very much, you usually make them worse." We anticipated that this espoused value would form a foundation around which more liberal and nonpunitive political-social views would cohere.

Results of Analyses: Political and Social Attitude Correlates. Students' espousal of the value of openmindedness was the single best discriminating variable between student activists and the complement ($p < .001$), and was a discriminator of more frequent drug use ($p < .10$). This value scale score relates positively to an involved and liberal student stance toward a plethora of social issues during the 1960s. (See Table 4.)

Similarly, mothers' and fathers' own espousal of openmindedness as a personal value was related significantly to their own liberal or nonpunitive attitudes toward seven of the nine 1969 measures of political-social attitudes.

The data show a general coherence of liberal and nonpunitive attitudes in the family, anchored to the extent of espoused personal valuation of openmindedness. Mother's openmindedness score predicts the espousal of openmindedness and tolerance as well as six of the nine 1969 political-social attitude scale scores of her husband, and relates significantly to three 1969 value scales of her adolescent children. Father's openmindedness score predicts significantly 5 of 12 scale scores of his wife, but none of the 1969 scale scores of his child. When, however, students' espousal of openmindedness score is used to predict parents' attitudes and values, the students' score relates to 6 of 12 measures of mothers' attitudes, and to 4 of fathers' 1969 scores.

In the 1970s espousal of openmindedness predicts most strongly social attitudes which have remained topical across the decade, e.g., opposition to capital punishment. Relationships between parents' 1969 espousal of openmindedness and their current views are fewer, but continue to show a liberal and nonpunitive slant. Students' openmindedness score, however, bears negligible or even negative relationships

Table 4. Political and Social Issue Correlates of Espousal of Openmindedness[a]

1969 items	Correlates with mothers' openmindedness score						Correlates with fathers' openmindedness score						Correlates with students' openmindedness score					
	w/own attitude		w/spouse's attitude		w/child's attitude		w/own attitude		w/spouse's attitude		w/child's attitude		w/own attitude		w/mother's attitude		w/father's attitude	
	r	p	r	p	r	p	r	p	r	p	r	p	r	p	r	p	r	p
Espoused openmindedness as a personal value	criterion		.23	.10	.29	.02	criterion		.23	.10	—	—	criterion		.29	.02	—	—
Espoused individual development as a personal value	.51	.001	—	—	.27	.04	—	—	—	—	—	—	.79	.001	—	—	—	—
Espoused tolerance as a personal value			.36	.02	NA		.29	.06	.46	.003	NA		NA		.32	.03	—	—
Positive attitude toward the hippie movement	.36	.005	.30	.04	.25	.05	.58	.001	—	—	—	—	.41	.001	.36	.005	.41	.002
Positive attitude toward civil disobedience	.47	.001	—	—	—	—	—	—	—	—	—	—	—	—	—	—	.31	.03
Positive attitude toward civil rights movement	.40	.002	—	—	—	—	.45	.002	—	—	—	—	—	—	—	—	—	—
Positive attitude toward black power movement	.41	.003	.30	.04	—	—	—	—	—	—	—	—	.40	.003	—	—	.24	.08
Positive attitude toward marijuana	.45	.001	.44	.001	—	—	.23	.10	.30	.04	—	—	.48	.001	—	—	—	—

Opposed the Vietnam War	.37 .03	—	—	.33 .04	—	—	—	.30 .02	—
Saw a need for social change in American society	—	.29 .07	—	.28 .08	—	—	.45 .001	.30 .02	—
Friends were politically liberal	—	.29 .06	NA	.29 .06	.25 .08	NA	NA	.23 .08	—
Believed university authorities should punish student protestors	−.38 .008	−.39 .005	NA	−.29 .04	−.28 .09	NA	NA	−.45 .001	−.35 .01
1979 items									
Opposes capital punishment	.37 .003	.42 .007	—	.46 .004	—	—	.34 .05	.32 .01	—
Supports legalization of marijuana	—	.34 .04	—	.39 .02	.25 .08	—	—	—	—
Favors Equal Rights Amendment	—	—	—	.47 .003	—	—	—	—	—
Supports liberal or left political party	—	—	—	—	.36 .01	.42 .04	—	.38 .003	—
Believes abortion should be available for those who want it	—	—	.31 .08	—	.43 .002	.35 .07	—	—	—
Favors amnesty for Vietnam War draft evaders	—	—	—	—	—	.33 .09	.42 .02	—	—
Supports publicly financed child-care facilities	.33 .008	—	—	—	—	—	—	.27 .03	—

(continued)

Table 4. (Continued)

1969 items	Correlates with mothers' openmindedness score						Correlates with fathers' openmindedness score						Correlates with students' openmindedness score					
	w/own attitude		w/spouse's attitude		w/child's attitude		w/own attitude		w/spouse's attitude		w/child's attitude		w/own attitude		w/mother's attitude		w/father's attitude	
	r	p	r	p	r	p	r	p	r	p	r	p	r	p	r	p	r	p
Sees a need for social change in American society	—	—	.31	.05	-.33	.09	—	—	—	—	—	—	—	—	—	—	—	—
Positive attitude toward alternative therapy movements	NA		NA		.36	.06	NA		NA		—		-.46	.01	NA		NA	
Positive attitude toward open or contractual marriage movement	NA		NA		—		NA		NA		—		-.38	.03	NA		NA	
Positive attitude toward health movements	NA		NA		—		NA		NA		—		-.53	.002	NA		NA	
Positive attitude toward gay liberation movement	NA		NA		—		NA		NA		—		-.41	.02	NA		NA	
Positive attitude toward ecology	NA		NA		.39	.04	NA		NA		—		—		NA		NA	

[a]NA signifies that respondent was not asked about this.

to involvement in organized political activity or to support for current social movements.

Discussion of Analyses: Political and Social Attitudes Correlates. It may come as no surprise that parents predict each other's attitudes and values better than they do the attitudes and values of their adolescent offspring, and that a more powerful pattern of mother–child than father–child relationships exists at this period in the family cycle. The more robust pattern that obtains when students' scores are used to predict parent political and social attitudes may indicate that, in general, parents' liberal and nonpunitive orientation is necessary but not sufficient for like value and attitude espousal by their children.

In 1979 the pattern of relationships, while retaining its general flavor, has become thin. Perhaps, as we mentioned previously, the press of private commitments or the near-universal endorsement of some views have weakened the link between political attitudes and a particular value structure.

Alternatively, as issues have changes contemporary efforts for social change often are directed more toward self-change than were the group actions of the 1960s. The meaning of involvement in social movements may have become quite different than it was. If self-change is the present goal, espousal of openmindedness may be shown clearly in actual lifestyle differences among cohort members rather than in group involvement differences. Insofar as our data have mirrored the waning of political directedness endemic to the 1970s, they may nonetheless show differences within these young adults which reflect the pervasive inward turning of efforts for social change.

Indeed, the character of contemporary lifestyle alternatives may be in part a consequence of the progress of the activist generation into a new lifestage. If, as Erikson (1950) posits, adolescence requires resolution of identity, then one may view the hippie and activist "identities" so prominent in the 1960s as responses of this cohort to identity concerns. The lifestage of young adulthood necessitates, in Erikson's view, attending to issues of intimacy. Current popular awareness of feminism, contractual marriage, gay liberation, communal living, and innovation approaches to family planning, childbirth and child care, coincides with the entry of this cohort into the life stage characterized by these intimacy-related concerns.

Results of Analyses: Personal Correlates. Students who in 1969 scored high on this scale now lead lifestyles which they see as less traditional ($p < .03$). They are more attentive to personal than to public issues ($p < .02$), and smoke marijuana with relatively greater frequency than students who scored lower on the 1969 value scale ($p < .02$).

The former students' scores relate as well to current priorities and

VALORY MITCHELL AND JEANNE H. BLOCK

behaviors of their parents. Mothers of high scorers are less concerned with popularity ($p < .09$), and the mother role has become less salient to them ($p < .09$). Fathers of high scorers are more likely to have changed some aspect of their thinking about marriage and children ($p < .07$). Both mothers ($p < .006$) and fathers ($p < .05$) of adolescents who espoused openmindedness are more likely to have tried marijuana.

Mothers who scored high on this scale see their children's lifestyles as less traditional ($p < .01$). These women are more likely to have changed some aspect of their thinking about marriage and children ($p < .02$). Their value score in 1969 is related to a current tendency to put less priority on social ease ($p < .03$) or on having a spouse who is admired ($p < .09$). The high scale scores of these women, perhaps as a consequence, predict their husband's expression of changed attitudes toward their careers ($p < .04$), with less concern about making a good income through his own efforts ($p < .08$).

Similarly, fathers who in 1969 scored high on this value scale tend now to put less priority on career accomplishments ($p < .09$) and prestige in the community ($p < .05$). Fathers' high score on this scale relates positively to the priority his wife places on meaningful relationships ($p < .003$), and negatively to the importance she sees in being good looking ($p < .04$).

Discussion of Analyses: Personal Correlates. We have presented some current personal correlates of each family member's score on this value scale in order to sketch some of the more personal ways the liberal and permissive orientation held by high scorers on espousal of openmindedness manifests in the present decade. Of particular interest is the interaction of the values of one individual with the style and priorities of other members of the family. For example, in the parent generation mother's value score is more strongly related to her husband's attitude toward his career than is his own value scale score; and the father's score (but not his wife's) predicts the extent of her concern with being good looking. Similarly, it is the openmindedness score of her offspring that relates to each parent's trying of marijuana.

While our findings can only hint at the directions and influences of individual members on the behavior of others in the family, future studies may find analysis of the interpersonal situation, such as we have demonstrated here, to be an enriching approach to the understanding of individual change and adaptation.

Results of Analyses: Intergenerational Relationship Correlates. In the 1960s the liberal orientation these families share contrasted with marked disagreement about political-social issues as they affected the individual adolescent. At that time students' espousal of openmindedness was negatively related to father–child agreement about marijuana use and

Table 5. Intergenerational Relationship Correlates of Espousal of the Personal Value of Openmindedness[a]

1969 items	Correlates with mothers' openmindedness score						Correlates with fathers' openmindedness score						Correlates with students' openmindedness score					
	w/own response		w/spouse's response		w/child's response		w/own response		w/spouse's response		w/child's response		w/own response		w/mother's response		w/father's response	
	r	p	r	p	r	p	r	p	r	p	r	p	r	p	r	p	r	p
Believed child fulfilled parent's aspirations in high school	−.33	.008	—	—	NA		—	—	−.24	.09	NA		NA		—	—	—	—
Parent agreed with child about child's general lifestyle and attitudes (sum score)	—	—	—	—	NA		—	—	—	—	NA		NA		—	—	−.28	.04
Parent agreed with child about child's academic program in college	—	—	—	—	NA		—	—	−.25	.10	NA		NA		—	—	—	—
Parent agreed with child about dangers of marijuana use	—	—	—	—	NA		—	—	—	—	NA		NA		−.27	.05	−.35	.02
Parent agreed with child about premarital sex	—	—	—	—	NA		—	—	—	—	NA		NA		−.30	.04	—	—
1979 items																		
Former student's personal values are a problem for parent	—	—	—	—	—	—	—	—	—	—	—	—	—	—	—	—	.33	.05

(continued)

Table 5. (Continued)

1969 items	Correlates with mother's openmindedness score						Correlates with father's openmindedness score						Correlates with student's openmindedness score					
	w/own response		w/spouse's response		w/child's response		w/own response		w/spouse's response		w/child's response		w/own response		w/mother's response		w/father's response	
	r	p	r	p	r	p	r	p	r	p	r	p	r	p	r	p	r	p
Current parent–child relationship is very close	—		—		—		—		—		—		—		—		—	
Former student's lifestyle is perceived as traditional	-.31	.01	-.44	.005	—		—		—		—		-.38	.03	-.30	.02	—	
Former student would turn to mother in a crisis	NA		NA		—		NA		NA		.59	.002	—		NA		NA	
Former student would turn to father in a crisis	NA		NA		—		NA		NA		.38	.06	—		NA		NA	
Mother and child agree substantially about student demonstrations	—		NA		—		NA		—		—		—		-.43	.001	NA	

Mother and child agree substantially about childrearing	—	NA	—	—	—	—	—	−.40	.03	—	NA
Mother and child agree substantially about child's occupational choice	—	NA	—	—	−.50	.01	—	—	—	—	NA
Mother and child agree substantially about child's choice of friends	−.24	.07	NA	—	—	—	−.36	.05	−.21	.10	NA
Mother and child agree substantially about marriage	−.22	.09	NA	—	—	—	—	—	−.26	.05	NA
Mother and child agree substantially about child's present lifestyle	−.25	.05	NA	—	—	—	—	—	—	—	NA
Father and child agree substantially about religion	NA	−.28	.10	—	NA	—	—	−.44	.01	NA	−.35	.03
Father and child agree substantially about childrearing	NA	—	—	—	NA	—	—	−.30	.10	NA	—	—

[a]NA signifies that respondent was not asked about this.

general lifestyle, and negatively related to mother–child agreement about marijuana use and premarital sex. (See Table 5.)

Mothers' espousal of openmindedness related to her feeling that her child had not entirely fulfilled her aspirations in high school; and fathers' score was associated with mother–child disagreement about the student's academic program.

By 1979 the intergenerational disagreement has become entrenched, as students' espousal of openmindedness in the prior decade predicts present disagreement with parents about student demonstrations, religion, marriage, childrearing, and choice of friends. Fathers of high-scoring former students are more likely to feel that their child's personal values are a problem, and mothers of high-scoring students see the current mother–child relationship as less close.

Mothers' espousal of openmindedness related negatively to mother–child agreement about marriage, choice of friends, and general lifestyle. Fathers' value scale scores were negatively related to parent–child agreement about religion and occupational choice, but strongly and positively related to their grown child's willingness to confide in either father or mother about personal crises.

Discussion of Analyses: Intergenerational Relationship Correlates. The correlational pattern which surrounds this value allegiance in the 1960s presents a somewhat sobering interpersonal portrait of the liberally oriented family. We feel impelled to reiterate before proceeding that the correlational trends reported here must be viewed more as hypotheses for further study than as well-documented cohort descriptions.

The pattern of relationships describes families who entered the 1960s relatively united in being politically involved, liberal, and valuing tolerance and personal growth. It has been usual to assume that perhaps as a result of this shared familial value orientation, young people in college during the late 1960s were open to ideas and forms of behavior which led to lasting dissension with their parents.

Recently the provocative commentaries of Lasch (1978) and others have raised anew a criticism of the socialization practices of this cohort, which they believe have led to the present political apathy and self-absorption of the so-called me generation. The current attention directed to Lasch's critique prompts us to consider the utility of his interpretation for our data. We introduce his viewpoint here because it seems to us that families which espouse a high personal valuation of openmindedness may have been particularly responsive to changing childrearing trends which, in Lasch's opinion, have undermined parental convictions. If so, Lasch's suppositions hold that parental valuations of openmindedness would imply an uncertainty and flagging self-trust which would lead them to lack consistency and clarity in articulating goals and standards for their children—a parental style which would presage an uncertain sense of self in the young. The adolescent of such parents would presumably be particularly disposed toward affiliating with groups which, while not violating parents' superordinate values, serve to bolster an ephemeral sense of efficacy and provide standards that define clearly, if transiently, an identity. In adulthood such young people would be especially prone to failures of commitment and to participation in pursuits such as alternative therapies and open marriage which Lasch sees as indicative of narcissistic self-preoccupation. Underlying these trends, he would predict an overinvestment of parents in their grown children's accomplishments as a way to validate and vindicate their success in the parent role. Insofar as women of this generation have invested in that role to the exclusion of other avenues of self-esteem, they would view their offspring's behavior with greater scrutiny.

Aspects of the correlational data can be used to support such an interpretation. That these parents and adolescents share liberal and non-punitive political-social attitudes, yet simultaneously disagree, may suggest a schism between the parents' generalized values and what they consider appropriate or acceptable in their own children. Inconsistency, as Loevinger (1959) also has suggested, may mark a style of socialization in which reactions to the child are determined more by parental conflicts and anxieties than by principle. While disagreement about lifestyle and personal choices need not affect the quality of relationship between the generations, there is evidence that it has done so. While fathers' espoused openmindedness appears to further current intergenerational trust, mothers' espoused openmindedness has apparently not facilitated a transcending of lifestyle differences.

Although some features of the data support Lasch's position, other facets of these data serve to make this interpretation more tenuous. That adolescents' value score predicts many of the political-social attitudes of parents suggests that communication and identification with these values was accomplished with some success. Dissension appears to have arisen when the young people attempted to forge a tangible identity through concrete actions in support of these shared abstract valuations. The disproportionate tendency for young people from these families to affiliate with political and social movements may be interpreted less as a response to parental amorphousness than as one manifestation of the group phenomenon which has long been characteristic of adolescence. Indeed the 1960s *Zeitgeist* of political activism has more often been cast as antithetical to the current "age of narcissism" (Lasch, 1978) than as its logical developmental precursor. In addition these young people are less likely than others in the cohort to endorse alternative therapies and open or contractual marriage, while showing no significant differences in marital or work status which might indicate a reluctance to partake in the commitments associated with adult adjustment.

While members of these families are more expressive of disagreements and dissatisfactions, when actual scores on these variables are examined it is evident that they are more compatible than not. The candid quality of their responses which is mirrored in the correlational data may therefore bespeak a less defensive style among high scorers than low scorers, rather than an atmosphere of conflict.

Finally, mothers of high scorers are likely to show shifts in their priorities away from investment in familial roles. While it is possible to see these priority shifts as responses to lack of perceived validation of their parenting, it seems equally plausible to see these mothers' changes as adaptive responses to the "empty nest" and to current feminist ideas, perhaps facilitated by their own espoused valuation of openmindedness.

In sum, then, these families do not present sufficient similarity to Lasch's description to corroborate his assertions.

ESPOUSAL OF FAITH IN THE POWER OF THE INDIVIDUAL VOICE

A second personal value, faith in the power of the individual voice, was measured by response to such items as: "I believe that a person like myself can have a voice in decisions made in Washington, D.C.," or "I am optimistic that the individual can change the world in which s/he lives." This value scale was selected because we felt it would be likely to capture a faith in the individual and the accountability of the individual which is conceptually associated with a conservative political-social world view.

Results of Analyses: Political and Social Attitudes Correlates. In 1969 students' scores on this value scale related strongly to both their own and their fathers' dim view of marijuana use and of the black power movement. High-scoring students were likely to support the Vietnam War. Their scores related as well to each parent's disapproval of the hippie movement. Mother's own scale score was associated with the opinion that the university should punish student protestors, and with her opposition to the civil rights movement, but related to a more positive attitude toward marijuana and the hippie movement in her child. Mother's score was a strong predictor of her husband's opposition to marijuana use, however. Father's scale score predicted his support of the Vietnam War and his wife's opposition to the civil rights movement, but did not relate significantly to the political-social attitudes of his child (see Table 6).

In the 1970s, extent of students' espousal of this value anchors a pattern of conservative attitudes in both themselves and their parents. Students' scores relate significantly to all family members' support for capital punishment, to both parents' opposition to amnesty for draft

Table 6. Political and Social Issue Correlates of Espousal of Faith in the Power of the Individual Voice[a]

1969 items	Correlates with mother's FPIV score						Correlates with father's FPIV score						Correlates with student's FPIV score					
	w/own response		w/spouse's response		w/child's response		w/own response		w/spouse's response		w/child's response		w/own response		w/mother's response		w/father's response	
	r	p	r	p	r	p	r	p	r	p	r	p	r	p	r	p	r	p
Espoused faith in the power of the individual voice	—	—	.32	.05	—	—	—	—	.32	.05	—	—	—	—	—	—	—	—
Espoused individual development as a personal value	—	—	—	—	.28	.05	—	—	—	—	—	—	—	—	—	—	—	—
Espoused tolerance as a personal value	—	—	—	—	—	—	.26	.10	—	—	—	—	—	—	—	—	—	—
Positive attitude toward hippie movement	—	—	—	—	.27	.05	—	—	—	—	—	—	—	—	-.35	.01	-.26	.07
Positive attitude toward civil rights movement	-.25	.10	—	—	—	—	—	—	-.27	.09	—	—	—	—	—	—	—	—
Positive attitude toward black power movement	—	—	—	—	—	—	—	—	—	—	—	—	-.45	.001	—	—	-.28	.05
Positive attitude toward marijuana	—	—	-.41	.007	.36	.05	—	—	—	—	—	—	-.48	.001	—	—	-.39	.005
Opposed the Vietnam War	—	—	—	—	—	—	-.32	.05	—	—	—	—	-.41	.001	—	—	—	—
Saw a need for change in American society	—	—	—	—	—	—	—	—	—	—	—	—	—	—	—	—	—	—

[a]Faith in the power of the individual voice has been abbreviated in table as FPIV. NA signifies that respondent was not asked about this.

(continued)

Table 6. (Continued)

	Correlates with mother's FPIV score						Correlates with father's FPIV score						Correlates with student's FPIV score					
	w/own response		w/spouse's response		w/child's response		w/own response		w/spouse's response		w/child's response		w/own response		w/mother's response		w/father's response	
	r	p	r	p	r	p	r	p	r	p	r	p	r	p	r	p	r	p
1969 items																		
Believed university authorities should punish student protestors	.51	.003	—		—		—		-.40	.03	—		—		—		—	
1979 items																		
Opposes capital punishment	-.27	.05	—		—		—		—		—		-.30	.10	-.32	.01	-.41	.01
Supports legalization of marijuana	—		—		—		—		—		—		—		-.29	.03	—	
Favors Equal Rights Amendment	-.25	.08	—		—		—		—		—		—		-.30	.02	—	
Supports left or liberal party	—		—		—		-.29	.09	—		—		—		—		—	
Opposes premarital sex	.33	.02	—		—		—		—		—		—		.28	.03	—	
Favors amnesty for Vietnam War draft evaders	—		—		—		—		—		—		—		-.34	.008	-.31	.06
Supports publicly financed child-care facilities	—		—		—		—		—		—		-.45	.01	—		—	
Sees a need for social change in American society	—		—		-.42	.04	NA		NA		NA		—		—		-.40	.02
Positive attitude toward physical fitness movement	NA		-.29	.09	.46	.02	NA		NA		NA		NA		NA		NA	

evaders, and to fathers' and children's opposition to publicly funded child care. In addition the former students' scores predict mothers' opposition to legalized marijuana, the Equal Rights Amendment, and premarital sex.

Mother's score related to her own support for capital punishment and her opposition to premarital sex and to the Equal Rights Amendment. Husbands of high-scoring mothers are unlikely to see a need for social change in American society. Father's 1969 scale score, however, predicts only his own more conservative political party affiliation.

Discussion of Analyses: Political and Social Attitudes Correlates. Although the network of correlations here is not as rich as is the pattern for the more liberal families, the espousal of faith in the power of the individual voice seems to characterize conservative attitudes and a relatively punitive orientation among both generations across the decade. As with the more liberal families there are more mother–child than father–child relationships, and students' value scores predict parents' political-social attitudes more successfully than parents' value scores predict the attitudes of their adolescent and adult children.

In the 1970s the correlates that reach significance retain a conservative flavor, and the former student's 1969 value scale score is a robust predictor of both parents' 1979 attitudes. At the same time, however, parents' scores have become poor predictors of their grown children's views: mother's score relates only to her child's disapproval of publicly funded child care and support for the physical fitness movement, and no significant relationships link father's value scores to his grown child's current political-social attitudes.

Thus while the former students' value espousal scores predict parents' current conservatism, conservative parents may be less likely to see continuity between their views and the current attitudes of their grown children. If, as suggested earlier, a number of the more avant-garde ideas and styles of the 1960s have become relatively commonplace among young adults in the 1970s, then it is precisely in the lack of relationship between the conservative elders and their offspring that these wider social changes might be most likely to be manifest. From this perspective, the accession of formerly radical ideas, attitudes, and behaviors to the mainstream of popular acceptance in the 1970s may have prompted a more profound disequilibration and destructuring of the assumptions and expectations of conservative families than did any contact with divergent views in the preceding decade.

Results of Analyses: Personal Correlates. Students who in 1969 scored high on faith in the power of the individual voice now lead lives which both they ($p < .002$), their mothers ($p < .10$), and their fathers ($p < .02$) see as more traditional. High scorers recall that career preparation was an important part of their college life ($p < .10$), and are unlikely to have changed any aspect of their thinking about their job or career ($p < .006$). Mothers of high scorers are less likely to have changed their attitudes about marriage and children ($p < .07$). These mothers place popularity ($p < .04$) and meaningful relationship ($p < .02$) in relatively higher priority than mothers of low scorers, and these priorities have gained importance for them over the last decade ($p < .04$, $p < .06$). These mothers are likely to recall that having a lot of money was a salient goal in the 1960s ($p < .03$). Students' scores were positively related to the importance that their fathers currently place on being a good leader ($p < .07$) and on having a spouse who is admired ($p < .08$), and to the relatively high priority fathers gave these goals in the 1960s ($p < .07$, $p < .08$). These fathers tend to feel that personal accomplishment in the arts is less important to them ($p < .08$).

Mother's own high score on this value scale in 1969 is related to the relatively low priority she places on career accomplishment ($p < .004$), being a good leader ($p < .07$), or making a good income through her own efforts ($p < .03$). Their high score on the value scale was also negatively related to employment outside the home when their children were young ($p < .003$). Mother's value score predicts that her husband will give high priority to feeling at ease socially ($p < .003$) and being important in the community ($p < .09$). Husbands of these women are less likely to have tried marijuana ($p < .07$). Children of mothers who scored high on this value scale are more likely to see high income as important in their job choice ($p < .08$), and are currently likely to use marijuana more frequently ($p < .02$).

The extent of father's espousal of faith in the power of the individual voice is related to a large number of his current personal goals. Father's 1969 value score is positively related to the importance he invests in feeling socially at ease ($p < .001$), important in the community ($p < .002$), good at sports ($p < .03$), popular and well-liked ($p < .06$), attractive to the opposite sex ($p < .02$), a good leader ($p < .07$), and to wanting meaningful relationships ($p < .001$). These fathers are more likely to be presently employed ($p < .002$). In recalling their personal priorities of 10 years ago father's value scale was significantly related to all of the above goals as well as the importance he recalls giving to the goal of being good looking ($p < .02$), politically effective ($p < .04$), having a lot of money ($p < .02$), giving help to others ($p < .08$), and being accomplished in his career ($p < .07$). High scores on this value scale are negatively related to having tried marijuana ($p < .07$), and positively related to continued espousal of faith that the voice of the average individual can be heard in national government ($p < .002$).

Father's scale score is negatively related to the priority his wife places on giving help to others now ($p < .09$) or 10 years ago ($p < .05$), but predicts the greater intensity of her desire to be politically effective ($p < .02$) and important in the community ($p < .04$). Wives of high scorers continue to share their spouses' faith that the average person can be heard on the national governmental level ($p < .02$) and are optimistic that an individual can change the world in which he or she lives ($p < .09$).

Father's high value score in 1969 relates to his grown child's report that career preparation was an important part of college life ($p < .01$). Children of high-scoring fathers are more likely to report being currently affected by the open or contractual marriage movements ($p < .05$) and the popular emphasis on per-capita population limitation ($p < .10$). They are less likely to feel that helping others is important in their job choice ($p < .02$), and are less likely to be professionally employed ($p < .07$), although their overall grade average while an undergraduate was higher than children of low-scoring fathers ($p < .04$).

Discussion of Analyses: Personal Correlates. These personal manifestations of faith in the power of the individual voice suggest the relationship between this value and both a traditional lifestyle and the assertion of a "rugged individualist" position in which agentic priorities and role-related status markers take precedence over more altruistic or relational concerns. Both parents aspire to fulfill conventional sex-role-related goals and emphasize the importance of esteem in the eyes of the generalized other. The stress on status, discipline, and self-control which previous research (Block, 1972) found to predominate in the childrearing practices of conservative parents is evinced in the continued tenacious striving of both parents to achieve a wide array of socially approved goals. The importance their children place on career training in college, and their unswerving aspiration toward employment which yields clear extrinsic rewards, may show a transgenerational continuity among family members which the paucity of social issue correlates might have masked.

In these family groups we again see indications that the value orientation of each individual supports and permits the options and obligations felt by other family members of the family. As we might anticipate, however, the investment in traditional familial and sex roles by each individual in the conservative family almost requires the corresponding role-related priority in other members of the unit. The personal correlates of high score on this value portray an almost archetypic conventional American family, with little indication of additions or modifications.

Results of Analyses: Intergenerational Relationship Correlates. In the 1960s the high-scoring conservative students agree with their fathers

Table 7. Intergenerational Relationship Correlates of Faith in the Power of the Individual Voice[a]

1969 items	Correlates with mother's FPIV score						Correlates with father's FPIV score						Correlates with student's FPIV score					
	w/own response		w/spouse's response		w/child's response		w/own response		w/spouse's response		w/child's response		w/own response		w/mother's response		w/father's response	
	r	p	r	p	r	p	r	p	r	p	r	p	r	p	r	p	r	p
Believed child fulfilled parent's aspirations in high school	.31	.02	–	–	NA		–	–	–	–	NA		NA		–	–	.26	.07
Parent agreed with child about child's general lifestyle and attitudes (sum score)	–	–	–.32	.05	NA		–	–	–	–	NA		NA		–	–	.33	.02
Parent agreed with child about child's academic program in college	–	–	–.37	.02	NA		–	–	–	–	NA		NA		–	–	–	–
Parent agreed with child about the dangers of marijuana use	–	–	–	–	NA		–.28	.08	–	–	NA		NA		–	–	.26	.10
Parents agreed with child about the value of student protests	–	–	–.28	.09	NA		–	–	–	–	NA		NA		–	–	–	–
Parent agreed with child about child's personal appearance and style of dress	–	–	–	–	NA		–	–	–	–	NA		NA		–	–	.37	.008
1979 items																		
Former student's personal values are a problem for parent	–	–	–	–	–		–	–	–	–	–		–		.22	.10	–	

Parent believes child has fulfilled parents' aspirations — −.24 .10 −.29 .10 — — — — — — — — — — .38 .02

Measure	Values
Parent believes child has fulfilled parents' aspirations	−.24 .10 −.29 .10 — — — — — — — — — — .38 .02
Former student's lifestyle is perceived as traditional	— — — — — — — — .52 .002 .22 .10 .38 .02
Mother and child agree substantially about student demonstrations	— NA .33 .08 — — — NA
Mother and child agree substantially about child's occupational choice	−.35 .01 NA — — — NA
Mother and child agree substantially about women's rights	−.28 .06 NA — — — NA −.37 .005 NA
Mother and child agree substantially about religion	−.32 .03 NA — — — NA
Father and child agree substantially about child's present lifestyle	NA −.48 .005 — — NA — — NA
Father and child agree substantially about religion	NA −.41 .02 — — NA — — NA −.37 .02
Father and child agree substantially about women's rights	NA −.43 .02 — — NA — — NA
Father and child agree substantially about child's occupational choice	NA −.42 .02 .42 .10 — NA — — NA
Father and child agree substantially about marriage	NA −.35 .05 .31 .10 — NA — — NA

[a]Faith in the power of the individual voice has been abbreviated in table as FPIV. NA signifies that respondent was not asked about this.

about lifestyle and attitudes, style of dress and physical appearance, and the dangers of marijuana use. Fathers of these young people were likely to feel that their children had fulfilled their aspirations in high school. Mother–child agreement and approval was independent of student's value scale score.

Mother's own scale score related to her belief that her child fulfilled her aspirations in high school. At the same time the husbands of high-scoring mothers report disagreement with adolescents surrounding academic program in college, the value of student protests, and general lifestyle. Fathers' score relates to the single variable of father–child disagreement about marijuana.

In the ensuing decade the value score correlates describe relationships in which agreement and approval are less likely to appear. The few relationships that surround the former student's value scale scores show that mothers now feel their children's personal values are a problem, and predict intergenerational disagreement over women's rights and religion. Fathers' scale score predicts only father–child agreement about marriage.

The conservative mothers' scale score, however, relates to significant mother–child disagreement about religion, women's rights, and child's choice of occupation. These mothers are likely to report that their grown child has come short of fulfilling their aspirations. Mothers' score also predicts current father–child disagreement about religion, women's rights, marriage, occupational choice, and general lifestyle. These fathers too feel that their child has not fulfilled their aspirations.

Discussion of Analyses: Intergenerational Relationship Correlates. This pattern of correlates supports our hypothesis that the conservative family, which weathered the 1960s with relative continuity, displays increasing dissension as the young people move into adulthood.

The conservative-conventional value orientation of parents seems to have kept them from altering long-held priorities despite the arrival of the "empty nest," changes in the social climate, or the press of psychological revaluations typical of mid-life. Mothers' disappointment in grown children may be particularly poignant since these women are especially invested in familial roles and continue to deemphasize other areas of potential personal accomplishment.

The young adults emerging from these families share their parents' traditional lifestyle and persistent striving toward socially sanctioned goals. However, this subgroup of the cohort, who avoided activism in the 1960s and who currently pursue highly individual rewards and concerns, seems to approach more closely the behavior patterns that Lasch describes in his commentary on the 1970s. They are more likely than other members of the cohort to seek out the alternative therapies and to be personally affected by open marriage and efforts to decrease the per-capita birth rate. Their university experience emphasized the functional role of education; work choice was predicated on the pragmatic concern of high-income potential, while altruistic motives were devalued. In the ensuing years these attitudes about career, as they report, have re-mained unchanged.

Parent–child disagreement regarding religion and women's roles may suggest that the pursuit of individual and extrinsic rewards by these young people is not as likely to be tempered by charitable fellow-feeling and the interpersonally sensitive orientation associated with spiritual values and the communal attributes of the traditional feminine role.

While these young people seem to typify the tenor of the 1970s as described by social critics, these families, whose socialization practices stressed discipline and self-control, seem least likely to have manifested parental confusion and diffusion of structure which Lasch identifies as the cause of the social malaise of the present decade.

Rather, the young adults of this group appear to act in accord with the focused and agentic orientation of their forebears. Continued faith in the "rugged individualist"—the ethos which anchored the family pat-terns described here—is the embodiment of such relatively undiluted agentic motives and goals.

CONCLUSIONS

The trends reported in the analyses above depict a young adult generation and a generation in mid-life as they continue the unsettling dialectical process of assimilating new notions into their established mo-tivational and value structures, and accommodate with greater or lesser ease to the press of a changing world and the internal demands and options of adult development.

In adulthood the adolescents whose political activism and "counter-culture" style attracted attention and concern seem generally to be oc-cupied with the prototypical tasks of their present developmental stage. While they did not accomplish the radical reformation of society which some may have wished, neither have they confirmed the dire predic-tions made about the viability of their personal futures.

Nassi and Abramowitz (1979), in an independently conducted study of former U.C. Berkeley free speech movement activists, find similar trends. Their sample also showed a decline in political activity and a shift toward personal and interpersonal concerns. Nonetheless

they feel that the group they studied continues to be a distinctive generational unit characterized by

> (a) the relative durability of the leftist political philosophy of the sixties; (b)
> the choice of occupation guided by political considerations in addition to
> conventional reward and status structures; and (c) the continuing struggle
> with the dilemma of maintaining moral ideals. (p. 34)

They suggest that the changes and continuities in the lives of former
student activists of this era be described as transitions rather than transformations—a conclusion which is descriptive of our sample of activists
as well.

In our study, most of this subsample of young people emerged from
families with a shared valuation of openmindedness, tolerance, and an
emphasis on personal development. Although the generations may disagree about the way these values are implemented in daily life, we are
impressed with the superordinate continuities that characterize these
families and distinguish them from the more conservative group. Both
generations retain liberal and nonpunitive political-social attitudes
across the decade. In their personal lives they show a willingness to
rethink and adapt their views of marriage, children, and career in response to changing life circumstances. Fathers of this group have begun
to turn from the primacy of career demands, while mothers indicate a
willingness to engage new priorities which have become available in the
mid-life stage of the family cycle. In so doing each parent may begin to
exercise qualities and skills which the demands of earlier role-related
priorities may have led them to leave undeveloped. The lesser intensity
of these parents' concern for esteem by the generalized other may facilitate the transcendence of sex-role conventions implicated in these mid-
life goal shifts. At the same time both these changes are indicative of the
internal restructuring which Loevinger (1976) describes as the passage
from conventional to autonomous levels of ego development.

Among the younger generation, this questioning of traditional role
expectations was implicit in the antiwar movement, and made explicit
both by the hippies and later, though quite differently, in feminist ideology. Both generations of these families then evince a willingness to take
advantage of life transitions as periods to explore and expand personal
options beyond the boundaries of previous expectations and dictates.

This developmental path, with its turnings and byways, stands in
sharp contrast to the relatively unswerving trajectory which characterizes both generations of the conservative family. At mid-life the conservative parents seem truly to be engaged in an attempt to conserve: to
preserve and maintain the goals and motivators which have guided
them in the past. Fathers of this group continue to strive for the many

accomplishments and status markers which the traditional masculine role demands, while mothers rarely venture outside a conventionally feminine pattern. This parental couple in mid-life thus interacts to accentuate each other's expectations of sex-role dichotomy. Guided by their faith that the individual can, and by implication should, accomplish through his own efforts, these parents adhere to a traditional familial organization which functions to facilitate father's achievement of socially recognized goals. The lives of young people from this familial milieu, not surprisingly, echo the directed striving, functional orientation, and concern for visible achievement markers which follow from this system of priorities.

While these young people, like their parents, prefer not to deviate from convention, many of the more visible trappings which formerly symbolized deviant ideologies have become both conventional and fashionable in the present decade. Divorced from the ideologies which spawned them, current fashions in music, dress, home furnishings, decor, and recreational activities have become the concrete markers of success and leisure which may attract these same relatively conventional young people today.

As the enjoyment of the body and of nature through such tangible items as waterbeds, hot tubs, and "recreational" drugs, and as participation in "self-awareness" and similar groups, have become both destigmatized and legitimated as popular leisure and social pursuits, they have been able to draw the participation of young people for whom they hold no prior ideological associations. At the same time they may have also, for many, vitiated into simple forms of self-indulgence for which the "Me generation" stands indicted by a number of social critics.

The increasing dissension of the conservative generations may stem in part from parents' fears that their children's acceptance of these fashions still carries the symbolic value it would have had in the 1960s. Similarly, because these current fads were first accepted by liberal adolescents, social critics of the 1970s seem to assume that present support for them continues to rest with that subgroup. Our data suggest otherwise.

However, any conclusions from our findings are drawn from a very limited data base. The inferences mentioned here may at best serve as suggestive hypotheses in future work. As interest in adult development becomes increasingly informed by studies of this and other cohorts, we may begin to formulate with greater confidence some answers to questions that have structured our study. We will be particularly interested in the lifespan implication of differences in the kind and extent of structures which characterize various socialization practices. The interaction of attitudes, goals, and values within members of the nuclear family may be a fecund ground for the study of adult change. Finally, changes in the implicit meaning of socially noticeable behaviors must be examined in order to understand more fully present and future personal and social change.

Acknowledgment

The author extends thanks to Christine E. Colbert for her insightful comments on the material reported here and for her critical readings of this manuscript.

REFERENCES

Baldwin, J. M. *Social and ethical interpretations of mental development.* New York: Macmillan, 1906.

Bakan, D. *The duality of human existence.* Chicago: Rand McNally, 1966.

Block, J. H. *The child-rearing practices report.* University of California at Berkeley: Institute of Human Development. 1965. (In mimeo)

Block, J. H. Generational continuity and discontinuity in the understanding of societal rejection. *Journal of Personality and Social Psychology,* 1972, *2,* 333–345.

Erikson, E. H. *Childhood and society.* New York: W. W. Norton, 1950.

Lasch, C. *The culture of narcissism.* New York: W. W. Norton, 1978.

Lewin, H. *A dynamic theory of personality.* New York: McGraw-Hill, 1935.

Loevinger, J. Patterns of parenthood as theories of learning. *Journal of Abnormal and Social Psychology,* 1959, *59,* 148–150.

Loevinger, J. *Ego development.* San Francisco: Jossey-Bass, 1976.

Nassi, A. J., & Abramowitz, S. I. Transition or transformation? Personal and political development of former Berkeley free speech movement activists. *Journal of Youth and Adolescence,* 1979, *8*(1), 21–36.

Neugarten, B. L. Adaptation and the life cycle. *Counseling Psychologist,* 1976, *6,* 16–20.

Piaget, J. *The construction of reality in the child.* New York: Basic Books, 1954.

Werner, H. *Comparative psychology of mental development.* New York: International Universities Press, 1948.

Wood, J. L. *The sources of American student activism.* Lexington, Mass.: Lexington Books, 1974.

Chapter 10

Past and Future of the Undergraduate Woman

Joseph Katz

Changes in Aspirations

If one looks only 20 years into the past, the changes in the aspirations of women undergraduates are substantial. Prof. Mabel Newcomer (1959), on the occasion of Vassar's Centennial, quotes the following from applications to Vassar College indicating that many students viewed college as preparation for serving one's future husband. "When I marry, I would like to converse with my husband's friends and business acquaintances with a mature and confident manner that can only come from a thorough education" (p. 67). Looking at Radcliffe, Newcomer (1959) reports that "The first Radcliffe students had to obtain books from the library by messenger after the library closed in the evening, and the books were returned by messenger when the library opened in the morning. Whether the students stayed up all night to read them is not recorded. Library facilities have improved over the years, but the Radcliffe women are still excluded from the Harvard undergraduate men's library. The explanation offered by the librarian, as late as the 1940s, was that the building had many alcoves and policing would be too expensive" (p. 198).

The quaintness of these statements, as they are perceived today, suggests the road that we have traveled. Undergraduate women's concept of who they are and what they can do has substantially altered. In a recent survey of ours 87% of the undergraduate women said that self-fulfillment through a career was important to them (Katz & Cronin,

Joseph Katz, Ph.D. • Human Development Department, State University of New York, Stony Brook, New York 11794.

1980). Women conceive the range of activity and aspirations open to them *by right* as wide for them as for men. By contrast, a very able undergraduate woman who was a research subject in 1961 declared that it was her ambition to be the first *vice-president* of the United States. Even a strong ambition then was for second place.

The new concept that women have of themselves has itself become an important force. The more assertive definitions that women, including undergraduate women, have given of themselves in recent years has been one factor that has led them to pursue more actively and successfully the realization of their rights. It has influenced the men to alter long-established attitudes and to begin their own redefinition of masculinity.The situation of women shows once more that society profoundly changes its behavior once its "victims" *actively* pursue their own interests.

SOME "WHY'S" OF THE CHANGES

Why did the new attitudes arise at the time they did? There were at least four favoring conditions. First, the student movement between 1964 and 1970 had as one of its main tenets the demand for people's greater participation in the social and educational structures that shaped them. Women were the last group to be singled out, after battles for voter registration and for a larger voice of students in university affairs. The inclusion of women came after women themselves had taken the initiative. One dramatic moment occurred during the "Vietnam Summer" of 1967 when a group of undergraduate women activists who had been assigned traditional secretarial duties by their male peers objected and asked that such work be shared and that women should equally participate in other activities, such as speaking, organizing, and negotiating (Keniston, 1968).

Second, there was the increasing concern with population growth. By 1968 the problems of overpopulation had been widely publicized and the then-new concept of zero population growth had gained wide hearing. It ended an era ushered in after World War II in which large families had become a social asset and seemed to be viewed as a psychological necessity. The ideological turn against large families probably was not only a consequence of rational considerations about limited room on "Spaceship Earth" but also of disappointment with the earlier idyllic visions of happy large families in the open spaces of the suburbs.

Third, by coincidence the 1960s also was the decade of the birth control pill. It promised safe and effective prevention of unwanted pregnancy. It gave women a much greater control over their own bodies and many age-old fears and taboos came tumbling down. Surveys we have conducted over the last nine years (Katz & Cronin, 1980) have shown consistently that college women are sexually more active than college men. In 1977 nonvirginity was nearly equal for both genders (about 75%), but 73% of the women as against 57% of the men reported themselves as *currently* having a sexual relationship. More dramatically still, the women engaged in sexual activity more frequently than the men (52% versus 40% said they had sexual intercourse five times a month or more often).

Fourth, women's share in higher education rapidly approached the 50–50 mark. In 1950 the percentage of women students had been 32%; 10 years later, 37%; 20 years later, 41%; and in 1978 it was 50% (Andersen, 1980, p. 58). Women's minority status in college was thus vanishing numerically as well. It is surprising that the impact of higher education on women's sense of self was so slow in coming. Over the years millions of women had received considerable training and exposure to ideas, including some very unconventional ones. Yet for a long time most of them accepted the abrupt halt at graduation of the development and expression of talents just discovered and tastes just acquired. Perhaps the "Vietnam Summer" young women activists who rebelled against being subservient were realizing ambitions that their mothers more or less unawares had nurtured themselves.

ACCOMPLISHMENTS

As one looks at the situation of undergraduate women in 1978 one can point to many accomplishments during the decade preceding it.

1. The proportion of female undergraduates, as just indicated, is equal to that of men. Because of the influx of older women, the rate of increase of female enrollments is currently larger than that of men (*Chronicle of Higher Education*, 1978).

2. The bachelor's degree no longer means the termination of higher education for as many women as it did in the past. About a quarter, for instance, of the entrants into medical schools now are women—up from 9% a relatively short time ago. In other graduate fields women are now represented in larger proportions.

3. The possibility of continued education casts a different light even on the undergraduate experience because women now can view their education in the larger context of accessibility to further personal and professional development. Previous barriers to part-time graduate study have lessened, with particular benefit for wome in the childrearing years. The motives for the facilitation of part-time study, just as for the

admission of older women students, are often not particularly feminist, but reflect the need for more students in a time of budgetary tightness. The effects, nevertheless, are greater opportunities for women.

4. During the last decade all of the most selective and renowned previously all-male colleges have become coeducational. While the number of these schools is small, their influence is great. They constitute something like national symbols and their going coeducational emphasizes that women are moving toward a place of preeminent equality.

5. The legal process in the form of affirmative action has come to the aid of women in higher education. As of now, the accomplishment is often more one of principle than reality, and the history of affirmative action has also been one of evasions. Nevertheless the fact that an obligation of moving toward greater representation of women among faculty and administrators is now an established principle of law has changed expectations and is beginning to affect social structures. Experience shows that it sometimes takes longer to change attitudes through persuasion or "education" than through having people exposed to new experiences that channel behavior in fresh ways. More women in positions of influence will mean that the realities of acquaintance, power, and politics will help to engender fresh behavior and attitudes. The greater presence of women professors and administrators also will provide encouragement for women students in their own aspirations.

6. On-campus opportunities for undergraduate women to develop and exercise leadership skills have increased in recent years. In the past women have been underrepresented in such undergraduate leadership positions as student government, the student newspaper, and other offices (Kreps, 1971, p. 55). But in a 1978 survey of four northeastern coeducational institutions, women and men in about equal proportions report having been elected to student offices and having worked on a school paper or magazine; more women than men report having been a member of a student–faculty committee. (This statement is based on unpublished figures from the Brown Project, 1980.)

A study of graduate students (Adler, 1976) indicates that women have tended to be excluded from the *informal* relationships that develop between professors and students. As most professors are male, social relations and friendships are more easily formed with male students. This seems less due to deliberate discrimination and more a function of the fact that camaraderie between the two genders, particularly for older faculty, is beset by long-established dividing walls, fears, and taboos. Similar barriers may exist for undergraduate women. The indications are, as we shall see, that the males now in college will find such camaraderie more easy to establish.

7. The past decade has seen a great expansion of women's studies.

The term "women's studies" in its present connotation did not even exist until recently . The significance of these studies has not been the addition of one more area of inquiry to the curriculum, but the infusion of a point of view into many areas of studies in which the neglect of women's presence, activities, and contributions meant not just gaps in our historical, social, and biological knowledge, but a distorted understanding of the phenomena in these fields (Howe, 1975).

8. The 1970s have seen important shifts in the attitudes of college males to women. Coresidential living (Katz, 1974, 1976; Reid, 1976) has been both cause and effect of changes in the student culture. Many male students who once would have viewed their female peers primarily as sex objects now see them as friends, colleagues, collaborators. The great majority of college men are supportive of the occupational aspirations of women. Two-thirds of all entering freshman men in 1980 disagree with the notion that the activities of married women are best confined to home and family (Astin, King, & Richardson, 1980, p. 24). Their attitudes change further during the college years. Many college men also are willing to face up to the consequences of their support. In 1977 three-fourths of the men surveyed by us (Katz & Cronin, 1980) said that they expected to spend as much time as their wives in bringing up their children. Slightly over half of them also expected to take an equal share in such domestic tasks as cooking. Two-thirds think that, ideally, *both* partners would provide the family income, and over half of the men declared themselves quite open to the idea of having their total financial support come from their mates for at least part of their lives. This represents, when compared to surveys of ours a few years earlier, a growing number of college males willing to give up the traditional role of being the sole financial provider.

As late as the middle 1960s college was widely regarded as a marriage market for women, with women being cast in the role of financial dependence. "Playing dumb" was part of the strategy for getting a man. A study at Stanford and San Jose State colleges in the mid-1960s (Leland, 1966) showed that there had been no change in several decades in the tendency of a large proportion of women to "play dumb" in front of men. Finding a man had been a primary occupational objective for women in a situation in which they were oriented toward and had access primarily to clerical, selling, nursing, and teaching jobs. Premature pregnancy or even sexual experience were considered a threat to entry into the housewife job market—one important reason for parietal rules. It is something of a new historical fact that today many college men agree with and support women's seeking a new autonomy and psychological equality. These attitudes are about to be tested in the world after college in which the continuing conservatism of social expectations and occupational structures may create discrepancies between college attitudes and later behavior.

It should also be noted that the enlarged occupational aspirations of women and their more autonomous conception of the female role implies no lessening of the traditional desire for marriage. In the 1978 survey of four educational and two single-sex northeastern colleges previously referred to (Brown Project, 1980, p. 103), less than 3.5% of the women seniors (and 3% of the men seniors) preferred to be single 10–15 years from now.

9. A consequence of women's enlarged sense of independence has been a major change in women's sexual behavior and attitudes. Particularly as birth control devices and legalized abortion greatly reduced the threat of unwanted pregnancy, women have shown a considerable rate of sexual activity, and pleasure in it. Surveys undertaken before 1960 (Bromley & Britten, 1938; Ehrmann, 1959; Kinsey, Pomeroy, Martin, & Gebhard, 1953) reported the incidence of sexual intercourse for college women to range from 13% to 33% (and for college men between 52% and 58%). A considerable portion of female premarital sexual activity was confined to her future husband and to a period of one or two years preceding marriage (Burgess & Wallin, 1953). In 1975 all but a small percentage of male *and* female students (Katz & Cronin, 1980) agreed that premarital sexual intercourse was permissible for males and females alike. Behavior has been consonant with these attitudes. In 1977, 72% of the college women surveyed by us reported premarital coital experience. The 1978 survey of six northeastern institutions shows a similar percentage (Brown Project, 1980, p. 74).

Even more remarkable is the fact, already referred to, that college women are considerably more active sexually than the men: more women than men report themselves as *currently* having a sexual partner and women also engage in sexual intercourse more frequently than the men. These findings are particularly surprising when held against traditional conceptions of femininity. It seems that once freed from certain social controls and consequences, women are less repressive, less guilt-ridden, more in tune with their feelings and sensuousness than before— and more than their male peers. This may help explain why consistently over the last decade more women than men describe themselves as enjoying sex. In 1977, 66% of the women and 50% of the men described their current sexual relationship as *very* satisfying emotionally (Katz & Cronin, 1980).

The understanding of women's sexuality gains an added dimension when one considers that college women continue to link the emotional and physical aspects of sex more than the men. In 1977, 58% of the women versus 23% of the men said that they would not have sexual intercourse if they were *only* physically attracted to their partner. Though there is still a considerable gap between women and men, it is noteworthy that a large percentage of college women find physical sex alone acceptable, and their numbers have been increasing in the last several years.

Our data suggest that because college women had freed themselves of past inhibitions and did not have to use sex as an enticement to marriage, they could afford to take a more detached view of sex. We find men pressuring for the security of a commitment and women resisting them until they could be more sure of the relation—or they never really wanted a lasting relationship with this particular partner. Women could also dare to expect a fuller emotional response from their male partners. As one of our interviewees put it: "It takes courage when you are sitting in a dark room and someone makes aggressive moves to say 'Wait a minute, let's talk about it and find out if we both feel the same way about the situation.'"

One further consequence of the changed relations between college men and women has been the waning of the "date." In the past the "date" was a highly ritualized arrangement, often oriented toward power and status and making the more genuine relationships of acquaintance or friendship more difficult. To some extent in the absence of a chaperone system it functioned as an informal control of sexual behavior. Today freer mutual visiting of men and women and informal, often spontaneous getting together of men and women, not necessarily in even gender ratio, have considerably increased the opportunities for expanded knowledge of men and women of each other.

TASKS AHEAD

One could exaggerate the changes that have taken place. Most undergraduate women find themselves in the presence of a still woefully small number of women faculty. The number of women in postgraduate studies is still far from proportionate in many fields. Traditional expectations about the role of wives are still common. The attitudes of many males in controlling positions—and that includes many male faculty—are still not actively supportive of women's aspirations to full equality. This situation is mirrored in our society at large. We have a Supreme Court with no women, and very few women in the Cabinet, the Senate, or the House. Most people seem to accept this as a matter of course without being conscious of the oddity that in a society that is half female so few females participate in government.

One must realize that the call for a system of education or for a society in which women share equally is, given our past, a large demand. It threatens long-established male social and psychological status and seems a threat to the male economic position. The signs from the undergraduate population are, as we have seen, encouraging. In addition to other responses already cited, in 1977, 71% of the men (and 73% of the women) answered yes to the question "Given the scarcity of jobs in today's market, do you favor equal job opportunities for women even if it should mean fewer jobs for men?" In another context, the potential for changed relationship between men and women was brought home with some force to those of us who observed the institution of coresidential living in college dormitories several years ago. The new living arrangements were immediately followed by relationships between the sexes that were more collegial, more mutually respectful than before. Obscene teasing, exhibitionistic attacks, and destructive put-downs on the part of males ceased and their place was taken by relationships in which each other's humanity became an object of discovery and enjoyment (Katz, 1974).

There are sufficient indications that male ambivalence continues. In the 1978 survey of the six northeastern institutions (Brown Report, 1980, p. 295) over 40% of female undergraduates reported to have felt uncomfortable at least once because of an intellectual "put-down," or a sexual joke, or a comment on their appearance by a male fellow student. Women's greater independence, their hiding their powers less, the greater demands they make on men for emotional responsiveness, fears of economic displacement—all these may contribute to male ambivalence. Colleges might make more deliberate attempts to help males to a fuller awareness and sorting out of their conflicting emotions.

There is work to be done on the part of women too. In the early 1950s the anthropologist Dorothy Lee used to ask her students at Vassar College what they expected their future mates to be like. Almost invariably they described them as more intelligent and otherwise superior to them. Lee then pointed out that as long as women expected such superiority of their men, it would contribute to a continued ascription of "inferiority" to women. Even today the indications are that many undergraduate women have a wavering sense of their legitimate rights to autonomy and equality. Women's continuing greater people-mindedness—in which one can hope more males will follow them—is also a source of confusion to them. Envisaging future family responsibilities seems to lead some of them to a diminution of their striving for autonomy. For others the real and seeming advantages of "passivity," of being taken care of, continue to exert some of their traditional appeal.

When one asks oneself what would be an appropriate response of educational institutions to today's undergraduate women, one realizes with some irony that most of the changes in the situation of undergraduate women described in this chapter have come about through a combination of new social conditions and autonomous developments in the youth culture. There was no deliberate educational policy that either foresaw or brought about these changes. So one might say that social forces have been working in favor of women's greater autonomy and that there can be some trust that they may continue to do so. Nevertheless, perhaps one can expect from educational policy-makers more than passivity. There are at least three areas where institutional efforts seem desirable.

1. The first one is to move with more speed toward a greater proportion of female faculty. This is a matter not only of simple justice, but also means that educational institutions would set a better example than they have until now of the possibility of equal participation by men and women in our society. The greater presence of women would give female students encouragements and models, and for men it would make intellect less sex-linked. Moreover a greater proportion of women professors would engender among the faculty an intellectual and psychological enrichment not dissimilar to that discovered by teachers in previously male institutions when their classes become coeducational.

2. The second area of effort is to ascertain through deliberate observation and through research existing discrimination and then respond to it. Some discrimination still exists in the form of crude and offensive assertions of prejudice by faculty and other personnel. Other discrimination consists in not making physical facilities, medical and other services, budgets for extracurricular activities available to women on equal terms with men or in consideration of women's special needs, e.g., the provision of gynecological services. Other discrimination has more the character of omission. These are a lack of effort or insufficient effort toward encouraging and equipping women to enter professions traditionally considered masculine. Recent attempts to further the mathematical training of college women are an example of facilitating women's entry into for them new professions.

3. The third area comprises the problems, anxieties, and opportunities engendered by the developing redefinition of gender roles described in this chapter. There is the conflict created for women by enlarged occupational opportunities and awareness of the continuing social and other obstacles to women's careers, particularly during the childrearing years. The absence of traditional guidelines brings fresh anxieties around such new social modes as living together or the considerably enlarged premarital sexual activity. The greater emotional and sexual intimacy of rather young people engenders problems which in the past were associated with marital conflicts. The greater sexual freedom has meant no diminution of many of the psychological problems

that have always characterized intimate relations, but they surface earlier now.

The traditional way of confronting such psychological problems is to call for counseling. But that call is often rhetorical, given the understaffing, and at times undertraining, of student affairs professionals. Some rethinking of the current trend to reduce student services is needed (Katz, 1979). It would also be desirable to increase the understanding by at least some faculty of the psychological problems their students confront in the area of gender roles. Such understanding, reflected in different faculty attitudes, would at least indirectly benefit the students.

There is a special opportunity in the fact that deeper problems in the relations between the genders surface more often now than before during the college years. It means that the attempt at understanding can be made in an educational setting and at a time of life when many basic decisions have not yet been made.

REFERENCES

Adler, N. Graduate women. In J. Katz & R. Hartnett, *Scholars in the making*. Cambridge, Mass.: Ballinger, 1976.
Andersen, C. J. (Compiler). *1980 fact book for academic administrators*. Washington, D.C.: American Council on Education, 1980.
Astin, A., King, M., & Richardson, G. *The American freshman: National norms for fall 1980*. Los Angeles: Cooperative Institutional Research Program, 1980.
Bromley, D. D., & Britten, F. H. *Youth and sex*. New York: Harper, 1938.
The Brown Project. *Men and women learning together: A study of college students in the late 70's*. Providence: Brown University, 1980.
Burgess, E. W., & Wallin, P. *Engagement and marriage*. Philadelphia: Lippincott, 1953.
Chronicle of Higher Education, 1978, 15(17), 1, 11.
Ehrmann, W. W. *Premarital dating behavior*. New York: Holt, 1959.
Howe, F. *Women and the power to change*. New York: McGraw-Hill, 1975.
Katz, J. Coeducational living: Effects upon male-female relationships. In D. A. DeCoster & P. L. Mable (Eds.), *Student development and education in college residence halls*. Washington, D.C.: American College Personnel Association, 1974.
Katz, J. Evolving male–female relations and their nurturance. *NASPA Journal*, 1976, 13, 38–43.
Katz, J. Collaboration of academic faculty and student affairs professionals for student development. In D. Tilley (Ed.), *The student affairs dean and the president: Trends in higher education*. Ann Arbor: ERIC Counseling and Personnel Services Clearinghouse, 1979.
Katz, J., & Cronin, D. Sexuality and college life. *Change Magazine*, 1980, 12, 44–49.
Keniston, K. *Young radicals; notes on committed youth*. New York: Harcourt, Brace and World, 1968.
Kinsey, A. C., Pomeroy, W. B., Martin, C. E., & Gebhard, P. H. *Sexual behavior in the human female*. Philadelphia: W. B. Saunders, 1953.
Kreps, J. *Sex in the marketplace*. Baltimore: Johns Hopkins University Press, 1971.

Leland, C. A. *Women-men-work: Women's career aspirations as affected by the male environment.*
    Doctoral dissertation, Stanford University, 1966.
Newcomer, M. *A century of higher education for American women.* New York: Harper, 1959.
Reid, E. A. Coresidential living: Expanded outcomes for women. *NASPA Journal,* 1976, *13,*
    44–56.

Chapter 11

Changing Sex Roles
College Graduates of the 1960s and 1970s

ABIGAIL J. STEWART AND PATRICIA SALT

Since the women's movement first began to heighten our awareness of the roles and relative status of men and women, it has become fashionable to monitor—and issue statements about—changes in these roles. Thus we periodically hear that women have made great strides but still have a long was to go. Or we hear that women have gone too far and have lost essential qualities which will leave the culture emptier. Or we hear that women have actually not moved any distance at all—the change is ephemeral, only occurring at the level of rhetoric and trivial outward display, but not at the level of real or significant behavior.

Obviously, part of the reason that it is so difficult to monitor change is that we are a part of it. Awareness of change may be the result of our own lack of movement personally while others change, or the result of our own personal movement while others do not change. If our changes are in synchrony with the changes of the culture as a whole we may overestimate the degree of change in the larger society. In short, the difficulty in assessing changes in sex roles is partly a result of our limited exposure to the entire culture, partly a result of the immediacy of our own personal experiences, and partly a result of the fact that the process of forming impressions of change involves comparing ourselves to a wider society we can only know incompletely.

ABIGAIL J. STEWART, PH.D. • Department of Psychology, Boston University, Boston, Massachusetts 02146.   PATRICIA SALT, PH.D. • Department of Psychiatry, Tufts University New England Medical Center, Boston, Massachusetts 02111.

MEASURING SEX-ROLE CHANGE: WHERE TO BEGIN?

In measuring sex-role change it is helpful to have a clear notion of what sex roles are. In general, statements which set out to define the nature of sex roles began as attempts to *describe* the consistent patterns of behavior associated with each sex. It is clear, however, that such descriptions take on a power of their own—they become, in short, prescriptions for the *correct* ways for men and women to behave. Challenging traditional sex-role definitions generally involves an alternative prescription, not merely an attack on the adequacy of former sex-role norms. Both traditional and newer definitions of sex roles then may be thought of as ideologies—visions of the way things could be, prescriptions for the way things should be, and predictions of the way things shall be. A review of alternative sex-role ideologies provides us with a set of different implicit hypotheses about the extent and direction of sex-role change.

CHANGES IN SEX-ROLE IDEOLOGY. The prevailing sex-role ideology at the beginning of this century held that the biological differences between men and women were naturally expressed in social role differences—that is, broad differences in life experiences and activities that "mirrored" biological differences (see Parsons, 1949; Zelditch, 1955/1968). Thus men were conceived to be more capable of instrumental, task-oriented behavior and to possess personality traits appropriate for this behavior (aggressiveness, toughness, etc.). Women were viewed as being more competent in the enactment of the expressive role behaviors involved in facilitating interpersonal harmony in the family, and as possessing personality traits appropriate for these role demands (warmth, nurturance, etc.).[1] It was argued that men and women properly occupied separate but equal spheres, and those spheres were reflected in social role definitions for men and women. The fact that men held virtually all positions of social power was felt to be reasonable since women had virtually exclusive power over the household, including children. Thus within a single dyad expressive and instrumental roles and traits were believed to be mutually complementary, creating a unit stronger than either element.

All revisions of sex-role ideology have begun with this traditional instrumental-expressive dichotomy as a starting point. Later notions have rejected the biological basis or social value of the traditional roles, or have questioned the separation of instrumental and expressive qualities into different roles, or have promoted reversal or merging of

---

[1]This differentiation has been captured in other terms. Bakan (1966) and Carlson (1972) use the concepts of agency and communion to discuss approximately the same phenomena.

roles, but the power of traditional sex-role ideology is manifest in the acceptance of its terms as the terms for discussion even of radical alternatives to it.

The beginning of significant change in this traditional sex-role ideology was rooted in a general commitment to equalitarianism. As it became increasingly unacceptable in American culture for individuals to be separated on the grounds of group identification (ethnic background, religion, race, and ultimately sex), increasing attention was paid to the real lack of equal opportunity for women in the educational and occupational spheres. This recognition was intensified by several observations. First, there was an increasing rejection of motherhood as the sole occupation for women, both because of the limits it imposed on their personal fulfillment (Dixon, 1969; Friedan, 1963; Rossi, 1964), and because of the destructive effects of powerful, frustrated mothers on the next generation (see Slater, 1968; Wylie, 1942). In addition there was an increasing loss of confidence in the "natural" basis of sex roles (reflected in Friedan's 1963, *The Feminine Mystique*, which persuasively argued that many aspects of "natural femininity" had been artificially produced and sold to American women).

The equalitarian sex-role ideology focused on the problems of equal access to higher education and the occupational marketplace (see Degler, 1964). According to this version of a new sex-role ideology, men and women should have equal rights and opportunities, though they might (or might not) have similar natures and talents, and might (or might not) make the same choices.

This ideology was quickly confronted by two new versions of the older sex-role ideology. Some argued that the price of experience in the male educational and occupational spheres would be the masculinization of female personality.[2] Success in the "man's world" would be bought at the price of harmony-promoting feminine virtues (see Erikson, 1964; McClelland, 1964; Roszak, 1969). This view required the (usually unstated) assumption that female personality characteristics were created, enhanced, and maintained by female experience (rather than female biology). Changes in experience would inevitably lead to changes in personality. Similarly, others argued that if men engaged in traditional female expressive activities—such as child care—they would be "feminized."

A new feminist biological sex-role ideology challenged this theory and proposed that female entrance into the male spheres of power and achievement would lead not to a transformation of female personality,

---

[2]A less frequently stated implicit ideology is that male participation in traditionally female activities will lead to feminization of male personality.

but instead to a transformation of those male demains (see, e.g., Dunbar, 1970; Firestone, 1970). Male conflict, braggadocio, and even war would be replaced with feminine conciliation, modesty, and peace. Thus the masculinization of feminine personality and the feminization of society (and perhaps also of men) remained alternative predictions and sex-role ideologies.

During the early 1970s a powerful ideological alternative emerged: androgyny (see especially Bem, 1974, 1975; Fasteau, 1975; Spence, 1977; Spence, Helmreich, & Stapp, 1975). According to this viewpoint, rigid sex roles are restrictive, confining, and limiting to both sexes. Instead of strict, polarized sex-roles, our cultural goal should be the mature integration of personality traits and/or behaviors previously assigned to one or the other sex into a unified, balanced individual of either sex. According to this vision, the harmony and balance previously attributed to the heterosexual dyad (expressive female and instrumental male) can be achieved within the alternately or simultaneously expressive and instrumental individual (see Sampson, 1977, for a critique of this view). The androgynous ideology predicts that both men and women will, and should, be transformed by sex-role change. This change will result, in the long run, in men and women who are *both* characterized by *both* instrumental and expressive traits and behaviors.

To summarize, several competing sex-role ideologies have developed over recent years. Traditional sex-role ideology argued that it is "natural" to assign the instrumental role and traits to men and the expressive role and traits to women. The equalitarian sex-role ideology proposed that men and women should have equal *access* to social roles, but specified nothing about the likely *outcome* of such equal access (in terms of the distribution of traits and behaviors by sex). The traditionalist view was restated in one way in nonbiological terms: sex-role change will lead to the "masculinization" of feminine personality and behavior. Feminist thinking transformed the original biological ideology: feminine personality will transform society (and possibly masculine personality and behavior). Finally, the new androgynous ideology states that sex-role change will permit the coexistence of both instrumental and expressive roles and/or traits in both male and female individuals (eventually presumably ending the need for any sex-role ideology). It is difficult to assess at this time the enduring strength of any one of the new sex-role ideologies, or indeed the persistent strength of traditional sex-role ideology. Adherents of particular ideologies observe particular trends as indicating the direction of social change. Others argue that although ideology may have changed, actual behavior has not changed at all. The fact that whether, how, and how much sex roles are changed and changing in America today is a topic of controversy suggests that we cannot determine the direction and depth of sex-role change by an examination of ideology alone, but instead must now examine changes in values, personality, and behavior in order to gauge the likely future of sex-role *ideology*.

UNDERSTANDING CHANGING SEX ROLES IN THE 1960s AND 1970s. One way to begin to understand sex-role change is to examine the behavior of a single group over time as individuals in the group attempt to respond to changed social conditions. Thus one might identify a single group of men and women who graduated from college during the early 1960s and who have coped, one way or another, with the past years of social change as they constructed families and careers. Clearly, developmental, longitudinal studies of this kind have great potential for providing an understanding of the changes in roles and ideology through the eyes of a single group, though it is difficult in such studies to separate the effects of different life-cycle tasks from the effects of social change. (Thus, do the women typically return to the work force in their middle 30s—if they do—because their major childrearing tasks are ended or because sex-role norms have changed?)

A second approach to identifying the direction and intensity of sex-role change (and the one used in this study) is to examine behavior and attitudes of comparable groups in different time periods. This approach does not permit an understanding of the effect of change on the individual (provided by the former approach), but it may offer an impression of the broad patterns of sex-role change, and permits us to rule out the effects of life-cycle changes. We have adopted this cross-sectional approach to understanding changing sex roles in three samples of graduates of one highly selective New England university. Clearly, any trends we can identify cannot be assumed to apply to all educational institutions or to the culture as a whole. Still, the graduates of such an institution are often thought of (or think of themselves) as cultural leaders. To the extent that these individuals are among those most likely to occupy positions of leadership and power, perhaps changes identified in successive generations of students will indicate the direction of broader social change.

Finally, though there are always limitations to studying only college students, it may be that in this case the youth and high level of educational achievement of the samples used are advantages. It is the young who have the smallest stake in the status quo, the least investment in things as they are. If we wish to understand what the future can hold, then it may be best to consult the young. Similarly, for those with more educational advantages life may be more a function of choices and preferences and less a function of necessity. Thus the life patterns actively *chosen* by those with more opportunities to choose may gradually become the patterns pursued by the wider culture.

In order to determine the *direction* of sex-role change among college students in the 1970s we began by assessing the *extent* of sex-role change. Given evidence of such change, we were in a position to evaluate several alternative hypotheses about the direction of change:

1. That only female college graduates had changed and they were more like male college graduates of the past (the "masculinization" hypothesis);
2. That only male college graduates had changed and they were increasingly like female college graduates of the past (the "feminization" hypothesis); and
3. That male and female college graduates had both changed, and were both developing in the direction of the androgynous ideal.

The possibility that achieving female graduates will transform society cannot be examined here, and the fact of increased equalitarianism is assumed, since the females were exposed to the same prestigious liberal arts education as their male counterparts. Operationally, the possibilities outlined above may be tested with our data by asking some specific questions. Were there more sex differences in the past than there are now (indicating that traditional sex roles have changed)? Do women and men both now behave more like either men or women behaved in the past (indicating that the "masculinization of feminine personality" or the "feminization of masculine personality" hypotheses may be correct)? Finally, do males show signs of increased expressive behavior and traits (and/or decreased instrumentality) and do females show evidence of increased instrumental behavior and traits (and/or decreased expressiveness)? If this last is true, then we would have evidence that "androgyny" better describes the personality and behavior of college graduates of the 1970s.

METHODS AND PROCEDURES

SUBJECTS. The samples in this study consist of three cohorts of college graduates (both male and female), covering a total time span of 18 years from the freshman year of the oldest cohort to graduation of the youngest (1960 to 1978). All subjects graduated from a competitive New England university. At original testing the oldest cohort was made up of the entire female class of 1964 and a one-third random sample of the males. The two other groups (the classes of 1975 and 1978) represented a random sample of their respective classes. These groups were selected as part of a larger study by the research office of the institution, which was familiar to the students as the office where standardized testing (e.g., the Graduate Record Examination, etc.) was done. The class of 1964 cohort originally included 244 women and 166 men. The class of 1975 cohort started with 48 women and 67 men, and the class of 1978 cohort is comprised of 75 women and 70 men.

METHODS. In this research we have made use of archival data and data collected for other studies, as well as data collected specifically for this project. To date the data have been drawn from three sources: (1) administration of a six-picture Thematic Apperception Test (TAT) during the fall of the freshman year (for the 1964 and 1978 cohorts); (2) completion of a mailed follow-up questionnaire, 2½ years after graduation (class of 1975 cohort); and (3) completion of a mailed follow-up questionnaire 10 years after graduation (class of 1964 cohort), but containing information about *each year* since graduation, and thus including information about 2½ years after graduation.

TAT ADMINISTRATION. The TATs were administered under neutral arousal conditions. The pictures chosen for the class of 1964 were originally selected for use with the males of this cohort, and were then used with the females so that direct comparisons could be made.[3] The class of 1978 was administered a *different* set of six pictures; the only picture common to both cohorts is one of a captain on a ship talking to another man. The scores from this picture are thus the only ones we are able to use for purposes of direct comparison of TAT-based personality variable scores between the 1964 and 1978 cohorts.

THE 2½-YEAR FOLLOW-UP PROCEDURE. In the late fall and early winter of 1977–1978 the subjects from the initial 1975 cohort were sent a letter and a questionnaire requesting their participation in the follow-up phase of this study. Since this cohort had not been studied intensively as a group and had not been prepared for a follow-up at this time, we were not sure what to expect about the response rate. In fact, since for some the only address available was the address of application, we were prepared for a

[3]Because these pictures were picked specifically for a male sample, and therefore include only two pictures with any female figures, an analysis of "picture differences" in motive and other imagery between pictures with and without female figures was carried out for our female sample. No systematic differences attributable to sex of stimulus figure were found in the intercorrelations of scores by pictures or in the correlations between TAT scores and criterion behaviors. It is true, however, that within the limits of these data it was not possible to assess the separate effects of cue value of the pictures, serial position of the pictures, and sex of stimulus figure. Therefore although no evidence was found of sex of stimulus figure effects, because this factor was confounded with serial position and cue value we cannot rule out sex of stimulus figure effects with any finality. Nonetheless, since there was no positive or clear-cut evidence dictating the selective exclusion of any of the pictures, we have retained scores for stories written to all of the pictures.

considerable attrition rate. However, including those we managed to reach by telephone and those to whom we sent a second copy of the questionnaire and a letter of reminder, our response rate is 66% for the men and 71% for the women. This compares favorably with usual rates for first-time mailed questionnaires.

The questionnaire was four pages long. It requested information about the subject's education, current occupation, marital status, education and occupation of spouse where applicable, and number of children (and if none presently, whether the subject plans, at this time, to have children at some time in the future). In addition subjects were asked to detail as fully as possible where they have lived and what activities have occupied their time for each year since college graduation. For the period of time since graduation, they were then asked to indicate the high points or most satisfying activities and the low points or most upsetting/disturbing aspects of that time. Subjects were also asked to specify the major events and/or people which/who influenced them, taking life as a whole. Subjects were also asked to indicate what, in retrospect, were the most enjoyable things or events and the most disappointing things or events that occurred while they were in college. Finally, we asked each subject to list what he or she would do in the next 10 years if he or she could do anything he or she wished.

THE 10-YEAR FOLLOW-UP PROCEDURES. In the spring of 1974 the subjects from the original 1964 cohort had been sent a letter and a questionnaire requesting their participation in the follow-up phase of this study. Of the women in the cohort, 50% of the original number responded; another 36% were unreachable (no address available, post office returned questionnaire, or unreachable by telephone at address given). Thus after 10 years a total of 122 women, or 78% of those who can be presumed to have received the questionnaire, responded.

The questionnaire was eight pages long. It asked for brief background information, information about current marital and family status, occupation, a detailed account of activities over the 10-year period (year by year), "high" and "low" points of the past 10 years, influences, a retrospective view of the satisfactions and disappointments of college, and a brief account of hopes and plans for the future 10 years.

Comparable information from the men of the cohort was obtained from two sources. A mailed questionnaire sent to the entire original class asked for brief background facts, a retrospective view of the satisfactions and disappointments of college, and "high" and "low" points of the last 10 years, as past of a longer questionnaire asking for other, unrelated information. Additional information, particularly about activities 2½ years after college, was obtained from the material contained in a book printed at the time of this class's fifth reunion. The amount and detail of this information thus varies greatly from subject to subject. Some follow-up information was obtained from these two sources for 43% of the original sample of males from the class of 1964.

CODING OF THE DATA. The TATS were scored for several *personality variables* using the scoring systems for *n* Achievement (McClelland, Atkinson, Clark, & Lowell, 1953/1958) *n* Affiliation (Heyns, Veroff, & Atkinson, 1958), and *n* Power (Winter, 1973). The first author scored all of the stories for all subjects. This scoring was in all cases carried out before any of the questionnaires were returned. Her reliability in scoring each system is demonstrated by the following rank-order correlations with expert scoring on prescored materials: *n* Achievement, *rho* = .96; *n* Affiliation, *rho* = .95; and *n* Power, *rho* = .97. All scoring was blind to the identity of the subject.

The follow-up questionnaires (both 2½ and 10-year follow-up) were coded blindly by the first author. The questionnaires were coded for two general categories of information for the purpose of this study: retrospective views of the college experience, including both positive and negative aspects; and life pattern variables chosen for analysis because the two cohorts (the class of 1964 and the class of 1975) could be most legitimately compared on them. Thus retrospective views of college at 2½ and 10 years *might* differ as a function of the length of time since college, but would both be retrospective and might not change greatly between the ages of 24 and 31. On the other hand, one's goals for the next 10 years (asked of both cohorts) would presumably depend heavily on one's activities for the past 10. Similarly, the high and low points of one's life since college (also asked of both samples) would depend a great deal on how much and what kind of "living" one had experienced.

Because the 1964 cohort had described their activities (marriage, children, school, work, etc.) for each year since college, we were able to extract their marital, parental, educational, and occupational status when they were 2½ years out of college (in January 1967) from the follow-up questionnaires. Thus we were able to code these activities and statuses in exactly the same way for both cohorts.

The variables selected for analysis here were coded as either present or absent for each subject. Codes for positive and negative aspects of college were initially developed simply to capture the types of issues mentioned by the initial class of 1964 samples. They proved both relevant and codable for the responses of the class of 1975. Responses indicating *the positive aspects of college* were coded as mentioning:

1. Peers (friends, people met)
2. Lifestyle (living in a dormitory, etc.)
3. Noncourse activities (working on the school paper, drama club, etc.)
4. Intimate relationship (boyfriend, etc.)

5. Personal achievements (senior thesis, graduating summa, etc.)
6. Faculty (a specific faculty member or a generalized statement)
7. Course (a particular course or some group of courses taken)

Individuals could and did mention more than one of these aspects of college.

The negative aspects of college were far more personal and idiosyncratic ("having mononucleosis my senior year"; "when my boyfriend went into the Peace Corps"; "after I broke my leg skiing"). However, we were able to code mention of:

1. Courses (again, a specific course or group of courses)
2. Personal failures (doing less well than expected or hoped)
3. Institutional abandonment (a sense that the institution was less than helpful or supportive in the individual's educational or occupational choice processes).

Again, individuals sometimes mentioned more than one of these.

The life pattern variables included indices of occupational, educational, marital, and parental status. These variables included:

1. Current status as a graduate student (any formal degree-granting program beyond the baccalaureate level)
2. Study toward or active involvement in any full-time professional career[4]
3. Specialization or advanced training or orientation of current occupation in traditionally male-dominated fields (medicine, law, academics, or business)
4. Whether married currently
5. Number of children, if any

Table 1 summarizes the data available and coded for each sample.

DATA ANALYSIS STRATEGY. Variables in all domains (personality, retrospective views of college, and life patterns) were classified as mainly reflecting instrumental or expressive concerns. This classification was clearly a crude one, and was meant only to convey the average relative weighting of goal- and task-oriented elements (instrumental) versus relationship and feeling-oriented elements (expressive). Thus, for example, "marriage" was considered to reflect "expressive" concerns on the average, though for any given individual it might also, or only, reflect instrumental concerns.

In the personality domain, achievement and power needs were

---

[4]This is drawn from the coding scheme for women's occupational aspirations reported in Stewart and Winter (1974).

Table 1. Summary of Data Available for Three Cohorts

Class of '64	Class of '75	Class of '78
Freshman TAT (1960) personality variables need for Achievement need for Power need for Affiliation		Freshman TAT (1974) personality variables need for Achievement need for Power need for Affiliation
10-year follow-up (1974) life-pattern variables (2½-year activities) Currently a graduate student Career specialization (medicine, law, academics, business) Full-time professional career Marital status Parental status	2½-year follow-up (1977) life-pattern variables (2½-year activities) Currently a graduate student Career specialization (medicine, law, academics, business) Full-time professional career Marital status Parental status	
Best aspects of college Peers Lifestyle Noncourse activities Intimate relationships Personal achievements Faculty Course	Best aspects of college Peers Lifestyle Noncourse activities Intimate relationships Personal achievements Faculty Course	
Worst aspects of college Course(s) Personal failure(s) Institutional abandonment	Worst aspects of college Course(s) Personal failure(s) Institutional abandonment	

viewed as having a substantial instrumental component, while affiliation was viewed as reflecting primarily an expressive need. It should be noted, however, that it may be that both instrumental and expressive needs can be and are satisfied via behavior that is appropriate to each sex role. In that case we would expect no sex differentiation in motives, only in their behavioral manifestation.

Concerns with the academic, work aspects of college (both positive and negative) were viewed as instrumental within the context of college students, while concerns with extracurricular, relational, and affective aspects of college were seen as largely expressive. Finally, graduate school and work activities were seen as elements of "instrumental" activity, while marriage and childbearing were seen as "expressive" activities.

Within the personality domain, analyses of variance were performed to assess overall cohort effects (indicating the possibility that both men and women had changed in the same ways between 1964 and 1978), sex effects (indicating overall sex differences across cohorts), and sex-by-cohort interactions (indicating the possibility of different changes for the two sexes between 1964 and 1978).

For the other variable domains, chi-square analyses were performed to assess the presence or absence of sex differences within each cohort. If sex-role change occurred between 1964 and 1975 we would expect a different pattern of sex differences within the two cohorts. "Masculinization" would be implied if there were fewer sex differences in 1975 and the women had increased instrumental expressions and decreased expressive ones. "Feminization" would be indicated by a reduction of instrumental concerns among men and an increase in expressive concerns. Convergence would be indicated if: (1) there were fewer sex differences in the 1975 cohort than in the 1964 one, and (2) the changes reflected both increased instrumentality in women and increased expressiveness in men.

RESULTS

PERSONALITY VARIABLES. As may be seen in Table 2, there is a substantial difference in the need for Achievement scores of the two cohorts, with the class of 1978 showing significantly lower scores than the class of 1964. There is, however, no significant difference between the sexes, and there is no significant cohort-by-sex interaction. There are no significant cohort or sex differences in need for Power, but there is a significant cohort-by-sex interaction. Women scored higher than men in n Power in 1964, but lower in 1978. In need for Affiliation there is a trend toward a main effect for cohort (the class of 1964 scoring higher) and a significant main effect for sex (women scoring higher). There is in addition a significant sex-by-cohort interaction, with the men scoring higher in the class of 1978 than in the class of 1964, but women scoring far lower in the class of 1978 than in the class of 1964.

Overall, then, both the needs for Affiliation and Power were lower in the 1978 cohort than they were in the 1964 cohort. The need for Affiliation scores were higher in females across the two cohorts. Finally, the pattern of sex differences was different for the two cohorts for both the power and affiliation motives. The power motive was higher in females in the class of 1964, but in males in the class of 1978. The affiliation motive was higher in females in both classes, but male scores

Table 2. Motive Scores on Picture #1 ("Ship's Captain") in the Classes of 1964 and 1978

	Mean scores (and standard deviation) on:		
Group	Need for Achievement	Need for Power	Need for Affiliation
Class of 1964 (freshman year)			
Men (N = 166)	−.39 (.74)	1.62 (1.84)	.08 (.44)
Women (N = 236)	−.25 (1.34)	2.05 (1.98)	.43 (.90)
Class of 1978 (freshman year)			
Men (N = 70)	−.90 (.51)	1.97 (1.37)	.13 (.48)
Women (N = 75)	−.95 (.23)	1.56 (1.34)	.15 (.39)
Effects			
F-value for cohort	39.08***	.16	3.02†
F-value for sex	.22	.01	7.80**
F-value for cohort by sex interaction	.95	5.78*	6.16*

†$p < .10$ *$p < .05$ **$p < .01$ ***$p < .001$.

in the class of 1978 were higher than male scores in the class of 1964, while female scores in the class of 1978 were lower than female scores in the class of 1964.

The hypothesis of change in the pattern of sex differences in personality variables is therefore supported for the needs for Power and Affiliation, but not for the need for Achievement. The "masculinization of female personality" hypothesis is not supported, since neither of the two significant sex-by-cohort interactions involves the exclusive shift of females toward the previously male pattern. The "androgyny" hypothesis is supported by the pattern of scores found for the need for Affiliation (lower scores for woman; higher scores for men, in 1978), but not for the needs for Achievement (where there was no change in pattern) or Power (where the change indicated a reversal, not convergence, of the sexes).

POSITIVE ASPECTS OF COLLEGE. We may compare the sexes in the 1964 and 1975 cohorts (both followed up longitudinally) in frequency of mentioning each of the seven coded "positive aspects of college." As may be seen in Table 3, there were significant differences between the sexes for four out of seven of the coded variables in the class of 1964 (achievements, peers, friends, noncourse activities, and intimate Relationship), and for none of the seven in the class of 1975. The hypothesis of sex-role change then seems to be generally supported.

Table 3. *Positive Aspects of College Experience: The Classes of 1964 and 1975*

	Instrumental			Expressive			
Group	Achievements	Faculty	Course	Peers, friends	Lifestyle	Noncourse activity	Relationship
Class of 1964							
Men (N = 94)	4	12	18	34	20	14	1
Women (N = 119)	27	19	29	20	13	28	33
Difference	-23	-7	-11	14	7	-14	-32
Chi-square[a]	17.58***	1.74	2.62†	4.53*	1.29	5.20*	32.57***
Class of 1975							
Men (N = 44)	14	2	21	46	11	30	30
Women (N = 34)	12	12	32	62	9	29	24
Difference	2	-10	-11	-16	2	1	6
Chi-square[a]	0.01	1.52	0.87	1.44	0.00	0.06	0.11

% listing as "good things about college"

[a]Chi-square values corrected for continuity where appropriate.
†$p < .10$ *$p < .05$ ***$p < .001$.

If we examine the direction of change, we can see that women more frequently listed *all but one* of the variables initially differentiating the sexes in the class of 1964. The pattern of scores indicates that women continued to list those aspects of college about as often in the class of 1975, but men listed them consistently more often. Thus the "masculinization of feminine personality" hypothesis is not supported by the direction of change in the pattern of scores between the sexes.

Finally, we may consider the specific content of the pattern changes. It is clear if we examine the data in this way that males listed the expressive aspects of college far less often than females in the class of 1964, but not in the class of 1975. However, women listed one instrumental goal more often than males in the class of 1964 (achievement), and another approached significance (course). Thus the "androgyny" hypothesis is supported by the apparent increase in valuing of expressive experience for men, and by the apparent increased valuing of instrumental courses by women (and decreased valuing by men). However, the high value attached to achievement by women in the class of 1964 (and the low value attached to it by men) is difficult to account for using the androgyny hypothesis. Nevertheless the class of 1975 showed a move away from sex differences in the valued aspects of college. In the expressive domain this move supported the androgyny hypothesis; in the instrumental domain the shift was not in line with any of the hypotheses discussed here.

NEGATIVE ASPECTS OF COLLEGE. We may also compare the sexes in frequency of mentioning each of the three coded "negative aspects of college," with "course" and "personal failures" being more related to the instrumental role, and "institutional abandonment" more related to the expressive role. As many be seen in Table 4, there was one highly significant sex difference in the class of 1964 (women listed "failure" more often), and none in the class of 1975 (supporting the hypothesis of sex-role change). In the case of "failure" (an instrumental aspect of college) there was a smaller sex difference in the class of 1975 because males scored higher than they had in the class of 1964.

The "androgyny" hypothesis may be seen as generally supported by the fact that men and women scored more similarly (less differently) in the class of 1975 than 1964. However, it is not supported by the fact that males showed *increased* distress over one instrumental aspect of college—"failure" (although their increase lessens the gap between their level of concern and the females' level).

LIFE PATTERN VARIABLES. As may be seen in Table 5, five of eight of the life pattern variables examined show significant sex differences in the class of 1964 (with one other showing a trend), while only one of the eight shows a difference in the class of 1975. In the class of 1964 men

Table 4. Negative Aspects of College Experience: The Classes of 1964 and 1975

	% listing as "bad things about college"		
	Instrumental		Expressive
Group	Course	Failure	Institutional abandonment
Class of 1964			
Men (N = 94)	12	11	7
Women (N = 120)	16	34	7
Difference	−4	−23	0
Chi-square[a]	0.44	14.81***	0.00
Class of 1975			
Men (N = 44)	2	21	7
Women (N = 34)	12	24	6
Difference	−10	−3	1
Chi-square[a]	1.52	0.00	0.09

[a]Chi-square values corrected for continuity where appropriate.
***$p < .001$.

show higher rates of graduate school attendence and professional-level career attainment. They also show higher rates of specialization in medicine, law, and business. In the class of 1964 women show a trend toward a higher rate of marriage, but there are no differences between the sexes in the rate of producing children or pursuing academic careers.

In the class of 1975 there are no sex differences in graduate school attendance, but there is a significant (though markedly reduced) difference in professional-level career attainment or preparation (with men showing a higher rate). There are, however, no significant differences in specialization rates for medicine, law, academics, or business. There are also no differences in the percentages married or with children. The smaller number of sex differences in the class of 1975 is largely the result of an increase in the rate of female educational and occupational attainment (rather than a decline in male attainment). That is, the hypothesis of sex-role change is clearly supported by these data. The hypothesis of "masculinization" is also clearly supported (female rates of occupational and educational attainment are approaching male rates, not vice versa). Finally, the "androgyny" hypothesis is not supported in that there is no evidence here that the sexes are "converging" from two directions, or that there is an increase in expressive role behavior in males parallel to the marked increase in instrumental role behavior in females. Indeed the most significant change in the expressive domain is a striking overall

Table 5. Career and Family Patterns: The Classes of 1964 and 1975

	% who are							
	Overall patterns		Instrumental				Expressive	
			Individual specialties					
Group	Graduate school	Full-time professional career[b]	Medical	Law	Academic	Business	Married	Children (if married)
Class of 1964								
Men (N = 72)	77	95	15	17	25	18	49	30 (of 30)
Women (N = 122)	43	45	6	3	28	0	63	27 (of 70)
Difference	24	50	9	14	−3	18	−14	3
Chi-square[a]	18.99***	42.97***	3.95*	11.90***	0.22	19.85***	3.11+	0.46
Class of 1975								
Men (N = 41)	66	97	24	20	17	17	15	17 (of 6)
Women (N = 31)	58	79	21	14	21	10	13	0 (of 4)
Difference	8	18	3	6	−4	7	2	17
Chi-square[a]	0.46	3.81*	0.13	0.39	0.15	0.63	0.06	0.74

[a]Chi-square values corrected for continuity where appropriate.
[b]Value of 4 in Stewart & Winter (1974) code.
+p < .10   *p < .05   **p < .10   ***p < .001.

drop in the rate of marriage for males and females in the class of 1975 as compared with the class of 1964, at least within 2½ years of graduation.

THE STABILITY OF EARLY LIFE PATTERNS. Since the members of the class of 1975 were only about 23 years old at the time they were followed up, it is reasonable to ask whether the life patterns they have established at this point are at all stable. Do the differences between the sexes which either do or do not show up at the age of 23 represent important, meaningful patterns of adult life? In order to estimate the degree of confidence we may have in the stability of these "early" life patterns, we have correlated the "early" life patterns of the class of 1964 (the 2½-year patterns analyzed comparatively above) with their own later, 10-year life patterns. The correlations between early and 10-year life patterns are presented for the two sexes in Table 6.

It is clear from these correlations that for both males and females there is considerable stability in level of professional attainment and in professional specialty between the ages of 23 and 31. There is, however, less stability in marital status over the period. If we can safely assume that the stability (or predictiveness) of life patterns from age 23 on has not changed from 1967 to 1978, we may have a relatively high degree of confidence in the meaning of the results we have examined for occupational life patterns, but a lower level of confidence in the results for family life patterns.

DISCUSSION

EVIDENCE FOR SEX-ROLE CHANGE. The overwhelming weight of the evidence indicates that the pattern of differences between the sexes has changed. The college students from the class of 1964 showed a far higher level of sex-role differentiation than did those from the classes of 1975 and 1978. Of the 21 comparisons of the sexes for each of the cohorts which have been presented in this chapter there were 12 significant sex differences for the class of 1964 but only 2 for the classes of 1975 and 1978 ($\chi^2 = 10.71$, $p < .01$).[5] In addition this trend toward less sex-role differentiation cut across several domains: personality traits or needs, positive and negative responses to college, and actual life patterns.

EVIDENCE FOR "MASCULINIZATION" AND "FEMINIZATION." In the areas of personality and positively valued aspects of college there is no real evidence supporting the "masculinization" hypothesis. Thus sex-role change in these two domains did *not* occur solely as the result of female shifts toward the previously male response style. Females in the

[5]This analysis assumes sex differences for both cohorts in the need for Power and only for the class of 1964 in the need for Affiliation (see Table 2).

Table 6. Relationship between Early and 10-Year Life Patterns for the Class of 1964

Variable	Men (N = 54) r	Women (N = 122) r
	Correlation[a] between variable measured after 2½ and 10 years among	
Marriage	.35*	.28**
Professional career[b]	.45**	.72***
Medicine	1.00***	.86***
Business	.77***	—
Law	.87***	.70***
Academics	.61***	.76***

[a]Phi coefficient.
[b]This category involves prediction from attendance at medical, law, or graduate school in the early period to having a career in medicine, law, or academics, respectively, at the time of the 10-year follow-up.
*p < .05   **p < .01   ***p < .001.

class of 1975 did show a lower level of distress with "expressive" negative aspects of college (as had the previous cohort of males); but on the other hand males in the class of 1975 showed an increased concern about instrumental values.

The masculinization hypothesis was, however, overwhelmingly supported by the evidence on educational and occupational attainments. In this area females' activities were clearly becoming increasingly like males' previous patterns, and there was no parallel shift in the males' activities. In the area of the positive aspects of college experience there was some evidence in favor of the "feminization" hypothesis. Men in the class of 1975 showed more concern in three of the four expressive areas than did their class of 1964 counterparts.

EVIDENCE FOR "ANDROGYNY." In very general terms, the lower level of sex differentiation in the class of 1975 could be considered evidence for androgyny. The androgynous ideal, however, has typically required more than merely an absence of sex-role stereotyping. The concept of androgyny has included the notion of an individual capable of integrating the traditionally male instrumental role and personality with the traditionally female expressive role and personality. Thus a stricter definition of androgyny demands evidence that males show increasing competence and concern in the expressive sphere and that females show a parallel increased competence and interest in the instrumental sphere.

In the personality variable domain we see support for the androgyny hypothesis in the shifts on the need for Affiliation. In the class of 1978 we find the men scoring higher on this expressive variable than the men in 1964, while at the same time women were scoring lower than had women in the class of 1964.

Similarly, men in the class of 1975 list far more positive aspects of college that are expressive (peers, friends, relationship, etc.) than had their 1964 counterparts, while women listed at least some more positive aspects of college that are instrumental (course). They also showed somewhat less concern about achievements. Men also showed a higher valuing of (instrumental) achievements in the class of 1975, and women showed a higher valuing of (expressive) peers or friends. Overall, though, two general trends—toward increased expressive values in men and toward increased instrumental values in women—can be identified in the data on positive aspects of college. In the area of negative aspects of college, though, the evidence is not so clear. This may, however, be due not to a "lack of androgyny" but to the low level of distress with instrumental aspects of college expressed by males in the class of 1964. This lack of distress in the older cohort may reflect stereotypically male stoicism rather than a geniune absence of concern, since the males did report less distress about *every* aspect of college.

There was no support for the androgyny hypothesis in the actual life patterns. Females show greatly increased activity in the instrumental sphere, but males show no increased activity in the expressive sphere. It is quite possible, though, that this is an artifact of the variables measured rather than a function of a real lack of change. The class of 1975 showed a greatly reduced tendency, overall, to marry and begin families at this early age. Very likely, expressive concerns are finding other, un-measured outlets in this cohort beyond traditional marriage and family. Thus though there is no evidence in favor of the androgyny hypothesis in terms of life patterns, we are concerned that expressive role activity has probably changed in *form* and not in *degree* for this younger cohort, and our variables are not sensitive to these new forms of expressive role activity.

CONCLUSION

The data presented in this chapter indicate that there are substantial differences in the sex-role-linked behaviors, traits, and values of the college students of the 1960s and the 1970s. The evidence in the area of behavior indicates that the "masculinization" of females hypothesis may be correct; that is, females' activities are more instrumental and like those engaged in by males in the past, but males' activities are not more expressive or more like females' activities in the past. The evidence in the area of traits and values, however, generally supports the "androgyny" hypothesis: men show increased expressive preoccupations and women show increased instrumental preoccupations. There does seem to be convergence of the sexes overall; the convergence is toward previously male activity but involves both instrumental and expressive values and needs. Because instrumentality is so closely and inevitably linked to action, female sex-role shifts may be far more obvious and easy to measure than male sex-role shifts toward increased expressiveness (represented in changes in values, traits, and styles of action, rather than in particular actions themselves). Moreover these data may point toward a complex definition of "androgyny." The fusion of expressive traits and values with instrumental action is one androgynous ideal that may even now be emerging as a real possibility for bright young college students.

Acknowledgment

We are grateful to David G. Winter for his assistance in securing and analyzing some of the data for males presented in this chapter, as well as for his helpful comments on the manuscript.

REFERENCES

Bakan, D. *The duality of human existence.* Chicago: Rand McNally, 1966.
Bem, S. L. The measurement of psychological androgyny. *Journal of Consulting and Clinical Psychology*, 1974, 42, 115–162.
Bem, S. L. Sex-role adaptability: One consequence of psychological androgyny. *Journal of Personality and Social Psychology*, 1975, 31, 634–643.
Carlson, R. Understanding women: Implications for personality theory and research. *Journal of Social Issues*, 1972, 28, 17–32.
Degler, C. Revolution without ideology: The changing place of women in America. In R. J. Lifton (Ed.), *The woman in America.* Boston: Beacon Press, 1964.
Dixon, M. The rise of women's liberation. In B. Roszak & T. Roszak (Eds.), *Masculine/feminine.* New York: Harper and Row, 1969.
Dunbar, R. Female liberation as the basis for social revolution. In R. Morgan (Ed.), *Sisterhood is powerful.* New York: Vintage, 1970.
Erikson, E. H. Inner and outer space: Reflections on womanhood. In R. J. Lifton (Ed.), *The woman in America.* Boston: Beacon Press, 1964.
Fasteau, M. F. *The male machine.* New York: Dell, 1975.
Firestone, S. *The dialectic of sex.* New York: William Morrow, 1970.
Friedan, B. *The feminine mystique.* New York: Dell, 1963.
Heyns, R. W., Veroff, J., & Atkinson, J. W. A scoring manual for the affiliation motive. In J. W. Atkinson (Ed.), *Motives in fantasy, action and society.* Princeton, N.J.: D. Van Nostrand, 1958.
McClelland, D. C. Wanted: A new self-image for women. In R. J. Lifton (Ed.), *The woman in America.* Boston: Beacon Press, 1964.
McClelland, D. C., Atkinson, J. W., Clark, R. A., & Lowell, E. L. A scoring manual for the

achievement motive (1953). In J. W. Atkinson (Ed.), *Motives in fantasy, action and society*. Princeton, N.J.: D. Van Nostrand, 1958.

Parsons, T. Age and sex in the social structure of the United States. In *Essays in sociological theory*. Glencoe, Ill.: Free Press, 1949.

Rossi, A. Equality between the sexes: An immodest proposal. In R. J. Lifton (Ed.), *The woman in America*. Boston: Beacon Press, 1964.

Roszak, T. The hard and the soft: The force of feminism in modern times. In B. Roszak & T. Roszak (Eds.), *Masculine/feminine*. New York: Harper and Row, 1969.

Sampson, E. E. Psychology and the American ideal. *Journal of Personality and Social Psychology*, 1977, *35*, 767–782.

Slater, P. *The glory of Hera*. Boston: Beacon Press, 1968.

Spence, J. T. Traits, roles and the concept of androgyny. Paper presented at Conference on Perspectives on the Psychology of Women, Michigan State University, May 1977.

Spence, J. T., Helmreich, R., & Stapp, J. Ratings of self and peers on sex-role attributes and their relation to self-esteem and conceptions of masculinity and femininity. *Journal of Personality and Social Psychology*, 1975, *32*, 29–39.

Stewart, A. J., & Winter, D. G. Self-definition and social definition in women. *Journal of Personality*, 1974, *42*, 238–259.

Winter, D. G. *The power motive*. New York: Free Press, 1973.

Wylie, P. *A generation of vipers*. New York: Farrar, Straus and Giroux, 1942.

Zelditch, M. Role differentiation in the nuclear family: A comparative study (1955). In N. Bell & E. Vogel (Eds.), *A modern introduction to the family*. New York: Free Press, 1968.

Chapter 12

Sex Differences in the Educational and Occupational Goals of Black College Students

Continued Inquiry into the Black Matriarchy Theory

JACQUELINE FLEMING

One of the events that has characterized the era under consideration is the ongoing, often lively discussion on the theory of a black matriarchy. This chapter will look at the history of this discussion through the era and then present data that should be relevant to testing the viability of one aspect of the theory.

Unwittingly, E. Franklin Frazier (1939) introduced the idea of the matriarchate among blacks and equated it with maternal households with husbands absent. He described it as one of the several family forms emerging just after slavery and estimated its prevalence as anywhere from less than 1% in rural farm areas to 31% in urban areas of southern cities. He referred to the self-reliance and self-sufficiency that Negro women learned during slavery, women who *must have been* [he claims] accustomed to playing the dominant role in the family and in marital relations (Chapter 7). With this description the idea of the black matriarchy was born, an idea that has kindled and rekindled the imaginations of social scientists and layman alike to this day. The mere mention of such a notion apparently had an inordinately intriguing appeal since

JACQUELINE FLEMING PH.D. • Department of Psychology, Barnard College, and Consulting Psychologist, United Negro College Fund, New York, New York 10021.

few authors seem to recall that in the same document Frazier also wrote a chapter on the downfall of the matriarchate, in which he observes that freedmen were exceedingly jealous of their newly acquired authority in family relations and insisted on a recognition of their superiority over women. He describes conditions under which male ascendancy very often became established in the family, a process encouraged by the new economic arrangements available to freedmen which favored male authority. Nonetheless the notion of the "downfall" was obviously less interesting for subsequent discussion, which seems to have been provoked only on the nature and "rise" of the black matriarchy.

As the "theory" goes, black women gained their ascendancy during slavery through the economic support of the family, an ascendancy which has allegedly led to a favoritism of the female child (see Staples, 1970). Kardiner and Ovesey (1951), for example, suggest that when black women work, the affective potential of the child is undermined; "she" automatically elevates the female role as provider and derogates the established role of the male. These authors assume that employment opportunities are better for black women and express concern about affecting economic changes necessary for the establishment of black patriarchal societies. As evidence of the psychological impact of the matriarchate on black males, they point out that most of the chief characters in black novels are women, with male fates being determined by them. Rohrer and Edmonson (1960) describe matriarchs as hostile to males and as openly expressing their preference for little girls. Gans (1970) depicts females as emasculating inasmuch as they treat men with disdain and hostility; upbringing in a predominantly female household is said to encourage ambivalence as to male functions and masculinity. Furthermore, Moynihan (1965) has linked female-headed households to the disintegration of the structure of black families.

While Frazier's notion of the matriarchate was a father-absent family, it has become a widely accepted assertion that even when the father is present the mother is the dominant member (Clark, 1965; Hyman & Reed, 1969). Schwartz's (1965) observation of several different family groups convinces him that it is maladaptive for status and authority to inhere in two different people—status in the mother because of her control of resources, and decision-making authority retained by the father. When the mother is present and the father weak, maladaptive consequences are the problems in the socialization particularly of male children evidenced by "some dissonance in the situation expressed by the boy" as well as more indication generally of delinquency and homosexuality. Ausubel (1956) claims that the black female child shows better personal and academic adjustment because she grows up in a matriarchal family atmosphere where girls are openly preferred and where greater sacrifices are made for their future. Grossack (1963) asserts that black females are provided with more educational opportunities and that the psychic castration of the black male is reflected in low educational attainments. Black women are judged to be better educated than black males (Bernard, 1966; Bressler & McKenney, 1968), to demonstrate superior scholastic performance (see Bernard, 1966; Jackson, 1973), to be more represented in high-status occupations (Scanzoni, 1971); and generally to be more successful than black males. One of the more quaint rationales for the relative success of black women has been described by Bock (1969) as something of a "farmer's daughter effect" where because women were freed in rural areas from the burdens of heavy labor, they had more opportunity to go to school and thus to enter and remain in mobility-line occupations.

In short, the largely observational, psychoanalytic, and imaginative contributions to the theory of the black matriarchy assert that:

1. Black females are dominant, with or without their men around.
2. This "abnormal" situation, i.e., the absence of patriarchy, creates psychological disturbances among black males and is responsible for the disintegration of the black family structure.
3. [Most relevant for the following discussion] There is good consensus that black girls are preferred over black boys to the extent that they receive more education, aspire to greater heights, have better jobs and make more money, and are, to be sure, a successful breed of women.

Allegedly, circumstances have culminated in an "unnatural superiority" of black women (Bernard, 1966).

Increasingly, more systematic evidence comparing the relative status of black men and women has found its way into the ongoing discussion. Those studies specifically concerned with educational and occupational issues will be given special attention here.

Bock (1969), in apparent support of the general theory, presents data showing that 7.7% of black women in the labor force are professionals while only 3.1% of black men are so classified. But he acknowledges that black women tend to be concentrated in a few female-dominated professions and his figures reveal that black female professionals earn only about three-fourths of what their male counterparts do. Feagin (1970) and Jackson (1973) have both shown through census figures that the alleged advantage of black women over black men in education is actually very slight, and obscures the fact that in terms of advanced degrees and elite professional attainment black males predominate. Factors that Jackson finds to account for the slight edge neither confirm nor deny any superiority of black women. Almquist (1973, 1975) further demonstrates that the earnings of black women, which were the lowest of the four sex × race groups studied, represented income losses due to racism and especially to sexism. Figures presented by Epstein (1973) actually show that while there are black women represented in their high-status professional communities, they are in a distinct minority.

In terms of occupational aspirations, Thorpe (1969), who controlled for social class, found that among North Carolina high school students black girls expressed higher aspirations than white girls or black boys, and Smith (1975) reviews studies that are generally said to indicate higher occupational aspirations among black women. However, neither Carter, Little, and Barabasz (1972), who also controlled for social class, nor Picou (1973) found sex differences among the black students in the seventh- and eighth-graders or high school seniors respectively. Turner (1971) found among subjects at predominantly white colleges that, relative to black men, black women expressed lower occupational aspirations. Also, Mednick and Puryear (1975) as well as Gurin and Gaylord (1976) discovered that at traditionally black colleges the attitudes of female students toward achievement goals were stereotypically feminine and surprisingly inconsistent with the image of the dominant black woman.

Considering the bulk of systematic evidence available on the educational and occupational status of black women relative to their men, there is little support for the general premises of the black matriarchy theory. However, as Kirkpatrick (1973) and Jackson (1973) have pointed out, there are sources of potential bias in many of these studies, such as the general absence of controls for social class or ability differences, that could affect the findings. Furthermore some of the research samples are small and look at students from particularized educational environments.

The purpose of the present study is to investigate the different aspects of educational and occupational goals among black men and women in a relatively large sample composed of students from a variety of educational backgrounds in order to determine what sex differences exist that cannot be attributed to social class or ability differences, and then to determine whether they provide support for the general theory or the recent data.

METHODOLOGY

SUBJECTS AND PROCEDURE. Subjects for the study were approximately 800 black college undergraduates from seven schools located in or near a major southeastern city. Represented in the sample were students from a variety of educational experiences: predominantly black and predominantly white institutions, state- and privately supported schools, liberal arts curricula as well as a technical institute, small colleges and large universities. All were subjects from a larger investigation of black students funded by the Carnegie Corporation (see Fleming, 1979). The sample was composed of 304 males and 496 females.

Subjects were recruited for the study in the spring of 1977 in cooperation with each of the seven schools by letters, phone calls, and announcements at general student meetings. Five dollars in cash and refreshments were offered as incentives for participation. Even so, the usual bias introduced by the self-selection process was surely operative as it is in most research. Turn-out rates of those students actually contacted ranged from 36% to 84%.

During large group testing sessions, a male and female experimenter administered a lengthy questionnaire along with several other instruments relevant to the purpose of the larger study which included the following questions on educational and occupational goals:

1. a. What is your major subject (or intended major)?
   b. Why have you chosen this particular major? That is, who or what has influenced you?

2. a. Are you seriously planning to go to graduate or professional school after college?
   b. If yes, what degree and course of study will you pursue?
   c. What obstacles might prevent you from carrying out your plans?

3. If you do not plan to go to graduate school, what are your plans after graduation?

4. a. What is your vocational objective? That is, what are your career plans?
   b. Why have you chosen this particular career? That is, who or what has influenced you?
   c. What obstacles might prevent you from carrying out your plans?

5. How do you think marriage will affect your career plans?

The sample size reflects the total number of subjects who provided codable answers to those questions.

From the answers given it was possible to extract and code the following 141 variables for all subjects:

19 major subjects
15 reasons for choosing the major subject
22 plans for graduate school

9 obstacles to graduate school plans
5 non-graduate school plans following graduation
25 career plans
15 reasons for vocational choice
9 obstacles to career plans
5 effects of marriage on career plans, and
15 summary measures

In addition, grades could be obtained for most of the subjects. (See the Appendix to this chapter for a complete list of the 141 variables coded.)

Given the importance in the literature on black families attached to social-class levels, it seemed necessary to control any initial sex differences that might appear for social-class background. Socioeconomic status (SES) was measured with an occupational rating scale developed by Martin Hamburger (1971) which utilizes a 7-point system and considers occupational title, education, and income. Ratings were given for head of household, and in cases in missing information, ratings were estimated from the available data.

It also seemed logical to control the findings for general aptitude (a combination of the math and verbal SAT scores) in addition to social class, especially since social class and general aptitude were not highly correlated in the total sample ($r = .13$, n.s.) and since there was a substantial sex difference in general aptitude in favor of males ($F = 35.936$, $p < .001$).

Results considered for discussion are those that hold at the .05 level of statistical significance across all three analyses described below. On the other hand when certain variables are expected to be strongly related to one or more covariates (such as the relationship between grades and aptitude) it may only be reasonable to consider controlled results as the best indication of "true" findings.

Each dependent variable was submitted to three analyses of variance (1) a one-way ANOVA with sex as the independent variable; (2) a one-way ANOVA with sex as the independent variable and SES as a covariate; and (3) one-way ANOVA with sex as the independent variable and aptitude as a covariate. Because of the large number of variables, only statistically significant results are presented in Table 1.

RESULTS

MAJOR SUBJECT. There are five significant results indicated for major subject or intended major (see Table 1). Surprisingly, more women are majoring in statistics, a category which includes computer science (.05 > p > .02). The remaining findings are in the expected direction: males

Table 1. Sex Differences in Educational and Occupational Goals

	Uncorrected mean		Uncorrected F ($N = 874$)	F corrected for SES	F corrected for APTI
	Male	Female			
Ambivalence *re* major	.05	.10	4.28*	3.79*	7.85***
Major Statistics, computer science	.00	.03	3.58	4.74*	5.23*
Engineering	.18	.07	24.93***	23.98***	17.90***
Social science	.05	.18	23.76***	19.17***	7.06**
Education	.02	.09	14.674***	12.12***	5.34*
Nursing	.00	.03	4.67*	4.68*	4.69*
Major traditionally female (i.e., social work, home economics, education, and nursing)	.02	.13	29.48***	22.76***	12.85***
Reason for major					
Helping others	.05	.10	6.99**	8.55**	8.50**
Liking children	.01	.06	8.34**	8.313**	4.298*
Dealing with people	.01	.07	17.37***	13.281***	10.32**
Grad school					
Engineering	.09	.02	16.45***	19.22***	14.46***
Social science	.04	.09	8.60**	6.70**	5.75*
Humanities	.01	.04	5.22*	7.79**	4.27*
Health-related field	.01	.04	4.29*	4.04*	6.69**
Grad school in traditionally female areas	.01	.09	24.21***	21.80***	10.14**
Obstacle to grad plans					
Marriage	.05	.10	6.41**	10.93***	10.07**
Specific career goal	.06	.17	21.03***	16.62***	8.94**
Career					
Business	.25	.14	15.40***	22.45***	4.48*
Entrepreneurship	.08	.03	10.04**	19.85***	4.89*
Engineering	.14	.04	21.99***	20.168***	24.97***
Math	.00	.03	6.28**	3.87*	2.65*
Social sciences	.02	.08	7.96**	7.12**	4.53*
Social work	.00	.03	12.07***	9.15**	9.43**
Nursing	.00	.03	5.88*	6.50**	4.56*
Reason for career					
Liking children	.02	.05	6.18**	7.60**	12.08***
Father	.07	.02	13.71***	10.99***	7.38**
Obstacle to career					
Marriage	.01	.07	15.54***	12.54***	10.45**

(continued)

Table 1. (Continued)

	Uncorrected mean		Uncorrected F (N = 874)	F corrected for SES	F corrected for APTI
	Male	Female			
Marriage					
No effect on career	.41	.48	3.57*	3.89*	7.39**
Will help career	.10	.03	14.19***	12.76***	4.86*
SES of career choice	1.52	1.65	5.78*	6.98**	6.24**
Male careers	.86	.59	61.38***		35.68***
Neutral career	.13	.26	16.10***		4.54*
Female career	.04	.20	36.04***		27.05***
Overall GPA	24.6	8.72	260.87***	253.18***	6.46**[a]
GPA in major	25.9	8.94	246.9***	220.32***	.93[b]

[a]Adjusted means: male = 22.8; female = 24.8.
[b]Adjusted means: male = 25.6; female = 26.9.
*$p < .05$ **$p < .01$ ***$p < .001$.

more often major in engineering ($p < .001$) while women were more likely to concentrate in social science (.01 > p > .001), education (.02 > p > .001), and nursing ($p < .03$). Thus with the exception of statistics the subjects in which sex differences are found indicate that males more often choose a traditionally male area while females show a preference for social sciences and two traditionally female subjects.

Looking at the reasons given for choosing the major subject, three significant results show that women more often do so in order to work or deal with people (.002 > p > .001), to help others (.008 > p > .004), and because they like children (.04 > p > .004). All of the findings then indicate more other-directed reasons among women for pursuing their particular subject matter.

Graduate School Plans. Table 1 also shows that in the category of plans for graduate school there were four significant results where more males chose graduate school in engineering ($p < .001$), while more women plan to pursue graduate education in the social sciences (.02 > p > .004), humanities (.04 > p > .005), and health-related fields (.04 > p > .01). It is perhaps worth noting that with the exception of social sciences, the subjects in which women tend to major more often than males are not directly translated into graduate study.

The one sex difference in obstacles to plans for graduate school plans shows that more women anticipate that marriage and sex-role pressures might interfere (.01 > p > .001).

There were no significant sex differences in the plans of these students not planning to pursue graduate study, be they work, work before returning to school, marriage, or just some form of relaxation.

CAREER PLANS. Among the seven significant results for career aspirations, another unexpected sex reversal occurred. More women aspired to careers in math and math-related fields such as statistics and computer science ($.05 > p > .01$). So certainly the proclivity of women toward math-related fields found for the major subject was not just a chance statistical finding. Indeed note that after all controls are instituted, the tendency for more women to be majoring in pure math approaches statistical significance ($p < .06$). There was, however, no difference between sexes in plans for graduate study in math-related fields.

For the remaining areas in which there are sex differences, males more often aspire to careers in business ($.03 > p > .001$), entrepreneurship ($.03 > p > .002$) and engineering ($p < .001$), while women more often plan for the sciences ($.03 > p > .005$), social work ($.003 > p > .001$), and nursing ($.03 > p > .001$). Thus, with the one exception noted, the general trend continues for more males at the career level to prefer some of the more exclusively male-dominated fields and for women to show inclination for social science and some of the traditional female-oriented occupations.

When asked to explain the reason for vocational choice, women more often gave liking children as the reason ($.01 > p > .001$), while males were more likely to say that their fathers provided encouragement or support, or acted as role models ($.01 > p > .001$). Note that this latter finding is contrary to existing literature claiming that any differential push within the family is from mothers to daughters.

When asked what might interfere with career plans, the only significant result was that women were more likely to mention marriage, children, and sex-role pressures ($.002 > p > .001$).

EFFECT OF MARRIAGE ON CAREER PLANS. One question investigated the anticipated effect of marriage on career plans. From the answers given, the following variables were coded: marriage (1) will have no effect on career; (2) will help career; (3) will delay career; (4) will make career harder; and (5) will interfere with career, i.e., stop it, change it, or lower goals. Two significant results indicated that women more often stated that marriage would have no effect ($.05 > p > .01$) and males were more likely to say that marriage would help their careers ($.03 > p > .01$).

There appears to be a contradiction in the degree to which marriage is spontaneously anticipated as an obstacle to career (and graduate school) plans and its perceived effect in response to a specific probe among the women. While there is the possibility of a defensive reaction to a specific probe on the effect of marriage, it seems more likely that the difference lies in the nature of the coding. The "obstacles" question was coded not only for marriage per se but also for general sex-role pressure and the anticipated impact of children, while the specific probe was limited to the effect of marriage alone. This implies that husbands may present no thwarting obstacle, but that marriage-related responsibilities are limiting factors.

SUMMARY MEASURES. The summary measures used are those not specific to any subject matter. In terms of grades, recall that the literature suggests that black women perform better than their male counterparts. However, for overall grade-point average (GPA) the first (uncorrected) analysis reveals that males do much better ($p < .001$), a finding that holds after a control for social class background ($p < .001$). After a control for aptitude women are found to perform better, though the strength of the findings is reduced ($p < .01$). For grades in the major subject, where motivation is presumably at a maximum, males again perform better on the first two analyses ($p < .001$), while there are no differences at all when variance due to aptitude is extracted ($p < .999$). So if one is talking about general impressions, as the literature does, the data show that in general males perform better, but when one considers individuals of roughly the same measured aptitude females perform better across subjects but show no advantage in the major, i.e., when motivation to succeed should be highest.

To assess some aspects of decision-making in the career selection process, variables were coded for indecision, ambivalence (giving two or more alternative choices) in choice of major, graduate plans, and career plans, as well as specificity of career plans (e.g., gynecologist in needy areas rather than "M.D."). Two significant results showed that women were more often ambivalent about the choice of major ($.05 > p > .005$), but were also more specific about career aspirations ($.003 > p > .001$). It appears that women may have a harder time deciding on their interests, but then have a clearer idea of what to do with their careers.

For the highest degree aspired to, there were no sex differences at all in whether students expected the terminal degree to be a bachelor's, master's level, or doctoral degree (M.D., Ph.D).

It was possible to assess traditionality of career choice by coding the percentage of women currently in that area according to the U.S. Bureau of Labor Statistics (1975), and then to categorize careers as either male dominated (i.e., with 0%–29% women), neutral (30%–59%), or female dominated (60%–100%). The results showed that women were significantly more likely to choose occupations with a large proportion of women ($p < .001$), less likely to choose careers in male-dominated areas ($p < .001$), and more likely to choose careers in neutral fields ($.03 > p > .001$) and in female-dominated areas ($p < .001$). These trends are of course consistent with the observed differences in specific subject matter.

Finally, the socioeconomic status level of career choice was rated according to the Hamburger Scale. Women were found to have significantly lower level aspirations than males ($.02 > p > .01$). Thus while the women would appear to be no less ambitious than the males insofar as desired attainment of terminal degrees is concerned, they nonetheless show a marked tendency to avoid careers in male-dominated areas in favor of those with more female representation and which also represent choices promising less prestige and remuneration.

DISCUSSION

The present study has considered a large number of variables related to the educational and occupational goals among a large sample of black students. It is certainly worth noting that there were many aspects of these goals in which no sex differences appeared. Most notable, a similar proportion of women plan to go on to graduate school, to attain advanced degrees, and to become doctors, lawyers, architects, scientists, and even politicians. It is only in a few of the last bastions of male supremacy that black women seem relatively unwilling to tread. So while the cumulative effects across all of the occupational choices creates a stereotyped picture of black women's aspirations, there are still a number of high-level professions whose ranks they will continue to enter. It is also notable that no sex differences in expected degree attainment were observed and that black women aspire to advanced degrees to the same extent as males, but the SES data indicate that the content of these advanced aspirations are imbued with less status and potential reward. Thus similar educational goals will in all likelihood not result in better jobs.

The one exception that flies in the face of the general trends is the seemingly greater penchant of black women for math-related careers. While no compellingly plausible explanation suggests itself, the trend is reminiscent of Ravenna Helson's (1971) work on creative women in general and creative female mathematicians in particular. She finds that abilities in math tend to be found among women who have somehow managed to escape from the mainstream American influences (via religion or foreign background) that thwart the development of such interests. Despite the total picture, then, perhaps there are such influences in the backgrounds of black women that surface in small but observable ways.

For men and women still in the learning state, career aspirations represent as yet unfilled wishes. Undoubtedly much will happen to them before their occupational choices become census statistics. But of all the obstacles envisioned as potential impediments to goal fulfillment (including grades, money, indecision, racial discrimination, or a competitive job market), only marriage and the presence of children were envisioned as more of a stumbling block to the women. (Note that the absence of sex difference in grades as an anticipated obstacle is entirely consistent with the absence of sex differences in performance in the major subject, those grades that contribute most heavily to future success.) It seems that men are more likely to see marriage as a stabilizing factor that enhances motivation to succeed, while for women the reproductive orientation and the inevitable energies consumed by it are realities that many women recognize. But it is not evident from these data that the potential loss of career momentum represents a particular strain to those women in question. Indeed of all the various reasons spontaneously given for wanting their careers, as well as pursuing subjects in their majors, women were more often inclined toward areas with an other-directed focus that reaffirmed their positive reproductive orientation.

It should be pointed out that there were no sex differences in career choice for reasons of status, financial need, interest, competence, or the challenge—thus belying some of the "unnatural" motives often differentially imputed to black women. Indeed the one other sex difference, showing that males much more often name their fathers as having provided impetus for the particular career choice, clearly provides contrary evidence to one of the more central aspects of the black matriarchy theory. There were no differences in the extent to which mothers or any other persons within the family were perceived as having differentially encouraged the famale students.

Thus the data presented here add to the body of literature that is dispelling many of the myths of the black matriarchy theory. For students in this particular sample the findings establish, without apparent bias from social class or ability considerations, that:

1. Black female students do not have higher career aspirations than their male counterparts with respect to status, prestige, or potential financial reward.

2. Despite some high-status professions, which these women show no inclination to avoid, the career goals of these female students are more often stereotypically feminine.

3. The relatively constricted ambitions of these women seem related to the reproductive orientation that has and perhaps always will be more true of women and represents a limiting factor for them (see Evans-Pritchard, 1956).

4. There is no evidence that the educational and occupational goals of these women are a product of favoritism or greater oppor-

tunity bestowed from mothers hostile to males, upon daughters bent on becoming matriarchs.

5. There is no substantial evidence that black female students in these colleges perform better scholastically than their male counterparts in areas of special interest that foreshadow career aspirations.

So far this discussion has purposely limited its comparisons in theory, previous research, and current results to black women relative to black men. The general theory specifically attacks the position of women relative to men and bases its maladaptive propositions on the alleged imbalance in male–female relations. Insofar as this comparison is the relevant one for the theory in question, the systematic research testing it in relation to educational and occupational status was found not to support the theory. The new data presented also show no support for a black female superiority, dominance, or ascendance vis-à-vis black men. Furthermore other recent studies also find no support for a matriarchal theory in terms of dominance in family relations (Blood & Wolfe, 1963; Geisman & Gerhart, 1968; Hyman & Reed, 1969; Mack, 1971). On this issue, then, the real pattern that has characterized the era under discussion is a steady downfall of the theory of the black matriarchy. It is a downfall in terms of systematic research evidence that was foreshadowed by Frazier's own chapter on the same subject, that he observed to be taking place in 1939. There is then virtually no evidence of a true black matriarchy and it is doubtful that the phenomenon (as described by the observationalists) was ever characteristic of black women.

If then it is so difficult to find systematic support for the black matriarchy theory, it may be worth speculating as to why such a notion has so captured the imaginations of social scientists and why it has been seized upon with an almost perverse fascination by laymen as well. What might it be about black women that makes them so vulnerable to "unnatural" indictments? The preceding discussion was limited to black male–female comparisons, but when comparisons are confined to differences between black and white women, the picture does change. Researchers do find that black professional women compared to their white counterparts earn a larger proportion (three-quarters) of what their male counterparts do than is true of white professional women (one-half) (Bock, 1969). According to Jackson (1973), the proportion of white women in the work force classified as professional (15%) is higher than that of black women (10%), but Epstein (1973) has shown that black women comprise a higher proportion of their respective high-status professional communities than do white women, and in certain professions black women earn a higher median income. While the overall earnings of black women are lower than those of white women (Almquist, 1973; Feagin, 1970), both Fichter (1967) and Kuvelsky and Obordo (1972) found a greater commitment to professional goals among high school and college students, respectively, in that roughly twice as many black women wished to combine full-time employment with the traditional roles of wife and mother. These findings are consistent with the stronger work orientation among black women elaborated on by Gump (1975) and their longer history of participation in the work force documented by Smuts (1971).

From the foregoing it does not seem that black women are guilty of having established a matriarchate that has evolved into an achievement syndrome, but are, perhaps, of working more and of displaying more self-reliance and instrumentality in the service of family functioning than their white counterparts. Black women have in effect traditionally violated many of the feminine norms of passivity and dependence, qualities admired by both black and white males alike, and the lack of which incites suspicion. Thus the "unnaturalness" of the black woman seems to lie in her historical inability to adhere to certain norms of feminity, not in her success at having effected a role reversal within the black family.

Summary

This study presents a historical overview of discussion on the theory of the black matriarchy, and then presents data relevant to a test of one aspect of the theory. According to some of the earlier psychoanalytic and observational contributions, black women were said to be dominant, with or without their men, and to outstrip black men in educational attainment, professional status, and income. However, according to more systematic research studies there is little support for the general premises of the black matriarchy theory. The present data from a large and varied population of college-age students demonstrate, without apparent bias from social class or ability considerations, that (1) black female students do not have higher career aspirations than their male counterparts with respect to status, prestige, or potential reward; and (2) to the extent that there are sex differences, the career goals of female students are more often stereotypically feminine owing to their reproductive orientation. Thus it does not seem that black women are guilty of having established a matriarchate that has evolved into an achievement syndrome, but are, perhaps, of working more and of displaying more self-reliance and instrumentality in the service of family functioning that their white counterparts.

REFERENCES

Almquist, E. M. The income losses of working black women: Product of racial and sexual discrimination. Paper presented at the American Sociological Association, New York, August, 1973.
Almquist, E. M. *Black women in the labor force: The experience of a decade.* Unpublished manuscript, North Texas State University, 1975.
Ausubel, D. P. Ego development among segregated children. *Mental Hygiene,* 1956, *42,* 362–369.
Bernard, J. *Academic women.* University Park, Penna.: Pennsylvania State University Press, 1966.
Bernard, J. *Marriage and family among Negroes.* Englewood Cliffs, N.J.: Prentice-Hall, 1966.
Blood, R. O., & Wolfe, D. M. *Husbands and wives: The dynamics of married living.* New York: Free Press, 1963.
Bock, E. W. Farmer's daughter effect: The case of the Negro female professional. *Phylon,* 1969, *30,* 17–26. (Also in A. Theodore, Ed., *The professional woman.* Cambridge, Mass.: Schenkman, 1971).
Bressler, T., & McKenney, W. Negro women in the United States. Paper presented at the annual meeting of the Population Association of America, Boston, 1968.
Carter, D. E., Little, C. A., & Barabasz, A. S. Comparative studies of Negro and white attitudes associated with educational-occupational aspirations. *Journal of Negro Education,* 1972, *41,* 361–364.
Clark, K. B. *Dark ghetto: Dilemmas of social power.* New York: Harper & Row, 1965.
Epstein, C. F. Positive effects of the double negative: Explaining the success of black professional women. In J. Huber (Ed.), *Changing women in a changing society.* Chicago: University of Chicago Press, 1973.
Evans-Pritchard, E. E. *The position of women in primitive societies and other essays.* London: Routledge & Kegan Paul, 1956.
Feagin, J. R. Black women in the American labor force. In C. V. Willie (Ed.), *The family life of black people.* Columbus, Ohio: Merrill, 1970.
Fichter, J. H. Career expectations of Negro graduates. *Monthly Labor Review,* 1967, *90,* 36–42.
Fleming, J. *The impact of predominantly white and predominantly black college environments of black students.* Third annual report to the Carnegie Corporation of New York. United Negro College Fund, September 1979.
Frazier, E. F. *The Negro family in the United States.* Chicago: University of Chicago Press, 1939.
Gans, H. J. The subcultures of the working class, lower class, and middle class. In E. O. Lauman et al. (Eds.), *The logic of social hierarchies.* Chicago: Markham, 1970.
Geisman, L. L., & Gerhart, U. C. Social class, ethnicity, and family functioning: Explaining some issues raised by the Moynihan report. *Journal of Marriage and the Family,* 1968, *30,* 480–487.
Gump, J. P. *Reality and myth: Employment and sex role ideology in black women.* Paper prepared for the conference on New Directions for Research on Women, Howard University, 1975.
Gurin, P., & Gaylord, C. Educational and occupational goals of men and women at black colleges. *Monthly Labor Review,* 1976, *99,* 10–16.
Grossack, M. M. (Ed.), *Mental health and segregation.* New York: Springer, 1963.
Hamburger, M. *A revised occupational scale for rating socio-economic status.* Unpublished manuscript, New York University, 1971.
Helson, R. Women mathematicians and the creative personality. *Journal of Consulting and Clinical Psychology,* 1971, *36,* 210–220.

Hyman, H. H., & Reed, J. S. "Black matriarchy" reconsidered: Evidence from secondary analysis of sample surveys. *Public Opinion Quarterly*, 1969, *33*, 346–354.

Jackson, J. J. Black women in a racist society. In C. V. Willie, B. M. Kramer, & B. S. Brown (Eds.), *Racism and mental health*. Pittsburgh: University of Pittsburgh Press, 1973.

Kardiner, A., & Ovesey, L. *The mark of oppression*. New York: World, 1951.

Kirkpatrick, J. L. Occupational aspirations, opportunities, and barriers. In K. S. Miller & R. M. Dreger (Eds.), *Comparative studies of blacks and whites in the United States*. New York: Seminar Press, 1973.

Kuvelsky, W., & Obordo, A. S. A racial comparison of teenage girls' protections for marriage and procreation. *Journal of Marriage and the Family*, 1972, *34*, 75–83.

Mack, D. Where the black matriarchy theorists went wrong. *Psychology Today*, 1971, *4*, 24.

Mednick, M. T. S., & Puryear, G. R. Motivational and personality factors related to career goals of black college women. *Journal of Social and Behavioral Sciences*, 1975, *21*, 1–30.

Moynihan, D. P. *The Negro family, a case for national action*. Washington D.C.: U.S. Government Printing Office, 1965.

Picou, J. S. Black-white variations in a model of the occupational aspiration process. *Journal of Negro Education*, 1973, *42*, 117–122.

Rohrer, J. H., & Edmonson, M. S. (Eds.), *The eighth generation: Cultures and personalities of New Orleans Negroes*. New York: Harper, 1960.

Scanzoni, J. J. *The black family in modern society*. Boston: Allyn & Bacon, 1971.

Schwartz, M. Northern United States Negro matriarchy: Status versus authority. *Phylon*, 1965, *26*, 18–24.

Smith, E. J. Profile of the black individual in vocational literature. *Journal of Vocational Behavior*, 1975, *6*, 41–59.

Smuts, R. W. *Women and work in America*. New York: Schocken Books, 1971.

Staples, R. The myth of the black matriarchy. *Black Scholar*, 1970, *1*, 9–16.

Thorpe, C. B. Status, race and aspiration: A study of the desire of high school students to enter a professional or a technical occupation. *Dissertation Abstracts*, 1969, *29*(10–A), 3672 (Abstract).

Turner, B. F. Perception of the occupational opportunity structure and socialization to achievement as related to sex and race. Paper presented at the meeting of the Eastern Psychological Association, New York, 1971.

Bureau of Labor Statistics, U.S. Department of Labor. *U.S. working women: A chartwork*. Bulletin 1880, 1975.

Appendix

Variables Coded for Educational and Occupational Goals

Major Subjects
  Math
  Statistics or computer science
  Science (physics, chemistry, biology, pre-med)
  Accounting
  Business (business administration, marketing, management)
  Engineering
  Architecture
  Political Science (also criminal justice, public relations)
  Economics
  Social Science (psychology, sociology, anthropology)
  English (also journalism)
  History
  Languages
  Social Work (also social welfare, social service)
  Home economics
  Education (also child development, special education)
  Nursing
  Communications (also broadcasting)
  Arts (includes fine and performing arts)

Reasons for Choosing Major
  Interest
  Knowledge (exposure, learning something)
  Competence (doing well, best subject)
  Challenge (difficult)
  Instrumental to work goal (needed for grad school; for good job)
  To make a contribution (a needed skill; for social change)
  Good job market (open market; good money)
  Race-related reasons (blacks needed; to help blacks)
  Dealing with people; working with people
  To help others (also, others need help)
  Liking children
  Family members (support or encouragement from; role modeling)
  Mother (support or encouragement from; role modeling)
  Father
  Person outside family

Graduate School Plans
  Medicine (includes dentistry and psychiatry)
  Law
  Business (M.B.A. and C.P.A.)
  Engineering
  Architecture
  Math (also statistics, computer science)

(*continued*)

Appendix   (Continued)

Graduate School Plans (Continued)
  Science
  Government (also political science, public administration)
  Economics
  Clinical psychology
  Social science (includes clinical psychology)
  Humanities (English, history, languages, philosophy)
  Journalism (also writing)
  Health-related fields (hospital administration, mental health)
  Legal-related fields (criminal justice, corrections)
  Social work (also social service)
  Education (also educational administration, counseling)
  Special education (therapy, pathology)
  Nursing
  Communications
  City planning
  Arts (fine and performing arts)

Obstacles to Graduate School Plans
  Number of obstacles envisioned
  Envisions no obstacles
  Money
  Ability (grades, acceptance to school)
  Indecision (lack of interest, changing interest, motivation)
  Good job offer
  Marriage (also sex-role pressures)
  Death (also bad health)
  Race-related obstacles

Non-graduate School Plans
  Work
  Work, then school
  To work way up (in business or a company, etc.)
  Marriage, (also children)
  Respite (rest, decide future, exploratory activity, have fun)

Career Plans
  Medicine
  Law
  Business
  Entrepreneurial (opening shop, opening business, owning business)
  Engineering
  Architecture
  Math (also statistics, computer science)
  Science
  Politics (also government, public administration)
  Economics
  Clinical psychology
  Humanities (English, history, languages, philosophy)
  Journalism (also writing, editing)
  Health-related fields (health administration, mental health)

Appendix   (Continued)

Career Plans (Continued)
Legal-related fields (criminal justice, corrections)
College professors
Education (secondary school teaching, school administration, library science)
Special education (therapy, learning disabilities, disturbed children)
Social work (also social service)
Nursing
Communications
City planning
Armed services
Arts (design, fine and performing arts)

Reasons for Career Choice
Status (also respect of profession)
Interest
Knowledge
Competence (good at it, will do a good job)
Challenge
To make a contribution
Race-related reasons (need blacks, blacks doing it, help blacks)
Working with people (meeting people, dealing with people)
To help others
Liking children
Family members (support or encouragement from; role modeling)
Mother
Father
Person outside family

Obstacles to Career Choice
Number of Obstacles
Envisions no obstacles
Money
Ability (grades, acceptance to school)
Indecision
Tight job market (competition)
Marriage (also children, sex-role pressures)
Death (also bad health)
Race-related obstacles (acceptance of blacks, etc.)

Effect of Marriage on Career Plans
No effect
Will help career
Will delay career
Will make career harder
Will interfere (stop it, change it, lower goals)

Summary Measures
Overall grade-point average (winter quarter)
GPA in major subject

(continued)

Appendix   (Continued)

Summary Measures (Continued)
Indecision about major
Ambivalence about major (gives two or more alternative choices)
Undecided plans for graduate school
Ambivalence about graduate school
Undecided career plans
Ambivalence about career plans
Specific career plans (e.g. "gynecologist in needy areas" versus "M.D.")
Highest degree planned is baccalaureate (B.A., B.S.)
Highest degree planned is masters level (M.A., M.S., M.B.A., C.P.A., etc.)
Highest degree planned is advanced (M.D., D.D.S., Ph.D., J.D.)
Percent of women in chosen profession
Career choice in male-dominated field (0%–29% women)
Career in neutral field (30%–59% women)
Career choice in female-dominated field (60%–100% women)
SES level of career choice

Chapter 13

Change and Constancy: A 100-Year Tale

Summary Reports by Discussants

RHONA RAPOPORT AND ROBERT RAPOPORT

A very different breed of women entered college in the mid-19th century as compared with today, and left it to enter a very different world. While much has changed, it often seems that a great deal is constant. The chapters presented here have looked at change. They are rich in detail and variegated. They portray this complexity in their substance. As we summarize we will try to extract a number of themes that seem to run through the book illustrating the kind of change and the continuities that seem to have occurred. They will explore the kinds of concerns that grip us as we stand questioning where we are going from here.

Four themes predominate, each with subthemes, each with a specific social and historical context. They can be summarized in four concepts, each expressed in a shorthand term as follows: (1) roles, (2) linkages, (3) values, and (4) consequences.

ROLES

There have been conspicuous changes in our ideas about men's and women's capacities, and the roles they can and should play in the family, in the labor force, and in society.

In the mid-19th century women were not assessed to be educable in

RHONA RAPOPORT, PH.D., AND ROBERT RAPOPORT, PH.D. • Institute of Family and Environmental Research, London N.W. 3, England.

the same sense as men. If they went to college, and many fewer did, it was to become cultured, not competent in a vocational sense.

As Jessie Bernard has detailed, the "ground rules" for the life careers and marital roles of men and women were clear and unequivocally different. Women's place was in the home, and marriage was forever, exclusive, dedicated to childrearing, and under the aegis of the paterfamilias. The changes in the ground rules of male–female role relationships have been piecemeal and uneven, sometimes even subject to reversals of direction.

Marriage and family remain an important source of people's personal satisfaction, as Douvan's chapter shows. Mary Jo Bane has documented the extent to which rising divorce rates affect this, and yet this trend is less catastophic than some doom-watchers imply. Individual marriages are less likely to be forever, but innumerable research reports indicate that remarriage is eagerly sought and widely practiced. Where marriages are retained intact, particularly among the longer married earlier generations, it may be, as Jessie Bernard suggests, that the longevity of the marriages has been bought through a toleration of occasional infidelity.

The Harris survey of 1975 and the Gallup poll of the same year document a general drop in popularity of childbearing and -rearing, as do the actual fertility data from government vital statistics. Yet more recent figures suggest a shift back. Domestic role definitions, division of labor, and patterns of decision-making depart widely from the Victorian ground rules, but there is considerable variation among individuals and groups.

A good deal of change has occurred in the three decades following World War II. Joseph Veroff's analysis of Michigan National Cross-Sectional Survey data from two points in this period provides insights into factors that seem to be associated with these changes. While more women are seeking and winning significant work roles in conjunction with whatever domestic roles they accept, men are simultaneously rebelling against the totality of domination that work roles have had in their lives. There is potential for a new complementarity here—but resistance and constraint as well. These operate at home and at work.

Jean Blumen's chapter analyzes some of the cultural constraints inhibiting women's attaining leadership roles in the workplace. Many of the chapters touch on some of the constraints hampering men's getting much out of (and putting much into) their family lives.

Social class and ethnic subcultural variations play a part in sex roles, as Jacqueline Fleming's chapter indicates. And while there may be little to support the notion of black matriarchy as a stabilized form of family structure going back to the plantation days, it is probably correct to say that black families are put under considerable strain when women take on and succeed in new roles, with new significance in the context of the black civil rights movement.

LINKAGES

Individuals, families, and communities all depend on the human impulse to connect. "Only connect," wrote John Donne in the 17th century, a refrain echoed by pastors, psychiatrists, and social scientists down the centuries to today. The prescription has gained in cogency as the malaise born of its absence deepens.

The ways in which individuals make connections outside their families, and the conceptions of what these connections should be, have unquestionably changed over the past 100 years for "young ladies of breeding and intelligence." A girl of "good background" may have been introduced to society through a "coming-out" event after which no holds were barred in the search for a suitable mate, through whom linkages among the major institutions of society would be sustained. Elite women's colleges in the 19th century may have served to a larger extent than today as filtering devices, sorting the more affluent, gifted, and intellectual aspirants to make a more efficient match with their male counterparts at affiliated male institutions. While coming-out events are still alive, neither the cocoon from which the aspirant emerges nor the goal or her subsequent quest are as clear.

Today's collegiate woman is more likely to develop interests and aspirations comparable to those of her male counterpart, with whom she shares many life experiences. Like her counterpart she may become intensely involved in political interests—for example, as Jeanne Block's data show, by participating in student agitations. Her own conception of how she should link herself to society is no longer confined to the pattern of vicarious participation through the accomplishments of a husband of substance and stature. She is likely to seek connections in her own right—with an occupation that might last throughout her life, with friends and associates who might be different from those of her family, and with other interests that reflect her separate personality. While men have been increasingly disenchanted with the degree of involvement that is expected from them at work—too often to the exclusion of other interests—women have become increasingly committed to and satisfied with work outside the home. At the same time Joseph Veroff shows how this increase in women's workplace participation can be accompanied by an apparently paradoxical increase in their dissatisfaction with their jobs. This is partly a measure of the discrepancy between women's new aspirations in the workplace and the capacity of occupations to absorb their skills and energies. In Veroff's terms, educational institutions have altered the press for self-actualization in work while not influencing the fabric of the work setting. Veroff cautions educators to think again about the messages they give to young people, presumably lest they add to the burden of their discontent. But the other side of the coin, perhaps more explored by those who concentrated on value issues, is to consider ways and means of influencing the fabric of the workplace, and along with it other social institutions which absorb young people.

The linkage issue is not an exclusively individual issue, any more than the "messages" issue is exclusively a responsibility of educators. When young couples marry they tend to be intensely preoccupied with one another, forging a marital bond of intimacy, in the terms used by Erik Erikson. When this work of bonding fails, there is rapid dissolution of the union, and it aborts. By far the highest proportion of divorces occurs in the first few years of marriage. But once the ties of intimacy are established and the marriage gets off the ground, new issues arise over which one of the partners should connect with which external connection. The traditional way of handling the complexities of this deceptively simple issue was for the wife to concern herself primarily with the family's local and kinship connections, and to concentrate on her duty to reproduce and rear offspring—the family's linkage to the future. Her husband, complementarily, was expected to link them to the larger social institutions of work, banking and finance, politics, and the macro social order. The entire family continues to be classified by both officials and fellows in the community according to the social status of the husband's occupation.

While all this is changing, it is changing unevenly and without a clear pattern of outcome. Many women wish to work continuously and eschew the tradition of accepting a social position dependent on that of their husbands. But neither they nor those who deal with them (including the Census Bureau) always know how to handle the ambiguities that emerge. We now have many families headed by women—not only, as in the past, through bereavement, but also through divorce. To continue to classify a woman in such a situation according to the link her ex-husband had with the occupational system is·ludicrous, yet this is widely practiced. There are many families in which both husband and wife sustain regular and continuous occupational careers on a more or less equal basis (in about 20% of marriages in which the wife work, her level of earning and social status is about the same or higher than her husband's). In "dual-career families" both husband and wife link the family to the outside world. The family may be enriched in noneconomic as well as economic ways, but there are new conflicts and strains to be managed. And there is often a divergence of values as well as purely logistical difficulties of coordinating two busy lives.

VALUES

The theme is a recurrent one in this volume, as it has been for men and women in the century just gone by. Every generation has experienced difficulty about the values of the oncoming generation. One of the recurrent themes in human history is the anxiety of the older generation about the "erosion" of values. The young, conversely, are often concerned with a search for new values, and the issue of how change can be brought about.

William Chafe has outlined some of the enduring values of American society, and has indicated how changes have often been brought about through the expression of implicit conflicts in the value system. Sometimes the conflicts are experienced within individuals as they search for personal solutions to such issues as the adoption of a particular model of sex roles and a pattern of behavior to enact the model. Abigail Stewart's and Patricia Salt's analysis of college graduates shows how this set of personal dilemmas works itself out in the life course of students emerging into the modern world. Jeanne Block's analysis of student protest movements depicts some of the forces underlying this form of expression of value conflicts. Jessie Bernard's analysis of the value dilemma in many long-standing marriages—between fidelity and longevity—is another manifestation. Carol Gilligan gets to the root of understanding the process of value choice within individuals growing up in families, and in so doing contributes not only to our understanding of a question that grips every successive generation, but also to our insight on specific value dilemmas.

Young people growing up in all societies and in all times become concerned with such value issues as how much attention to give to fulfilling social obligations versus freedom for personal expression and how much to tolerate in others behavior which one feels is unacceptable for oneself. While these and other moral dilemmas are part and parcel of growing up in a social context, they have come to have particular poignancy for women today as a result of the evolving conceptions of equality between the sexes. People are asking, with ever greater concern, questions like: Will the pursuit of equality between the sexes mean an end to what we have cherished in family life? Will women bring a new value emphasis on nurturance, cooperation, and human interdependence to the workplace, or will they be taken over by the individualistic and competitive values that have ruled the lives of men at work? What kind of person do we wish to produce in our families, educational institutions, and through the operation of policies, legislation, and mass media communications? Should women come to look and act more like men? men more like women? both like something entirely new? or should variability and flexibility be encouraged—from each according to his or her bent? Each value orientation has its appeal, and its drawbacks.

Is there any way that we can interpret events that will tell us which value orientation is likely to prevail? Is there any point in trying to shape the course of the development of social values, or should young people today concentrate on their personal lifestyles?

CONSEQUENCES

History provides instances which could support various answers to the questions raised. We may be in the midst of an evolutionary process which will produce a continuation of the trends detected without further upheaval. Families and educators concerned with influencing the orientation of young people might as well concentrate on how best to accommodate the inevitable greater equality between the sexes.

A contrasting position holds that the emphasis on equality has gone too far, and a correction will inevitably settle in according to which women will return to their more "natural, biologically determined" roles and men will continue to pursue their own "natural" lines of interest unencumbered by the threats and inconveniences of women's assertiveness. One proponent of this view has recently asserted that there is no such thing as a dual-career family; one partner will always have just a job, while the other builds a career. The speaker meant that the "other" would be male. The data of this conference make it apparent that this is by no means inevitable. Aside from the demographic materials presented by Nathan Keyfitz showing women's relentless march toward greater equality—however short it still falls from an ultimate ideal—there are also the data presented by Elizabeth Douvan, based on the Michigan national surveys. Men and women are both more open to the idea that people can combine occupational and familial roles in various ways. While a backlash against egalitarian trends may be inevitable, it does not signify a *reversal* of the evolutions we have been discussing.

Cross-cutting the various theories and models of the change process is the issue of *who* should do *what* about it. This book has brought together individuals who are in fact trying to do something about the trends at different levels. Research on men's and women's motivations, growth patterns, relationships, and behavioral performance is one approach—and it must be seen as having a value/political element. Clinical work, conversely, has research implications of its own.

A more direct and explicit attempt to apply the insights and findings presented in this volume is seen in the work of policy-makers (who were not present at the conference, but toward whom many of our comments have been addressed), and educators like Matina Horner, who is implementing this vision in the field of education. Conferences have a way of raising more questions than they can answer, particularly multidisciplinary conferences, and especially conferences which attempt to straddle research and action. Matina Horner picks up the challenge of her colleagues in her assault on the decade ahead with her research recommendations for the 1980s.

Index

Abortion
  demographic analysis, 7–8
  legalization of, as indicator of
    changes in social attitudes,
    7, 268
  and moral judgments of women,
    43–46
  and sexual behavior of women, 268
Accidental deaths, sex distribution
  of, 12
Adults, effects of divorce on, 192
Affirmative action
  and placement of women in higher
    education, 266

Baldwin, J. M., dialectic of personal
  growth, 223
Barnard, C. I., on authority, 65
Beecher, C., 106
Benedict, R., 99
Berkeley, University of California at
  study of social and personal values
    of students, 324–369
Bernard, J., on psychological effects
  of marriage, 203–206
Birth control. See Contraception
Birth rate
  analysis of future trends in, 8–9,
    10–11
  in Canada, 10
  and changes in social attitudes,
    27–28

Birth rate (cont.)
  as factor in changing women's life-
    styles, 5
  in France, 11
  in Germany, 11
  in Soviet Union, 10
  in United States, 5, 6, 27
  among unmarried women and ad-
    olescents, 9
Blacks
  abortion among, 8
  divorce and separation among, 185
  educational and occupational
    goals, 297–311
  marriage rate among, 9
  as part of labor force, 13, 299
  sex differences in educational and
    occupational goals, 297–310
  sex equity in education among, 12

Canada
  birth rate compared with that of
    United States, 10
Centrality, and performance of family roles, 209–213
Change and constancy, summary reports regarding, 317–322
Charismatic leadership, 65
Charity, involvement of Victorian
  women in, 102, 103
Children
  attitude of drug users toward, 233